Global Governance and Local Peace

Why do international peacebuilding organizations sometimes succeed and sometimes fail, even within the same country? Bridging the gaps between the peacekeeping, peacebuilding, and global governance scholarship, this book argues that international peacebuilding organizations repeatedly fail because they are accountable to global actors, not to local institutions or people. International peacebuilding organizations can succeed only when country-based staff bypass existing accountability structures and empower local stakeholders to hold their global organizations accountable for achieving local-level peacebuilding outcomes. In other words, the innovative, if seemingly wayward, actions of individual country-office staff are necessary to improve peacebuilding performance. Using in-depth studies of organizations operating in Burundi over a fifteen-year period, combined with fieldwork in the Democratic Republic of the Congo, Nepal, South Sudan, and Sudan, this book will be of interest to scholars and students of international relations, African studies, and peace and conflict studies as well as policy makers who aim to improve their rate of peacebuilding success.

SUSANNA P. CAMPBELL is an assistant professor at American University's School of International Service. She has published extensively on international intervention in conflict-affected countries, focusing on how global governance organizations interact with the microdynamics of conflict and cooperation. Professor Campbell has been awarded scholarly and policy grants for her research, including from the United States Institute of Peace. She has led large evaluations of international intervention in conflict-affected countries, including for the United Nations and the World Bank, and conducted extensive fieldwork in sub-Saharan Africa and globally. Her scholarship has contributed to demonstrated policy change at the global and local levels.

T0371066

Global Governance and Local Peace

Accountability and Performance in International Peacebuilding

Susanna P. Campbell

CAMBRIDGE
UNIVERSITY PRESS

CAMBRIDGE
UNIVERSITY PRESS

University Printing House, Cambridge CB2 8BS, United Kingdom

One Liberty Plaza, 20th Floor, New York, NY 10006, USA

477 Williamstown Road, Port Melbourne, VIC 3207, Australia

314-321, 3rd Floor, Plot 3, Splendor Forum, Jasola District Centre, New Delhi - 110025, India

79 Anson Road, #06-04/06, Singapore 079906

Cambridge University Press is part of the University of Cambridge.

It furthers the University's mission by disseminating knowledge in the pursuit of education, learning and research at the highest international levels of excellence.

www.cambridge.org
Information on this title: www.cambridge.org/9781108407632
DOI: 10.1017/9781108290630

First published 2018
First paperback edition 2019

A catalogue record for this publication is available from the British Library

Library of Congress Cataloging in Publication data
Names: Campbell, Susanna P., 1974– author.
Title: Global governance and local peace : accountability and performance in international peacebuilding / Susanna P. Campbell.
Description: Cambridge CB2 8BS, United Kingdom ; New York, NY : Cambridge University Press, 2018. | Includes bibliographical references and index.
Identifiers: LCCN 2017041360 | ISBN 9781108418652 (hardback)
Subjects: LCSH: Peace-building–International cooperation. | International agencies.
Classification: LCC JZ5538 .C353 2018 | DDC 303.6/4–dc23
LC record available at https://lccn.loc.gov/2017041360

ISBN 978-1-108-41865-2 Hardback
ISBN 978-1-108-40763-2 Paperback

Contents

Figures

Tables

Acknowledgments

This book presents research that I conducted between 2002 and 2016. Over these fifteen years, it benefited from the contributions of many smart people who gave their time and energy toward this project. I am grateful to each one of them.

Numerous staff of CARE Burundi, the United Nations, the United Kingdom's Department for International Development (DFID), and the Burundi Leadership Training Programme (BLTP) gave their time, their trust, and their documents. Because of the sensitive nature of the material discussed in this book, I cannot reveal their names. They are the heroes of this story. They take these complex and rigid organizations and make them work in highly complicated and fluid contexts. And, at times, this work makes a real difference in people's lives.

I also want to thank my Burundian friends. They helped me to understand what was behind the scenes, to accept the complexity, to listen, to learn, and to laugh. They told me their dreams for peace in Burundi and how much they had invested in its success, and how disappointed they were when it began to fail.

This book began during my time at the Fletcher School at Tufts University. Peter Uvin deeply understood the underlying idea from the start and offered unwavering support for the project and its completion. Toni Chayes pushed me toward excellence and was always convinced that organizations matter. Karen Jacobsen showed me how to transform a complex topic into an elegant and refined research design. Kimberly Howe, Dipali Mukhopadhyay, and Christof Kurz helped me to laugh and stay "on the ball," providing highly useful feedback on very early drafts.

During my time as a post-doctoral researcher at the Saltzman Institute of War and Peace Studies at Columbia University and at the Centre on Conflict, Development, and Peacebuilding at the Graduate Institute in Geneva, I received excellent feedback on the manuscript and its related papers. I am grateful to Michael Doyle, Page Fortna, Bob Jervis, Roy Licklider, and Jack Snyder for their highly valuable feedback while I was at Columbia. In Geneva, Keith Krause, Oliver Jütersonke, and Sandra

Reimann ensured that I had a conducive home for research. While there, I received very helpful feedback on early versions of the manuscript from Ravi Bhavnani, Thomas Biersteker, Karsten Donnay, Stephanie Hofmann, Keith Krause, Annabelle Littoz-Monnet, and Emily Meierding.

Several other scholars read different versions of this manuscript and provided me with essential advice. Miles Kahler and Debra Avant provided detailed and constructive inputs on this manuscript during the final stages, helping to push it out the door. Michael Barnett was particularly helpful at both the beginning and the end of this process, providing targeted feedback that made the manuscript demonstrably better. Séverine Autesserre not only provided essential support for my initial idea for this manuscript but also read the entire first draft several iterations ago and gave me highly detailed, constructive, and supportive feedback for which I am grateful. Naazneen Barma, Lynn Eden, Michael Findley, Bob Keohane, Elisabeth King, David Lake, Amanda Murdie, Roland Paris, Ole Jacob Sending, Timothy Sisk, Stephen Stedman, Kate Weaver, and Christoph Zürcher all read chapters of this book, providing excellent recommendations and helping to shape this book's form and content.

I presented versions of this book at several invited talks, including at Uppsala University's Department of Peace and Conflict Research, Folke Bernadotte Academy, the Saltzman Institute of War and Peace Studies (SIWPS) seminar series at Columbia University, the Graduate Institute's Political Science Colloquium, the AGORA V series at the University of Warwick, the Bopst Center for Peace and Justice at Princeton University, the Institute for Political Science at the University of St. Gallen, the Centre for Security Studies at the Swiss Federal Institute of Technology in Zurich (ETH Zurich), and the Center on International Security and Cooperation (CISAC) at Stanford University. The inputs that I received at each presentation advanced and improved this manuscript, and I am grateful for the investment the participants made in my work.

The research from this book was supported by several grants, including a United States Institute of Peace Dissertation Fellowship, a Swiss National Science Foundation Early Post-Doctoral Grant, a Swiss National Science Foundation Project Grant, and a Swiss Network for International Studies project grant. It would not have been possible to conduct the extensive field research presented in this book without these generous grants.

Two anonymous reviewers provided astute feedback that helped reshape the manuscript. Nigel Quinney provided highly constructive advice and guidance in the final stages of the revisions. Several talented research assistants also worked on this project: Mira Fey, Anca Paducel, Gena Robinson, and Brandon Sims. I am grateful for their detailed and precise work.

My family has watched this book emerge as an initial idea and grow into a massive, multiyear project, supporting me all along the way without questioning the breadth or the depth of my venture. My dad read and provided careful editorial inputs on multiple iterations of this manuscript, bringing his keen eye, everlasting enthusiasm, and clear voice. My mom reminded me to continue to rest, sleep, and laugh as I dove into yet another enormous undertaking. My stepmom encouraged me to travel the world and tell my story. This is part of it. My husband, Matthias, made this book possible in so many ways, patiently and persistently encouraging me to make it as good as possible and, at the same time, get it out into the world. In one of her earliest games, my daughter pretended to write a book. I loved showing her this process and am grateful for the joy and laughter that she helped me maintain along the way.

Abbreviations and Acronyms

ACABQ	Advisory Committee on Administrative and Budgetary Questions
ADC-Ikibiri	Alliance of Democrats for Change in Burundi
AMIB	African Union Mission in Burundi
BCPR	Bureau of Crisis Prevention and Recovery
BINUB	Integrated United Nations Mission to Burundi or United Nations Integrated Office in Burundi
BLTP	Burundi Leadership Training Program
BNUB	United Nations Office in Burundi
CENI	National Independent Electoral Commission
CNDD-FDD	National Council for the Defense of Democracy-Forces for the Defense of Democracy
DAC	Development Assistance Committee
DDR	Disarmament, Demobilization, and Reintegration
DFID	Department for International Development
DFS	Department of Field Support
DPA	Department of Political Affairs
DPKO	Department of Peacekeeping Operations
DRC	Democratic Republic of the Congo
DSRSG	Deputy Special Representative of the Secretary-General
ERSG	Executive Representative of the Secretary-General
FAB	Burundian Armed Forces
FAO	Food and Agriculture Organization
FCO	Foreign Commonwealth Office
FDN	National Defense Force
FEWER	Forum on Early Warning and Early Response
FRODEBU	Front for Democracy in Burundi
GDP	Gross Domestic Product
HC	Humanitarian Coordinator
ICG	International Crisis Group
ILO	International Labour Organization

IMC	Implementation Monitoring Committee
INGO	International Non-Governmental Organization
IO	International Organization
JSC	Joint Steering Committee
Ligue ITEKA	Burundian Human Rights League
M&E	Monitoring and Evaluation
MDG	Millennium Development Goals
MDRP	Multi-donor Reintegration Program / Multi-country Demobilization and Reintegration Program
MONUC	United Nations Organization Mission in the Democratic Republic of Congo
MP	Member of Parliament
MSD	Movement for Solidarity and Democracy
NGO	Non-Governmental Organization
OAG	Observatory of Governmental Action
OCHA	Office for the Coordination of Humanitarian Affairs
OHCHR	Office of the United Nations High Commissioner for Human Rights
OLUCOME	Organization for Combating Corruption and Financial Misappropriations
ONUB	United Nations Operation in Burundi
OTI	Office of Transition Initiatives
Palipehutu-FNL	Party for the Liberation of the Hutu People-National Forces of Liberation
PBA	Peacebuilding Architecture
PBC	Peacebuilding Commission
PBF	Peacebuilding Fund
PBSO	Peacebuilding Support Office
PNB	Burundian National Police
PRSP	Poverty Reduction Strategic Plan
RC	Resident Coordinator
RR	Resident Representative
SNR	National Intelligence Services
SRSG	Special Representative of the Secretary-General
UNAIDS	Joint United Nations Programme on HIV/AIDS
UNCT	United Nations Country Team
UNDAF	United Nations Development Assistance Framework
UNDP	United Nations Development Programme

UNESCO	United Nations Educational, Scientific, and Cultural Organization
UNFPA	United Nations Population Fund
UN-Habitat	United Nations Human Settlements Programme
UNHCR	United Nations High Commissioner for Refugees
UNICEF	United Nations International Children's Emergency Fund
UNIFEM	United Nations Development Fund for Women
UNOB	United Nations Office in Burundi
UNSC	United Nations Security Council
UNSG	United Nations Secretary-General
UPRONA	Union for National Progress
USAID	United States Agency for International Development
WFP	World Food Program
WHO	World Health Organization
WWICS	Woodrow Wilson International Center for Scholars

Introduction

> Organizations are more than instruments; they are themselves bundles of desires.[1]
>
> Browne and Wildavsky, 1983

I lost at poker that night. My fellow players were used to high stakes. They were Nairobi "hacks" – foreign correspondents who hopped from war zone to war zone in search of the next story. The riskier the situation, the better the tale. It was September 2000, and I had just found out I would move to Burundi to work for the United Nations (UN). Burundi was in the midst of a civil war. I would live in Bujumbura, the capital city, where high mountains on two sides of the city provided the perfect terrain for rebel groups to lob mortar shells into government buildings.

On the third side, Lake Tanganyika stretched out like a glistening ribbon wrapping the Democratic Republic of the Congo (DRC), also embroiled in war. At night, I would watch tracer fire shoot across the sky – black, black, black, black, then red – marking the persistent struggle for control of the state and its resources between the rebels and the Burundian Army.

I had spent the previous four years working on international peace-building policy.[2] In the 1990s, many international actors adopted policies committing themselves to building peace in war-torn countries.[3] These "global governors" wanted to transform war-torn states into those that could sustain peace through rule of law, market-based economies,

---

[1] Angela Browne and Aaron Wildavsky, "Implementation as Exploration (1983)," in ed. Jeffrey L. Pressman and Aaron Wildavsky, *Implementation: How Great Expectations in Washington Are Dashed in Oakland* (Berkeley: University of California Press, 1984), 252.

[2] I worked for the Center for Preventive Action of the Council on Foreign Relations, a US foreign policy think tank, and the Forum on Early Warning and Early Response (FEWER), a global network that linked researchers in conflict-prone countries with actors outside of the country who could advocate to prevent violence and build peace.

[3] See, in particular, Boutros Boutros-Ghali, *Agenda for Peace: Preventive Diplomacy, Peacemaking and Peacekeeping* (New York: United Nations, 1992); and the report of the Carnegie Commission on Preventing Deadly Conflict, *Preventing Deadly Conflict: Final Report* (New York, NY: Carnegie Corporation of New York, 1997).

and liberal democracy.[4] I wanted to see for myself if global organizations could foster this type of local change. So, the news that I was going to Burundi simultaneously thrilled and terrified me.

The Nairobi hacks did not show much sympathy for either sentiment. I boarded the flight to Bujumbura a few days later.

International Organizations (IO), International Non-Governmental Organizations (INGO), and bilateral donors give their offices in war-torn countries – "country offices" – the authority to implement and oversee most of their peacebuilding activities.[5] As a UN staff person and, subsequently, as a researcher, I saw that these country offices were not equally successful at peacebuilding, a reality that existing scholarship did not address. For example, in Burundi in 2009, the UN peacekeeping mission implemented several highly successful projects that helped to reintegrate former combatants into society, combine former enemy forces into a relatively cohesive new military, and establish an independent human rights commission.[6] During the same year, the United Nations Development Programme (UNDP) implemented several well-intentioned yet harmful projects, including one that reduced the credibility of the newly established Burundian National Police.[7] This variation in country-office performance is not unique to these organizations or to Burundi. During my subsequent research in the DRC, Nepal, South Sudan, and Sudan, I also saw a high degree of variation in the success and failure of peace-building projects, regardless of the type of activity, the location, or the point in time.

To explain variation in peacebuilding success and failure, this book presents a new typology of country-office performance, outlining four types of country offices: *peacebuilding learners, micro-adaptors, sovereignty* reinforcers, and *stagnant players*. Organizational performance, in the most general sense, refers to whether an organization achieves its aims.[8] Country-office performance, thus, describes whether a country office

---

[4] Global governors are "actors who exercise power across borders for purposes of affecting policy." Deborah D. Avant, Martha Finnemore, and Susan K. Sell, eds., *Who Governs the Globe?* (Cambridge, UK: Cambridge University Press, 2010), 2.

[5] By bilateral donor, I mean the aid agency of a state that gives aid bilaterally to another country. In this book, I do not address the behavior or performance of private contractors, state military organizations, or national Non-Governmental Organizations.

[6] For a detailed assessment of these interventions, see Susanna P. Campbell, "Independent External Evaluation: Peacebuilding Fund Projects in Burundi," Evaluation (Bujumbura: BINUB, 2010), accessed December 17, 2017, www.unpbf.org/wp-content/uploads/Independent-Evaluation-Burundi.pdf.

[7] Campbell, "Independent External Evaluation: Peacebuilding Fund Projects in Burundi."

[8] Tamar Gutner and Alexander Thompson, "The Politics of IO Performance: A Framework," *Review of International Organizations* 5, no. 3 (2010): 227–48.

achieves its aims in the country in which it intervenes. In this book, I focus on a minimal measure of country-office performance: organizational learning. In this book's typology, only one type of country office, the peacebuilding learners, is likely to achieve its peacebuilding aims. The other three types may pursue peacebuilding activities, but are unlikely to attain their desired peacebuilding outcomes. Over time, a country office may move between these four types, potentially becoming a peacebuilding learner if it creates informal local accountability and has formal accountability that prioritizes peacebuilding.

I use the term "local" in contrast to "global," referring to the people and events within a country, synonymous with "domestic" or "subnational."[9] The people and institutions that make up the local are, of course, complex and multifaceted; there is a high degree of heterogeneity. In fact, peacebuilding interventions aim to create sustainable peace, in part, by ensuring that the conflict-affected state and society no longer exclude particular groups from political participation or economic benefit. In other words, global peacebuilders try to ensure that local institutions represent the heterogeneity of local perspectives, with the implication that country offices should also ground their global interventions in this diverse local reality.

I developed the typology presented in this book by studying twenty-eight cases of country-office performance in Burundi, between 1999 and 2014.[10] Using original data, including over three hundred interviews, I identified two necessary and jointly sufficient conditions for country-office performance – informal local accountability and formal peacebuilding accountability – and the causal mechanisms at play. In developing this typology, I assessed the explanatory value of alternative hypotheses for peacebuilding success and failure – the conflict environment, organizational culture and practices, type of

---

[9] For excellent syntheses of the debates around the "local" in international peacebuilding, see Séverine Autesserre, "International Peacebuilding and Local Success: Assumptions and Effectiveness," *International Studies Review* 19, no. 1 (2017): 114–32; and Vanessa Newby, "Power, Politics and Perception: The Impact of Foreign Policy on Civilian-Peacekeeper Relations," *Third World Quarterly* (June 2017): 1–16.

[10] In research design terms, this is a typological theory. For descriptions of this approach, see Andrew Bennett, "Causal Mechanisms and Typological Theories in the Study of Civil Conflict," in ed. Jeff Checkel *Transnational Dynamics of Civil War* (Cambridge, UK: Cambridge University Press, 2014), 205–30; Bennett, "Complexity, Typological Theory, and Research Design," Power Point (May 2015); David Collier, Jody LaPorte, and Jason Seawright, "Putting Typologies to Work: Concept Formation, Measurement, and Analytic Rigor," *Political Research Quarterly* 65, no. 1 (2012): 217–32; and Colin Elman, "Explanatory Typologies in Qualitative Studies of International Politics," *International Organization* 59, no. 02 (2005): 293–326.

activity, and amount of resources.[11] The twenty-eight cases of country-office behavior in my sample enabled me to build the typology and validate each type using additional cases. I then examined the generalizability of my typology to other country offices operating in Burundi, the DRC, Nepal, South Sudan, and Sudan and found support for my findings there as well.

In this book, I argue that the variation in country offices' peacebuilding performance results, in part, from informal local accountability arrangements made by individual country-office staff. For country offices to achieve local-level change, they have to delegate authority to a representative group of local stakeholders who hold the country office accountable for achieving its local aims. This *informal local accountability* gives the country office the local-level feedback necessary to *identify* actions that may reduce the gap between its global peacebuilding aims and local peacebuilding outcomes. *Formal accountability that prioritizes peacebuilding* above other aims incentivizes the country office to *take these actions*. Over time, these feedback loops are likely to build local buy-in for the peacebuilding activity and possibly even "local ownership," a constant and elusive goal of international intervention.[12]

To create informal local accountability, however, country-office staff must circumvent standard operating procedures put in place by their headquarters or donors. This circumvention is necessary because country offices are designed to respond to the demands of their headquarters and donors, not to those of local stakeholders. Country offices are held accountable for delivering the goods and services mandated and funded by their headquarters and donors, regardless of whether local-level demand for them exists.[13] Good country-office performance, thus, requires seemingly "bad behavior" by individual staff members who break or bend rules to create informal local accountability. As one UN staff person wrote

---

[11] For discussion of alternative explanations of peacebuilding success and failure, see Séverine Autesserre, *Peaceland: Conflict Resolution and the Everyday Politics of International Intervention* (Cambridge, UK: Cambridge University Press, 2014); Autesserre, *The Trouble with the Congo: Local Violence and the Failure of International Peacebuilding*, Vol. 115, (Cambridge, UK: Cambridge University Press, 2010); Susanna P. Campbell, David Chandler, and Meera Sabaratnam, eds., *A Liberal Peace? The Problems and Practices of Peacebuilding*, (London: Zed, 2011); and Michael Doyle and Nicholas Sambanis, *Making War and Building Peace: United Nations Peace Operations* (Princeton, NJ: Princeton University Press, 2006).

[12] For a detailed discussion of the concept of local ownership and the way it is manifest in United Nations Peace Operations, see Sarah B. K. von Billerbeck, *Whose Peace? Local Ownership and United Nations Peacekeeping* (Oxford, UK: Oxford University Press, 2016), 114–26.

[13] Bertin Martens et al., *The Institutional Economics of Foreign Aid* (Cambridge, UK: Cambridge University Press, 2002).

in the *New York Times*: "Too often, the only way to speed things up is to break the rules."[14]

The basic implication of this book is that IOs, INGOs, and bilateral donors are, ironically and unintentionally, designed to fail at peacebuilding. Their country offices are not structured to receive the diverse local-level feedback necessary for them to achieve positive peacebuilding performance. Consequently, these global governors succeed at peacebuilding only when well-placed country-office staff take the risk of grounding the organization's global peacebuilding priorities in the local reality.

The importance of informal local accountability for international peacebuilding means that effective global governance relies, at least to some degree, on the local governance of global actors. Efforts to strengthen peacebuilding performance solely through top-down accountability requirements and external evaluations are, thus, unlikely to have the desired results. To positively perform, international peacebuilders need to delegate authority to local actors who have little power in the global system. But the ability of country offices to delegate this authority to local actors hinges on innovative and entrepreneurial staff who use their own agency to bridge the divide between the global and local. The improved peacebuilding performance of global governors, thus, rests on their ability to create conducive environments for these innovative staff to operate.

In the following sections, I first discuss in more detail the measure of country-office performance used in this book: organizational learning. I then give an overview of the population of study, describing the different types of peacebuilding activities and the broader population of country offices who implement them. Next, I discuss the importance of studying the peacebuilding performance of these country offices for our broader understanding of peacebuilding success and failure, as well as for the performance of global governance actors. I follow this discussion with a review of the existing literature on peacebuilding and global governance, which largely overlooks the performance of individual country offices. I then provide an overview of this book's typological theory, outlining why the combination of (1) the presence or absence informal local accountability and (2) the presence or absence of formal peacebuilding accountability produces four typical types of country offices: peacebuilding learners, micro-adaptors, sovereignty reinforcers,

---

[14] Anthony Banbury, "I Love the U.N., but It Is Failing," *New York Times*, March 18, 2016, accessed December 17, 2017, www.nytimes.com/2016/03/20/opinion/sunday/i-love-the-un-but-it-is-failing.html.

and stagnant players. Next, I discuss this book's findings, the broader significance of these findings, and the data, research design, and methods employed to generate them. I close by giving an overview of the remaining chapters of this book.

Country-Office Performance as Organizational Learning

The measure of organizational performance used in this book is *organizational learning of the country office*.[15] Some definitions of organizational learning refer to how an organization processes information about its actions, context, or outcomes, but do not consider how the organization acts on this information.[16] I use a measure of organizational learning that identifies the *actions* taken by the country office as the manifestation of learning.[17] In taking these actions, the country office is not simply adapting to the context without information about its successes and failures. *Country-office learning involves actions intended to reduce the gap(s) between the country office's aims and outcomes*, which requires that the organization receive feedback about the outcomes it has, or has not, achieved.[18] For the purpose of this book, I focus on learning in relation to the country office's peacebuilding aims, although I discuss the generalizability to other types of aims in the concluding chapter. I measure performance in terms of *whether the country office acts to reduce the gap between its peacebuilding aims and outcomes*. In the research section at the end of this chapter, I outline the precise conditions of this measurement.

Organizational learning is a minimal measure of peacebuilding performance – a necessary but insufficient condition for a country office to achieve its peacebuilding aims. Peacebuilding strives to transform the

---

[15] Organizational performance, as opposed to staff or policy-level performance, describes whether the organization achieves a set of organization-wide goals. For a fuller discussion of organizational performance, see Colin Talbot "Performance Management" in ed. Ewan Ferlie, Laurence E. Lynn Jr., and Christopher Pollitt, *The Oxford Handbook of Public Management* (Oxford, UK: Oxford Handbooks Online, 2007), 494.

[16] For further discussion of organizational learning, see Chris Argyris, *On Organizational Learning* (Boston: Blackwell, 1992); George Huber, "Organizational Learning: The Contributing Processes and the Literatures," *Organization Science* 2, no. 1 (1991), 88–115; and Jack S. Levy, "Learning and Foreign Policy: Sweeping a Conceptual Minefield," *International Organization* 48, no. 2 (1994), 279–312.

[17] This definition is based on the work of Argyris, *On Organizational Learning*.

[18] For discussion of the difference between learning and adaptation, see Jonathan Fox and L. David Brown, eds., *The Struggle for Accountability: The World Bank, NGOs, and Grassroots Movements* (Cambridge, MA: MIT Press, 1998), 11–14, who refer to Peter Haas, *Saving the Mediterranean: The Politics of International Cooperation* (New York: Columbia University Press, 1990); and Peter Haas, "Introduction: Epistemic Communities and International Policy Coordination,"*International Organization* 46, no. 1, (1992), 1–35.

institutions that contributed to war into those that can sustain peace. This is a highly ambitious agenda, which is subject to high rates of failure.[19] Peacebuilding activities are assumed to be different from simpler tasks, such as food delivery, that do not aim to change behaviors.[20] The success or failure of any international peacebuilding activity is potentially due to many different factors, including the conflict environment, the preferences of local actors, the preferences of international actors, and the availability of sufficient and appropriate resources. At a minimum, however, a country office needs to take actions to reduce the emergent gap between its transformative ambitions and the changing local reality. Country offices that learn are thus more likely to achieve their peacebuilding aims than those that do not learn.[21]

As I discuss further in Chapter 1, organizational learning is important for all organizations but is likely to be particularly important to peacebuilding for at least four reasons. First, peacebuilding aims to change a changing context. Peacebuilding takes place in dynamic war-affected contexts. The institutions and actors that it aims to transform are in flux. A country office first has to figure out how to localize its global aims in that context. Then, it has to adjust these aims as the context changes, and its initial assessment and plans quickly become outdated. As Lise Morjé Howard found in her work on UN peacekeeping, this "field-level learning" is necessary precisely because global aims have to be localized within a context that keeps changing.[22] Second, we are not able to predict the precise causes of peace in a particular country. Learning, therefore, offers the country office the opportunity to figure out whether its activities seem to fit the particular conflict-affected context. Third, because peacebuilding aims to support change that local actors will sustain, it requires the buy-in of local actors. Organizational learning by the country office requires informal local accountability that

[19] Doyle and Sambanis, *Making War and Building Peace.*

[20] For discussion of the difference between simple and complex tasks in international intervention, see Stephen D. Krasner and Thomas Risse, "External Actors, State-Building, and Service Provision in Areas of Limited Statehood: Introduction," *Governance* 27, no. 4 (October 2014): 545–67.

[21] For further discussion of the role of organizational learning in peacebuilding performance, see Susanna P. Campbell, "Organizational Barriers to Peace: Agency and Structure in International Peacebuilding" (PhD dissertation, Tufts University, 2012); Susanna P. Campbell, "Routine Learning? How Peacebuilding Organizations Prevent Liberal Peace," in ed. Campbell et al., *A Liberal Peace?* 89–105; and Susanna P. Campbell, "When Process Matters: The Potential Implications of Organizational Learning for Peacebuilding Success," *Journal of Peacebuilding and Development* 4, no. 2 (2008): 20–32.

[22] Lise Morjé Howard, *UN Peacekeeping in Civil Wars* (Cambridge, UK: Cambridge University Press, 2008).

is also likely to engender local buy-in and ownership. Fourth, the standard implementation practices of IOs, INGOs, and bilateral donors are based on the assumption that if one develops a project description with the right analysis, the right strategy, the right project aims, and the right measurement indicators and anticipate the right risks, that project will achieve its desired outcomes.[23] Organizational learning enables country offices to correct these inflexible, supply-driven templates and adapt their peacebuilding interventions to the changing local reality.

The framing of peacebuilding performance as organizational learning is related to the policy goal of "conflict sensitivity," a goal that peacebuilding, development, and humanitarian actors have widely adopted.[24] For an organization to be conflict-sensitive, it has to (1) understand the conflict dynamics in which it operates; (2) understand the relationship between its interventions and these dynamics; and (3) take actions in response to this understanding to reduce its negative contribution and increase its positive contribution to conflict dynamics. If a country office learns in relation to its peacebuilding aims, it is thus also likely to qualify as conflict-sensitive.

Peacebuilding: Multiple Actions and Actors

Peacebuilding is an umbrella term that describes a wide range of interventions that country offices undertake to reduce the risk that a conflict-prone country will lapse or relapse into violent conflict. These interventions aim to address inequality that corresponds to ethnic, religious, gender, or other social cleavages; build domestic conflict management and service delivery capacities in the economic, security, justice, and governance sectors; improve society–society relations by enhancing social cohesion and building trust among social groups; and improve state–society relations by building trust in and the legitimacy of the government.[25] These interventions can take place before, during, or after the outbreak of civil

---

[23] For a discussion of these programming patterns, see Dennis Dijkzeul, "Programs and the Problems of Participation" in ed. D. Dijkzeul and Y. Beigbeder, *Rethinking International Organizations: Pathology and Promises* (Oxford, UK: Berghahn, 2004), 197–233.

[24] See International Alert, Saferworld, and FEWER, "Conflict Sensitive Approaches to Development, Humanitarian Assistance and Peacebuilding: A Resource Pack" (London, 2004), 3.

[25] These peacebuilding "theories of change" were developed by the UN Peacebuilding Fund; see www.unpbf.org/application-guidelines/what-is-peacebuilding/.

war or political violence.[26] They can include peacekeeping, statebuilding, conflict resolution, development, humanitarian, human rights, or other types of interventions.[27]

Since the 1990s, when UN Secretary-General Boutros Boutros-Ghali called for increased international peacebuilding, there has been rapid growth in the number of IOs, INGOs, bilateral donors, and other global actors engaged in local peacebuilding.[28] In any given conflict-affected country, there are dozens, if not hundreds, of global governors implementing peacebuilding activities at the local level. A country office's peacebuilding activities largely correspond to its organization's core mandate or area of expertise, reflecting "deeply rooted organizational mandates rather than 'best practices' born from empirical analysis."[29]

A single country office may implement humanitarian, development, and peacebuilding activities, making it potentially difficult to distinguish between them.[30] The basic difference between these types of activities is their ultimate aim. International development and humanitarian assistance aim to work *around* conflict dynamics. Peacebuilding aims to work directly *on* conflict dynamics.[31]

The causes of civil war and political violence are so multifarious that almost any type of activity implemented in a war-torn country can be labeled as a peacebuilding activity, given the appropriate

---

[26] For a justification of this broad conceptualization of peacebuilding, see Advisory Group of Experts, *Review of the United Nations Peacebuilding Architecture* (New York: United Nations, June 29, 2015).

[27] For a discussion of these different types of activities and their potential contradictions, see Charles T. Call and Elizabeth M. Cousens, "Ending Wars and Building Peace: International Responses to War-Torn Societies," *International Studies Perspectives* 9 (2008): 1–21; Susanna P. Campbell and Jenny Peterson, "Statebuilding," in ed. Roger Mac Ginty, *Handbook of Peacebuilding* (London: Routledge, 2013), 336–46; Roland Paris and Timothy D. Sisk, *The Dilemmas of Statebuilding: Confronting the Contradictions of Postwar Peace Operations (Security and Governance)* (New York: Routledge, 2009); and Oliver Richmond and Jason Franks, *Liberal Peace Transitions: Between Statebuilding and Peacebuilding* (Edinburgh: Edinburgh University Press, 2009).

[28] For this articulation of peacebuilding, see Boutros Boutros-Ghali, *Supplement to the Agenda for Peace* (New York: United Nations, 1995).

[29] Michael Barnett, Hunjoon Kim, Madalene O'Donnell, and Laura Sitea, "Peacebuilding: What Is in a Name?" *Global Governance* 13, no. 1 (2007): 53.

[30] Several humanitarian organizations, such as the International Commission of the Red Cross (ICRC) and Doctors Without Borders (MSF), focus on only life-saving humanitarian assistance and protection in order to maintain humanitarian neutrality. Most other large humanitarian organizations, however, consider themselves to be multi-mandate organizations and engage in peacebuilding activities as well as humanitarian and development work.

[31] For this articulation of the difference between peacebuilding, development, and humanitarian activities, see Jonathan Goodhand, "Violent Conflict, Poverty and Chronic Poverty," Chronic Poverty Research Centre Working Paper, no. 6, *SSRN Electronic Journal* (May 2001): 1–49.

transformative spin.[32] For example, rebuilding roads, constructing schools, training judges, providing assistance to refugee populations, building local courts, equipping police forces, providing seed funding for small businesses, establishing truth and reconciliation commissions, launching military attacks, developing taxation offices, and training leaders in conflict resolution techniques could all qualify as peacebuilding activities. The implementing organization simply has to claim that the activity addresses a potential driver of conflict or peace in the recipient country.[33]

Although a broad set of activities could qualify as peacebuilding, a fixed set of supply-driven activities has emerged as the field has grown. Standardization, professionalization, and measurement have disciplined this crowded field. These activities focus on (1) reform of the security sector (police, military, and intelligence); (2) reform of the judicial system; (3) development of mechanisms to address crimes committed during the war ("transitional justice"); (4) development of conflict resolution capacities and representative state institutions ("good governance"); and (5) fostering of economic and infrastructure development at all levels of society ("socio-economic foundations").[34]

Just because an activity is labeled as a peacebuilding activity, of course, does not mean that it builds peace, or influences its determinants, however defined. Peacebuilding is an experiment. Before an activity is implemented, no one knows whether or not it will achieve its desired peacebuilding outcome, or whether that outcome will have the hypothesized effect on violent conflict or peaceful cooperation in the recipient country. "Peace" and its constituent elements are still hotly debated in both policy and scholarly circles, not to mention in conflict-affected

---

[32] See David Mason and Sara McLaughlin Mitchell, eds., *What Do We Know about Civil Wars?* (New York: Rowman and Littlefield, 2016), for a synthesis of the literature on the causes of civil war and its recurrence; and Charles T. Call, *Why Peace Fails: The Causes and Prevention of Civil War Recurrence* (Washington, DC: Georgetown University Press, 2012), for discussion of the importance of political exclusion in the onset of civil wars and the failure of peace agreements.

[33] For this conceptualization of peacebuilding, see CDA Collaborative Learning Projects, *Reflecting on Peace Practice (RPP): Participant Training Manual* (Cambridge, MA: CDA Collaborative Learning Projects, 2008).

[34] Among the many documents that describe this standard set of peacebuilding activities, these two provide helpful syntheses: Daniel Serwer and Patricia Thomson, "A Framework for Success: International Intervention in Societies Emerging from Conflict," in ed. Chester A. Crocker, Fen Osler Hampson, and Pamela Aall, *Leashing the Dogs of War: Conflict Management in a Divided World* (Washington, DC: United States Institute of Peace Press, 2007); and Dan Smith, *Towards a Strategic Framework for Peacebuilding: Getting Their Act Together*, Royal Norwegian Ministry of Foreign Affairs (Brattvaag, Norway: Hatlehols AS, 2004).

countries themselves.[35] To understand the conditions under which the international peacebuilding experiment works, we need first to understand the performance of individual country offices – the agents of international peacebuilding at the local level.

Why Country-Office Performance Matters

To assess success and failure, peacebuilding and peacekeeping scholarship tends to focus on annual country-level outcomes, such as the number of battle deaths, not the outcomes that directly result from the actions of a particular country office or group of country offices.[36] This provides an intuitive narrative – international peacebuilding succeeds if war ends and fails if significant violent conflict continues – but it belies the nature of war-to-peace transitions.[37] It imagines war-to-peace transitions as linear processes where war stops with a peace agreement, a transitional phase begins and ends, and peace is established. In reality, peaceful cooperation and violent conflict coexist and coevolve, iterating back and forth as different actors within the country vie for power.[38] In countries attempting to transition out of civil war, violent conflict and peaceful cooperation simultaneously reinforce and undermine each other. Groups and individuals regularly alter their positions and strategies. Porous borders and international politics insert new players into a dynamic process of war making, statebuilding, and peacebuilding.[39] These

---

[35] For a synthesis of the debate on the conceptualization and measurement of peace, see "Presidential Special Issue on Exploring Peace" *International Studies Review* 19, no. 1 (2017), accessed December 17, 2017, https://academic.oup.com/isr/issue/19/1.

[36] For example, Doyle and Sambanis, in *Making War and Building Peace*, measure the success of UN peace operations in terms of a battle death threshold of below twenty-five per year and the Polity democracy scale measure of at least eight.

[37] Countries in which peacebuilding takes place are usually attempting "war-to-peace" transitions. War-to-peace transition refers to the process by which a country begins to emerge from full-scale war and attempts to transition to self-sustaining peace. These transitions can last decades and are often subject to setbacks, recurrence of violent conflict, and the coexistence of violent conflict and peaceful cooperation. Many countries end their war-to-peace transition with renewed war.

[38] For discussion of the coexistence and coevolution of violent conflict and peaceful cooperation, see Susanna P. Campbell, with Michael G. Findley, and Kyosuke Kikuta, "An Ontology of Peace: Landscapes of Conflict and Cooperation with Application to Colombia," *International Studies Review* 19, no. 1 (2017): 92–113.

[39] For discussion of these dynamics, see Stathis N. Kalyvas, *The Logic of Violence in Civil War* (New York: Cambridge University Press, 2006); Ayoob Mohammed, "State Making, State Breaking, and State Failure," in ed. Chester A. Crocker, Fen Osler Hampson, and Pamela Aall, *Leashing the Dogs of War: Conflict Management in a Divided World* (Washington, DC: United States Institute of Peace, 2007); and Dipali Mukhopadhyay, *Warlords, Strongman Governors, and the State of Afghanistan* (Cambridge, UK: Cambridge University Press, 2014).

important changes in local institutions, conflict, and cooperation fall under the radar of aggregate measures of conflict and peace.

Instead of focusing on the success or failure of the collective of peace-building interventions in a country, I take an actor-centric perspective, identifying the performance of individual country offices.[40] I analyze when and why IO, INGO, and bilateral donors learn in relation to their peacebuilding aims, and then investigate how this learning influences the possible achievement of their aims within the country.

Understanding the performance of IO, INGO, and bilateral country offices matters because this is the operational unit through which peace-building takes place. For most intervening organizations engaged in conflict-affected countries, the country office carries the primary responsibility for achieving the organization's aims in that country. These offices analyze the local context, provide headquarters with crucial information about this context, and help develop the organization's strategy for that country, often writing the first draft of this local strategy.

Country offices coordinate with the host government and with other IO, INGO, and bilateral donor country offices.[41] They hire staff and consultants. They procure supplies – cars, computers, food, construction materials, and other local and international goods. They negotiate regularly with government officials, civil society actors, local communities, and, at times, rebel or militia groups. They monitor the implementation of activities and evaluate whether or not these activities achieve the organization's aims. In other words, country offices carry out global governance at the local level; they "create issues, set agendas, establish and implement rules or programs, and evaluate and/or adjudicate outcomes" on the ground.[42]

By identifying the causes of country-office peacebuilding performance, this book focuses on the factor that is most within an intervening organization's control – its own behavior. Rather than focusing on the distant effect of all intervenors, or the effect of UN peacekeeping operations on the number of battle deaths, this book analyzes intervening organizations' actual engagement with the local contexts that they aim to influence.[43]

---

[40] This approach responds to Avant et al.'s *Who Governs the Globe* call for scholars to take an actor-centric perspective to the study of global governance.

[41] The term "host government" is often used to refer to the government of the country in which international actors are intervening. The term is used frequently within the United Nations, which views its country-level offices as guests of the host government.

[42] Avant et al., *Who Governs the Globe?* 2.

[43] In so doing, it builds on the excellent work of Howard, *UN Peacekeeping in Civil Wars*, as well as my previous publications: Campbell, "When Process Matters"; and Campbell, "Routine Learning?"

Identifying how and why different country offices perform is crucial precursor to understanding their contribution to subnational outcomes in civil war as well as more aggregate national-level outcomes, such as levels of violence or degrees of democracy.[44] If a country office does not contribute to its own peacebuilding aims, then it is not likely to contribute intentionally to a more distant measure of peace in a specific subnational locale or at the national level.

Limits of Existing Analyses

The literature on international peacebuilding has two broad approaches.[45] The first approach is commonly referred to as the "liberal peace critique" and is highly critical of the entire international peacebuilding enterprise for imposing liberal democratic institutions, the rule of law, and a market-based economy on war-torn countries.[46] The second approach is the one in which this book is situated, and which critical peace scholars tend to refer to as the "problem-solving" literature.[47] This scholarship does not take a normative stand on the international peacebuilding enterprise, but examines the conditions under which international peacebuilding may or may not work. This problem-solving literature is also often highly critical of international peacebuilding, but diverges from the majority of critical peace scholarship in that it seeks to explain both

---

[44] For the use of these national-level performance measures, see Doyle and Sambanis, *Making War and Building Peace.*

[45] For a synthesis of the main arguments in these two approaches, see Campbell et al., *A Liberal Peace?*

[46] This literature is vast. For examples of the work of three of the most prominent scholars in this vein, see David Chandler, "Back to the Future? The Limits of Neo-Wilsonian Ideals of Exporting Democracy," *Review of International Studies* 32, no. 3 (2006): 475–94; Roger Mac Ginty, *International Peacebuilding and Local Resistance* (London: Palgrave, Macmillan, 2011); and Oliver Richmond, *A Post-Liberal Peace* (New York: Routledge, 2012).

[47] For some of the most influential new work in this area, see Autesserre, *Peaceland*; Naazneen Barma, *The Peacebuilding Puzzle: Political Order in Post-Conflict States* (Cambridge, UK: Cambridge University Press, 2016); Michael Barnett and Christoph Zürcher, "The Peacebuilder's Contract: How External State-Building Reinforces Weak Statehood," in ed. Timothy Sisk and Roland Paris, *The Dilemmas of Statebuilding: Confronting the Contradictions of Postwar Peace Operations* (Abingdon, UK: Routledge, 2009), 23–52; Kathleen Jennings, "Life in a 'Peace-kept' City: Encounters with the Peacekeeping Economy," *Journal of Intervention and Statebuilding* 9, no. 3 (2015): 269–315; Milli Lake, "Building the Rule of War: Postconflict Institutions and the Micro-Dynamics of Conflict in Eastern DR Congo," *International Organization* 71, no. 2 (2017), 281–315; Astri Suhrke, *When More Is Less: The International Project in Afghanistan* (New York: Columbia University Press, 2011); and Jeni Whalan, *How Peace Operations Work: Power, Legitimacy and Effectiveness* (Oxford, UK: Oxford University Press, 2013), 19–48.

positive and negative peacebuilding outcomes. In the following paragraphs, I discuss how the problem solving peacebuilding and peacekeeping scholarship and global governance scholarship view country-office performance.

Most of the international peacebuilding and peacekeeping literature either treats all country offices as a single monolithic unit or focuses only on UN peacekeeping operations. This literature makes crucial contributions, but still leaves many open questions due to the omission of a crucial variable: the performance of individual country offices. The peacebuilding and peacekeeping literature explains when and why the presence of well-resourced UN peacekeeping operations leads to fewer battle deaths each year, but does not account for the potential influence of the hundreds of global governors that operate alongside and collaborate directly with these operations.[48] This literature argues that the shared culture and practices of international intervenors prevent them from stopping war or building peace, but it does not explain the potentially wide differential in the performance of the multitude of country offices operating in a single conflict-affected country.[49] It explains the importance of organizational learning for UN peacekeeping operations, but does not explain why country offices learn or whether other IOs, INGOs, or bilateral donors exhibit similar learning patterns.[50] It argues that the supply-driven peacebuilding templates implemented by global governors stifle both national peacebuilding capacity and local democratic processes, but does not investigate instances when these templates may be altered to fit the local context.[51]

[48] See Kyle Beardsley and Kristian Skrede Gleditsch, "Peacekeeping as Conflict Containment," *International Studies Review* 17, 1 (2015): 67–89; Doyle and Sambanis, *Making War and Building Peace*; Virginia Page Fortna, "Does Peacekeeping Keep Peace? International Intervention and the Duration of Peace after Civil War," *International Studies Quarterly* 48, no. 2 (2004): 269–92; Fortna, *Does Peacekeeping Work? Shaping Belligerents' Choices after Civil War*, Princeton, NJ: Princeton University Press, 2008); and Michael Gilligan and Ernest J. Sergenti, "Do UN Interventions Cause Peace? Using Matching to Improve Causal Inference," *Quarterly Journal of Political Science* 3, (2008): 89–122.

[49] See Séverine Autesserre, "Hobbes and the Congo: Frames, Local Violence, and International Intervention," *International Organization* 63, no. 2 (2009): 249–80; Autesserre, *Peaceland;* and Autesserre, *The Trouble with the Congo*.

[50] See Howard, *UN Peacekeeping in Civil Wars*.

[51] See Michael Barnett, "Building a Republican Peace: Stabilizing States after War," *International Security* 30, no. 4 (2006): 87–112; Virginia Page Fortna, "Peacekeeping and Democratization," in ed. Anna Jarstad and Timothy Sisk, *From War to Democracy* (Cambridge, UK: Cambridge University Press, 2008), 39–70; Roland Paris, *At War's End: Building Peace after Civil Conflict* (Cambridge, UK: Cambridge University Press, 2004); Béatrice Pouligny, *Peace Operations Seen from Below: UN Missions and Local People*

The extensive literature on civil war has embraced the importance of examining subnational behavior, motivations, and events. Surprisingly, this subnational perspective has is not reflected in much of the literature on intervention in civil war. Civil wars emerge and persist because of decisions made by rebel groups, political leaders, and local-level populations, leading to outcomes that are visible at the national level – such as the number of battle deaths or the signing of a peace agreement – as well as outcomes that may not be captured by national-level measures, such as robust and innovative community-level institutions.[52] Even though peacebuilding often takes place in the midst of civil war and aims to affect the behaviors of rebel groups, political leaders, and local-level populations, few scholars have investigated how international peacebuilders engage with the dynamic local reality. Even Autesserre's important work on international engagement with local conflict dynamics does not explain why or how different country offices engage with these local dynamics in different ways.[53]

Much of the global governance scholarship, for its part, overlooks the behavior of country offices because it focuses on the global level: on global accountability; decision-making at IO, INGO, and bilateral donor headquarters; headquarter-level bureaucratic pathologies; and the emergence and adoption of global norms.[54] It largely assumes that

(Bloomfield, CT: Kumarian, 2006); Astri Suhrke, "Reconstruction as Modernisation: The 'Post-Conflict' Project in Afghanistan," *Third World Quarterly* 28, no. 7 (2007): 1291–1308; and Susan Woodward, "Do the Root Causes of Civil War Matter? On Using Knowledge to Improve Peacebuilding Interventions," *Journal of Intervention and Statebuilding* 1, no. 2 (2007): 143–70.

[52] For syntheses of these arguments, see Campbell et al., "An Ontology of Peace," 1–22; Stathis N. Kalyvas, "The Ontology of 'Political Violence': Action and Identity in Civil Wars," *Perspectives on Politics* 1, no. 3 (September 2003): 475–94; and Oliver Kaplan, Resisting War: How Communities Protect Themselves, (Cambridge, UK: Cambridge University Press, 2017).

[53] Autesserre, "Hobbes and the Congo;" Autesserre, *Peaceland*; and Autesserre, *The Trouble with the Congo.*

[54] See, for example, Michael Barnett and Martha Finnemore, "The Politics, Power, and Pathologies of International Organizations," *International Organization* 53, no. 4 (1999): 699–732; Michael Barnett and Martha Finnemore, *Rules for the World: International Organizations in Global Politics* (Ithaca, NY: Cornell University Press, 2004); Martha Finnemore and Kathryn Sikkink, "International Norm Dynamics and Political Change," *International Organization* 52, no. 4 (1998): 887–917; Ruth Grant and Robert O. Keohane, "Accountability and Abuses of Power in World Politics," *American Political Science Review* 99, no. 1 (2005): 29–43; Darren G. Hawkins, David A. Lake, Daniel L. Nielson, and Michael J. Tierney, *Delegation and Agency in International Organizations* (Cambridge, UK: Cambridge University Press, 2006); Tana Johnson, *Organizational Progeny* (Oxford, UK: Oxford University Press, 2014); Margaret E. Keck and Kathryn Sikkink, *Activists beyond Borders: Advocacy Networks in International Politics* (Ithaca, NY: Cornell University Press, 1998); Barbara Koremenos, Charles Lipson, and Duncan

the performance of a country office is either determined by the preferences of the organization's principals – their founders, member states, headquarters, and/or donors – or by competing norms or other social factors that lead to dysfunctional bureaucratic practices. The global governance literature largely overlooks the potentially independent behavior of country offices.

For much of the global governance scholarship, accountability to an organization's principals is valued as inherently good.[55] When an organization complies with the preferences of its headquarters and donors, it succeeds; when it does not comply, it fails. This literature labels deviations from principals' preferences as "agency slack," arguing that such undesirable behavior undermines the ability of the agent to achieve the principals' preferred outcome.[56] A handful of assessments of IO, INGO, and bilateral donor country offices, however, reveal heterogeneous country-level decision-making even within one organization, pointing to the importance of studying the behavior of global governors at the local level.[57]

This book does less to dispute the claims of the existing peacebuilding, peacekeeping, and global governance literature than to argue that they have overlooked a critical part of the picture – country-office performance – and are thus omitting important variables that help explain the local peacebuilding performance of global governors. If some organizations contribute to positive outcomes in a war-torn country and others contribute to negative outcomes, then it is important to understand which organizations are more likely to contribute to which outcome and why. How can a single country office succeed at one point in time and fail at

Snidal, "The Rational Design of International Institutions," *International Organization* 55, no. 4 (October 2001): 761–99; Barbara Koremenos, Charles Lipson, and Duncan Snidal, *The Rational Design of International Institutions* (Cambridge, UK: Cambridge University Press, 2004); David A. Lake, "Delegating Divisible Sovereignty: Sweeping a Conceptual Minefield," *Review of International Organizations* 2, no. 3 (2007): 219–37.

[55] For a synthesis of these arguments, see Michael Barnett, "Accountability and Global Governance: The View from Paternalism," *Regulation and Governance* 10, no. 2 (June 2016); 134–48; and Daniel Nielson, Michael J. Tierney, and Catherine E. Weaver, "Bridging the Rationalist–Constructivist Divide: Re-Engineering the Culture of the World Bank," *Journal of International Relations and Development* 9, no. 2 (2006): 107–39. For a notable exception to this trend, see Alexander Cooley and James Ron, "The NGO Scramble: Organizational Insecurity and the Political Economy of Transnational Action," *International Security* 27, no. 1 (2002): 5–39.

[56] See, for example, Hawkins et al., *Delegation and Agency*, 824–5; and Mark A. Pollack and Emilie Hafner-Burton, "Mainstreaming Gender in the European Union: Getting the Incentives Right," *Comparative European Politics* 7, no. 1 (April 2009): 114–38.

[57] See Doyle and Sambanis, *Making War and Building Peace*; Howard, *UN Peacekeeping in Civil Wars*; Lake, "Building the Rule of War"; and Michael Lipson, "Performance under Ambiguity: International Organization Performance in UN Peacekeeping," *Review of International Organizations* 5, no. 3 (September 2010): 249–84.

another point in time in the same country? How can one country office fail and another one succeed in the same country at the same point in time? In spite of the vast literature on civil war, international peacekeeping, international peacebuilding, and global governance, we do not understand why country offices engage differently with host country contexts or how this engagement influences their performance.

By answering these questions, this book supports numerous critiques of international peacebuilding by explaining why country offices perform poorly. But it also supports claims of peacebuilding success by explaining the conditions under which country offices achieve positive peacebuilding performance. A detailed understanding of the reasons for the variation in the performance of country offices is important not only for existing scholarship but also for policy makers and practitioners who seek to improve the effectiveness of international peacebuilding interventions. In the following section, I outline this book's main claims about the causes of country-office peacebuilding performance.

Explaining Peacebuilding Performance: A Typology

Two conditions are necessary for IO, INGO, and bilateral donor country offices to contribute to their peacebuilding aims in a particular country. First, country offices must prioritize their peacebuilding aims; that is, they must prioritize accountability for their peacebuilding goals, rather than humanitarian or development goals. I refer to this organizational characteristic as *formal peacebuilding accountability*. Second, country offices must delegate informal accountability to local stakeholders, which I refer to as *informal local accountability*. Feedback from a representative group of local actors (through informal local accountability) provides information about the organization's work and its relationship to local conflict dynamics. Formal accountability primarily for peacebuilding incentivizes the country office to pay attention to this conflict-related information and adjust its interventions so that they are more relevant to the evolving local conflict dynamics. Together, these top-down and bottom-up accountability mechanisms enable the country office to take real-time action to reduce the gap between its peacebuilding aims and its peacebuilding outcomes, or learn. Learning, in turn, increases the likelihood that the organization will contribute to its peacebuilding aims in a dynamic conflict-affected context.

As discussed earlier in this Introduction, I measure country-office peacebuilding performance in terms of organized learning. Given that the success or failure of a peacebuilding intervention depends on multiple factors beyond the country office's control, organizational learning by the country office in relation to its peacebuilding aims is a necessary but insufficient condition for it to achieve these aims. In the case study chapters, I demonstrate the role that formal and informal accountability play in organizational learning and the potentially positive relationship between this organizational learning and a country office's achievement of its peacebuilding aims.

Formal Accountability: Responsiveness to the Organization's Principals

An organization's *formal accountability routines* hold it responsible for achieving its aims.[58] Organizations seek to guide their own behavior using targets, or aims.[59] In IOs, INGOs, and bilateral donors, the organization's principals – governing boards, member states, donors, headquarter bureaucracy – establish these aims. These principals give country offices the authority, as their agents, to achieve these aims in a particular country. They establish formal accountability routines that link the organization's headquarters and country offices, stipulating the incentive structure for the organization's country offices. These accountability routines constrain the behavior of each country office, hold it responsible for meeting the organization's aims in that country, and ensure that it complies with the organization's overall standards.[60] Accountability routines are a type of organizational routine, or the standard operating procedures that are replicated throughout an organization and govern the standard behavior of its component parts, including country offices.[61]

Formal accountability routines influence how the country office views the context in which it operates, what information it internalizes about this context, what responses it deploys in this context, and how headquarters assesses its effectiveness, or performance, in this context.[62] Formal

---

[58] For a discussion of accountability and its manifestations and measurement, see Fox and Brown, eds., *The Struggle for Accountability*. For a discussion of the manifestation of accountability as routines in closed, hierarchical organizations, see Johan P. Olsen, "Democratic Order, Autonomy, and Accountability," *Governance: An International Journal of Policy, Administration, and Institutions* 28, no. 4 (2015): 430.

[59] For a discussion of the role argets in organizational learning, see Barbara Levitt and James G. March, "Organizational Learning," *Annual Review of Sociology* 14, no. 1 (1988): 319–40.

[60] For a synthesis of the role of accountability and delegation in global governance, see Grant and Keohane, "Accountability and Abuses of Power in World Politics"; and David A. Lake, "Rightful Rules: Authority, Order, and the Foundations of Global Governance," *International Studies Quarterly* 54, no. 3 (2010): 587–613.

[61] For a discussion of the role of organizational routines in organizational behavior, see Levitt and March, "Organizational Learning," 326.

[62] For a discussion of the role of accountability in organizational behavior and learning, see Alnoor Ebrahim, *NGOs and Organizational Change: Discourse, Reporting, and Learning*

accountability routines are manifest in the vertical micro-level interactions between the principals of IOs, INGOs, and bilateral donors and the country office. They can take the form of project and financial reports; project proposals; daily email and phone communications; meetings; reviews and assessments; visits from donors, members of the governing board, or headquarters-level staff, as well as other hierarchical interactions.

The hierarchical formal accountability structure of IOs, INGOs, and bilateral donors leads to the predominance of upward accountability. Generally, the country office's principals are located outside of the country in which it operates, and often have limited knowledge of the local contexts that the country office encounters. The dominance of upward accountability, manifest in formal accountability routines, raises a crucial challenge for country offices: they are not incentivized to respond to diverse local-level feedback about the effectiveness of their activities.[63] They are incentivized to respond to the preferences of their principals and to deliver goods and services to local-level actors. This focus on upward accountability seems to have become even more pronounced as international peacebuilding, like other areas of international intervention, has become professionalized, solidifying formal accountability routines and reducing opportunities for innovation.[64]

Most IOs, INGOs, and bilateral donors agree that local ownership of their interventions is important; nonetheless, their formal accountability routines still incentivize listening to, responding to, and fulfilling the requirements of their principals outside of the conflict-affected country.[65] Without feedback from local institutions and the incentive

---

(Cambridge, UK: Cambridge University Press, 2003); Alnoor Ebrahim, "Accountability Myopia: Losing Sight of Organizational Learning," *Nonprofit and Voluntary Sector Quarterly* 34, no. 1 (2005): 56–87; Lynn Eden, "'Getting It Right or Wrong': Organizational Learning about the Physical World," in ed. M. Leann Brown, Michael Kenney, and Michael Zarkin, *Organizational Learning in the Global Context* (Aldershot, UK: Ashgate, 2006), 197–216; and Levitt and March, "Organizational Learning."

[63] For support for this claim, see Alnoor Ebrahim, "Accountability in Practice: Mechanisms for NGOs," *World Development* 31, no. 5 (2003): 813–29; Clark Gibson et al., *The Samaritan's Dilemma: The Political Economy of Development Aid* (Oxford, UK: Oxford University Press, 2005); Bertin Martens et al., *The Institutional Economics of Foreign Aid*; and Andrew Natsios, "The Clash of Counter-Bureaucracy and Development" (Washington, DC: Center for Global Development, 2010).

[64] For a discussion of similar trends in democracy assistance, see Sarah Bush, *The Taming of Democracy Assistance* (Cambridge, UK: Cambridge University Press, 2015).

[65] On the importance of listening to a variety of actors within a country, see the CDA's Collaborative Learning Project, *Time to Listen: Hearing People on the Receiving End of International Aid* (Cambridge, MA: CDA Collaborative Learning Projects, 2012). While most country offices are told to build some "local ownership" for their activities, they often lack formal guidelines for how this ownership should take place. For a detailed discussion of the challenges facing local ownership, see von Billerbeck, *Whose Peace?*

to respond to this feedback, country offices cannot take informed actions to reduce the gap between their global aims their outcomes in the local context, or learn. Organizational learning in a dynamic context requires real-time feedback about the effect of the organization's activities, as well as regular actions to reduce the gap between the organization's peacebuilding aims and actual effects of its peacebuilding activities.[66]

To help ensure that country offices achieve headquarters' aims, headquarters may require country offices to conduct periodic external evaluations, a formal accountability routine. While these evaluations may provide crucial information about intervention outcomes and incentivize the country office to respond to this information, evaluations often take place at the end of a project and are usually conducted by external consultants who are present in the country for only a few weeks. As a result, evaluations rarely provide the direct, diverse, and real-time local feedback necessary for the country office to adjust its peacebuilding activities to the rapidly changing local context that it aims to influence, or to create the type of buy-in from local actors that is likely to be necessary for change in local institutions.[67]

Given that the formal accountability routines that govern the behavior of country offices do not incentivize local feedback, how can we explain the instances when country offices receive and respond to representative's local-level feedback?

Informal Local Accountability: Giving Authority to Diverse Local Stakeholders

Country offices can counterbalance the upward pull of formal accountability routines by creating informal local accountability. *Informal local accountability* takes place when the country office delegates authority to a diverse group of local stakeholders, giving them influence over the way that the country office's peacebuilding interventions are implemented.[68]

---

[66] For a detailed discussion of the role of feedback in organizational learning, see Argyris, *On Organizational Learning*; and Browne and Wildavsky, "Implementation as Exploration."

[67] For a discussion of the importance and challenge of diverse local buy-in, or local ownership, see von Billerbeck, *Whose Peace?*; CDA Collaborative Learning Projects, *Time to Listen*; John Paul Lederach, *Building Peace: Sustainable Reconciliation in Divided Societies* (Washington, DC: United States Institute of Peace, 1997); and Roger Mac Ginty, "Hybrid Peace: The Interaction between Top-Down and Bottom-Up Peace," *Security Dialogue* 41, no. 4 (2010): 391–412.

[68] For discussions of the importance of the implementation phase of peacebuilding, see Campbell, "When Process Matters"; CDA Collaborative Learning Projects, *Time to Listen;* and Ben Oppenheim and Johanna Soderstrom, "Citizens by Design? Explaining

Like informal governance mechanisms, informal local accountability can manifest in different ways.[69] The defining factor is that informal local accountability gives a diverse group of local actors the authority to sanction the country office for failing to achieve its aims in the country context. Of course, these different local actors could seek to co-opt the peacebuilding intervention.[70] This is why the integration of a diverse group of local stakeholders is a key component of informal local accountability is so important; it creates the opportunity for these local accountability routines to mitigate, rather than exacerbate, intergroup cleavages.[71]

Peacebuilding interventions aim to address the social and political cleavages within and between the conflict-affected state and society. In countries with strong state institutions and strong state–society relations, country offices may be able to rely on the government to convey the diverse perspectives of its population.[72] But these are not the countries in which most civil war and peacebuilding take place. Instead, peacebuilding often takes place in relatively underdeveloped countries where different political and armed actors openly contest the nature of political institutions, the distribution of the state's resources, and the rights of the population.[73] Consequently, to receive local feedback from a representative group of local stakeholders in its interventions, a country office has to actively seek out diverse stakeholder perspectives and establish

Ex-Combatant Satisfaction with Reintegration Programming," *Journal of Development Studies* (2017): 1–20.

[69] For a discussion of informal governance, see Thomas Christiansen and Christine Neuhold, eds., "International Handbook on Informal Governance," *Journal of Common Market Studies* 51, no. 6 (2013): 1196–1206; Randall Stone, *Controlling Institutions: International Organizations and the Global Economy* (Cambridge, UK: Cambridge University Press, 2011); and Randall Stone, "Informal Governance in International Organizations: Introductions to the Special Issue," *Review of International Organizations* 8, no. 2 (2013), 121–36.

[70] For discussion of the role of cooptation in peacebuilding, see Barma, *Peacebuilding Puzzle*; and Barnett and Zürcher, "The Peacebuilder's Contract."

[71] For a critique of local feedback mechanisms, see Séverine Autesserre, "Paternalism and Peacebuilding: Capacity, Knowledge, and Resistance in International Intervention," in ed. Michael N. Barnett, *Paternalism beyond Borders* (Cambridge, UK: Cambridge University Press, 2017).

[72] For a discussion of the particular challenges of governance and international cooperation in conflict-affected states, see Department for International Development, *Building Peaceful States and Societies: A DFID Practice Paper* (London: Department for International Development, 2010); Daniel Esser, *Do No Harm: International Support for State Building* (Paris: Organization for Economic Cooperation and Development, 2010); Sue Unsworth, *An Upside Down View of Governance* (Washington, DC, and London: Institute of Democracy Studies, 2010); and World Bank, *World Development Report 2011: Conflict, Security, and Development* (Washington, DC: World Bank, 2011).

[73] For a discussion of the relationship between poor governance and civil war, see Barma, *Peacebuilding Puzzle*; and Barbara F. Walter, "Why Bad Governance Leads to Repeat Civil War," *Journal of Conflict Resolution* 59, no. 7, (2014): 1242–72.

informal local accountability routines to solicit their feedback and investment in the intervention.

To create informal local accountability, individual country-office staff
have to bypass some of the formal accountability routines that the organization's principals created to hold the country office accountable. Even
if these formal accountability routines prioritize peacebuilding interventions, they incentivize externally, supply-driven peacebuilding that
is largely unresponsive to local dynamics or needs. Implementing locally
relevant peacebuilding interventions, therefore, requires that the country
office invest in informal local accountability that is, by definition, not
incentivized by the organization's upward accountability. As a result,
positive peacebuilding performance depends, in part, on country-office
staff who bend or break the formal accountability routines intended to
make the country office perform.

Integrating Formal and Informal Local Accountability: Four Types

While informal local accountability determines whether or not a country
office receives feedback from a representative group of local stakeholders, the focus of formal accountability determines which feedback
the organization responds to. Intervening organizations view the country
context through the lens of their own priorities.[74] Just as lawyers view
problems through the lens of the law, country offices view the country
context through the priorities set by their principals. If a country office's
formal accountability routines prioritize peacebuilding, which I refer to
as *formal peacebuilding accountability*, then it is likely to view the country
context primarily through a peacebuilding lens. Likewise, if a country
office's formal accountability routines prioritize development, it is likely
to view the context primarily through a development lens. This implies
that a country office will be forced to choose among humanitarian,
development, and peacebuilding aims.

As depicted in Figure I.1, treating formal peacebuilding accountability
and informal local accountability as dichotomous variables produces four
possible types of country offices: *peacebuilding learners, micro-adaptors, sovereignty reinforcers*, and *stagnant players*. In this typology, formal accountability
routines either prioritize peacebuilding or prioritize other non-
peacebuilding aims, such as development or humanitarian assistance;

---

[74] For discussion of how organizational priorities shape organizational learning, see Lynn Eden,
Whole World on Fire: Organizations, Knowledge, and Nuclear Weapons Devastation (Ithaca, NY:
Cornell University Press, 2004); Eden, "'Getting It Right or Wrong'"; Levitt and March,
"Organizational Learning"; and Dianne Vaughan, *The Challenger Launch Decision: Risky
Technology, Culture, and Deviance at NASA* (Chicago: University of Chicago Press, 1996).

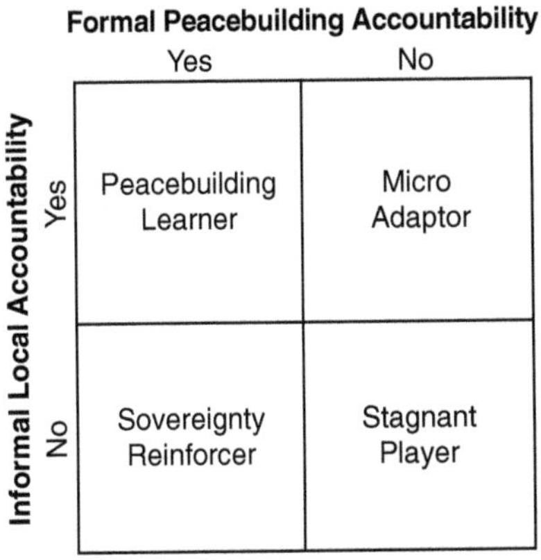

Formal Peacebuilding Accountability

	Yes	No
Yes	Peacebuilding Learner	Micro Adaptor
No	Sovereignty Reinforcer	Stagnant Player

Informal Local Accountability

Figure I.1. Types of Country Offices

informal local accountability either exists or does not exist. Because a country office's formal and informal local accountability routines may change over time, a single country office may move from one type to another over time.

When a country office has both formal peacebuilding accountability and informal local accountability, it is a *peacebuilding learner*. Only peacebuilding learners are likely to achieve their peacebuilding aims. The other three types of country offices – sovereignty reinforcers, micro-adaptors, and stagnant players – are not likely to achieve their peacebuilding aims. Country offices that prioritize formal peacebuilding accountability but lack informal local accountability routines are *sovereignty reinforcers*. These country offices are likely to reinforce the policies of the host government at the expense of local actors who are not well represented or well served by the state. Country offices that have strong informal local accountability routines but lack formal peacebuilding accountability are *micro-adaptors*. They are likely to understand local institutions, but they are unlikely to directly address the conflict dynamics in these institutions. Country offices that lack both informal local accountability routines and formal peacebuilding accountability are *stagnant players*. They are likely to implement the same set of activities from one year to the next without adjusting to the evolving conflict dynamics in the country.

Overview of Findings

As discussed in further detail in the research design section that follows, I developed this book's typological theory by studying the behavior of five country offices at six crucial turning points in Burundi between 1999 and

2014. This gave me twenty-eight cases of country-office performance because two of the country offices were not operational during the first phase. The case study organizations include the four Security-Council mandated United Nations peace operations deployed to Burundi between 1999 and 2014, which I refer to collectively as the UN Missions, the United Nations Development Programme (UNDP) office in Burundi, the United Kingdom's Department for International Development (DFID) office in Burundi, CARE International's office in Burundi, and the Burundi Leadership Training Program (BLTP) of the Woodrow Wilson International Center for Scholars.

As depicted in Table I.1, the peacebuilding performance of these five country offices varied significantly throughout Burundi's war-to-peace transition. In only nine out of twenty-eight cases were the country offices peacebuilding learners, acting regularly to align their global peacebuilding aims and activities with the preferences of local stakeholders. In the other nineteen cases, the country offices fell into one of the three other types of country-office behavior and failed to demonstrate a clear contribution to their peacebuilding aims.

This variation in country-office performance was not determined by the existing explanations for peacebuilding success and failure: the intensity of the conflict-related hostilities, the capacity of the host government, or the structural or cultural features of the country offices.[75] It was not determined by whether the country office was an IO, INGO, or bilateral donor or by its degree of hierarchy, degree of decentralized authority, founding mandate, size, or staff training curriculum, all alternative explanations for organizational performance from the global governance and organizational learning literatures.[76] The positive peacebuilding performance of these twenty-eight cases was determined by the presence of two necessary and jointly sufficient characteristics: formal peacebuilding accountability and informal local accountability. The creation of informal local accountability, in turn, was due to the initiative of country-office staff who were willing to invest time and resources, often with high

---

[75] Autesserre, "Hobbes and the Congo"; Autesserre, *Peaceland*; Autesserre, *The Trouble with the Congo*; and Doyle and Sambanis, *Making War and Building Peace*.

[76] Argyris, *On Organizational Learning*; Ariane Berthoin-Antal, Uwe Lenhardt, and Rolf Rosenbrock, "Barriers to Organizational Learning," in ed. M. Dierkes et al., *Handbook of Organizational Learning and Knowledge* (Oxford, UK: Oxford University Press, 2000), 865–85; M. Leann Brown and Michael Kenney, "Organizational Learning: Theoretical and Methodological Considerations," in ed. Brown et al., *Organizational Learning in the Global Context*, 1–20; Eden, "'Getting It Right or Wrong'"; Eden, *Whole World on Fire*; Levitt and March, "Organizational Learning"; James G. March and Herbert Simon, *Organizations, Second Edition* (Cambridge, UK: Blackwell Business, 1993); and Koremenos et al., "The Rational Design of International Institutions."

Table I.1. *Overview of Case Studies*

	Phase I: Jan. 1999– Oct. 2001	Phase II: Nov. 2001– Nov. 2003	Phase III: Dec. 2003– Aug. 2005	Phase IV: Sept. 2005– Apr. 2009	Phase V: May 2009– May 2010	Phase VI: June 2010– Apr. 2014
UN Missions	Peacebuilding Learner	Sovereignty Reinforcer	Peacebuilding Learner	Sovereignty Reinforcer	Sovereignty Reinforcer	Sovereignty Reinforcer
UK DFID	n/a	Peacebuilding Learner	Peacebuilding Learner	Stagnant Player	Stagnant Player	Stagnant Player
BLTP	n/a	Peacebuilding Learner	Peacebuilding Learner	Micro-adaptor	Peacebuilding Learner	Peacebuilding Learner
UNDP	Stagnant Player	Stagnant Player	Stagnant Player	Sovereignty Reinforcer	Sovereignty Reinforcer	Stagnant Player
CARE	Stagnant Player	Stagnant Player	Stagnant Player	Peacebuilding Learner	Micro-adaptor	Micro-adaptor

transaction costs, to empower a representative group of local stakeholders to hold the country office accountable for achieving its global peacebuilding aims at the local level.

Relevance for Policy Action

Understanding peacebuilding through this typology challenges the
conventional wisdom about the performance of global governance organizations. While the existing scholarly and policy discussions of accountability in IOs, INGOs, and international donors largely assume that
accountability is inherently good, this book shows that strong formal
accountability alone can create a disincentive for country-office staff to
engage with the local institutions that they aim to transform, in turn
decreasing the likelihood that the country office will achieve its peacebuilding aims.[77]

The literature on global governance generally describes IOs as the
most accountable global actors; INGOs are seen as the least accountable global actors because of the weaker state-based constraints on
their policies or practices.[78] The case studies in this book indicate
that, on the one hand, the accountability of IOs to states at the global
level may constrain their relevance to the local conflict dynamics that
they aim to influence. On the other hand, the lack of global constraints on of INGOs may give them the greatest potential for true
local accountability to the populations that they aim to serve. An
examination of the country-level behavior of these global governors
thus calls into question key assumptions in the existing literature
about their effectiveness.

The performance of key actors in global governance also has a strong
bearing on the legitimacy of these actors in both the local and the global
arenas. As Gutner and Thompson have noted, "performance is the path
to legitimacy, and thus our ability to understand performance – what it is
and where it comes from – is crucial."[79] This book identifies a crucial
paradox: the legitimacy of IOs, INGOs, and bilateral donors is derived in
part from their willingness to delegate their authority (through informal
local accountability) to local actors who are unrepresented by the

---

[77] Grant and Keohane, "Accountability and Abuses of Power in World Politics" 29–43;
and Judith G. Kelley and Beth A. Simmons, "Politics by Number: Indicators as Social
Pressure in International Relations," *American Journal of Political Science* 59, no. 1
(2015): 55–70.
[78] Grant and Keohane, "Accountability and Abuses of Power in World Politics," 29–43.
[79] Gutner and Thompson, "The Politics of IO Performance."

institutions of global governance.[80] Effective global governance may, therefore, require increased local governance of global actors.

Because of the high density of country offices deployed in conflict-affected countries, we can think of international peacebuilding as a petri dish in which to study how key global governance actors interact, coexist, and cooperate among themselves and with domestic institutions.[81] By analyzing the organizational routines that IO, INGO, and bilateral donor country offices replicate in different country contexts, the findings presented here shed light on the broader behavioral patterns of these organizations. This book's findings on the country-office performance of IOs, INGOs, and bilateral donors engaged in peacebuilding, therefore, should be relevant to these organizations' behavior in less tumultuous contexts as well, as discussed in more detail in this book's Conclusion.

By investigating how different intervening organizations respond to the same context, this book focuses on the aspect of international peacebuilding that intervening organizations have the greatest capacity to change: their own behavior. As a result, these findings are relatively easy to translate into concrete policy recommendations for IOs, INGOs, and bilateral donors. The specific recommendations that result from these findings are described in detail in the concluding chapter of this book.

Data, Research Design, and Methodology

This book presents an explanatory typology of country-office peacebuilding performance.[82] I develop this typology using twenty-eight cases of country-office behavior in one country, identifying the necessary and jointly sufficient conditions for their positive peacebuilding performance, or lack thereof.

I employ a nested, longitudinal case study design to examine the behavior of the country offices of five diverse intervening organizations – two IOs, two INGOs, and one bilateral donor – in relation to changes

---

[80] Jeff Colgan and Robert Keohane, "The Liberal Order Is Rigged," *Foreign Affairs* (April/May 2017), accessed December 17, 2017, www.foreignaffairs.com/articles/world/2017-04-17/liberal-order-rigged.

[81] Barnett and Zürcher, "The Peacebuilder's Contract."

[82] For a discussion of typologies, see David Collier, Jody LaPorte, and Jason Seawright, "Putting Typologies to Work: Concept Formation, Measurement, and Analytic Rigor," *Political Research Quarterly* 65, no. 1 (2012), 217–32; Colin Elman, "Explanatory Typologies in Qualitative Studies of International Politics," *International Organization* 59 (2005), 293–326; and Alexander L. George and Andrew Bennett, *Case Studies and Theory Development in the Social Science* (Cambridge, MA: MIT Press, 2004), chapter 11, 233–262.

in the country environment during six distinct phases in Burundi's war-to-peace transition from 1999 to 2014.[83] The primary unit of analysis is the country office during one phase in Burundi's war-to-peace transition. Each new temporal phase is triggered by a large shift in Burundi's conflict dynamics. The case study organizations each identified these shifts as meriting an updated peacebuilding strategy and approach. As discussed in further detail in the following pages and in Chapter 2, I assess whether the case study organizations responded to their own contextual triggers for organizational learning in relation to Burundi's evolving war-to-peace transition. Because two of the country offices were not operational during the first temporal phase, there are twenty-eight cases through which I assess country-office peacebuilding performance.

From among the broader universe of IOs, INGOs, and bilateral donors engaged in peacebuilding in Burundi between 1999 and 2014, I used the diverse case selection approach to select the five organizational cases. I describe each of these organizations in more detail in the respective case study chapters, and outline the case study selection strategy in the following pages.

As I review in the following sections, my causal inference strategy uses case study selection purposively to rule out alternative explanations, identify the necessary and sufficient conditions for the outcome of interest validate the theoretical mechanism through causal process-tracing in multiple cases, and identify the scope conditions under which the theory is valid.

Data

This book draws on original primary data that I gathered over a fifteen-year period, including over three hundred semi-structured interviews, participant observation, and archival analysis of internal documents from each of the case study organizations.[84] I used a stratified purposive sampling strategy to ensure that I gathered data from staff at all levels of seniority, key former staff from the case study organization, headquarters-based staff, and local partners of each case study

---

[83] This research design is nested in the sense that the primary unit of analysis – the country office – operates within (is nested within) the country case of Burundi. It is longitudinal in that it measures the behavior of the five country offices at six different points in time in one country. For discussion of this type of case study design, see Robert K. Yin, *Case Study Research: Design and Methods* (Thousand Oaks, CA: Sage, 2009), 29, 50.

[84] See https://dataverse.harvard.edu/dataverse/susannacampbell for a full description of the interview sample. In line with the informed-consent agreement that I made with each interviewee, I have anonymized all interviews and only refer to them by the organization or organizational type, year, location, and the code that I assigned to each interview.

organization in Burundi.[85] In addition to in-depth research into the five case study organizations, I conducted interviews with the broader population of IO, INGO, and bilateral donor country offices in Burundi, key informants from Burundian civil society, and staff responsible for Burundi at each case study organization's headquarters.

I gathered these data through research trips to Burundi in 2002, 2004, 2008, 2009, and 2013 as well as through interviews conducted with headquarters staff in Geneva, London, New York, and Washington, D.C. between 2004 and 2016. As an external evaluator for three of the case study organizations – the BLTP, the UN Missions, and UNDP – I was given access to internal documents and allowed to participate in internal meetings, providing important insight into the inner workings of these organizations. The other two organizations – DFID and CARE International – gave me very open access to their staff and internal meetings, enabling me to conduct comparable analyses.

Developing and Validating a Typological Theory

To develop and refine my typological theory, I used original data about the case study organizations and the broader organizational population, as discussed above, as well as archival documents about Burundi's evolving context between 1999 and 2014.[86] I used these data to identify two necessary and jointly sufficient conditions for the four different types of country-office behavior, and examined the influence of alternative explanations for organizational learning and peacebuilding success and

---

[85] Stratified purposive sampling means that you select the categories, or strata, of people who you want to talk with from within the broader population of potential interviewees and then ensure that you have a representative group of individuals from each stratum. In this case, I wanted to interview the same categories of people across each of the case study organizations and within the broader population of IO, INGO, and bilateral donor country offices engaged in peacebuilding in Burundi. Michael Quinn Patton, *Qualitative Research and Evaluation Methods*, 3rd ed. (Thousand Oaks, CA: Sage, 2001), 240.

[86] Andrew Bennett provides a nice description of the process of typological theory development, which I employed: "Constructing a typological theory involves both deductive and inductive reasoning. Deductively, the analyst defines the dependent variable of interest and uses prior theories ... to identify the relevant independent variables. The analyst then creates a typological space (or what is known in logic as a 'property space') that consists of all the possible combinations of the variables. Inductively, the analyst begins placing known cases into the typological space according to preliminary knowledge of the values of the variables in those cases. The analyst can then iterate between what was theorized *a priori*, what is known empirically, and what is learned from additional empirical study, refining the typological space and possibly re-conceptualizing variables to higher or lower levels of aggregation depending on the complexity of the space and the analyst's research goals." Bennett, "Causal Mechanisms and Typological Theories in the Study of Civil Conflict," 221–2.

failure. I then used process tracing to identify the specific causal mechanisms operating in each of the four types of country offices. Because I had twenty-eight cases in total, and multiple cases per type, I was able to build the initial theory for each type of country office with at least one case and then validate that theory with one or more additional cases for each type. In other words, I was able to use my relatively large number of cases to validate my causal inference claims for each component of the typology and for the overall theory underlying the typology. After building and testing my typological theory in Burundi, I then conducted more than ninety interviews to test the plausible relevance of this theory with the same types of country offices operating in other conflict-affected countries – the DRC, Nepal, South Sudan, and Sudan – validating my theory there as well.

Research Design

The typological theory presented here claims that two factors, formal peacebuilding accountability and informal local accountability, are necessary and jointly sufficient for organizational learning in relation to the country office's peacebuilding aims.

The *dependent variable* is a measure of organizational performance: organizational learning. This dichotomous variable is defined as whether or not the organization took regular actions to narrow the gap between its peacebuilding aims and outcomes. I measured whether the country office had taken clear actions to reduce the gap between the majority of its peacebuilding activities and peacebuilding aims and whether the country office had altered its overall peacebuilding aims within one year of the beginning of a new phase in Burundi's transition.

Organizational learning is both a process and an outcome measure.[87] The presence of organizational learning shows that its precursor exists: a process by which the organization internalizes information about its outcomes and evaluates their relationship to its aims. But because organizational learning is measured by whether or not an action takes place, it is also an outcome-based measurement. I argue that this performance outcome – actions to narrow the gap between its aims and outcomes – is, in turn, necessary although insufficient, for the country office to achieve its desired outcomes in a particular local context, which in this instance is manifest in the achievement of its peacebuilding aims.

---

[87] Gutner and Thompson, "The Politics of IO Performance."

The two dichotomous *independent variables* are formal peacebuilding accountability routines (or the lack thereof) and informal local accountability routines (or the lack thereof). I measured a country office's formal peacebuilding accountability routines by whether communications (e.g., mandates, reports, proposals, emails, visits) between headquarters and the country office prioritized peacebuilding above other potential aims (e.g., humanitarian aims, development aims). I measured a country office's informal local accountability routines by whether if the country office had established mechanisms to consult regularly with and delegate problem-solving authority to a representative group of domestic actors beyond the host government, donors, and other actors to which the organization was formally accountable.

Organizational Case Selection

As is recommended for typological theorizing, I used the diverse case selection approach.[88] The diverse case selection approach allowed me to "capture the full range of variation along the dimension(s) of interest."[89] I selected the five case study organizations from among the broader population of IO, INGO, and bilateral donor country offices that implemented peacebuilding activities in Burundi over the period of this study: 1999 to 2014.[90] I selected case studies that gave me full variation in the dichotomous values on my two independent variables, and that represented typical examples of these types of organizations within the broader universe of cases in Burundi.[91]

The twenty-eight cases of country office behavior also provided me with variation in key alternative explanations for organizational learning and peacebuilding success and failure, which I discuss in detail in this book's conclusion. Over the fifteen-year period, the case study organizations varied in key organizational features – size, degree of hierarchy, core mandate, and related formal organizational routines. They also varied in more dynamic features – leadership, staffing, funding sources and amounts, project goals and strategies, procedures intended to improve

---

[88] John Gerring, "Case Selection for Case-Study Analysis: Qualitative and Quantitative Techniques," in ed. Janet M. Box-Steffensmeier, Henry E. Brady, and David Collier, *The Oxford Handbook of Political Methodology*, p. 651.

[89] Gerring, "Case Selection for Case-Study Analysis: Qualitative and Quantitative Techniques," 651.

[90] See https://dataverse.harvard.edu/dataverse/susannacampbell for a list of the universe of cases from which I selected the case study organizations and the complete record of this research design and data collection process.

[91] For a description of this diverse case selection technique, see Gerring, "Case Selection for Case-Study Analysis: Qualitative and Quantitative Techniques," 651–2.

peacebuilding performance, and informal organizational routines. This variation allowed me to systematically examine whether or not my hypothesized causal explanation or other alternative hypotheses explained the peacebuilding performance of the case study organizations.

Because the case study organizations had to agree to be case studies for this research, the case selection strategy may be biased toward organizations that have a certain degree of openness and are, thus, more likely than other organizations to engage in organizational learning.[92] Each organization had to agree to share its internal documents with me, allow me to interview any of its staff and partners, and ask observers about its work.

Country and Event Selection

The selection of one country allowed me to control for the general country environment and examine how the case study organizations interacted with the same context. I selected Burundi as the country environment because, up until 2014, it had undergone a relatively typical war-to-peace transition and there was an important focus on peacebuilding throughout the period under study. As one of the two pilot countries selected by the UN Peacebuilding Commission (PBC), Burundi was an important test case for global governors' overall pursuit of local peacebuilding. During the fifteen-year period under study in this book, Burundi iterated between improvements and significant setbacks in its political and security situation, presenting important nonlinear variation. Burundi's low level of strategic importance for most IOs, INGOs, and bilateral donors also allowed me to isolate formal accountability routines from the potentially erratic influence of strategic interest from the organizations' principals.

As discussed in detail in Chapter 2, this analysis begins in 1999, when Burundi's peace process was relaunched after the removal of regionally-imposed sanctions, and ends in 2014, just prior to Burundi's descent into intense political violence. I identify six phases in the Burundian conflict that were each widely recognized by international and national actors alike as launching a new trend in Burundi's war-to-peace transition. These phases represent shifts in the political and security environment that were identified by the case study organizations and the broader organizational population as turning points to which they should adapt.[93] I assess whether or not they did so.

---

[92] Argyris, *On Organizational Learning.*

[93] I identified these key events and new trends through systematic review of the country-level documents posted on Reliefweb (https://reliefweb.int/), the primary clearinghouse for information on crisis-affected countries used by international humanitarian and

Scope Conditions

The theory presented in this book should apply to the broader population of IOs, INGOs, and bilateral donors that establish country offices in conflict-affected countries for the purpose of achieving peacebuilding aims. It should be most relevant to IOs, INGOs, and bilateral donors that delegate authority to their country offices than to those that fully centralize authority at headquarters.

This book focuses on formal organizational characteristics that IOs, INGOs, and bilateral donors are likely to replicate in each country in which they intervene. Specifically, formal accountability routines are replicated from one country office to the next within a particular IO, INGO, or bilateral donor, but because of institutional isomorphism, are also likely to be replicated across the broader population of country offices intervening in conflict-affected countries.[94] The outcome of interest – organizational learning – is an organizational behavioral outcome that can exist regardless of the country context, making these findings applicable to other types of complex country-office aims that also require high rates of organizational learning.[95] In particularly hostile country contexts, organizational learning may, in fact, lead the organization to decide that peacebuilding interventions are no longer feasible.

By focusing on organizational attributes and behaviors that may be replicated from one country office to the next, I identify parameters that are likely to be found in other IO, INGO, and bilateral donor country offices operating in other conflict-affected countries. By using a diverse case selection strategy, described previously, I select a typical case of each type in my typological theory, making the findings for each case study broadly generalizable to the other organizations that occupy that same type. Gerring argues "the diverse-case method probably has stronger claims to representativeness than any other small-N sample," and "has the additional advantage of introducing variation on the key variables of interest."[96] By ensuring that I have at least two cases per type, I am able to compare within a single type and, thus, validate the theory for each type. Subsequent to building the theory in Burundi, I tested its

---

peacebuilding actors. I then used the Delphi method to validate these findings with key informants in Burundi.

[94] See Paul DiMaggio and Walter Powell, "The Iron Cage Revisited: Institutional Isomorphism and Collective Rationality in Organizational Fields," in *The New Institutionalism in Organizational Analysis*, ed. Paul DiMaggio and Walter Powell (Chicago: Chicago University Press, 1991), 64–5.

[95] See Matthew Andrews, Lant Pritchett, and Michael Woolcock, *Building State Capability: Evidence, Analysis, and Action* (Oxford, UK: Oxford University Press, 2017);

[96] Gerring, "Case Selection for Case-Study Analysis: Qualitative and Quantitative Techniques,"652.

plausibility in other contexts through additional research in the DRC, Nepal, South Sudan, and Sudan, showing that it has diverse geographical relevance, even in countries where global governors have much higher levels of strategic interest.[97]

As I discuss in more detail in the conclusion, this theory is also likely to shed light on the behavior of IOs, INGOs, and bilateral donors that aim to achieve complex development and humanitarian aims. International peacebuilding is a difficult case of country-office performance precisely because its goals are so ambitious. Yet, because of the large number and diverse mandates, structures, and size of organizations engaged in peacebuilding, international peacebuilding also represents an ideal lens through which to examine the local behavior of a wide variety of actors in global governance.

Organization of the Book

Chapter 1 develops this book's full theoretical framework that I have just previewed. In Chapter 2, I explain the background and environment in which the case study analysis took place, describing the ebbs and flows in fifteen years of Burundi's war-to-peace transition.

Chapter 3 focuses on the peacebuilding performance of IOs that relates, in particular, to their accountability to the states that created them. It investigates the behavior of the four peace operations mandated by the United Nations Security Council in Burundi between 1999 and 2014, which I refer to as the UN Missions, and the efforts of the United Nations Development Programme (UNDP) Burundi Country Office over the same period.

Chapter 4 outlines the common characteristics of INGOs engaged in peacebuilding, including their lack of formal accountability to states. By design, INGOs may have greater potential to respond to the changing dynamics in a war-torn country and to a wide group of local and national stakeholders. Chapter 4 analyzes two INGOs operating in Burundi between 1999 and 2014: CARE International's Burundi office and the Burundi Leadership Training Program (BLTP) of the Woodrow Wilson International Center for Scholars.

Chapter 5 discusses the characteristics of bilateral donor agencies, drawing on the growing literature on the political economy of development aid and examining its relevance for intervention in conflict-affected

---

[97] For discussion of the role of strategic interest in international aid allocation patterns, see Alberto Alesina and David Dollar, "Who Gives Foreign Aid to Whom and Why?" *Journal of Economic Growth*, 5(1) (2000): 33–63.

countries. It describes the crucial case of the United Kingdom's Department for International Development (DFID), one of the donors most committed to doing conflict-sensitive development in fragile and conflict-affected states.

The conclusion synthesizes the book's main argument: that IOs, INGOs, and bilateral donors are designed to fail at peacebuilding but sometimes succeed because of the interaction between formal peace-building accountability and informal local accountability, made possible by the efforts of innovative country-level staff circumventing standard operating procedures. It also addresses potential alternative explanations. It then discusses the relevance of the book's theory for IOs, INGOs, and bilateral donors operating in areas other than peacebuilding and in countries other than Burundi, based on additional research conducted in the DRC, Nepal, South Sudan, and Sudan. It closes by presenting concrete recommendations for policy makers and practitioners and discusses open questions that could inform future research.

1   Local Peacebuilding and Global Accountability

By focusing on a new level of analysis – the country offices of IOs, INGOs, and bilateral donors – this book addresses a crucial under-researched question: How does variation in the characteristics of country offices influence their ability to achieve positive peacebuilding performance? This chapter answers this question by providing a typology that explains the variation in peacebuilding performance described in the subsequent case studies. It begins by describing the relationship between organizational learning and peacebuilding, followed by a discussion of the difficulty of organizational learning, particularly for global organizations that are not incentivized to receive or respond to feedback from local actors. The chapter then proceeds to describe how, even in the face of such constraints, some organizations achieve positive peacebuilding performance through informal local accountability routines developed by innovative country-level staff.

Organizational Learning as Peacebuilding Performance

The concept of organizational performance used in this book focuses on an intermediate measure of performance: organizational learning of the country office in relation to its peacebuilding aims. *Organizational learning* refers to actions taken to reduce the gap between an organization's aims and its outcomes.[1] Organizational scholars claim that organizational learning is a necessary condition for the achievement of outcome-level aims.[2] In highly dynamic contexts – such as countries recovering from war – an organization's policy implementation plan may quickly become disconnected from the rapidly changing

---

[1] Chris Argyris, *On Organizational Learning* (Boston: Blackwell, 1992).
[2] Argyris, *On Organizational Learning*; Lise Morjé Howard, *UN Peacekeeping in Civil Wars* (Cambridge, UK: Cambridge University Press, 2008); and Jeffrey L. Pressman and Aaron Wildavsky, eds., *Implementation: How Great Expectations in Washington Are Dashed in Oakland* (Berkeley: University of California Press, 1984).

environment.[3] In such contexts, regular actions to reduce the gap between the organization's aims and outcomes become necessary for positive organizational performance.

Organizational performance describes whether an organization achieves a set of organization-wide goals.[4] An organization can have process-focused aims, such as internal coordination among different departments. It can have outcome-focused aims at the project-level, such as reintegrating a group of ex-combatants into their communities. Or it can have more distant impact-level aims, such as building sustainable peace.[5] However, the successful achievement of internal process-related goals does not necessarily lead to the achievement of outcome- or impact-related aims. In the words of Gutner and Thompson, "At best, process performance is a necessary but not sufficient condition for favorable outcomes."[6] An organization can have a good process with a bad outcome, or a good outcome with a bad process. Furthermore, the successful achievement of project-level outcomes does not automatically lead to macro-level impact. For example, an organization may have a well-implemented ex-combatant disarmament project but not achieve sustainable peace. Likewise, one can have sustainable peace in spite of failed ex-combatant disarmament projects.

Most scholarship on International Organizations (IO), International Non-Governmental Organizations (INGO), or bilateral donor interventions in a country has evaluated an organization's effectiveness in terms of national-level (i.e., macro-level) outcomes, such as a reduction in the number of annual battle deaths or an end to war.[7] As discussed in the Introduction, the problem with using national-level measures to assess the performance of an individual organization is that national-level

---

[3] Angela Browne and Aaron Wildavsky, "Implementation as Exploration (1983)," in ed. Pressman and Wildavsky, *Implementation: How Great Expectations in Washington Are Dashed in Oakland*, 232–53.

[4] Ewan Ferlie, Laurence E. Lynn Jr., and Christopher Pollitt, *The Oxford Handbook of Public Management* (Oxford: Oxford Handbooks Online, 2007).

[5] This entire paragraph draws on Gutner and Thompson's the pathbreaking article on IOs and organizational performance: Tamar Gutner and Alexander Thompson, "The Politics of IO Performance: A Framework," *Review of International Organizations* 5, no. 3 (2010): 227–48.

[6] Gutner and Thompson, "The Politics of IO Performance," 236.

[7] Virginia Page Fortna, "Peacekeeping and Democratization," in *From War to Democracy*, ed. Anna Jarstad and Timothy Sisk (Cambridge: Cambridge University Press, 2008), 39–70; Michael Doyle and Nicholas Sambanis, *Making War and Building Peace: United Nations Peace Operations* (Princeton, NJ: Princeton University Press, 2006); Séverine Autesserre, *The Trouble with the Congo: Local Violence and the Failure of International Peacebuilding* (Cambridge, UK: Cambridge University Press, 2010); and Séverine Autesserre, "Hobbes and the Congo: Frames, Local Violence, and International Intervention," *International Organization* 63, no. 2 (2009): 249–80.

outcomes may result from the actions of multiple domestic or international actors, which these studies do not account for. They show correlation, not causation, making it difficult to identify specific actions by an IO, INGO, or bilateral donor that might have contributed to the national-level (i.e., macro-level) outcome.

As discussed in the Introduction, organizational learning is both a process and an outcome measure.[8] It does not measure the impact of the project at the project-level or the national-level. Instead, it focuses on a process and outcome that are necessary, but insufficient, for project-level impact. From the presence of organizational learning one can infer that its precursor exists: a process by which the organization internalizes information about its outcomes and evaluates the gap between the outcomes achieved and the organization's aims. Organizational learning is also an outcome-based measurement that measures whether an organizational action was taken. These actions taken by the organization to narrow the gap between its aims and outcomes are, in turn, necessary (although insufficient) to achieve the organization's aim in that particular context. For an organization pursuing peacebuilding country-office organizational learning is a necessary condition for the organization to achieve its peacebuilding aims.

The Importance of Organizational Learning for Peacebuilding

Although organizational learning is important for all organizations, it seems to be particularly important for organizations engaged in peacebuilding.[9] Howard, in her work on UN peacekeeping, argues that success "is not based on learning discrete, concrete 'rules of the game,' because the game is constantly changing. When the UN learns on the ground, it acquires the ability to adapt to the changing contexts of civil wars – the organization engages with its environment and invents mechanisms to understand it."[10] Organizational learning is necessary for peacebuilding because of at least six characteristics of international peacebuilding.

First, international peacebuilding aims to change a changing context. Peacebuilding takes place in highly dynamic war-torn contexts that experience frequent change in the public and private institutions that peacebuilding aims to affect. Given "the difficulty of understanding

---

[8] Gutner and Thomson, "The Politics of IO Performance," 236.
[9] Susanna P. Campbell, "When Process Matters: The Potential Implications of Organizational Learning for Peacebuilding Success," *Journal of Peacebuilding and Development* 4, no. 2 (2008): 20–32; and Howard, *UN Peacekeeping in Civil Wars*.
[10] Howard, *UN Peacekeeping in Civil Wars*, 19.

post-conflict dynamics and the even greater difficulty of correctly predicting the impact of one's actions upon them, error is very likely."[11] Without adjusting their policies and activities to new and evolving country contexts, IOs, INGOs, and bilateral donors are unlikely to change the context in the way they intend.[12]

Second, peacebuilding is highly experimental. No one knows exactly what causes "peace." As a result, policy guidelines and scholars have repeatedly argued that IOs, INGOs, and bilateral donors should question whether or not their activities fit the needs and capacities of a particular context.[13] By receiving feedback about whether their activities are having the intended effect in a country, country offices have the opportunity to adapt their approach and question whether it was the right approach in the first place. This continual refinement requires that "peacebuilders confess to a high degree of uncertainty" in what they are doing and how they will achieve the desired ends.[14]

Third, by definition, peacebuilding requires the buy-in of local actors. Because international peacebuilding aims to contribute to sustainable change in local institutions, its success depends in part on whether country offices create local-level demand for their specific peacebuilding activity and build the buy-in among local actors necessary to sustain the change that international actors initiate.[15] "[E]ven where enforcement is used at the outset, the peace must eventually become self-sustaining, and consent needs to be won if the peace enforcers are ever to exit with their work done."[16] To understand the perspective of the local actors and

---

[11] Peter S. Uvin, "Difficult Choices in the New Post-Conflict Agenda: The International Community in Rwanda after the Genocide," *Third World Quarterly* 22, no. 2 (2001): 185.

[12] Michael Barnett et al., "Peacebuilding: What Is in a Name?" *Global Governance* 13, no. 1 (2007): 35–58; Susanna P. Campbell, "Routine Learning? How Peacebuilding Organizations Prevent Liberal Peace," in *A Liberal Peace? The Problems and Practices of Peacebuilding*, ed. Susanna P. Campbell, David Chandler, and Meera Sabaratnam (London: Zed, 2011), 89–105; and International Alert, Saferworld, and Forum on Early Warning and Early Response (FEWER), *Conflict Sensitive Approaches to Development, Humanitarian Assistance and Peacebuilding: A Resource Pack* (London: International Alert, 2004), 3.

[13] Campbell, "Routine Learning?"

[14] Michael Barnett and Christoph Zürcher, *The Peacebuilder's Contract: How External State-Building Reinforces Weak Statehood* (Stanford, CA: Stanford University Press, 2007), 31–2.

[15] Mary B. Anderson, Dayna Brown, and Isabella Jean, *Time to Listen: Hearing People on the Receiving End of International Aid* (Cambridge, MA: CDA Collaborative Learning Projects, 2012); Séverine Autesserre, *Peaceland: Conflict Resolution and the Everyday Politics of International Intervention* (Cambridge, UK: Cambridge University Press, 2014); and Campbell, "When Process Matters."

[16] Doyle and Sambanis, *Making War and Building Peace*, 56.

encourage these actors to sustain the change initiated by the peacebuilding activity, country offices need to gradually alter their activities in response to local actors' shifting capacities and preferences, or engage in organizational learning.[17] Without this level of responsiveness, country offices are unlikely to develop trust with the local stakeholders whose collaboration is necessary for the success of their peacebuilding interventions. As Talentino finds, "if local actors distrust third parties, they will remain fearful, suspicious, and unwilling to compromise."[18]

Fourth, peacebuilding aims to change behaviors and institutions in a war-torn country. Where international development and humanitarian assistance work through or around existing institutions *in* conflict-affected countries without attempting to alter the status quo, peacebuilding works directly *on* conflict-affected institutions, attempting to metamorphose them from enablers of civil war to sustainers of equitable peace.[19] Achieving these transformative goals in a highly dynamic context implies that implementing organizations regularly adjust both their aims and their means, or that they learn.[20] According to Browne and Wildavsky's study of public sector organizations:

If change – altered relationships among participants leading to different outcomes – is the idea behind implementation, the continuous adjustment of objectives is called for just as much as the modification of instruments for attaining them. Implementation ceases being static; it becomes dynamic by virtue of incorporating learning of what to prefer as well as how to achieve it.[21]

Fifth, country offices may exist for decades in a conflict-affected country. During this time, the country is likely to undergo changes that significantly alter the political and economic landscape: new elections, the establishment of security, the outbreak of armed violence, the implementation of power-sharing arrangements, for example. To maintain their relevance to the needs and preferences of local institutions, country offices need to adjust and readjust their aims and approaches to align with the new contexts.

Sixth, the professionalization of the international peacebuilding industry has increased the need for organizational learning by country offices. Intervening organizations tend to replicate a standard list of peacebuilding

---

[17] Campbell, "When Process Matters."

[18] Andrea Kathryn Talentino, "Perceptions of Peacebuilding: The Dynamic of Imposer and Imposed Upon," *International Studies Perspectives* 8, no. 2 (2007): 154.

[19] Jonathan Goodhand, "Violent Conflict, Poverty and Chronic Poverty," *SSRN Electronic Journal* Chronic Poverty Research Centre Working Paper, no. 6 (May 2001), 1–49.

[20] Angela Browne and Aaron Wildavsky, "Implementation as Exploration," in *Implementation*, ed. Pressman and Waldavsky, 232–56.

[21] Browne and Wildavsky, "Implementation as Exploration," 234.

activities from one country to the next, using the same organizational procedures and staff capacities. To adapt standardized approaches to the local realities, country offices have to engage in organizational learning.

In sum, without organizational learning, global governors are highly unlikely to localize their peacebuilding ambitions. Peacebuilding is too complex a task and the contexts in which it takes place too dynamic for a country office to achieve its peacebuilding aims simply by implementing its activities as planned. For these global actors to contribute to their local-level peacebuilding aims, their country offices need to take regular actions to align their peacebuilding approach with the context during both the preparation and implementation phases, or, in other words, they need to engage in organizational learning in relation to their peacebuilding aims.

Barriers to Organizational Learning

Organizational learning is not easy.[22] The importance of organizational learning to international peacebuilding presents significant challenges for country offices. The organizational learning process includes a series of steps, "beginning with the taking of an action, followed by the monitoring of the outcomes of the action, their interpretation, and then some modification of the propensity to repeat the action."[23] Learning does not simply describe the intake, processing, or sharing of information.[24] It refers to the process that leads the organization to take actions to reduce the gap between its aims and its outcomes. To learn, an organization must have evidence about this gap and it must take action based on this evidence to improve the likelihood that the organization will achieve its aims in the future.[25] To do so, the organization requires effective feedback mechanisms from the actors and institutions it aims to affect.

Organizational learning involves varying degrees of difficulty, but peacebuilding seems to require the most difficult type of learning:

---

[22] Barbara Levitt and James March, "Organizational Learning," *Annual Review of Sociology* 14, no. 1 (1988), 319–340; and Ariane Berthoin Antal, Uwe Lenhardt, and Rolf Rosenbrock, "Barriers to Organizational Learning," in *Handbook of Organizational Learning and Knowledge*, ed. M. Dierkes, A. Berthoin Antal, J. Child, and I. Nonaka (Oxford: Oxford University Press, 2000), 865–85.

[23] James G. March, "Learning and the Theory of the Firm," in *Explorations in Organizations*, ed. James G. March (Stanford, CA: Stanford Business Books, 2008), 85.

[24] Argyris, *On Organizational Learning*; and Jack S. Levy, "Learning and Foreign Policy: Sweeping a Conceptual Minefield," *International Organization* 48, no. 2 (1994).

[25] Argyris, *On Organizational Learning*, 67.

double-loop learning.[26] When an organization engages in *single-loop learning*, it simply adjusts the way that it implements an activity without questioning the relevance of the activity to the context.[27] In other words, the organization may alter the order in which it carries out tasks or the people it involves, but it does not question whether or not it should implement that particular activity in that particular context. *Double-loop learning* means that the organization alters its overall aim and approach to make both its aims and its activities more relevant to the context in which the organization is operating.[28] Frequent double-loop learning is important for organizations that aim to alter their behavior in highly dynamic contexts. But double-loop learning is difficult for many organizations because it requires that the organization engage with information about both its successes and its failures in an open and non-defensive way.[29]

The literature does not tell us which organizations will learn and which will not.[30] The organizational literature indicates that the size of the organization, the degree of hierarchy, the degree of decentralization, and the founding mandate of the organization may influence how and when the organization learns, but does not tell us which combination of characteristics makes organizations better or worse learners.[31] Howard identifies the importance of learning for the fulfillment of UN

[26] Campbell, "When Process Matters."

[27] Argyris, *On Organizational Learning*. 68.

[28] Argyris, *On Organizational Learning*, 67–68.

[29] Argyris, *On Organizational Learning*; and Chris Argyris and Donald A. Schon, "Organizational Learning: A Theory of Action Perspective," (Boston, MA: Addison-Wesley, 1978).

[30] Lynn Eden, "'Getting It Right or Wrong': Organizational Learning about the Physical World," in *Organizational Learning in the Global Context*, ed. M. Leann Brown, Michael Kenny, and Michael Zarkin (Aldershot, UK: Ashgate, 2006), 197–216; Lynn Eden, *Whole World on Fire: Organizations, Knowledge, and Nuclear Weapons Devastation* (Ithaca, NY: Cornell University Press, 2004); Levitt and March, "Organizational Learning"; James G. March and Herbert Simon, *Organizations*, 2nd ed. (Cambridge, MA: Blackwell Business, 1993); Chris Argyris and Donald A. Schon, *Organizational Learning: A Theory of Action Perspective* (Boston, MA: Addison-Wesley, 1978); and Stephen Krasner and Thomas Risse, "External Actors, State-Building, and Service Provision in Areas of Limited Statehood: Introduction," *Governance* 27, no. 4 (October 2014): 545–67.

[31] M. Leann Brown and Michael Kenney, "Organizational Learning: Theoretical and Methodological Considerations," in *Organizational Learning in the Global Context*, ed. M. Leann Brown, Michael Zarkin, and Michael Kenney (Hampshire, UK: Ashgate, 2006), 1–20; Eden, "'Getting It Right or Wrong'"; Eden, *Whole World on Fire*; David A. Lake, "Delegating Divisible Sovereignty: Sweeping a Conceptual Minefield," *Review of International Organizations* 2, no. 3 (2007): 219–37; Berthoin Antal, Lenhardt, and Rosenbrock, "Barriers to Organizational Learning"; Argyris, *On Organizational Learning*; Levitt and March, "Organizational Learning;" March and Simon, *Organizations*; and Barbara Koremenos, Charles Lipson, and Duncan Snidal, "The Rational Design of International Institutions," *International Organization* 55, no. 4 (2001): 761–99.

peacekeeping mandates, but does not identify the organizational characteristics that facilitate this learning or examine the degree to which organizational learning is important for other parts of the United Nations, IOs, INGOs, or bilateral donors.

Although potentially any organization could learn, scholarship points to two significant barriers to organizational learning that are particularly relevant to IO, INGO, and bilateral donor country offices: organizational learning is bounded by the organization's mandate; and global governors are not structured to receive feedback from the local institutions and actors that peacebuilding aims to influence.

Why Organizational Learning Is Bounded

Organizations learn what they know.[32] Learning in organizations is constrained by the organization's primary purpose, the type of knowledge it values, and the overall worldview that this purpose and knowledge give the organization. Organizations use routines to hold themselves accountable for achieving their purpose, which, in turn, reinforces the importance of this purpose and further builds staff knowledge that corresponds to this purpose.

For IOs, INGOs, and bilateral donors, the knowledge and corresponding accountability routines are determined at headquarters and are translated into routines that these organizations replicate from one country to the next. These routines, and thus what the organization learns, are grounded in each organization's primary purpose or overall mandate, whether economic development, life-saving humanitarian assistance, peacebuilding, or some other focus.

Eden observes that organizational purpose and knowledge are generally developed during "the creation of organizations, and during periods of organizational upheaval [when] actors articulate organizational goals and draw on and modify existing understandings, or knowledge, of the social and physical environment in which [they] must operate."[33] This purpose and knowledge, which is translated into organizational routines and aims, determines "what counts as a problem, how problems are represented, the strategies to be used to solve those problems, and the constraints and requirements placed on possible solutions."[34] Organizational routines are the organization's standard operating procedures.[35]

---

[32] Levitt and March, "Organizational Learning"; and Campbell, "When Process Matters."
[33] Eden, *Whole World on Fire*, 49–50.
[34] Eden, *Whole World on Fire*; and Eden, "'Getting It Right or Wrong,'"198.
[35] Levitt and March, "Organizational Learning," 326.

An organization responds to information that it "thinks" is important. In other words, an organization pays attention to information that it understands based on its existing knowledge-laden routines, discards what it does not understand, and takes action in the ways that it has trained its personnel to respond.[36] The logic of organizational action, therefore, involves "matching procedures to situations more than it does calculating choices."[37] As mentioned in the Introduction, just as a lawyer pays attention to information about legal issues and responds with legal solutions, an organization views and responds to its environment through its own particular lens. This bounded rationality is mirrored at the level of individual staff members within the organization who also observe their environment through their own particular lenses, which usually reflect the organization's lens.[38]

The importance of organizational knowledge, routines, and aims in determining organizational behavior makes IOs, INGOs, and bilateral donors fundamentally supply driven. They respond to a context with only what they have to supply.[39] As the saying goes, "if you have a hammer, everything looks like a nail." Intervening organizations are predisposed to repeat the same types of actions and implement the same types of activities in spite of shifts in their country context, particularly if they do not integrate feedback from stakeholders within the country context.

Because the majority of the organizations that do international peacebuilding were founded to implement development, humanitarian, or traditional peacekeeping activities, their organizational knowledge and routines are geared toward development, humanitarian, and traditional peacekeeping responses.[40] Because most of these organizations focus most on what they deliver, not the outcome or impact of these interventions on their hypothesized determinants of peace, they do not often integrate the local feedback necessary to shift their knowledge, routines, and aims to enable them to be more effective peacebuilders. These organizations' resistance to change is further compound by their focus on global, not local, accountability.

Upward Accountability and Local Feedback in Global Governance

Bilateral donors, IOs, and INGOs are designed to achieve the aims set by their principals based mostly outside the war-torn country – their

---

[36] Eden, *Whole World on Fire*; and Eden, "'Getting It Right or Wrong,'"198.
[37] Levitt and March, "Organizational Learning," 320.
[38] Herbert Simon, *Administrative Behavior*, 4th ed. (New York: Free Press, 1997).
[39] Barnett et al., "Peacebuilding: What Is in a Name?" 35–58.
[40] Barnett et al., "Peacebuilding: What Is in a Name?" 35–58.

member states, governing boards, and headquarters bureaucracies – not to localize these aims so that they achieve the type of change they desire in the conflict-affected country. IO, INGO, and bilateral donor country offices are, thus, upwardly accountable.[41] Global governors are accountable for supplying activities that correspond to their principals' aims, but they are not responsible for ensuring that these activities achieve local-level outcomes that correspond to these aims.

Accountability is the implication "that some actors have the right to hold other actors to a set of standards, to judge whether they have fulfilled their responsibilities in light of these standards, and to impose sanctions if they determine that these responsibilities have not been met."[42] For IO, INGO, or bilateral donor country offices, the goals set by their principals against which their performance is judged is their set of standards. The "actors who have the right" to hold a country office accountable are the organization's principals located primarily outside of the host country, not the populations in war-torn countries.

International relations scholars generally assume that a country office positively performs when it complies with its formal accountability routines and that it fails to perform when the country office does not.[43] Accountability is viewed as the primary way that the organization can achieve its principals' aims, or perform. When agents do not comply with the principals' preferences, this is viewed as "agency slack" that undermines the achievement of these preferences.[44]

Organizational theory argues that accountability is manifest in routines: the rules, "procedures, technologies, beliefs, and cultures [that] are conserved through systems of socialization and control."[45] Accountability routines are intended to ensure that the organization achieves the aims set by its principals, forming links in the chain of delegation.[46] Accountability routines thus determine the country office's aims, the source of the feedback about its achievement of its aims, and, therefore, the focus of the country office's learning and performance.

---

[41] Alnoor Ebrahim, "Accountability Myopia: Losing Sight of Organizational Learning," *Nonprofit and Voluntary Sector Quarterly* 34, no. 1 (2005): 56–87.

[42] Ruth Grant and Robert Keohane, "Accountability and Abuses of Power in World Politics," *American Political Science Review* 99, no. 1 (2005): 29.

[43] Darren G. Hawkins et al., *Delegation and Agency in International Organizations* (Cambridge, UK: Cambridge University Press, 2006).

[44] Hawkins et al., *Delegation and Agency in International Organizations*, 24–5.

[45] Levitt and March, "Organizational Learning," 326.

[46] Hawkins et al., *Delegation and Agency in International Organizations*, 24–5; and Lake, "Delegating Divisible Sovereignty," 222.

Bilateral donors, IOs, and INGOs are given authority by their governing boards and by the host country to intervene in the transformation of this country's domestic institutions.[47] Interference in the domestic affairs of a state is most often discussed in relation to UN peace operations: "Multidimensional, second-generational peacekeeping pierces the shell of national autonomy by bringing international involvement to areas long thought to be the exclusive domain of domestic jurisdiction."[48] To receive the rational-legal authority to carry out business in a country, bilateral aid agencies, IOs, and INGOs must sign agreements with their host government to establish offices there, implement aid programs, and supply their staff with the appropriate legal documents to reside there.[49] But no formal mechanism obliges these global actors to be accountable to the population in the host countries. Particularly in countries emerging from civil war, where democratic institutions are often still weak, accountability to the host government does not ensure that intervening organizations serve the interests of the broader population.[50] In these fragile states, reinforcing the power and authority of the government may solidify existing divisions in society, many of which may have contributed to the initial outbreak of war.[51] The specific way that IOs, INGOs, and bilateral donors are authorized to intervene varies by organization type.

An IO receives its authority to intervene from the member states that established it. The IO member states may include the government of the war-torn country in which the IO intervenes. The IO member states authorize the IO to intervene in the war-torn country, decide on its mandate, decide on the country office's core budget in the country, and decide when the IO will leave. The IO headquarters, in turn, advises the member states on each of these decisions, oversees the implementation of the mandate decided upon by the IO member states, and monitors regular reporting from the country office about progress made toward achieving this mandate. These sources of authority correspond to the direction of the organization's accountability routines global to local.

Bilateral donors are authorized by their political leadership to contribute a particular amount and type of funding to a country and are given

---

[47] Grant and Keohane, "Accountability and Abuses of Power in World Politics," 29–43; David Lake, "Rightful Rules: Authority, Order, and the Foundations of Global Governance," *International Studies Quarterly* 54, no. 3 (2010): 587–613.
[48] Doyle and Sambanis, *Making War and Building Peace*, 312.
[49] Lake, "Rightful Rules."
[50] Philip Gourevitch, "Coming to Terms," *New Yorker*, June 22, 2015.
[51] Krasner and Risse, "External Actors."

permission by the host government to establish a country office and distribute aid there.[52] The organizational aims of bilateral donors are established by their legislators, political leaders, and headquarters. Country offices report to their headquarters and their political leadership on their progress toward these aims. Shifts in political leadership in the donor country may lead to significant changes in aid policy and the specific aims that each country office is expected to achieve.

An INGO's governance board gives it authority to intervene in a war-torn country; the governance board may be made up of private individuals, government representatives, or representatives of private corporations.[53] INGOs are often funded by a combination of core funding that their headquarters distributes and funding that bilateral or multilateral donors give directly to the organization's country office, subcontracting INGOs to achieve their aims in that country.[54] An INGO's aims and formal accountability routines are therefore determined both by its headquarters and by the bilateral and multilateral donors that sign contracts with the INGO to implement particular activities in that country.

In the literature on global governance, accountability to states is generally considered to be a good thing. Grant and Keohane, comparing IOs, INGOs, states, and companies, argue that IOs are the most accountable global organization because they are accountable to a range of states that delegate authority to them to pursue the states' aims at the global level.[55] On the other hand, INGOs are viewed as the least accountable because they are neither accountable to states nor to populations.[56] INGOs are accountable only to their independently constituted boards, which are made up of a varying range of actors, including private individuals, as discussed above.

The scholarship on the political economy of international aid argues that accountability to principals outside the country may actually undermine the performance of country offices. Normally, in private- or public-sector organizations, the organization improves the good or service that it delivers based on feedback from the consumer of the good or service.

---

[52] Clark C. Gibson et al., *The Samaritan's Dilemma: The Political Economy of Development Aid* (Oxford: Oxford University Press, 2005).

[53] Alexander Cooley and James Ron, "The NGO Scramble: Organizational Insecurity and the Political Economy of Transnational Action," *International Security* 27, no. 1 (2002): 5–39; Alnoor Ebrahim, *NGOs and Organizational Change: Discourse, Reporting, and Learning* (Cambridge, UK: Cambridge University Press, 2003); and Ebrahim, "Accountability Myopia."

[54] Cooley and Ron, "The NGO Scramble."

[55] Grant and Keohane, "Accountability and Abuses of Power in World Politics," 29–43.

[56] Grant and Keohane, "Accountability and Abuses of Power in World Politics," 38.

This feedback tells the organization whether or not the good or service is "performing" in the way that the organization intends. The organization's governance structure seeks to hold the providers of the good or service accountable for responding to this feedback, using accountability routines, and therefore improve the quality of the good or service provided. If the recipient of the good or service is not satisfied, she or he can theoretically respond through interaction with public officials or by refusing to purchase the product.

In international aid, however, the feedback loop between the local recipients and international decision makers is broken.[57] The recipient of a good or service does not have the authority to impose sanctions on the IO, INGO, bilateral donor, or private contractor providing the good or service. There is no formal accountability routine that runs to the local population. Although the host government has the authority to refuse the money, the population has no formal feedback mechanism to which the IO, INGO, bilateral donor, or private contractor must respond. The population cannot formally sanction the IO, INGO, bilateral donor, or private contractor, and therefore cannot hold these global actors accountable for delivering high-quality local goods or services. The population does not have the formal authority to hold global organizations accountable for their local performance. In the words of Bert Martens et al.:

> [A] unique and most striking characteristic of foreign aid is that the people for whose benefit aid agencies work are not the same as those from whom their revenues are obtained; they actually live in different countries and different political constituencies. This geographical and political separation between beneficiaries and taxpayers blocks the normal performance feedback process.[58]

The structure of formal upward accountability in IOs, INGOs, and bilateral aid donors undermines their local-level performance because local actors do not have the authority or formal accountability routines through which to influence the performance of international intervenors. Local stakeholders are not authorized to hold global actors accountable for achieving their local-level aims. Country offices are incentivized to communicate regularly with their headquarters and principals, not with the populations they are attempting to help.

When communicating with their headquarters, country offices often report easily quantifiable deliverables: the amount of money they spend,

---

[57] Bertin Martens et al., *The Institutional Economics of Foreign Aid* (Cambridge, UK: Cambridge University Press, 2002).
[58] Martens et al., *The Institutional Economics of Foreign Aid*, 14.

the quantity of supplies they procure and deliver, the number of things they build, the number of people they train. These indicators allow country offices to demonstrate compliance with the plan that they agreed upon with their principals – that they spent the money in the way intended. But, these indicators do not demonstrate whether or not the country office contributed to their desired change in local institutions – the ultimate purpose of all of the easily quantifiable deliverables.[59] As a result, global governors often lack systematic feedback about whether or not their country offices are achieving their desired local-level aims, and their country offices have few formal incentives to respond to local-level feedback when they receive it.[60]

Without feedback or strong incentives to respond to feedback from diverse local stakeholders, how can country offices learn in relation to the local context?[61] As discussed previously, organizational learning by the country office is a necessary condition for the country office to achieve its aims in dynamic environments, especially for country offices that pursue complex aims such as peacebuilding. If country offices do not take actions to reduce the gap between their supply-driven aims and their outcomes in the local context, or learn, they are not likely to achieve these aims at the local level.[62] Instead, they are likely to implement supply-driven activities that may be largely irrelevant to the needs of local stakeholders.[63] One would, thus, expect these global governors to fail at local peacebuilding. How, then, can we explain instances of positive peacebuilding performance by country offices at the local level?

Peacebuilding Performance: A Typology

In this book, I argue that IOs, INGOs, and bilateral donors overcome their predisposition for poor peacebuilding performance when they possess two necessary and jointly sufficient characteristics: informal accountability to local stakeholders and formal accountability that prioritizes peacebuilding. Throughout this book, I refer to these two characteristics as informal local accountability and formal peacebuilding accountability. These two characteristics together create a upward and downward accountability dynamic that enables the country office to learn in relation to its peacebuilding aims. Country offices that are

---

[59] Ebrahim, *NGOs and Organizational Change*; Martens et al., *The Institutional Economics of Foreign Aid*; and Gibson et al., *The Samaritan's Dilemma*.
[60] Ebrahim, "Accountability Myopia"; and Gibson et al., *The Samaritan's Dilemma*.
[61] Ebrahim, "Accountability Myopia."
[62] Ebrahim, "Accountability Myopia"; and Campbell, "When Process Matters."
[63] Cooley and Ron, "The NGO Scramble."

peacebuilding learners are more likely than other organizations to achieve their peacebuilding aims.

The concurrence of upward and downward accountability enables the country office to take regular actions to align its international peacebuilding aims and approach with the dynamic preferences of the local institutions that it aims to transform. Informal local accountability routines (i.e., downward accountability) give a representative group of local stakeholders the authority to assess the relevance of the country office's peacebuilding activities and recommend changes to increase their effectiveness. Formal peacebuilding accountability routines (i.e., upward accountability) incentivize the country office to respond to this local feedback and question the continued relevance of its peacebuilding approach to the local context.

Rule-breaking or rule-bending behavior by individual country-office staff is, in turn, necessary for the creation of informal local accountability routines. Contrary to the assumption of existing scholarship, this book argues that at the country level, agency slack can be a good thing – in other words, bad behavior may be necessary for good performance.[64]

To achieve the ambitious peacebuilding goals set out by their principals, IO, INGO, and bilateral donor country offices must circumvent rigid accountability routines, created by these same principals, that prioritize upward accountability and inhibit feedback from the local populations these country offices aim to help. Innovation by individual country-office staff outside of the behaviors incentivized by formal accountability routines is necessary for the creation of informal local accountability. Clearly not all rule-breaking or rule-bending behavior by country-office staff improves peacebuilding performance. But rule-breaking or rule-bending behavior that establishes informal accountability to a representative group of local actors does seem to improve peacebuilding performance, particularly when the principals prioritize peacebuilding.

Informal Local Accountability

Informal local accountability takes place when the country office delegates authority to local stakeholders who represent the diversity of

---

[64] Hawkins et al., *Delegation and Agency in International Organizations*, 8, 28 identifies two types of agency slack: *shirking*, in which agents simply minimize their effort to achieve their principals' preferences; and *slippage*, in which agents take initiatives that align with their own policy preferences, not those of their principals. The type of bad behavior described here falls within the latter category and involves initiative by individuals within the country office that is outside of and/or undermines the accountability routines set up by the organization's principals to govern the behavior of its country offices.

local interests in the country office's peacebuilding intervention(s).[65] Like informal governance, "informal procedures may take a variety of forms."[66] The defining characteristic of informal local accountability is the delegation of authority to local actors to affect the direction and content of the country office's peacebuilding interventions. Local stakeholders and country-office staff may use a variety of strategies to produce informal local accountability, such as local evaluations, monitoring groups, regular consultations, or other systematic mechanisms to help guide the implementation of interventions.[67] For example, when implementing a dialogue initiative among political parties in Burundi, the United Nations gave a representative group of participants the authority to monitor the effectiveness of the dialogue sessions and determine the direction of future sessions.

These accountability routines are informal in that they are not required by the country office's principals or related "officially sanctioned channels."[68] Moreover, no local actor, other than key individuals in the host government, has the authority to impose formal sanctions if he or she judges that the IO, INGO, or bilateral donor has not met its commitments.

---

[65] There is a rich discussion in the peacebuilding literature about the heterogeneity of local opinion and perspective. Scholars have argued that there is not one "local" or one perspective (Campbell, Chandler, and Sabaratnam, eds., *A Liberal Peace?*). This is true of all populations but may be particularly true of populations in war-torn countries where the war and violent conflict have further divided groups along ethnic, religious, socio-economic, gender, and/or other categories. The concept of informal local accountability proposed here takes this reality into account because it is defined by whether or not the stakeholders represent the diversity of the local actors with a direct stake in the peacebuilding intervention. By representing the diversity of stakeholders, they are more likely to help direct the intervention toward everyone's collective interest rather than the interest of one particular group, fulfilling the primary underlying "theory of change" of most peacebuilding interventions.

[66] Randall Stone, *Controlling Institutions: International Organizations and the Global Economy* (Cambridge, UK: Cambridge University Press, 2011), 13.

[67] For example, for a project that is implemented at the community level, this group could include a stratified purposive or random sample of community members – addressing the potential gender, ethnic, religious, and generational cleavages that exist in the community; representatives of informal governance structures, such as community committees; and local government representatives.

[68] See Gretchen Helmke and Steven Levitsky, "Informal Institutions and Comparative Politics: A Research Agenda," *Perspectives on Politics* 2, no. 4 (2004), 705. Many IOs, INGOs, and bilateral donors argue that they build "local ownership" in the countries in which they intervene. In reality, this often translates into contractual agreements between the host government and the organization rather than involvement of the broader society or the diverse stakeholders in any particular intervention. For a detailed discussion of some of the contradictions inherent in the UN's application of local ownership, see Sarah B. K. von Billerbeck, *Whose Peace? Local Ownership and United Nations Peacekeeping* (Oxford: Oxford University Press 2016).

Even though informal local accountability is informal in the sense that it occurs outside of it possesses the main constituent elements of accountability: it gives local stakeholders the informal right to hold the country office accountable for achieving its own peacebuilding aims in accordance with local standards, to judge whether it has achieved these aims and standards, and to impose some type of sanction if it determines that these aims and standards have not been met.[69] The power of local stakeholders to sanction the country office derives in part from the poor understanding that many country offices have about the local contexts.[70] Local stakeholders can incentivize the country office to achieve its own peacebuilding aims, for example, by providing detailed, representative feedback and well-constructed suggestions for improving the quality of the intervention. Local stakeholders can sanction a country office for not complying, for example, by providing recommendations that seek to undermine the intervention, refusing to provide feedback, or providing inaccurate feedback.

Formal Peacebuilding Accountability

Although informal local accountability determines whether or not the country office receives feedback from local stakeholders, formal accountability routines determine the feedback to which the country office responds.[71] As discussed earlier, country offices view the country context through the lens of their organizational priorities.[72] Organizational priorities are set by the organizations' principals, whether member states, donors, legislators, political leaders, or private individuals, and translated into formal accountability routines. Formal accountability routines are manifest in the vertical micro-level interactions between the principals of the IO, INGO, or bilateral donor and their country offices. They may take the form, for example, of project and financial reports; project proposals; daily email and phone communications;

---

[69] This definition of informal local accountability paraphrases the definition of accountability given by Ruth Grant and Robert Keohane, "Accountability and Abuses of Power in World Politics," *American Political Science Review* 99, no. 1 (2005): 29.

[70] Autesserre, *Peaceland*; Béatrice Pouligny, "Civil Society and Post-Conflict Peacebuilding: Ambiguities of International Programmes Aimed at Building 'New' Societies," *Security Dialogue* 36 (2005): 495–510.

[71] Formal accountability routines also create incentives within headquarters. But in this book, I focus on the incentives created for the country office. For discussion of headquarters incentives in relation to democracy promotion, see Sarah Bush, "The Argument: Structure, Agency, and Democracy Promotion," *The Taming of Democracy Assistance: Why Democracy Promotion Does Not Confront Dictators* (Cambridge, UK: Cambridge University Press: 2015), 22–52.

[72] Levitt and March, "Organizational Learning"; and Eden, "'Getting It Right or Wrong.'"

meetings; and visits from donors, members of the governing board, or headquarters-level staff.[73]

Many intervening organizations engaged in peacebuilding also implement humanitarian, development, or human rights activities and thus possess multiple potential country-office priorities. When their principals, and the formal accountability routines that they create, prioritize peacebuilding above other potential priorities, country offices are more likely to respond to local feedback about their peacebuilding outcomes.[74]

A Typology of Country-Level Performance

In this book, I treat formal peacebuilding accountability and informal local accountability as dichotomous variables: each variable has only two possible values. A country office can either have formal peacebuilding accountability or it can have formal accountability that prioritizes another type of aim, such as a development or humanitarian aim. A country office can either have informal local accountability – meaning that it delegates authority to a representative group of local stakeholders to hold the country office accountable for delivering peacebuilding aims that are relevant to these stakeholders – or not.

The different combinations of these two variables lead to four possible types of country-office performance: peacebuilding learners, micro-adaptors, sovereignty reinforcers, and stagnant players. Because both formal and informal local accountability can vary within a single country office over time, a single country office may move between these organizational types.

Peacebuilding learners have both informal local accountability and formal peacebuilding accountability (see Figure 1.1). These country offices take regular actions to reduce the gap between their peacebuilding aims and their peacebuilding outcomes, or learn in relation to their peacebuilding aims. Peacebuilding learners do not just learn in relation to one project or activity, but do so across the majority of their peacebuilding interventions. Of the four types of country-office

---

[73] Martha S. Feldman and Brian T. Pentland, "Reconceptualizing Organizational Routines as a Source of Flexibility and Change," *Administrative Science Quarterly* 48, no. 1 (2003): 94–118.

[74] Prioritizing peacebuilding above other potential priorities means that country offices pay attention to the dynamics of conflict and cooperation in the country context, rather than simply to development or humanitarian indicators. Even though peace is arguably a determinant of, and determined by, development, human rights protection, and sustainable livelihoods, intervening organizations tend to focus on much more proximate outcomes that directly reflect their organizational priorities.

FORMAL PEACEBUILDING ACCOUNTABILITY

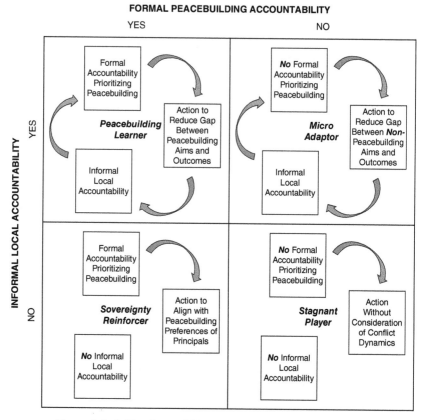

Figure 1.1 A Typology of Country-Office Performance

performance, peacebuilding learners is the only type that is likely to achieve positive peacebuilding performance.

In highly dynamic contexts, the overall country environment changes, as does the peacebuilding intervention itself as it aims to create change in the changing local context. Organizations that simply implement their peacebuilding activities as planned, without regularly attempting to align them with the changing context, are less likely to achieve the desired peacebuilding outcomes in that context.[75]

---

[75] Most intervening organizations do their analysis of the country context and plan the details of their project at least one year before implementation begins. This means that by the time these organizations begin to implement their activity, the analysis on which they based their activity is often out of date.

The literatures on peacebuilding, international aid, and global governance have largely overlooked the behavior exhibited by peacebuilding learners, focusing instead on explaining peacebuilding failure.[76]

Micro-adaptors are country offices that do not prioritize formal peacebuilding accountability but do have informal local accountability. Microadaptors prioritize development, humanitarianism, human rights, or some other non-peacebuilding aim. Micro-adaptors can learn, responding to information from local stakeholders and acting to reduce the gap between their aims and outcomes. But micro-adaptors do not learn in relation to their peacebuilding aims.

Micro-adaptors pay attention to feedback on indicators of development and basic human needs, such as the quality of water, basic nutrition levels, or primary education levels. Micro-adaptors do not aim to address directly indicators of social or political conflict such as ethnic discrimination or the absence of civic participation of disenfranchised groups. These indicators are of course not mutually exclusive. A country office could, for example, measure the degree to which different ethnic groups have access to potable water. But organizations must make choices about what information they pay attention to, and these choices are determined by the organization's top priorities and codified in their formal accountability routines.

Micro-adaptors are likely to work *in* conflict dynamics, not *on* them.[77] They do not aim to address *directly* the causes of *conflict* or peace in the country. Even though micro-adaptors may have peacebuilding aims, because peacebuilding is not the primary focus of the country office, most of their activities are unlikely to work toward these peacebuilding aims.

The peacebuilding and global governance literatures have largely overlooked the behavior of micro-adaptors, with the exception of a handful of pieces on humanitarian and development INGOs that describe how they tend to work around, not on, conflict.[78]

---

[76] One exception is the work of Howard (*UN Peacekeeping in Civil Wars*), who identifies organizational learning as a necessary condition for UN peacekeeping missions to fulfill their mandates. Howard, however, does not explain the specific causes of this behavior at the country level, instead arguing that it is due to freedom and flexibility offered by headquarters to the country office. See also David Chandler, "Back to the Future? The Limits of Neo-Wilsonian Ideals of Exporting Democracy," *Review of International Studies* 32, no. 3 (2006): 475–94.

[77] Goodhand, "Violent Conflict, Poverty and Chronic Poverty."

[78] Goodhand, "Violent Conflict, Poverty and Chronic Poverty"; Alex de Waal, "Mission without End? Peacekeeping in the African Political Marketplace," *International Affairs* 85, no.1 (2009): 99–113; and Mary Anderson, *Do No Harm: How Aid Agencies Can Support Peace, or War* (Boulder, CO: Lynne Rienner, 1999), 37–54.

Sovereignty reinforcers possess formal peacebuilding accountability but lack informal local accountability. These country offices lack regular feedback from local stakeholders and therefore respond primarily to feedback from their headquarters, donors, and the host government. They reinforce the sovereignty and preferences of the host government, largely ignoring the preferences of civil society and the broader population.

Sovereignty reinforcers' focus on the preferences of the host government matters for peacebuilding because peacebuilding aims to transform the relationship between the state and society.[79] The inability of the state to peacefully govern the whole of society is considered central to the emergence and continuation of civil war and violent conflict.[80] Sovereignty reinforcers may adapt their peacebuilding interventions, but only primarily in relation to the preferences of the state.

Much of the peacebuilding and aid literature discusses the behavior exhibited by sovereignty reinforcers. Autesserre, for example, describes intervening organizations that are hidden behind razor-wire-rimmed walls and interact only with other expatriates; their isolation leads to a poor understanding of the societies they inhabit and aim to transform.[81] Much of the literature on UN peacekeeping also describes this type of behavior and the inability of UN peacekeeping staff to create real "local ownership" beyond the host government as a result.[82]

Stagnant players are country offices that lack both formal peacebuilding accountability and informal local accountability. They tend to implement the same activities throughout the different stages of a country's war-to-peace transition without adapting to changes in the overall conflict dynamics or the specific local institutions that they work with. Without local-level feedback about their outcomes, they lack the information

---

[79] Organization for Economic Cooperation and Development, Development Assistance Committee (OECD-DAC), "Supporting Statebuilding in Situations of Conflict and Fragility: Policy Guidance," DAC Guidelines and Reference Series (Paris: OECD, February 28, 2011), 90; and Department for International Development (DFID), "Building Peaceful States and Societies: A DFID Practice Paper" (London: DFID, 2010).

[80] David Mason and Sara McLaughlin Mitchell, eds., *What Do We Know about Civil Wars?* (New York: Rowman and Littlefield, 2016).

[81] Autesserre, *Peaceland.*

[82] Pouligny, "Civil Society and Post-Conflict Peacebuilding"; Kathleen Jennings, "Life in a 'Peace-kept' City: Encounters with the Peacekeeping Economy," *Journal of Intervention and Statebuilding* 9, no. 3 (2015): 296–315; Jeni Whalan, *How Peace Operations Work: Power, Legitimacy and Effectiveness* (Oxford: Oxford University Press, 2013), 19–48; von Billerbeck, *Local Ownership and United Nations Peacekeeping*, 114–26; and Béatrice Pouligny, *Peace Operations Seen from Below: UN Missions and Local People* (Bloomfield, CT: Kumarian, 2006).

necessary to take actions to reduce the gap between their aims and outcomes. Because their headquarters does not prioritize peacebuilding above other aims, they have few incentives to adapt to conflict-related dynamics.

Constructivist scholars have often written about this type of country-office behavior.[83] For example, Uvin argues that apolitical development agencies strengthened the Rwandan state, which helped enable it to carry out the 1994 genocide.[84] Other scholars argue that, at the very least, this type of country-office behavior blindly finances the host government's policies, encouraging the government to be less accountable and responsive to its population.[85]

Conclusion

This book challenges the trend in the international relations literature to study differences among global governors only at the global level. Previous studies of intervening organizations have focused on headquarters-level behaviors, without examining how the key institutions in global governance intervene at the country level. The majority of the literature on the structure of IOs takes a rationalist perspective, focusing on the ways in which states exercise their preferences by selecting particular elements of institutional design when forming IOs.[86] This rationalist perspective extends to much of the scholarship on principal–agent relationships in IOs, which views states as the principals and IOs as the agents designed to fulfill the wishes of their principals.[87] Some constructivist scholars have begun to study IOs as autonomous actors whose bureaucratic cultures and pathologies give them some independence from their member states.[88]

In isolation, neither a focus on state preferences nor a focus on bureaucratic behavior tells the full story of country-office behavior. By

---

[83] Michael N. Barnett and Martha Finnemore, *Rules for the World: International Organizations in Global Politics* (Ithaca, NY: Cornell University Press, 2004); Autesserre, *The Trouble with the Congo*; and Autesserre, *Peaceland*.

[84] Barnett and Finnemore, *Rules for the World*.

[85] Todd Moss, Gunilla Pettersson, and Nicolas van de Walle, "An Aid-Institutions Paradox? A Review Essay on Aid Dependency and State Building in Sub-Saharan Africa," Working Paper no. 74 (Washington, DC: Center for Global Development, January 2006), 1–28.

[86] Koremenos, Lipson, and Snidal, "The Rational Design of International Institutions."

[87] For an overview of current application of principal-agent theory to International Organizations, see Hawkins et al., *Delegation and Agency in International Organizations*.

[88] Michael Barnett and Martha Finnemore, "The Politics, Power, and Pathologies of International Organizations," *International Organization* 53, no. 4 (1999): 699–732; and Barnett and Finnemore, *Rules for the World*.

examining the relationship between formal peacebuilding accountability routines and informal local accountability routines within country offices, this book integrates the claims of both rationalist and constructivist scholars. It identifies the important role played by member states in determining the behavior of country offices, but also shows how informal local accountability routines that are not directly controlled or mandated by member states may be necessary for positive country-office performance. It identifies the importance of bureaucratic pathologies, manifest in formal accountability routines, but also shows instances in which individual country-office staff circumvent these routines and contribute to positive peacebuilding outcomes.

In so doing, this book provides a detailed analysis of the independent behavior of IO, INGO, and bilateral donor country offices that is largely absent from political science literature. Furthermore, it points to the crucial role played by individual country-office staff in creating the informal local accountability routines that are necessary for positive peacebuilding performance.

2   The Country Context: Burundi from 1999 to 2014

> We have just entered a new phase. The people of Burundi must know this; they must know that no more time must be lost in so senseless and futile a conflict and that the time has come for political realism and collective responsibility so that Burundi may become a land of milk and honey, where each citizen has the capacity to realize his or her potential in complete freedom and justice.[1]   President Pierre Buyoya
> January 23, 1999

This chapter describes one country context in which international peacebuilding took place: Burundi from 1999 to 2014. The chapter begins in 1999 after the removal of a regional embargo reinvigorated Burundi's peace process and ends in 2014 as Burundi was preparing for its 2015 elections. At numerous turning points in between, Burundians and international observers declared, "Burundi is at a crossroads."[2] Each of these critical turning points ushered in a new phase in Burundi's war-to-peace transition. Between phases, the political and security dynamics changed significantly. Within each phase, the political and security dynamics remained relatively consistent. Prior to each new phase, it was unclear if a new phase would advance Burundi toward peace or toward violence and renewed war.

This book does not seek to make causal claims about the impact of international intervention on Burundi's war-to-peace transition in general. Rather, Burundi serves as the backdrop for an analysis of the peacebuilding performance of five global governors engaged in peacebuilding in Burundi. This book uses a minimal measurement of performance:

---

[1] Government of Burundi, "Letter Dated 1 February 1999 From the Permanent Representative of Burundi to the United Nations Addressed to the President of the Security Council – S/1999/106" (UN Security Council, February 2, 1999), 3.

[2] UN News Centre, "Ban Lauds Burundians for Gains in Consolidating Peace," June 9, 2010, accessed December 20, 2017, http://goo.gl/I4WK7a; and Filip Reyntjens, "Again at the Crossroads: Rwanda and Burundi, 2000–2001," *Current African Issues* (Nordic Africa Institute, Uppsala, Sweden, May 2001).

organizational learning. An organization learns when it takes actions to reduce the gap between its aims and outcomes.[3] For the purpose of this book, organizational learning occurs when the country office takes regular actions across its programs to reduce the gap between its peacebuilding aims and its outcomes. This gap may emerge because the activities were not suited for the context in the first place or because the context changed and the activities were no longer suited for the context.

This chapter discusses six major phases in Burundi's war-to-peace transition between 1999 and 2014 as well as the events that triggered each one.[4] Each case study organization and the broader group of intervening organizations engaged in peacebuilding in Burundi identified these six phases as crucial turning points. As outlined in the Introduction, this book investigates whether or not the five case study organizations engaged in organizational learning across most of their country office within one year after the initiation of a new phase.

Chapters 3, 4, and 5 assess the five case study organizations' peacebuilding performance during each of the six phases, asking: Did these country offices make changes across their activities to reduce the gap between their peacebuilding aims and outcomes within one year of the initiation of a new phase? Such an approach does not impose an arbitrary measure of performance, but instead assesses the case study organizations according to their own criteria, asking: Did the country offices adjust to the major changes that they identified as being important?

This chapter proceeds by, first, providing a brief background on Burundi. It then discusses the initiation of each new phase, the dynamics within each phase, and the implications of these dynamics for the trajectory of Burundi's war-to-peace transition.

Background

Burundi is a small, hilly country nestled in Africa's Great Lakes region. Burundi is one of the most densely populated and poorest countries in

---

[3] Chris Argyris, *On Organizational Learning* (Boston: Blackwell, 1992).

[4] I identified major turning points in Burundi's war-to-peace transition by studying the analyses of the context that intervening organizations conducted. I identified big shifts in the environment through a systematic review of country-level documents posted on Reliefweb, including newswire stories; reports from the UN; reports from human rights organizations, such as Human Rights Watch; reports from conflict analysis organizations, such as the International Crisis Group (ICG); and unpublished conflict analyses conducted by the case study organizations. I then validated these findings with a range of experts on Burundi.

the world.[5] From independence from Belgium in 1962 until 2001, Burundi was ruled by a Tutsi clan from Bururi Province that monopolized the state, the military, and the economy and used violence, intimidation, and exclusion to maintain power. The Bururi clan's tight grip on power and violent tactics led to intense oppression of the majority Hutu population, exclusion of other Tutsis from government, and several waves of massacres and reprisals (1965, 1972, 1988, and 1991) involving Hutus against Tutsis and vice versa.[6]

These episodes of ethnic violence in Burundi culminated in the outbreak of civil war in 1993. In June 1993, Burundians elected a Hutu intellectual, Melchior Ndadaye, as their first president. In October 1993, Burundian Army officers assassinated Ndadaye and two other prominent Hutu politicians. These events sparked large-scale massacres of the minority Tutsi population and deadly reprisals by the Tutsi-run army against the majority Hutu population. The country descended into a civil war fought between the Burundian Army (Forces Armées Burundaise) and two Hutu rebel groups, the Forces Nationales de Libération du Peuple Hutu (Palipehutu-FNL, or FNL) and the Conseil National pour la Défense de la Démocratie (CNDD-FDD). By 1999, an estimated two hundred thousand Burundians had been killed in the fighting and approximately one million more had been forced to flee their homes.

---

[5] According to UN figures, Burundi's population density was 353.9 people per square kilometer in 2012. See United Nations Statistics Division, "Burundi Country Profile" *UN Data* (2015), accessed December 20, 2017, http://goo.gl/odvLav. The country ranked 180th out of 187 countries on the 2014 Human Development Index. See UN Development Programme, "Burundi Country Profile: Human Development Indicators," accessed December 20, 2017, http://goo.gl/qA4n8N.

[6] The ethnic composition of Burundi's population is as follows: 85 percent Hutu, 14 percent Tutsi, and 1 percent Twa. See African Studies Center, University of Pennsylvania, *East Africa Living Encyclopedia*, "Burundi: Ethnic Groups," accessed December 20, 2017, www.africa.upenn.edu/NEH/bethnic.htm. In 1965, the Hutu military units revolted, giving way to an armed conflict, during which Hutu peasants killed about five hundred Tutsi, followed by Tutsi counterstrikes that resulted in the death of an estimated five thousand Hutus. In 1972, Hutu insurgents attempted a coup and attacked Tutsi civilians that led to systematic massacres of Hutus by the Tutsi-dominated army (eighty thousand to one hundred thousand Hutus are estimated to have been killed). In 1988, as a result of disorganized rural violence by politically and socially discontented Hutu against Tutsis in the northern Ntega and Marangara communes, the Tutsi-dominated army conducted unpremeditated massacres of Hutus. (Between five thousand and twenty thousand or as many as fifty thousand Hutus are estimated to have been killed.) In November 1991, the radical Party for the Liberation of the Hutu People launched attacks in northern towns in the hope of provoking a general Hutu uprising that resulted in the death of three hundred Tutsi and one thousand Hutus. See *Minorities at Risk*, "Chronology for Hutus in Burundi" (2010), accessed December 20, 2017, www.mar.umd.edu/chronology.asp?groupId=51601.

Although Burundi's civil war was fought through an ethnic lens, it was rooted in fierce competition for control over the Burundian state and its resources. Burundi's hierarchical social structure and strict deference to authority that originated in its precolonial feudal system continued to pervade politics, governance, and everyday life. The Belgian colonial politics of "divide and rule" and international aid policies of the 1980s solidified the patronage system, making control of the state the primary avenue toward wealth for oneself and one's kin.[7] During Burundi's war and peace process, Burundian politicians competed desperately to be at the top of the totem pole, with little concern for the many Burundians sidelined from power and its benefits.

Phase I: The Unexpected Success of the Arusha Process: January 1999 to October 2001

In January 1999, the Regional Peace Initiative on Burundi lifted sanctions that had been imposed on the country since 1996. Rwanda, Zaire, Kenya, Tanzania, Ethiopia, and Uganda had established the sanctions against Burundi to protest the 1996 coup by President Buyoya and to force all parties to the conflict to enter multiparty negotiations.[8] International donors supported the sanctions by freezing approximately US $300 million in development aid.[9] On January 23, 1999, the regional heads of state lifted the sanctions in part to reinforce the positive progress made in Burundi's Arusha peace negotiations.[10] International donors, in turn, pledged to increase the amount of "expanded humanitarian aid" to Burundi.[11]

---

[7] Adam Branch and Zachariah Mampilly, *Africa Uprising: Popular Protest and Political Change* (London: Zed, 2015); Alex de Waal, "Mission without End? Peacekeeping in the African Political Marketplace," *International Affairs* 85, no. 1 (2009): 99–113; and Rene Lemarchand, "Burundi: Ethnic Conflict and Genocide," (Washington, DC: Woodrow Wilson International Center for Scholars, 1994), 206.

[8] *All Africa Press Service*, "Regional Leaders to Impose Sanctions on Burundi" (August 8, 1996), accessed December 21, 2017, http://goo.gl/iBnW7B; and International Crisis Group (ICG), "Burundi under Siege: Lift the Sanctions Re-Launch the Peace Process," Africa Report series, no. 1 (Brussels: ICG, April 28, 1998), accessed December 20, 2017. www.justice.gov/sites/default/files/eoir/legacy/2014/09/29/icg_04271998.pdf.

[9] Alexis Sinduhije, "Burundi Faces Economic Woes Despite Sanctions End," *Reuters AlertNet* (1999), accessed December 20, 2017, http://goo.gl/MBHa87.

[10] ICG, "Burundi: Internal and Regional Implications of the Suspension of Sanctions International Crisis Group," Africa Report series, no. 3 (Brussels: ICG, May 4, 1999), accessed December 20, 2017, http://goo.gl/Mz071H.

[11] ICG, "Burundi: Internal and Regional Implications."

Many observers saw the suspension of the sanctions against Burundi in January 1999 as "a major shot in the arm for the peace process," but the shot quickly wore off.[12] For most of 1999, although the nineteen parties to the Arusha peace process met regularly, they did not make much progress. The mediator, Julius Nyerere, and international donors funding the talks became frustrated with the slow pace. Nyerere criticized the parties at the talks for "wasting time, money, and hope."[13] An international donor commented that it was difficult to guarantee continued funding for peace talks when "many of the participants seem to treat it as a free holiday."[14] Many people argued that the high per diems paid at the Arusha talks became a disincentive for the participating parties to come to agreement, particularly as several "Arusha mansions" of participating politicians were under construction in Bujumbura.[15]

As the peace talks stalled, intense fighting continued between the government, on one side, and the CNDD-FDD and FNL rebel groups, who were excluded from the Arusha talks, on the other. Although the Burundians were by far the most affected by the war, some internationals became targets. On October 12, 1999, the UNICEF representative from Chile, a Dutch World Food Program (WFP) logistics officer, and seven Burundian staff members were killed by rebels during a visit to a *regroupement* camp in Rutana Province.[16] Their deaths sent shockwaves throughout the international community in Burundi. The United Nations evacuated all nonessential personnel and reduced its activities to a minimum.[17] Combined with the lack of progress in the peace process and the desolate situation for so many Burundians, the murder of the UN staff made Burundi's prospects seem even gloomier. "Hope is in short supply in Burundi these days,"

---

[12] Refugees International, "Give Burundi a Chance" (Washington, DC: Refugees International, November 30, 1999), accessed December 20, 2017, http://goo.gl/IWIhq6.

[13] *Agence France-Presse*, "Burundi Negotiators to Meet for Consultations" (October 1, 1999), accessed December 31, 2017, http://goo.gl/IDGVxa; and Reuters, "Burundi Peace Talks End in Deadlock," *Reuters AlertNet* (July 16, 1999), accessed December 20, 2017, http://goo.gl/eYKkAq.

[14] Agence France-Presse, "Burundi Negotiators to Meet."

[15] Informal discussions in Bujumbura, 2000 and 2001.

[16] UN Country Team, "Press Statement on the Incident Resulting in the Deaths of Two UN Staff Members in Rutana Province (Burundi) 12 Oct 1999" (Burundi: United Nations, October 13, 1999), accessed December 20, 2017, http://goo.gl/IThcmS. The "regroupment" camps were created to clear civilians out of rebel-held areas so that the Burundian military could better target the rebels.

[17] UN Department of Public Information, "Press Briefing by Special Representative on Burundi," press release (Bujumbura: United Nations, October 19, 1999), accessed December 20, 2017, http://goo.gl/sVsnEf.

said Kathleen Cravero, the UN Humanitarian Coordinator and one of the few survivors of the Rutana murders.[18]

Julius Nyerere, the former Tanzanian president who had led the Arusha negotiations, died of leukemia in London that same October. Nelson Mandela became the new chief mediator, and his appointment injected new energy into the peace process. On August 28, 2000, nineteen parties signed the Arusha Peace and Reconciliation Agreement for Burundi (the Arusha Agreement).[19] The Arusha Agreement contained relatively comprehensive guidelines for Burundi's three-year transitional government and the creation of new institutions. It offered two major solutions to Burundi's war: power sharing and equitable economic development. The power-sharing arrangements addressed the ethnic origins of the war, whereas Protocol IV of the agreement outlined a comprehensive plan for reconstruction and development. Mandela ensured that the socioeconomic dimension was covered in the Arusha Agreement. He believed strongly that Burundi's conflict was rooted in its poverty and inequality and that addressing social and economic inequalities would be the foundation of Burundi's peacebuilding process: "It must be possible for the people of Burundi to materially distinguish between the destructiveness of conflict and the benefits of peace."[20]

However, the Arusha Agreement was missing two crucial components: a cease-fire and a decision on who would lead during Burundi's three-year transition period. In spite of Mandela's efforts, the CNDD-FDD and the FNL refused to sign on to an agreement that they had not participated in drafting.[21] As a result, the Arusha Agreement was an agreement among all the other major and minor political parties in Burundi, but not among those who were actually engaged in battle: the Burundian Army, the CNDD-FDD, and the FNL. Such a gaping hole in the agreement made it impossible to implement without additional agreements on the cease-fire and on transitional leadership.

---

[18] UN Department of Public Information, "Briefing by Humanitarian Coordinator for Burundi," press release (New York: United Nations, December 3,1999), accessed December 20, 2017, http://goo.gl/L7haa1.

[19] Initially, only eighteen parties signed the agreement, although the nineteenth signature soon followed.

[20] Nelson Mandela, Donor Conference on Burundi, Paris, December 6–7, 2000. Citation available at ICG, "A Framework for Responsible Aid to Burundi," Africa Report series, no. 57 (Brussels: ICG, February 21, 2003), 9, accessed December 20, 2017, www.crisis group.org/africa/central-africa/burundi/framework-responsible-aid-burundi.

[21] ICG, "Burundi after Six Months of Transition: Continuing the War or Winning Peace?" Africa Report series, no. 46 (Brussels: ICG, May 24, 2002), accessed December 20, 2017, www.crisisgroup.org/africa/central-africa/burundi/burundi-after-six-months-transition-continuing-war-or-winning-peace.

By mid-2001, intense fighting and indiscriminate attacks on civilians were occurring in thirteen of Burundi's seventeen provinces.[22] The success of the peace process in the neighboring Democratic Republic of the Congo (DRC) and the associated rebel disarmament processes there seemed to be contributing to the escalation of conflict in Burundi.[23] The CNDD-FDD and the FNL were also growing stronger as they recruited new members and appeared to be coordinating their operations.[24] In May 2001, Jan Van Eck, a Burundi analyst at the Centre for International Policy Studies in Pretoria, and the International Crisis Group (ICG) warned that Burundi was "sliding once again towards widespread civil war."[25] Burundians had hoped that the Arusha Agreement would bring peace; instead, they faced the threat of a war that could engulf the entire Great Lakes region.[26] A regional observer summed up the general mood about Burundi in June 2001: "If it's not the rebels, politics and poverty will bring the country down."[27]

In July 2001, a meeting of the Regional Peace Initiative on Burundi designated Burundi's president, Pierre Buyoya, as the transitional president and Domitien Ndayizeye, a key player in Burundi's major Hutu party, FRODEBU, as the vice president for the first eighteen months of Burundi's planned three-year transition period.[28] For the second half of the transitional period, the Hutu parties that participated in the Arusha process would choose the new president and the Tutsi parties would choose the vice president.

Such agreement on transitional leadership made Burundians and international actors hopeful that the Arusha Agreement could be implemented. However, first a protection force had to be established to guarantee the physical safety of politicians returning from exile to take part in

---

[22] ICG, "Burundi: Breaking the Deadlock," Africa Report series, no. 29 (Brussels: ICG, May 14, 2001), 2, accessed December 20, 2017, www.crisisgroup.org/africa/central-africa/burundi/burundi-breaking-deadlock.

[23] Simon Denyer, "Analysis: Burundi Slides Back towards All-out War," *Reuters AlertNet* (May 15, 2001), accessed December 20, 2017, http://goo.gl/CwQLJf.

[24] ICG, "Burundi: Breaking the Deadlock," 1.

[25] ICG, "Burundi: Breaking the Deadlock," ii.

[26] *Pan African News Agency*, "80% des burundais préoccupés par la guerre civile dans le pays" (June 5, 2001), accessed December 20, 2017, http://goo.gl/E5sQoJ.

[27] *Integrated Regional Information Networks*, "Burundi: IRIN Focus: Containing the Crisis" (June 28, 2001), accessed December 20, 2017, http://goo.gl/lAQIT8.

[28] UN Security Council, "Statement Issued by the Government Following the Fifteenth Summit Meeting of the Regional Peace Initiative on Burundi (S/2001/752)," letter to the Security Council (Bujumbura: United Nations, July 31, 2001), accessed December 20, 2017, http://goo.gl/FXGdjF.

the new government.[29] Because of their roles as both perpetrators and victims of the war, many of these exiled politicians feared for their lives. UN Secretary-General Kofi Annan indicated that without a cease-fire, UN troops would not be deployed for this task, leaving the regional peace initiative and South African mediators searching for other options.[30]

In October 2001, just a few days before President Buyoya and Vice President Ndayizeye were to be inaugurated, the South African Special Protection Unit, comprising seven hundred troops, arrived in the country. Nelson Mandela had convinced the South African Army to deploy this unit to protect approximately 150 politicians returning to Burundi to be part of the transitional government.[31] Not all Burundians welcomed the troops. Extremists on both sides objected to their deployment, with Tutsi hard-line groups calling on Burundians to attack the troops.[32] In spite of threats, the South African troops arrived without incident, and the transitional government was inaugurated on November 1, 2001.

In sum, between January 1999 and October 2001, Burundi's peace-building process experienced extreme highs and lows. The Arusha peace negotiations advanced, faltered, and advanced again. Violence escalated, civilians fled the violence, and violence raged even more. Just as the country seemed about to descend into full-scale war, there was a breakthrough in the Arusha negotiations and the transitional national government was inaugurated. For distant observers and Burundian analysts alike, this phase offered few moments of certainty as to whether Burundi would advance toward war or peace.

Aid for Peace

As Burundi's peace process and ongoing war vied for attention, another conflict was brewing: the battle over the resumption of aid to Burundi.

---

[29] ICG, "Burundi: One Hundred Days to Put the Peace Process Back on Track," Africa Report series, no. 33 (Arusha, Bujumbura, Nairobi, Brussels: ICG, August 14, 2001), 1, accessed December 20, 2017, www.crisisgroup.org/africa/central-africa/burundi/burundi-one-hundred-days-put-peace-process-back-track.

[30] ICG, "Burundi: One Hundred Days," 3.

[31] *Agence France-Presse*, "S. African Troops Arrive in Burundi for VIP Protection Force" (October 28, 2001), http://goo.gl/orFfFh.

[32] Claire Keeton, "Burundi Still Volatile Despite Transition Installation: Analysts," *Agence France-Presse*, (October 31, 2001), http://goo.gl/JfPO2C; and *Integrated Regional Information Networks*, "Burundi-South Africa: SA Troops Face 'Delicate Mission'" (October 30, 2001), accessed December 20, 2017, https://reliefweb.int/report/burundi/burundi-south-africa-sa-troops-face-delicate-mission. The intention had originally been to have a mixed Hutu–Tutsi protection force, but the parties were unable to agree on the composition of the force. The International Protection Force was intended to be a stopgap measure, and their responsibility would be taken over by the Burundian force. This never happened.

The level of attention that Burundi's war and peace process received from states around the world seemed to be at odds with this tiny country's geostrategic importance. Regional heads of state saw Burundi as a potential success story and an island of stability in a region fraught with conflict.[33] International actors hoped to assuage their guilt from not acting to prevent Rwanda's 1994 genocide by trying to prevent genocide in Burundi.[34]

Once the embargo was lifted in January 1999, international actors and the Burundian government advocated tirelessly for the resumption of aid to the impoverished country.[35] In January 2000, Marc Nteturuye, Burundi's permanent representative to the United Nations, declared:

We also expect the international community to accompany the peace process along the way, to be on the side of the Government and help them to conduct the peace process to a safe harbor. The peace process needs political support, but it also needs economic assistance and support for reconstruction.[36]

While the peace process, war, and struggle for aid persisted, the Burundian people suffered. The war, sanctions, and withdrawal of aid had made an already impoverished people dirt poor. The gross domestic product (GDP) per capita in 2001 was estimated at US $120, down from an average of US $240 between 1980 and 1985.[37] Rapidly escalating fighting forced hundreds of thousands of Burundians to flee their homes and to move far away from their fields and communities. With more than two hundred thousand dead from the war, people were traumatized and vulnerable. Insecurity and drought further reduced the capacity to live decently, resulting in waves of malnutrition, disease, and death.

The state was also suffering, although to a different degree. Not only did it have less money to spend, but the money was worth less. Over the period when the sanctions were in place – 1999 to 1996 – inflation

---

[33] ICG, "Burundi under Siege"; and ICG, "Burundi: Implications of the Suspension of Sanctions."

[34] Michael S. Lund, Barnett R. Rubin, and Fabienne Hara, "Learning from Burundi's Failed Democratic Transition, 1993–1996: Did International Initiatives Match the Problem?" in *Cases and Strategies for Preventive Action* (New York: Century Foundation, 1998), xii, 247; and ICG, "Burundi under Seige."

[35] ICG, "Burundi: Proposals for the Resumption of Bilateral and Multilateral Co-Operation," Africa Report series, no. 4 (May 4, 1999), accessed December 20, 2017, www.crisis group.org/africa/central-africa/burundi/burundi-proposals-resumption-bilateral-and-multi lateral-co-operation.

[36] UN Department of Public Information, "Press Conference by Permanent Representative of Burundi," press release (Burundi: United Nations, January 14, 2000), accessed December 20, 2017, http://goo.gl/C3lwRT.

[37] UN Security Council, "Interim Report of the Secretary-General to the Security Council on the Situation in Burundi" (New York: United Nations, November 14, 2001), accessed December 20, 2017, http://goo.gl/6cc00x.

continued to rise steadily. In 1996 alone, export earnings dropped 50 percent and the cost of imports increased by 25 percent.[38] The budget deficit swelled, and the black market flourished as people in power found ways around the embargo. The only stable income for the state was from beer: the Arabarudi Brewery in Bujumbura remained largely unaffected by the war and continued to provide 60 percent of its profits to the government.[39]

The desperate economic situation made the resumption of aid even more urgent.[40] Because the Burundian war was largely a conflict over scarce resources, resolving the conflict required a larger pie that could serve more people more effectively.[41] Prior to 1996, aid provided more than 80 percent of total investment in the country.[42] Because not all parts of the country were embroiled in war, organizations such as Refugees International argued that investing in programs in secure areas of the country would "build momentum for peace by focusing people on the future instead of the past."[43] Nonetheless, very little of this type of investment took place.

In spite of their financial and political commitment to Burundi's peace process, Western donors were reluctant to provide development or peacebuilding aid to Burundi. Without an end to the war in sight, donors questioned whether a state with such a weak administration, pervasive cronyism, and nepotism was ready for development assistance, much less direct budgetary support. The resumption of development aid, after all, meant supporting one side of the conflict by pouring money into the coffers of the government.

It was not the need for money that was in question, but rather whether giving money to this government was appropriate and how renewed aid would shift the balance of power.[44] Donors also feared that aid would encourage the war by giving the government more money with which to purchase weapons. The coexistence of Burundi's peace process and its civil war reinforced donor skepticism.

---

[38] "Economic Sanctions against Burundi Suspended," *Africa Recovery* 12, no. 4 (April 1999), accessed December 20, 2017, www.un.org/en/africarenewal/subjindx/124sanc.htm.

[39] ICG, "Burundi under Siege," 36.

[40] ICG, "A Framework for Responsible Aid to Burundi."

[41] ICG, "Burundi: Proposals for the Resumption of Bilateral and Multilateral Co-Operation."

[42] ICG, "Burundi: Proposals for the Resumption of Bilateral and Multilateral Co-Operation," 3.

[43] Refugees International, "Give Burundi a Chance."

[44] ICG, "A Framework for Responsible Aid to Burundi."

Donors had used the promise of development aid to entice Burundian politicians to sign the Arusha Agreement, but once that happened, donors moved the goalpost and promised to release aid only after the transitional government had been inaugurated. The general debate around the resumption of aid to Burundi, however, led to widespread agreement on the importance of peacebuilding – or the use of international aid and intervention to build the foundation of an equitable peace – from the early stages of Burundi's peace process.

Phase II: Peace with War: November 2001 to November 2003

On November 1, 2001, Burundi's transitional government, with Pierre Buyoya as its president, was inaugurated for a three-year period. The inauguration of the transitional government marked a crucial shift in Burundi's war-to-peace transition. Implementing the Arusha Agreement seemed possible, as did ethnic power sharing in Burundi. In spite of the significant progress marked by this event, crucial challenges remained.

The Arusha signatory parties had chosen the transitional president, the vice president, and twenty-six ministers. Once these parties, many of them former enemies, were in the new government, they continued many of the same political battles that had preoccupied them during the Arusha talks – but now they did not have Mandela to mediate their disagreements.[45]

It took the new government two months to agree to appoint the transitional National Assembly, the body responsible for passing the legislation required for Arusha's reforms. The implementation of the Arusha Agreement was already behind schedule at this point, and stagnation only worsened. Although the Arusha Agreement provided a framework for Burundi's transitional institutions and major reforms, the transitional government had to work out the details.[46] It had to implement institutional reforms while occupying new institutions – in other words, write the rule book while playing the game. At the same time, government representatives had to manage their own constituencies, many of whom were wary of this new partnership and what it might cost them.

The Arusha Agreement mandated the Implementation Monitoring Committee (IMC) to oversee Burundi's three-year transitional period and ensure that the key benchmarks stipulated in the agreement were

[45] ICG, "Burundi after Six Months of Transition," 2.
[46] ICG, "Burundi after Six Months of Transition," 8.

met.[47] The IMC was comprised of signatories of the agreement and was headed by Berhanu Dinka, the special representative of the United Nations Secretary-General to Burundi. Unfortunately, although the IMC held regular meetings and followed the evolution of political events in the country, it was not able to force the government to implement the Arusha Agreement. According to an International Crisis Group report, "The IMC is being transformed into a credit society for its members, a small forum for perpetual negotiations, where the parties procrastinate with no consciousness of the urgency of their task or the suffering of the people of Burundi."[48]

During this time, the battle between the Burundian Army and the rebel groups raged on. In fact, just after the government's inauguration, both the army and the rebels launched new offensives against each other. Suddenly it seemed the negotiation table and the battlefield had merged. Each side attempted to weaken the other on the battlefield in order to strengthen its stance at the negotiating table. Although cease-fire talks between the transitional government and the rebel groups continued, the rebels remained reluctant to agree to a cease-fire before their conditions were met. The Economist Intelligence Unit commented: "It is the insurgency itself which gives the rebels their political leverage."[49]

The Burundian people continued to be exasperated by the slow implementation of the Arusha Agreement and the escalating fighting. According to Joseph Ndayizeye of Ligue ITEKA, Burundi's foremost human rights organization at the time, people believed the politicians had caused the conflict and had little trust that they would fulfill the promises made at Arusha.[50] Bad governance is "the root cause of all the problems we are facing now ... hatred, deprivation, nepotism, corruption, and an almost feudal style of leadership," he said.[51] The state, after all, was the main route to wealth, and the transitional government seemed to be "more concerned with bringing the dividends of peace to themselves, not their people."[52]

---

[47] UN Information Service, "Secretary-General Appoints Berhanu Dinka as His Special Representative for Burundi," biographical note (New York: UN, July 24, 2002), accessed December 20, 2017, http://goo.gl/DA5c3x. At the time of Dinka's appointment, he was the secretary-general's special representative and regional humanitarian advisor for the Great Lakes region.

[48] ICG, "Burundi: Breaking the Deadlock," 25.

[49] Economist Intelligence Unit, "Burundi Economic and Political Outlook" (London: Economist Intelligence Unit), accessed February 9, 2012, http://goo.gl/nXHJDI.

[50] Anaclet Rwegayura, "Burundi: Famine Hits Hard as Fighting Continues in Burundi," *Pan African News Agency*, (October 4, 2000), accessed December 20, 2017, http://goo.gl/G9gqBd.

[51] Rwegayura, "Burundi: Famine Hits Hard."

[52] ICG, "A Framework for Responsible Aid to Burundi," 13.

The Burundian people had hoped that the Arusha Agreement would bring an end to the war and a badly needed influx of aid. Instead, all they saw was more war, abuse, and poverty:

> Burundians do realize that, in fact, the main cause of the conflict is the control of the resources which are extremely limited. The control of resources is so crucial that it becomes more and more a question of life and death. You will keep in your mind that the state is the principal employer and the principal source of economic resources. That's why every political protagonist would like to rush after power.[53]

Miraculously, Burundi's war-to-peace transition advanced. On May 1, 2003, President Buyoya handed the presidency over to his vice president, Domitien Ndayizeye, who became the first Hutu president to remain in office for a full tenure. As the primary holder of political, financial, and military power in Burundi, the Burundian Army had played a key role in enabling this transition.[54] In October and November 2003, cease-fire agreements were signed between the largest faction of the CNDD-FDD and the transitional government, immediately improving security throughout the country. Only one rebel group now remained outside Burundi's peace process: Agathon Rwasa's faction of the FNL.

Phase III: Peace, Transition, and War: December 2003 to August 2005

On November 23, 2003, President Domitien Ndayizeye formed a new twenty-seven-member cabinet that included Pierre Nkurunziza, the leader of the biggest rebel faction (CNDD-FDD), as the minister of good governance and state inspection and three other CNDD-FDD representatives as members of parliament who carried some ministerial responsibility, thus marking the integration of Burundi's rebel groups into government.[55] The removal of the embargo in January 1999 marked the beginning of Burundi's exit from war; the inauguration of the transitional government in November 2001 marked the start of the implementation of Burundi's peace agreement; the integration of the CNDD-FDD into Burundi's government marked the attainment of negative peace, or the absence of violent political conflict, in much of Burundi's territory.

---

[53] Fabien Nsengimana, "Briefing on BLTP Activities" (Washington, DC: Woodrow Wilson Center, January 16, 2008), 2, accessed December 20, 2017, http://goo.gl/Hm8SUu.
[54] Interview with observer O11, Bujumbura, March 25, 2009.
[55] ICG, "End of the Transition in Burundi: The Home Stretch," Africa Report series, no. 81 (Brussels: ICG, July 5, 2004), accessed December 20, 2017, www.crisisgroup.org/africa/central-africa/burundi/end-transition-burundi-home-stretch.

It established security throughout most of the country for the first time since the outbreak of the war in 1993.

The transitional government rapidly sped up its implementation of the Arusha Agreement after the CNDD-FDD joined. To abide by the transition's three-year time frame, democratic elections would have to be held by October 31, 2004. To do this, the transitional government would have to reach a cease-fire agreement with the FNL, which still refused to participate in official cease-fire talks.[56] The transitional government would also have to implement the cease-fire agreements signed in November 2003 by Nkurunziza's CNDD-FDD and the agreements signed by two smaller factions of the CNDD-FDD and FNL in 2002.

The implementation of these agreements required that the rebel combatants be either demobilized or integrated into the National Defense Force, which had been agreed to in the Arusha Agreement but had not yet been created. The rebel groups would also have to transform themselves into political parties. The government and international community would have to facilitate the return of displaced people and refugees so that they could vote in the elections. An interim post-transitional constitution, which would guide the government after the first postwar elections, would have to be agreed upon and adopted by referendum. Several other laws would have to be adopted, and five rounds of elections would have to be organized: the referendum, two local-level elections, and the National Assembly and Senate elections.[57] The president would be appointed by the Senate and the National Assembly.

A well-functioning government would have had difficulty completing all these tasks within such a short time frame (eleven months). For Burundi's transitional government, the challenge seemed next to impossible. On the political side, there was enormous tension between the CNDD-FDD and FRODEBU, the main Hutu party. The main Tutsi party, UPRONA, took FRODEBU's side. The CNDD-FDD believed that it had done all the fighting, but the Arusha Agreement gave FRODEBU, which was not linked to an armed group, the rewards.[58] Now that both FRODEBU and the CNDD-FDD were part of the transitional government, their historic conflict became a major impediment to governance and preparation for the upcoming elections. CNDD-FDD party members felt that they had a greater chance of winning if elections

---

[56] ICG, "End of the Transition in Burundi."

[57] For more information about the 2005 elections, see ICG, "Elections in Burundi: The Peace Wager," Africa Briefing series, no. 20 (Brussels: ICG, December 9, 2004), accessed December 20, 2017, www.crisisgroup.org/africa/central-africa/burundi/elections-burundi-peace-wager.

[58] ICG, "End of the Transition in Burundi," 13–16.

were held at the time called for in the Arusha Agreement. The less time party members spent in government, the less they would be tarnished by people's negative perception of the transitional government.[59] FRODEBU party members believed that they would be at an advantage by delaying the elections.[60] As the political infighting continued, it became increasingly clear that the elections would be delayed.

In the end, politics were also personal.[61] People feared for their lives and those of their families. They feared that their access to wealth and their ability to pay off their debt would be taken away.[62] They feared they would lose the personal prestige that they had gained through their positions in government and lose all that they had fought for if they did not hold onto power.

For the Burundian people, the political antics increased fears about the elections. The previous round of democratic elections, in 1993, had led to waves of violence and death and the onslaught of the war. "The Tutsis are afraid, and the Hutus are afraid," the International Crisis Group observed. "How can you think that there is nothing to be afraid of when those who are supposed to reassure us say they too are worried about the situation?"[63] The continued fighting between the Burundian Army and the FNL rebel group made peace seem a distant possibility. A UN report described the level of deterioration:

[E]xecutions of civilians, torture, sexual violence, illegal and arbitrary detention continue, with impunity, primarily targeting the civilian population ... Both FNL and joint FAB/CNDD-FDD forces have been accused of grave violations of international humanitarian law and human rights, as well as looting and subjecting the population to a constant state of fear.[64]

Although the two military groups were engaged in joint operations and the cease-fire between the Burundian Army and the CNDD-FDD was holding, the integration of the rebel forces and the army into a new National Defense Force was stalled.[65] This hiccup posed a threat to the forthcoming elections. If the rebel groups were not integrated into the

---

[59] ICG, "End of the Transition in Burundi."

[60] ICG, "End of the Transition in Burundi."

[61] Interview with observer O10, Bujumbura, July 10, 2002.

[62] Interviews conducted in Bujumbura, 2002, for ICG report "A Framework for Responsible Aid to Burundi."

[63] ICG, "Elections in Burundi," no. 63. From an interview conducted by the ICG in Kirundo or Ngozi province in October 2004.

[64] UN Security Council, "First Report of the Secretary-General on the United Nations Operation in Burundi (ONUB)" (New York: United Nations, August 25, 2004), 9–10, accessed December 20, 2017, http://goo.gl/4LlZsY.

[65] ICG, "End of the Transition in Burundi," 9.

National Defense Force, the military would not be under the full control of civilian authority, challenging the legitimacy of the newly elected government. Furthermore, many Hutus would feel threatened by the persistence of an all-Tutsi military.[66] Many analysts believed that the issues blocking the integration of the rebel and military forces were so intractable that they would preclude the implementation of the Arusha Agreement and a peaceful end to the transition.[67]

Several issues prevented the rebel groups and the Burundian Army from being integrated into a new National Defense Force. First, the parties could not easily come to agreement on who qualified as a combatant. Second, they were unable to agree on how the different positions within the rebel groups, political movements, and the Burundian Army would be harmonized to ensure that each group had power within the integrated defense forces and that each individual had the ability to carry out his or her task. Third, the integration process was delayed in part because the Burundian Army was engaged in a counterinsurgency campaign against the FNL and did not want to go into cantonment or give up their heavy weapons. Fourth, the reintegration of former combatants into society was delayed because of the weak capacity of the National Commission for Demobilization, Reinsertion, and Reintegration.

For long-time observers of Burundi's politics, the army's decision to support the Arusha Agreement, rather than to try to block it, was "extraordinary."[68] It was a "clear sign that the Arusha process had created a change" in power and politics in Burundi.[69] The army leadership supported the reforms outlined in Arusha because it believed that it would fare best if it depoliticized itself.[70] The Tutsi parties were gradually losing political ground, and, according to the ethnic power-sharing provisions of the Arusha Agreement, they would need to be transformed into integrated Hutu–Tutsi parties. An all-Tutsi army, the driver of the war, would not fare well under Hutu leadership. The army saw that it would gain by transforming itself into an integrated force that would be more palatable to Burundi's new leadership. The disarmament of army and rebel combatants officially began in December 2004, more than a month after elections were originally scheduled to take place. The remaining issues preventing the formation of the new defense

---

[66] ICG, "End of the Transition in Burundi."
[67] Interview with observer O11, Bujumbura, March 25, 2009.
[68] Interview with observer O11, Bujumbura, March 25, 2009.
[69] Interview with observer O11, Bujumbura, March 25, 2009
[70] ICG, "End of the Transition in Burundi," 9.

force were regulated by presidential decree on May 11, 2005, less than a month before the communal elections.

On June 1, 2004, the United Nations Mission in Burundi (ONUB) was established to help organize the elections and oversee the disarmament and demobilization of Burundi's rebel groups. The first contingent of troops was the African Union Mission in Burundi's 2,612 troops, which were "re-hatted" in blue UN hats.[71] The Burundian government, South Africa, and the Regional Initiative had been campaigning for several years for the UN to send a peacekeeping force.[72] While the UN Security Council and Secretariat debated whether to send troops, the South Africans and the African Union had stepped in to fill the need for a protection and peacekeeping force. Without them, it is unlikely that Burundi's peacebuilding process would have advanced so smoothly.

ONUB collaborated closely with the South African mediators and the Regional Initiative to help the transitional government pass the necessary legislative reforms to organize elections in June, July, and August 2005, bringing the transitional phase to an end. "ONUB's close and regular contact with the regional heads of state [who] had influence with Burundi's political leaders played a decisive role in curbing isolated political attempts to sink the process."[73]

On August 19, 2005, Pierre Nkurunziza, the former head of the largest faction of the CNDD-FDD, became Burundi's new president in elections that were widely recognized as being free, fair, and largely peaceful. Nkurunziza and his party won by a big margin.[74] International oversight of Burundi's transitional phase officially ended on August 9, 2005, with the final meeting of the Implementation Monitoring Committee. Burundi had made it through another highly tumultuous and action-packed phase in its war-to-peace transition. Nonetheless, challenges remained. A UN assessment mission remarked:

The nature of the Burundian economy has been a factor in the hostilities, which can, simply put, be considered as competition between the haves and have-nots in a zero-sum game. Many of the assessment mission's interlocutors

---

[71] Henri Boshoff, Waldemar Vrey, and George Rautenbach, *The Burundi Peace Process: From Civil War to Conditional Peace*, Institute for Security Studies Monograph 171 (Pretoria: Institute for Security Studies), 7, accessed December 20, 2017, https://iss africa.org/research/monographs/the-burundi-peace-process-from-civil-war-to-conditional-peace.

[72] The Regional Initiative for Burundi included many of the same African states that had imposed initial sanctions on Burundi: Uganda, Rwanda, the DRC, South Africa, Tanzania, Ethiopia, Zambia, and Mozambique.

[73] Boshoff, Vrey, and Rautenbach, *Burundi Peace Process*, 113.

[74] Peter Uvin, *Life after Violence: A People's Story of Burundi* (London: Zed, 2009), 20.

stressed that in Burundi, even more so than in other post-conflict countries, the equitable expansion of economic and social opportunities is essential for a sustainable peace.[75]

Phase IV: Hope, Party Politics, and the Consolidation of Power: September 2005 to April 2009

The 2005 elections were a huge success. They brought an end to Burundi's nine-year peace process and ushered in a legitimate, sovereign government chosen by the people. Hope was in the air – hope for the fulfillment of basic needs, prosperity, security, sustainable peace, and reconciliation. This hope was shared by peasants, politicians, international civil servants, and regional leaders. The new government saw itself as the voice of the people, who until now had been mere pawns of the political class. Writing at the time, scholar Peter Uvin observed:

The government clearly sees itself as a fresh break in Burundi's history: a government representing the majority of the people, inclusive and negotiated, and connected to the ordinary people in ways in which no previous government was ... [The president's] first decision – free elementary schooling for all Burundians – exemplified this perfectly: In a country where social exclusion took place through highly unequal access to education, and in which the war had further destroyed the education system, the decision constituted a radical and visible break with the past ... deeply appreciated by ordinary people everywhere.[76]

In October 2005, less than two months after being elected, the Burundian government notified the United Nations that it wanted ONUB to withdraw and the UN to focus on development, not on peacekeeping or peacebuilding.[77] The government was taking its cue from Rwanda, which had liberally used its sovereign authority to revoke the right of intervening organizations and individuals to work there.[78] The Burundian government's decision to expel ONUB was one of the first indications that it would take Rwanda's approach and, perhaps more surprisingly, that this approach would work. But while the international

---

[75] UN Security Council, "Report of the Secretary-General on Burundi" (New York: United Nations, March 16, 2004), para. 26, accessed December 20, 2017, http://goo.gl/zjyvBT.

[76] Uvin, *Life after Violence*, 21–2.

[77] Stephen Jackson, *The United Nations Operation in Burundi (ONUB): Political and Strategic Lessons Learned*, Independent External Study (New York: Conflict Prevention and Peace Forum, July 2006), accessed June 6, 2017, www.peacekeepingbestpractices .unlpb.org/PBPS/Library?ONUB%20Lessons%20Learned.pdf.

[78] Interview with observer O12, via telephone, May 4, 2010.

community viewed Rwanda as an efficient and effective development partner, it saw the Burundian government as enmeshed in corruption, human rights violations, and dirty party politics from the beginning of its tenure.[79]

The tensions and competition that had preoccupied the CNDD-FDD, FRODEBU, UPRONA, and the other parties during the transitional phase continued to infuse the post-2005 government. During Nkurunziza's first year in office, the CNDD-FDD consolidated its control over the government and its companies; jailed prominent members of the opposition, civil society, and media; and used torture and summary executions to silence critics and ensure control over the state and its wealth.[80] For example, in violation of the interim constitution, Nkurunziza gave FRODEBU and UPRONA fewer ministries than those to which they were entitled.[81] He filled most of the technical and directorial posts in the government and state-run companies with CNDD-FDD members before establishing the commission that was supposed to ensure that these appointments were merit based.[82] CNDD-FDD governors dismissed FRODEBU communal administrators in violation of the law on communal administration.[83]

In July and August 2006, the government threw several prominent opposition politicians – including the former president Domitien Ndayizeye – into jail on charges that they were attempting to stage a coup. These charges were widely viewed as unsubstantiated.[84] Three of the politicians – all Tutsi – were tortured, rekindling ethnic tensions simmering beneath the growing interparty warfare.[85] The mere mention of a coup rekindled many Hutus' fear of a repeat of the 1993 coup that had triggered the war.[86]

The newly integrated National Defense Force sought to resolve the ongoing conflict with the FNL by defeating the FNL on the battlefield. To augment the National Defense Force's fight, the National Intelligence Services and the newly created Burundian National Police

---

[79] Interviews with members of the international community 1.33 and 1.34, Bujumbura, March 18 and 19, 2009.
[80] ICG, "Burundi: Democracy and Peace at Risk," Africa Report series, no. 120 (Brussels: ICG, November 30, 2006), accessed December 20, 2017, www.crisisgroup.org/africa/central-africa/burundi/burundi-democracy-and-peace-risk.
[81] ICG, "Burundi: Democracy and Peace at Risk," 7.
[82] ICG, "Burundi: Democracy and Peace at Risk."
[83] ICG, "Burundi: Democracy and Peace at Risk."
[84] ICG, "Burundi: Democracy and Peace at Risk," 3.
[85] ICG, "Burundi: Democracy and Peace at Risk."
[86] ICG, "Burundi: Democracy and Peace at Risk," 2–3.

rounded up suspected FNL supporters, including local administrators, militants, and some FRODEBU supporters and jailed, tortured, and executed them.[87]

The government began to crack down on Burundian media and civil society. The ICG stated, "Given the weakness of the opposition and the CNDD-FDD's dominance of the state institutions, the strongest opposition to the new government has come from the press and civil society."[88] Key civil society leaders and journalists were jailed for speaking out against the government, acts that were condemned by international observers: "The Committee to Protect Journalists is alarmed by the ongoing campaign of intimidation by the authorities in Burundi against radio stations that have cast doubt on a government claim to have uncovered a coup plot."[89]

In reaction to the violent, oppressive tactics that came to characterize the CNDD-FDD government, a party congress voted in early 2007 to remove the party leader, Hussein Radjabu, from power and replace him with a more moderate personality.[90] Several of Radjabu's political supporters defected from the CNDD-FDD and formed their own party block, depriving the CNDD-FDD of its majority in the National Assembly. To protest the unwillingness of Nkurunziza to give a fair share of posts in government, FRODEBU and UPRONA took advantage of the CNDD-FDD's newfound weakness and prevented legislation from being passed by the National Assembly, essentially stalling the government.[91] A game of tit-for-tat followed, with the old and new guard continually trying to punish each other for bad behavior.

A compromise was reached in November 2007 that led to the establishment of a new government that gave FRODEBU and UPRONA the posts that the constitution promised them.[92] The UN Integrated Office in Burundi's (BINUB) Cadre de Dialogue project organized targeted meetings (see Chapter 4), and the Executive Representative of the Secretary-General (ERSG) and his top advisors engaged in quiet diplomacy that

---

[87] ICG, "Burundi: Democracy and Peace at Risk," 4; UN Security Council, "Sixth Report of the Secretary-General on the United Nations Operation in Burundi" (New York: United Nations, March 21, 2006), 8.

[88] ICG, "Burundi: Democracy and Peace at Risk," 9.

[89] Committee to Protect Journalists, "CPJ Condemns Continuing Harassment of Radio Journalists" *Committee to Protect Journalists* (October 2, 2006), accessed December 20, 2017, http://goo.gl/RNxUK1.

[90] ICG, "Burundi: Restarting Political Dialogue," Africa Briefing series, no. 53 (Brussels: ICG, August 19, 2008), 3, accessed December 20, 2017, www.crisisgroup.org/africa/central-africa/burundi/burundi-restarting-political-dialogue.

[91] ICG, "Burundi: Restarting Political Dialogue," 4.

[92] ICG, "Burundi: Restarting Political Dialogue," 5.

apparently contributed to this breakthrough.[93] Unfortunately, the cooperative atmosphere did not last. In May 2008, Burundi's Constitutional Court backed a decision by President Nkurunziza to replace Radjabu's dissident group of CNDD-FDD members of parliament, allowing the CNDD-FDD to dominate the National Assembly, removing any necessity for them to negotiate with FRODEBU and UPRONA.[94]

The battles between the CNDD-FDD and FRODEBU and UPRONA were, in part, a conflict between new and old civil servants. Former government officials and observers repeatedly complained about the lack of experience and training of CNDD-FDD officials and the fact that posts were allocated on political, not meritocratic, grounds.[95] Many of the politicians from FRODEBU and UPRONA as well as Tutsi members of the army had been trained in Burundi and abroad. They had run a well-functioning, if impoverished, civil service. They had participated in years of negotiations. Through all this, the leadership had become accustomed to political compromise. CNDD officials had not. Uvin observed:

Much of the government is also rather inexperienced in managing a major bureaucracy, with all this implies in terms of contradictory messages, unclear policies, problems with the donor community, etc. . . . They are not helped in this respect by the fact that the experienced senior civil servants in the bureaucracy belong to the two losing political parties and hence often do nothing to help the new government, rather enjoying seeing it fail.[96]

When the CNDD-FDD government was elected, members of the government and the international community treated it with what the CNDD-FDD interpreted as a lack of respect. This impression reinforced the CNDD-FDD's defensiveness and unwillingness to compromise:

They did not treat [Nkurunziza] with proper respect. I think that set the tone for the problems. [The government was] not prepared to have the international community tell them what they should be doing.[97]

FRODEBU and UPRONA had a similarly condescending approach:

Since 2007, these two parties have often behaved like parties of notables, convinced of their intellectual and social superiority and underestimating the 'members of the maquis' of the CNDD-FDD.[98]

---

[93] United Nations, "Report of the Technical Assistance Mission to BINUB," UN Restricted (New York: United Nations, September 19, 2007), 4.
[94] ICG, "Burundi: Restarting Political Dialogue," 7.
[95] This message was conveyed repeatedly during interviews in Burundi in December 2008.
[96] Uvin, *Life after Violence*, 22.
[97] Interview with observer O13, via telephone, October 12, 2011.
[98] ICG, "Burundi: Restarting Political Dialogue," 13. The term *maquis* refers to rebel groups and is derived from the guerilla groups in the French Resistance.

The tumultuous political context distracted politicians and civil servants from what should have been their main task: governing. During its first year in office, the CNDD-FDD was plagued by corruption scandals that contributed to the turmoil within the CNDD-FDD and worsened its relationships with opposition parties and donors.[99] Between 2005 and 2010, Burundi dropped from 130th to 170th on the Transparency International's Corruption Perceptions Index.[100] If, as Uvin argues, the civil war showed that "nobody in power gave a damn about the needs and interests of the majority of the population," then the period from 2005 to 2009 reinforced this belief, as increased levels of corruption were combined with growing oppression and monopolization of power – this time by the new guard.[101] In spite of Nkurunziza's claims to serve the interests of Burundian people, his tenure in office demonstrated otherwise.

Although the parties within the government were fighting with one another, the National Defense Force was much more united in its ongoing battles with the FNL. The FNL and the government had signed a comprehensive cease-fire agreement on September 7, 2006, but fighting between the two forces continued, as did the arrest and abuse of people known to be allied with the rebels.[102] Pressured by Tanzania, the FNL signed a new cease-fire declaration on May 26, 2008.[103] This declaration led to regular discussions between the FNL, represented by Agathon Rwasa, and President Nkurunziza and eventually to the demobilization of FNL combatants and the allocation of government posts to FNL representatives in 2009.[104]

In the face of political games and increasing corruption, most Burundians continued to struggle to survive. Although the end of fighting in most of the country after November 2003 established a degree of security that most Burundians had not experienced for a decade, increasing crime and banditry brought a different type of insecurity.[105] The economic climate offered financial benefits for some, but poverty was too pervasive and its origins too deep to be altered in just a few years. The gross

---

[99] ICG, "Burundi: Democracy and Peace at Risk," 7; and ICG, "Burundi: Restarting Political Dialogue."

[100] Transparency International, "Policy_Research/Surveys_Indices/CPI," *Transparency International Corruption Perceptions Index*, accessed April 20, 2012, http://goo.gl/DPmRNw.

[101] Peter Uvin, "Corruption and Violence in Burundi," *New Routes* 14 no. 3 (2009): 17, accessed December 20, 2017, www.academia.edu/630689/Corruption_and_Anti-Corruption_in_Peacebuilding_Toward_a_Unified_Framework.

[102] ICG, "Burundi: Restarting Political Dialogue," 9.

[103] ICG, "Burundi: Restarting Political Dialogue," 10.

[104] ICG, "Burundi: Restarting Political Dialogue."

[105] Uvin, *Life after Violence*, 46.

national income per capita, adjusted for inflation, was US $210 in 1990, US $90 in 2003, US $110 in 2006, and up to US $170 in 2009.[106] For many Burundians, the post-transition period brought increased financial hardship because of the high rates of inflation and growing numbers of people – returning refugees and more international staff – competing for land and housing.[107]

After the 2005 elections, international aid increased from a low of US $38 million in 1996 to US $180 million in 2005 and then up to US $264 million by 2009.[108] The number of international players grew significantly. Donors and INGOs were anxious to help Burundi capitalize on the success of its peace process and prevent the country from sliding back into war.

In October 2006, Burundi was selected as one of the first two countries on the agenda of the UN's newly created Peacebuilding Commission (PBC). The PBC was established to prevent countries from returning to war by helping donors focus on core peacebuilding priorities, coordinating their efforts, and ensuring that the country had the necessary resources to carry out its peacebuilding priorities.[109] The selection of Burundi as a country of focus for the PBC brought new donors to Burundi – most notably Norwegians, Dutch, and Japanese. It also encouraged Burundi's more traditional donors – Belgium, the European Commission, the United States, the World Bank, France, the United Kingdom, and Germany – to increase support to the country.[110]

At the same time as international aid increased, the unified stance of African states and international donors began to disappear. The crucial political support that Burundi had received from the South African facilitation team and the Regional Initiative gradually dissolved. Before 2005, the Regional Initiative and the South African facilitation team had convened the Burundian government and the rebel groups time and time again and pressured them to stick to their commitments. After 2005, the Regional Initiative was torn apart by competition among the various states involved and disagreement on their goals for Burundi.[111] Although South Africa continued to lead negotiations with the FNL, its rivalry

---

[106] World Bank, "Data Catalog," accessed February 9, 2012, http://goo.gl/NsPR.
[107] Informal discussions, Bujumbura, 2009.
[108] Organisation for Economic Co-operation and Development, Development Assistance Committee, "QWIDS—Query Wizard for International Development Statistics," accessed February 9, 2012, http://goo.gl/XMNIu.
[109] Report of the High-Level Panel on Threats, Challenges and Change. "A More Secure World: Our Shared Responsibility," A/59/565 (December 2, 2004), 69.
[110] Interviews with key informants in international community, Bujumbura: 1.30, March 19, 2009; 1.31, June 5, 2010.
[111] Interview with observer O14, via telephone, December 9, 2011.

with Tanzania broke the cohesion between South Africa's efforts and those of the Regional Initiative.[112]

The international community tried to maintain its oversight of Burundi's peacebuilding process by establishing a Partners Forum in September 2005, but the government objected on the grounds that the forum duplicated the efforts of the National Committee on Aid Coordination. The international community responded by reducing the ambitions of this forum. BINUB was supposed to play a prominent role in coordinating the international community, in part on behalf of the PBC, but did not make coordination a priority. The ERSG of BINUB preferred a much quieter type of diplomacy than what was viewed as the abrasive and condescending approach of many international donors.[113]

The Burundian government tried to discourage a coherent approach among the international community and continuously reminded it that Burundi, as a sovereign country, would not respond to pressure. Many donors felt they were at the mercy of their Burundian government counterparts and had few levers to influence the government's behavior other than delaying the distribution of funds. Many donors seemed to be more committed to Burundi's peacebuilding success than Burundian politicians were. Donors "are tired, but they can't let it fail because if they do it is their failure," an observer noted. "It was a real success. Now they want to see if they can save it."[114]

INGOs, too, faced great difficulty doing peacebuilding after 2005, much more than they had experienced prior to the elections. The government began cracking down on INGOs, holding back work permits and INGO registration permissions because the government believed INGOs were receiving money that should go directly to the government.[115] As a result, many INGOs were reluctant to overtly engage in peacebuilding or other seemingly political projects: "INGOs pay attention to not having a direct political role. They know that the situation is delicate now."[116] In reality, many donors were holding back funds from the Burundian government and funding INGOs instead because of increasing corruption, human rights violations, ongoing fighting with the FNL, and uncertainty as to what the 2010 elections would bring.[117]

---

[112] Interview with observer O12, via telephone, May 4, 2010.
[113] Interview with UN staff member 1.7, Bujumbura, March 19, 2009.
[114] Interview with observer O11, Bujumbura, March 25, 2009.
[115] Interview with observer O11, Bujumbura, March 25, 2009.
[116] Interview with observer O11, Bujumbura, March 25, 2009.
[117] Interviews with international donors 1.30 and 1.31, Bujumbura, March 19, 2009 and June 5, 2009.

Phase V: Peace, Political Violence, and New Elections: May 2009 to April 2010

In April 2009, Agathon Rwasa, the leader of the FNL, officially demobilized his rebel group. Burundi's war was finally over. By June 2009, FNL members were given their long-awaited positions in government. The demobilization and integration of FNL combatants into the security forces was under way. After almost sixteen years of death, destruction, and displacement, Burundi's political parties and rebel groups were integrated into its government. Theoretically, violence would no longer be necessary because political parties would resolve their conflicts peacefully within the halls of government.

The end of Burundi's war had come in phases – the Arusha Agreement was signed in 2000, the transitional government was inaugurated in 2001, the CNDD-FDD joined the transitional government and demobilized in 2003, democratic elections were held in 2005, and the FNL joined the government and security forces in 2009. With each phase, signs of peace and prosperity appeared. Beach clubs opened along Bujumbura's sandy Lake Tanganyika coast. Well-off Burundians dined by the pool. Expatriates played weekly beach volleyball games, oblivious to the death and destruction that had taken place so recently just a few miles away. Only a few years earlier, gunshots and mortar shells had echoed from the surrounding hills. Restaurants and roads had crumbled into ruin. Now Bujumbura was once again becoming a holiday paradise. Tourism was taking off, and Burundi was being downgraded on travel threat lists. New businesses flourished. Streets were repaved. In Bujumbura, at least, there were visible signs that Burundi was truly in a post-conflict phase. With the integration of the FNL into the government, this trend became irrefutable. The war was over, at least for the time being.

During the fifteen-year peace process, Burundians had built a vibrant civil society, an impressive independent media, and a culture of openness and dialogue. Among its neighbors – Rwanda, the DRC, Kenya, and Uganda – Burundi was the only real multiparty democracy.[118] But the memories of war were still vivid for many Burundians, and violence still pervaded much of society. Domestic violence grew. Mob justice was common in the face of a corrupt and ineffective judicial system.[119] A CARE Burundi staff member described the situation:

---

[118] Human Rights Watch, "Pursuit of Power: Political Violence and Repression in Burundi" (New York: Human Rights Watch, May 2009), 11.

[119] ICG, "Burundi: Ensuring Credible Elections," Africa Report series, no. 155 (Brussels: ICG, February 12, 2010), accessed December 20, 2017, www.crisisgroup.org/africa/central-africa/burundi/burundi-ensuring-credible-elections.

With the end of the conflict, people still aren't afraid to kill. They learned that experience during the conflict. People live the horrible situations of conflict and now they aren't afraid to do other stuff. People have much more courage because they participated in the murders in the crisis. Many men were trained and even the community was trained to be armed and to kill people. Even youth and women were trained. This greatly increased the violence in households. We never lived like this before the war.[120]

Political violence increased. The CNDD-FDD and the FNL began this trend in 2008 and 2009 while they were still in cease-fire talks, launching attacks and targeted assassinations at each other's supporters.[121] These attacks continued even after the FNL was integrated into the government and registered as a political party. In the lead-up to the 2010 election cycle, the CNDD-FDD and the FNL attacked and counterattacked each another's supporters. They created gangs made up of demobilized combatants and the multitude of unemployed youth.[122] The political violence was most vitriolic between the CNDD-FDD and the FNL, but soon many other parties became involved. They each amassed their own gangs and used violence and intimidation in their pursuit of electoral victory.[123] They committed numerous pre-electoral abuses, which Human Rights Watch reported as:

Campaigning before the legally authorized campaign period; assassinations; arbitrary arrests; verbal confrontations; fraud in distributing the identity documents required to vote; restrictions on free assembly; bribes and vote-buying; use of state vehicles for campaign purposes; physical confrontations; disturbance of party meetings; and hiring and firing based on political affiliation.[124]

Human Rights Watch and local election monitors reported "that CNDD-FDD members – including state officials – are responsible for the majority of the abuses, which include personal attacks, arbitrary arrests, and what appears to be a politically motivated murder."[125] The CNDD-FDD was uncomfortable sharing power, continuing to employ the authoritarian decision-making structure and tactics that it had honed through years of warfare.[126] The CNDD-FDD was projected to win the 2010 elections, and it wanted to continue to control

---

[120] Interview with CARE staff member C1, Bujumbura, June 8, 2009.
[121] Human Rights Watch, "Pursuit of Power."
[122] ICG, "Burundi: Ensuring Credible Elections."
[123] ICG, "Burundi: Ensuring Credible Elections."
[124] Human Rights Watch, "'We'll Tie You Up and Shoot You'" (New York: Human Rights Watch, May 14, 2010), 11, accessed December 20, 2017, http://goo.gl/6vxbA7.
[125] Human Rights Watch, "'We'll Tie You Up and Shoot You,'" 4.
[126] ICG, "Burundi: Ensuring Credible Elections."

communal-level governance and maintain the two-thirds majority in the National Assembly that allowed it to pass legislation without consideration for the other parties.[127]

The pre-electoral violence and abuse increased the likelihood of political violence during the election cycle. But this time around, there would not be international peacekeepers to ensure security as there had been in 2005. Security would be left up to Burundi's corrupt and poorly trained police force.[128] International election observers would be present, but they would have little capacity to prevent violence or intimidation. They could simply report on it. The capacity of BINUB was weakened with the expulsion of its head, the ERSG Youssef Mahmoud, in late 2009 because he was accused of supporting the National Independent Electoral Commission (CENI) at the expense of government interests. He was the third representative of the UN Secretary-General in a row to be asked to leave Burundi. With Mahmoud's departure, the government ensured that the UN would be unable to keep a close eye on its conduct during the elections.[129]

As before, the government tried to silence the civil society and media. Assassinating the vice president of Burundi's main anticorruption NGO – the Organization for Combating Corruption and Financial Misappropriations (OLUCOME) in April 2009 – and leaving his body displayed in front of his house was a particularly audacious action.[130] Senior members of the security forces were the suspected culprits.[131] The Human Rights Watch analyst in Burundi was kicked out of the country after publishing a report in May 2009 on growing political violence.[132] Despite intense intimidation and arrests of members of civil society and the media, independent media and key civil society actors remained active for the time being and continued to report on and challenge the conduct of the government.

The international community was relatively unresponsive to the increasing political violence and limits on political freedom. It was focused on the organization and outcome of the elections. The

---

[127] Human Rights Watch, "'We'll Tie You Up and Shoot You,'" 4.
[128] Interview with key informant O12, via telephone, May 4, 2010.
[129] ICG, "Burundi: Ensuring Credible Elections," 21.
[130] Human Rights Watch, "Burundi: Find Killers of Anti-Corruption Activist" (New York: Human Rights Watch, April 16, 2009), accessed December 20, 2017, https://goo.gl/Dwo3Io.
[131] ICG, "Burundi: Ensuring Credible Elections," 7.
[132] Human Rights Watch, "Closing Doors? The Narrowing of Democratic Space in Burundi" (New York: Human Rights Watch, November 23, 2010), accessed December 20, 2017, http://goo.gl/VIKfSa.

international community was expecting a successful electoral period, although several donors were skeptical.[133]

In the face of clear political intimidation, targeted political assassinations, imprisonment of opposition candidates, and other acts intended to influence the outcome of the elections, on what grounds could the international community judge the elections as free and fair? It seemed that international technical assessment classified the elections as free and fair.[134] In other words, if the elections were technically sound and did not lead to large-scale violence, then the elections would be judged as legitimate. The same standard had been applied in 2005. Uvin observed the following:

Note that what was mainly peaceful about these [2005] elections was the day they were held. There was significant intimidation before the elections, as the parties fought the CNDD-FDD (which possessed parallel administrations throughout most of the country) for local control. Afterwards, the usual mechanisms of cooptation and intimidation allowed further solidifying of power. Hence, democratic elections are sandwiched between non-democratic processes, but the international community needs only the day itself to allow itself to congratulate itself on its beautiful success.[135]

Phase VI: A One-Party State and a New Rebellion: May 2010 to December 2014

The first round of elections in Burundi's 2010 electoral cycle – commune-level elections – was held on May 24, 2010. These elections were not accompanied by serious violence.[136] They were, however, strategically important for all participating political parties. The communal councils approved all nominations of senior civil servants and elected the Senate, which would therefore determine the number of seats and positions allocated to each party.[137]

The CNDD-FDD won the communal-level elections by 64 percent. The opposition parties responded to the results by declaring "massive electoral fraud."[138] When the opposition complained of fraud, neither the government, the CENI (the National Independent Electoral Commission),

---

[133] Interviews with international donors to Burundi 1.30, 1.31, March 2009.
[134] Interviews with key international donors to Burundi 1.30, 1.31, March 2009.
[135] Uvin, *Life after Violence*, 69, n. 6.
[136] ICG, "Burundi: From Electoral Boycott to Political Impasse," Africa Report series, no. 169 (Brussels: ICG, February 7, 2011), accessed December 20, 2017, http://goo.gl/5GKjmt.
[137] ICG, "Burundi: From Electoral Boycott to Political Impasse."
[138] ICG, "Burundi: From Electoral Boycott to Political Impasse," i.

nor international election observers investigated the specific allegations or responded to the opposition candidate's complaints.[139] The CENI refused to make vote tallies available to the opposition as required by law.[140] Independent investigations into the allegations revealed that fraud "was not at a level that would have significantly altered the election results."[141]

The opposition parties formed a coalition – l'Alliance des Démocrates pour le Changement au Burundi (ADC-Ikibiri) – and demanded that the CENI be dismissed and the commune-level elections be annulled or they would not rejoin the electoral process. The international community responded to the opposition's complaints by declaring the elections to be free and fair and calling on the opposition parties to rejoin the electoral process.[142] Burundian civil society largely echoed the same refrain. The ADC-Ikibiri boycotted the remaining three rounds of elections, including those for president and parliament. There was practically no coverage of the elections in the international press, and what news there was called them a success.

The Burundian government responded with conviction. In early June 2010, the government banned all meetings by opposition parties. Grenade attacks were launched in several locations, unattributed to either the government or the opposition. Police surrounded the residence of Agathon Rwasa, the head of the FNL, who subsequently fled to an undisclosed location. Other opposition leaders were captured by the National Intelligence Services, and several of them were tortured.[143]

Meanwhile, the presidential elections were held on June 28, with the only candidate, Pierre Nkurunziza, winning with 91 percent of votes. In spite of the opposition's withdrawal, the election cycle continued to move forward as planned, with only the CNDD-FDD, UPRONA, and several other small parties close to the CNDD-FDD participating.[144] The government attempted to silence media and civil society through imprisonment and other strategies.[145] Leaders of opposition parties fled the country. By the end of the election cycle in September 2010, the CNDD-FDD had a secure hold on all branches and levels of government. Burundi had become a one-party state. Appointments in the Senate and the National Assembly strictly followed the constitution's

---

[139] Human Rights Watch, "Closing Doors?" 20–1.
[140] Human Rights Watch, "Closing Doors?" 21.
[141] Human Rights Watch, "Closing Doors?" 20.
[142] ICG, "Burundi: From Electoral Boycott to Political Impasse," 19.
[143] Human Rights Watch, "Closing Doors?"
[144] ICG, "Burundi: From Electoral Boycott to Political Impasse," 6.
[145] Human Rights Watch, "Closing Doors?"

quotas for ethnic and gender balance, although these quotas did not address the intra-Hutu conflict that was now simmering.

The international community and regional actors interested in Burundi continued to follow the situation but did not attempt to influence its course. Many had decided that the elections were a Burundian problem and that the CENI should sort it out.[146] UN Secretary-General Ban Ki-moon visited Burundi on June 9, 2010 and declared, "It is imperative that these elections be a success. Burundi has an opportunity to become a success story and a model for the continent."[147] The international community and the Regional Initiative believed that they could help to make Burundi's elections a success by pressuring the opposition to rejoin the electoral process and ignoring any infractions against them. Human Rights Watch observed:

> The international community wanted to show at all costs that Burundi's elections were a success. But it wasn't true. There were serious human rights abuses, there was torture, all the opposition leaders are hiding or going into the bush – that's not a success. But, when the opposition complained, the diplomats treated the opposition like they were worthless. And when we criticized the CENI's lack of transparency, the diplomats didn't want to hear it.[148]

After the electoral cycle ended in September 2010, the security and political situation continued to deteriorate. Attacks and assassinations, targeted at both the CNDD-FDD and people allied with the opposition parties, continued. In mid-2011, the international community began to raise concerns about the situation. A letter signed by ambassadors of European Union (EU) countries with offices in Burundi declared that the "United Nations has received serious and detailed information about at least twenty cases of extrajudicial killings as well as several dozen cases of torture reportedly committed by security officials between June 2010 and March 2011."[149] It called for the government to stop this practice and to prosecute suspected criminals.[150]

By November 2011, there was incontrovertible evidence that a new rebellion had been created, was based in the DRC, and was collaborating with the rebel groups that continued to fight there.[151] The Observatoire de l'Action Gouvernementale, a well-respected Burundian watchdog

---

[146] Interview with observer O15, June 2010.
[147] UN News Centre, "Ban Lauds Burundians."
[148] Human Rights Watch, "Closing Doors?" 50.
[149] Agence France-Presse, "AFP: Western Envoys Raise Concerns over Burundi Killings," June 3, 2011.
[150] Agence France-Presse, "AFP: Western Envoys Raise Concerns over Burundi Killings."
[151] Integrated Regional Information Networks, "Burundi: A New Rebellion?" November 30, 2011.

organization, reported that at least three hundred members of the FNL had been killed by the government security forces or the CNDD-FDD's youth wing, Imbonerakure, since May 2011.[152] It also reported that violence was being directed toward another opposition party, the Mouvement pour la Solidarité et la Démocratie, run by former journalist Alexis Sinduhije.[153] Arrests and intimidation of journalists and civil society members – who received little protection from the justice system – continued.[154] The CNDD-FDD was preparing for the next round of presidential elections in 2015, although President Nkurunzia's determination to run for an unconstitutional third term began to create increased fragmentation and dissent in his party.

Peace is reversible. Shortly after the official end to Burundi's sixteen-year civil war, Burundi began descending again toward increased violence and war. In May 2010, Burundi's war-to-peace trajectory took a decidedly undemocratic turn that led to the exclusion of almost all opposition parties from government, a significant increase in targeted political assassinations, and the emergence of a new rebel movement. There was no peace process anymore. The international community was present on the ground but resigned to the situation, afraid of leaving for fear of being blamed for Burundi's possible descent into war. So it stayed, watching as a new rebellion emerged and as authoritarianism became increasingly rooted, with the 2015 elections looming.

Conclusion

The key events discussed in this chapter launched Burundi into new phases in its peacebuilding process. Prior to each phase, no one knew if Burundi would strengthen institutions that would solidify its peace or reinvigorate institutions that would lead the country into renewed war. Burundi's peace process was considered a success by many because five out of these six phases strengthened institutions that were thought to be determinants of a just peace, enshrined in the Arusha Agreement. The last phase, however, led to decidedly negative changes in Burundi's institutions and the erosion of the spirit of power-sharing as well as many of the freedoms represented in Arusha.

The removal of the regional embargo in January 1999 gave new energy to the Arusha peace talks and made it possible for donors to give

---

[152] Integrated Regional Information Networks, "Burundi: A New Rebellion?"
[153] Integrated Regional Information Networks, "Burundi: A New Rebellion?"
[154] Integrated Regional Information Networks, "Burundi: A New Rebellion?"

peacebuilding and development funding to Burundi.[155] The inauguration of the transitional government in November 2001 proved that politicians were committed to trying to implement the Arusha Agreement, signed in August 2000. It opened the opportunity for international actors to support the government in implementing the reforms outlined in Arusha and to increase momentum behind the ongoing negotiations with the rebel groups.

The integration of the largest rebel group, the Nkurunziza arm of the CNDD-FDD, into the transitional government in November 2003 established security throughout most of Burundi and gave international actors the opportunity to work in provinces that they had been cut off from because of the fighting. It also signaled that the parties to the conflict were committed to peace: "For the first time in years, the country seems to be headed towards a genuine end to the conflict."[156]

The inauguration of Pierre Nkurunziza as president of Burundi in August 2005 on the heels of free, fair, and peaceful elections showed Burundians that peace was possible. The previous democratic elections, in 1993, had sparked war. Fears of a recurrence pervaded the collective Burundian conscience. The inauguration of Nkurunziza offered an opportunity for international actors to help the Burundian state and society address the causes of the conflict and begin to rebuild the social fabric and institutions destroyed by the war. Unfortunately, hope soon dissipated as the CNDD-FDD increasingly attempted to sideline challengers and silence Burundi's civil society and media.

Integration of the FNL rebel group into the government and military that began in April 2009 finally brought Burundi's lingering war to an end. It offered an opportunity for the international community to support the long-delayed integration of the FNL into Burundi's institutions and to help prevent violence and tension from escalating in the lead-up to the 2010 elections or during the elections themselves.

The 2010 elections launched Burundi as a seemingly authoritarian democracy, with only one party in power. Withdrawal of the opposition

---

[155] Between 1993 and 1999, several donors funded the Arusha peace talks but did not give anything other than humanitarian assistance to NGOs in Burundi and did not give any money directly to the Burundian government. Several donors – namely DFID and USAID – funded INGOs to engage in unofficial mediation (Track II or Track 1½ diplomacy) in Burundi, whereas others funded innovative dialogue interventions by a few INGOs, such as Search for Common Ground and International Alert. But very little money went to the Burundian government or to address the enormous socioeconomic needs, trauma, or distrust among the Burundian people. For more details on the period from 1993 to 1999, see Lund, Rubin, and Hara, "Learning from Burundi's Failed Democratic Transition," 47–91.

[156] ICG, "End of the Transition in Burundi," 1.

from the 2010 elections led to the election of Nkurunziza as the leader of a de facto one-party state that engaged in increasingly authoritarian tactics, and intimidation of the population, opposition, civil society, and free press, which further eroded the freedoms that had been enmeshed in the Arusha peace process. This culminated in 2014 in fragmentation and tension within the CNDD-FDD as the 2015 elections loomed on the horizon.

For international actors intervening in Burundi, taking peacebuilding actions in response to each of these critical junctures was risky. If they waited for certainty that their actions would deliver intended results, then they missed the window of opportunity to influence the situation. In many cases, organizations were not willing to risk taking actions to reduce the gap between their peacebuilding aims and outcomes. However, as the next three chapters show, many individuals were willing to stick their necks out, to try something new and innovative, and to coerce their organizations into supporting them in this effort. Those who were most effective were able to anticipate changes in the peacebuilding context because they had established informal local accountability routines, and able to respond to unanticipated changes because they had formal accountability routines that prioritized peacebuilding. If their actions did not actually reduce the gap between their aims and outcomes, either they revisited their assumptions and altered their approach again or their interventions became irrelevant to the new phase in Burundi's evolving war-to-peace transition.

3   INGOs in Peacebuilding: Globally Unaccountable, Locally Adaptive

The first International Non-Governmental Organization (INGO) that I worked for, the Forum on Early Warning and Early Response (FEWER), went bankrupt. Our office was located above a brewery on Brick Lane in London, an -area that was being gentrified by hipsters. The brewery doubled as our meeting room. FEWER aimed to bridge the divide between national Non-Governmental Organizations (NGOs) in conflict-torn countries and INGOs and think tanks in Western countries. The national NGOs would provide information and analysis about the potential escalation of violent conflict. Then, the INGOs and think tanks in Western countries would use the national NGOs' conflict early warning information to advocate for Western governments and International Organizations (IOs) to respond. FEWER's big ideas broke down in practice, and it was unable to raise sufficient funds to cover its core costs. As with most INGOs, it was plagued by fundraising problems, mission creep related to new projects that it acquired to fill funding gaps, and accountability challenges that plague all organizations with such diverse constituencies.

The scholarship on INGOs describes them as the least accountable type of global governor.[1] Because they are not accountable to states or to populations, INGOs are viewed as more likely than IOs, for example, to abuse their power. Relatedly, scholars describe INGOs as driven by the whims and preferences of their donors.[2] INGOs are believed to be so focused on raising money from any available source that they do not pursue consistent strategies, or respond consistently to the needs of the people whom they claim to help.

---

[1] Ruth W. Grant and Robert O. Keohane, "Accountability and Abuses of Power in World Politics," *American Political Science Review* 99, no. 1 (April 4, 2005): 29–43.
[2] Alexander Cooley and James Ron, "The NGO Scramble: Organizational Insecurity and the Political Economy of Transnational Action," *International Security* 27, no. 1 (2002): 5–39; and Alnoor Ebrahim, *NGOs and Organizational Change: Discourse, Reporting, and Learning* (Cambridge, UK: Cambridge University Press, 2005).

INGOs' lack of consistent sources of global accountability, however, has a potential upside. In comparison to bilateral donors and IOs, INGOs are considered more adaptable. Bilateral donors are constrained by their domestic constituencies and the agreements they have made with other states. IOs are constrained by their mandates and the preferences of the states that created them. INGOs, however, are not accountable to any one group of states or a particular domestic constituency. They are created by public and private actors to fulfill a particular (usually moral) purpose. This purpose can change. Their governance structure can change. The issues that they promote can change. Their donors and related formal accountability structures can change.

How do the dual characteristics of weak global accountability and greater potential for adaptability influence INGO performance at the country level? In this chapter, I show that INGOs' lack of singular accountability to states may, in fact, enable their country offices to develop informal local accountability routines more easily than IOs or bilateral donors. The lack of global constraints on INGOs creates an environment in which entrepreneurial country-office staff may have a lot of room to maneuver and innovate, particularly if they can secure funding to do so. Country-office staff could use their agency to create strong informal local accountability routines and, relatedly, develop strong relationships with key actors at both the community and state level. If INGO country offices are also able to find donors who fund peacebuilding interventions (creating formal peacebuilding accountability), then they are likely to learn in relation to their peacebuilding aims. This organizational learning, in turn, significantly increases the chance that the INGOs will achieve their local peacebuilding aims.

In this chapter, I use an in-depth examination of two INGOs – the Burundi Leadership Training Program (BLTP) and CARE International's Burundi office (CARE Burundi) – over a fifteen-year period to explain how informal local accountability, formal peacebuilding accountability, and organizational learning can manifest in INGO country offices and influence their achievement of peacebuilding outcomes. The BLTP and CARE Burundi represent two typical types of INGOs engaged in international peacebuilding: one that focuses solely on conflict resolution and dialogue processes (the BLTP), and one that is a multimandate INGO (CARE Burundi), meaning that that it can

Table 3.1. *BLTP and CARE Burundi Country-Office Behavior*

	Phase I: Jan. 1999– Oct. 2001	Phase II: Nov. 2001– Nov. 2003	Phase III: Dec. 2003– Aug. 2005	Phase IV: Sept. 2005– Apr. 2009	Phase V: May 2009– May 2010	Phase VI: June 2010– Apr. 2014
BLTP	n/a	Peacebuilding Learner	Peacebuilding Learner	Micro-adaptor	Peacebuilding Learner	Peacebuilding Learner
CARE	Stagnant Player	Stagnant Player	Stagnant Player	Peacebuilding Learner	Micro-adaptor	Micro–adaptor

simultaneously implement humanitarian, development, and peace-building activities.[3]

As Table 3.1 shows, the BLTP and CARE Burundi tended to fall into the peacebuilding learner and micro-adaptor categories, in part, because they were able to create informal local accountability routines. Compared to the IO and bilateral donor case studies discussed in this book, these two INGOs seemed to find it easier to create informal local accountability. I contend that INGOs' weak global accountability to states creates more opportunities for informal local accountability. In other words, INGOs' weak global ties may, in fact, enable them to form stronger local ties that are necessary for local-level performance.

This chapter discusses existing scholarship on INGO performance. It then examines the behavior and peacebuilding performance of the BLTP, followed by a similar analysis of CARE Burundi. It concludes with a comparison of the two INGOs and discusses the implications of

---

[3] Most of the research on INGOs has focused on their role in human rights networks. Human rights INGOs are viewed as having strong connections to local communities that suffer from human rights violations and to the domestic constituencies of powerful Western states. INGOs defend the rights of these disenfranchised communities by shaming the state into responding. They use their strong networks with sympathetic governments and IOs to increase the pressure on the rights-violating government. In this book, I talk about a different type of INGO. I focus on development, humanitarian, and peacebuilding INGOs that deliver goods and services at the country level. These INGOs may have an overall advocacy arm as well, but in this book, I study their service provision capacity. On human rights advocacy NGOs, see Margaret E. Keck and Kathryn Sikkink, *Activists beyond Borders: Advocacy Networks in International Politics* (Cambridge, UK: Cambridge University Press, 1998); Amanda Murdie and David R. Davis, "Shaming and Blaming: Using Events Data to Assess the Impact of Human Rights INGOs," *International Studies Quarterly* 56, no. 1 (2012): 1–16; and Wendy H. Wong, "Pushing against Boundaries: How Non-Governmental Organizations Link the Politics of Human Rights to Poverty," *International Studies Review* 13, no. 4 (2011): 660–2.

this analysis for the broader universe of service delivery INGOs engaged in peacebuilding.

INGOs: Pawns or Agents?

Since the 1990s, the number of INGOs working in international peace-building has expanded dramatically, following the upward trend in the overall growth of INGOs.[4] This growth is due, in part, to the increased demand by IOs and bilateral donors for INGOs to help deliver goods and services at the country level. This demand has led to an increasingly symbiotic functional relationship among IOs, bilateral donors, and INGOs, with INGOs relying on bilateral donors and IOs for resources, whereas IOs and bilateral donors rely on INGOs to deliver assistance at the local level.[5] "Wary of giving too much to governments in the developing world, unwilling to expand their own bureaucratic operational infrastructure, donor states have turned to service INGOs as a solution for implementing aid and providing relief in humanitarian crises."[6]

In spite of the symbiotic relationship among INGOs, IOs, and bilateral donors at the country level, some scholars consider INGOs to be among the least accountable actors in world politics. Much international relations scholarship views international authority as resting solely with states that have political authority – or "rightful or legitimate rule" – conferred on them by their governance systems, whether democratic or authoritarian.[7] States delegate this authority to IOs, which are then held accountable by these same states for carrying out the tasks assigned to them.[8]

Unlike IOs, INGOs are directly accountable only to their internal governance structures – made up of private individuals, firms, and/or some states – and to the individuals, IOs, firms, and bilateral donors that fund their operations. The two main sources of accountability for INGOs are fiscal accountability to their funders, to whom INGOs must provide financial reports, and reputational accountability to the broader public, who may also finance these INGOs and in whose eyes the INGO wants

---

[4] Michael Barnett, "Humanitarianism Transformed," *Perspectives on Politics* 3, no. 4 (2005): 723–40.

[5] Kim D. Reimann, "A View from the Top: International Politics, Norms and the Worldwide Growth of NGOs," *International Studies Quarterly* 50, no. 1 (2006): 45–68.

[6] Reimann, "A View from the Top," 64.

[7] David A. Lake, "Rightful Rules: Authority, Order, and the Foundations of Global Governance," *International Studies Quarterly* 54, no. 3 (2010): 587–613.

[8] Grant and Keohane, "Accountability and Abuses of Power in World Politics."

to maintain a good reputation.[9] Even though many INGOs claim to represent the interests of disenfranchised populations, these populations do not have the authority to hold INGOs accountable for serving their interests.

Several scholars argue that the predominance of fiscal accountability in INGOs has led them to function according to market logic, similarly to how firms operate.[10] Cooley and Ron argue that, rather than being moral actors motivated only by their normative aims, INGOs are similar to most other private contractors.[11] These authors contend that INGO behavior is motivated by competition with other INGOs for increasingly scarce, short-term grants from donors. They argue that INGOs' focus on gaining contracts and securing donor funding pushes "all other concerns – such as ethics, project efficacy, or self-criticism – to the margins."[12]

Other research into the behavior of INGOs shows that this upward accountability to donors undermines INGOs' capacity to respond to the needs of their beneficiaries.[13] INGOs' focus on fiscal accountability to donors, these scholars contend, encourages INGOs to concentrate on achieving indicators of their donors' success – such as the amount of money spent, the amount of goods delivered, financial compliance with audit criteria, or the advancement of other key institutional goals, such as meeting the Millennium Development Goals (MDGs).[14] According to this scholarship, this incentive structure, in turn, inhibits organizational learning in service delivery INGOs because they are not incentivized to gather the feedback from their beneficiaries that is necessary for them to learn and improve their country-based outcomes.[15] These scholars argue that the short-term nature of funding arrangements between INGOs and donors also encourages a short-term vision by INGOs, rather than longer-term strategies that may enable them to address structural issues in their environments, such as the root causes of conflict.[16]

---

[9] Grant and Keohane, "Accountability and Abuses of Power in World Politics."
[10] Cooley and Ron, "The NGO Scramble."
[11] Cooley and Ron, "The NGO Scramble."
[12] Cooley and Ron, "The NGO Scramble," 16.
[13] Ebrahim, *NGOs and Organizational Change.*
[14] Ebrahim, *NGOs and Organizational Change,* 157.
[15] Cooley and Ron, "The NGO Scramble"; and Ebrahim, *NGOs and Organizational Change.*
[16] Ebrahim, *NGOs and Organizational Change,* 157; and Erica Johnson and Aseem Prakash, "NGO Research Program: A Collective Action Perspective," *Policy Sciences* 40, no. 3 (2007): 233; Fiona Terry, *Condemned to Repeat? The Paradox of Humanitarian Action* (Ithaca, NY: Cornell University Press, 2002).

Although the role of fiscal accountability explains important aspects of INGO behavior, I argue that that fiscal accountability does not fully explain INGO country-office behavior. These formal accountability routines, alone, do not explain the variation in INGO performance exhibited by the two INGOs described in this chapter. It explains failed INGO projects, but not successful ones.

This chapter shows that although INGO formal accountability routines incentivize country offices to be unresponsive to the local context and people whom they aim to "help," they do not explain the full range of INGO country-office behavior. Key staff within INGO country offices can play a crucial role in establishing informal local accountability routines that delegate authority to a representative group of local stakeholders. Combined with formal peacebuilding accountability, this informal local accountability can enable the INGO country office to learn in relation to its peacebuilding aims and, at times, achieve them.

In the following sections, I describe the behavior of the BLTP and CARE Burundi between 1999 and 2014 and analyze how their formal accountability routines and informal local accountability routines, or lack thereof, steered each organization toward and away from positive peace-building performance.

The Burundi Leadership Training Program (BLTP)

Howard Wolpe established the BLTP in 2002 "to increase the ability of the country's ethnically polarized leadership to work together in consolidating its post-war transition."[17] Wolpe, who died in 2011, was a former United States representative from Michigan. He was also a former US presidential special envoy to the Great Lakes region of Central Africa and the US delegate to Burundi's Arusha and Lusaka peace talks. He subsequently became the director of the Africa Program at the Woodrow Wilson Center for International Scholars (WWCIS), the Washington, DC–based think tank, where he started the BLTP. Over the twelve-year period that this case study covers, the BLTP had between six and twelve staff, split between Washington, DC, and Bujumbura. This makes the BLTP by far the smallest of the cases studied in this book.

---

[17] Woodrow Wilson International Center for Scholars (WWICS), "Proposal for Renewing and Expanding the World Bank/WWICS Partnership in Post-Conflict Burundi" (Washington, DC: WWICS, July 2004), 1.

During the Arusha peace talks, Wolpe was struck by the poor negotiation skills of the vast majority of the Burundian parties.[18] He argued that if they had been trained in basic negotiation skills, they would have been better able to articulate their positions, understand the perspectives of the other parties, and find common ground. After Burundi's transitional government was inaugurated on November 1, 2001, and charged with implementing key provisions of the Arusha peace agreement, Wolpe saw a crucial opportunity to strengthen the conflict resolution skills of members of the new government. As discussed in Chapter 2, Burundi's transitional government was made up of political parties and former armed groups who had spent years fighting each other on the battlefield and in peace negotiations. Without any further preparation, these individuals were charged with collaboratively governing Burundi, including undertaking a highly ambitious set of legal, procedural, and political reforms and organizing democratic elections that would end their hold on power.

Even though the members of Burundi's transitional government had agreed to govern together, many were visibly afraid of one another.[19] Only when some degree of openness and understanding among former enemies was achieved, Wolpe argued, could these individuals begin to govern together.[20] "War creates a situation where people are convinced that their own survival can only come at the expense of the other. The challenge is trying to change the culture that war creates."[21] The establishment of the transitional government made people's survival dependent on one another. The task, Wolpe argued, was to help them understand this new relationship and give them tools to work together constructively. "I believe that fundamentally people will never alter the way they behave toward one another unless they see that as a matter of self-interest."[22]

---

[18] The description of the Burundi Leadership Training Program (BLTP) presented draws on more than thirty-five interviews, participant observation, and thorough analysis of internal documents that I conducted for an evaluation of the BLTP that I did with Peter Uvin in 2004 – Peter Uvin and Susanna P. Campbell, "The Burundi Leadership Training Programme (BLTP): A Prospective Assessment" (Washington, DC: World Bank, 2004) – as well as more than a dozen additional interviews and internal document review that I conducted subsequent to this evaluation.

[19] Participant observation, BLTP Workshop in Ngozi, Burundi, May 18–19, 2004.

[20] Howard Wolpe, "Response to Draft Evaluation of the BLTP by Peter Uvin and Susanna P. Campbell" (Washington, DC: WWICS, July 2004).

[21] Wolpe, "Response to Draft Evaluation."

[22] Marianne McCune, "Relearning the Peace (Interview with Howard Wolpe)" Homelands Productions, accessed December 21, 2011, http://homelands.org/stories/relearning-the-peace/.

To carry out his vision, Wolpe brought together a team of highly skilled individuals with deep knowledge of Burundi, politics, conflict resolution and dialogue methods, and the preferences of Western donors.[23] This team helped the BLTP to establish strong informal local accountability routines from the outset, consulting regularly with a wide variety of political stakeholders and ensuring that their inputs were integrated into the initial design and implementation of BLTP activities.

The BLTP team included Eugene Nindorera, a Tutsi, who had been the minister of human rights during the war and was revered by Hutus, Tutsis, and the international community for his determined defense of the human rights of all Burundians. He brought moral authority, political prestige, and a true insider's knowledge and understanding of the political actors. The BLTP team also included Fabien Nsengimana, who had a similar, if more low-key, profile. As a former advisor to President Buyoya, he was well versed in Burundi's politics and leadership, and even though he lost his father and siblings in the massacres of 1972, he was strongly committed to peace. As a former teacher and administrator, training and project management came naturally to him. Elizabeth McClintock, a specialist in Harvard's Getting to Yes conflict resolution techniques, brought a deep knowledge of conflict resolution and dialogue methods to the BLTP team; and Steve McDonald, a veteran of development assistance in Africa, was the BLTP's highly skilled administrator and fundraiser. This small but formidable team was committed to Wolpe's vision and had the skill set, networks, and credibility to see it through.

The World Bank Post-Conflict Fund provided the BLTP with an initial grant of US $1 million – a significant amount of money for a series of training workshops.[24] The World Bank was looking for a way to support reconciliation in Burundi during the transitional phase, and a project led by a prominent US politician presented the perfect opportunity. The support from the World Bank Post-Conflict Fund gave the BLTP formal accountability routines that prioritized peacebuilding. Unlike the rest of the World Bank, the Post-Conflict Fund prioritized peacebuilding outcomes above development outcomes, and its formal accountability routines thus required its grantees to demonstrate their accountability to peacebuilding-related aims.

---

[23] See BLTP, "Fabien Nsengimana," BLTP website, accessed December 21, 2017, http://goo.gl/uKmzxm; McCune, "Relearning the Peace (Interview with Howard Wolpe)."

[24] Uvin and Campbell, "The Burundi Leadership Training Programme (BLTP): A Prospective Assessment."

In sum, the BLTP began its interventions in Burundi with both strong informal local accountability and formal peacebuilding accountability. In the next section, I describe how and why the BLTP's behavior evolved over Burundi's war-to-peace transition and how this change related to alterations in its formal and informal local accountability.

The BLTP's Trajectory

The BLTP was formed for the Burundian context that existed in Phase II of Burundi's war-to-peace transition. It was staffed by highly skilled individuals who created strong informal local accountability routines and was initially funded by the World Bank's Post-Conflict Fund during Phase II of Burundi's war-to-peace transition. As depicted in Table 3.2,

Table 3.2. *The Burundi Leadership Training Program*

	Informal Local Accountability	Formal Peacebuilding Accountability	Country Office Type	Result
BLTP Phase I: Jan. 1999– Oct. 2001	n/a	n/a	n/a	n/a
BLTP Phase II: Nov. 2001– Nov. 2003	Yes	Yes	Peacebuilding Learner	Actions to reduce gap between peacebuilding aims and outcomes
BLTP Phase III: Dec. 2003– Aug. 2005	Yes	Yes	Peacebuilding Learner	Actions to reduce gap between peacebuilding aims and outcomes
BLTP Phase IV: Sept. 2005– Apr. 2009	Yes	No	Micro-adaptor	Actions to reduce gap between *non*-peacebuilding aims and outcomes
BLTP Phase V: May 2009– May 2010	Yes	Yes	Peacebuilding Learner	Actions to reduce gap between peacebuilding aims and outcomes
BLTP Phase VI: June 2010– Apr. 2014	Yes	Yes	Peacebuilding Learner	Actions to reduce gap between peacebuilding aims and outcomes

this combination of informal local accountability and formal peace-building accountability enabled the BLTP to be a peacebuilding learner during Phases II and III, helping it to achieve its aim of improving the capacity of Burundi's transitional leaders to govern together more effectively.

After Burundi's 2005 elections (launching Phase IV), many donors lost interest in peacebuilding, which meant that the BLTP lost its formal peacebuilding accountability routines. During Phase IV, the BLTP sustained strong informal local accountability, but its formal accountability routines did not incentivize the BLTP to respond to the changed nature of Burundi's war-to-peace transition. Instead, the BLTP largely continued to do what it had done in the past. The BLTP adjusted its interventions to feedback from participants, but did not alter its overall approach in response to the post-2005 political context. The BLTP was a micro-adaptor during Phase IV.

During Phases V and VI, the BLTP found new peacebuilding donors, sustained its informal local accountability, and, once again, became a peacebuilding learner. As a result, it helped, once again, to improve the capacity of Burundi's leadership class to govern together across ethnic and political party lines.

In the next sections, I discuss in more detail the BLTP's behavior during each of these phases and subsequently analyze the reasons for this behavior.

BLTP as a Peacebuilding Learner

As discussed in the previous sections, the BLTP was designed to be a peacebuilding learner. From the outset, it had strong informal local accountability routines and formal peacebuilding accountability. It maintained these characteristics during Phases II and III of Burundi's transition; it was not yet operational in Burundi during Phase I. During each phase, it took regular actions to reduce the gap between its peacebuilding aims and outcomes. In response to the big shift in Burundi's political context that catalyzed Phase III, the BLTP also shifted its approach to target new opportunities that emerged in this new context.

The initial aim of the BLTP (during Phase II of Burundi's transition) was to train one hundred leaders from "diverse ethnic, social, and institutional backgrounds" in methods designed to help them put themselves in the shoes of the "other," to engage in joint problem solving, and to improve their capacity to listen and communicate with each other.[25] The

---

[25] Wolpe, "Response to Draft Evaluation"; WWICS, "Proposal for Renewing and Expanding the World Bank/WWICS Partnership."

leaders were selected through a laborious process in which Burundians were asked to identify the most influential leaders, for good or for bad, in Burundi.[26] Through three week-long training sessions that sequestered approximately thirty leaders at a time in the northern town of Ngozi, the BLTP took ninety-five leaders through a process that was informative for most and transformative for many.[27]

The leaders the BLTP "trained" represented the breadth of Burundi's political and social spectrum. They included representatives from Burundi's transitional government, the Burundian military, rebel groups that had already been integrated into the military, national NGOs, and the media. Participants even included some individuals affiliated with the FNL rebel movement and splinter factions of the CNDD-FDD, both of which remained outside the transitional government and in open combat with the Burundian military at the time.

The effect of the BLTP training on some of the participants was profound. It was particularly visible for those who had not directly participated in the Arusha negotiations.[28] The delegates to Arusha had attended numerous rounds of discussions with their political and military opponents; the non-Arusha attendees had not had this experience.

The BLTP trainings asked former opponents to sit in the same room during the day and dine and drink together at night for several days. It asked them to engage in role-playing games, physically placing themselves in the social position of another group. It required them to negotiate with one another from this newly diminished or newly augmented position of power for the duration of the game.

Within the broader hostile political environment that existed at the time in Burundi, the relationships and sense of community developed among BLTP participants created a space for this broadly representative group of leaders to have conversations that, participants argued, were not possible in any other sphere.[29] The BLTP trainings were considered successful by participants and observers not only because they exposed participants to basic conflict resolution techniques, but because participants learned these techniques by practicing them with their (former) enemies:

---

[26] Uvin and Campbell, "The Burundi Leadership Training Programme," para. 58; interview with BLTP staff member B7, Washington DC, October 29, 2008.

[27] Uvin and Campbell, "The Burundi Leadership Training Programme."

[28] Uvin and Campbell, "The Burundi Leadership Training Programme."

[29] Interviews with BLTP participants, Bujumbura, June 2004; see Uvin and Campbell, "The Burundi Leadership Training Programme," para. 45

In all honesty, this is not about leadership training. This is about breaking down barriers between people so that they are able to address their problems jointly. It is interest-based negotiations. It is making people understand that they are not going to progress if they don't get along. That is an element of leadership. Our objective wasn't training leaders. It was taking leaders who are in this position via history and making them better able to work together.[30]

The political context in Burundi shifted again at the end of 2003, setting the stage for Phase III of Burundi's war-to-peace transition. The BLTP responded by taking key actions to reduce the gap between its peacebuilding aims and outcomes in this new context. It continued to be a peacebuilding learner.

In November 2003, the leader of the largest rebel group, Pierre Nkurunziza of the CNDD-FDD, was integrated into the transitional government, bringing an end to fighting in most of the country. The next step set out in Burundi's peace agreements was to demobilize the CNDD-FDD combatants and integrate a portion of them into a new National Defense Force, which would be made up of 50 percent soldiers from the existing Burundian Armed Forces and 50 percent soldiers from the demobilized rebel groups. Even though Burundi's Arusha Agreement had specified the general composition of the new National Defense Force, it had not specified exactly what posts and grades would be assigned to each armed force and to individuals within each force. In other words, Burundi's peace process had not solved the problem of the "status of combatants" when integrating a state military and former rebel organizations, with such different types of training and experience, into one cohesive military. The CNDD-FDD rebel group and Burundian military had to figure out how to solve this problem on their own.

In early 2004, to negotiate the "status of combatants," the Burundian Army and the CNDD-FDD established negotiation teams and charged them with figuring out how to integrate the two armed forces. Unfortunately, these negotiators reached a stalemate. If the negotiation teams could not reach an agreement on how to integrate the two armed forces, then the implementation of the Arusha Agreement would be stalled.

Several of the military officers who had participated in the BLTP's initial leadership training workshops approached Wolpe to suggest that the BLTP help break the deadlock in the negotiation about the "status of combatants":

The BLTP came at a very important time. We were at the last negotiations with the CNDD-FDD ... I thought [using the BLTP training] was a great

---

[30] Interview with BLTP staff member B10, by telephone, November 16, 2011.

idea. It could help push us forward with the negotiations. If the military can meet together and accelerate the process, then that can help push forward the politicians.[31]

The BLTP took the Army negotiators and the CNDD-FDD negotiators through modified versions of its leadership training, after which the negotiation teams reached an agreement around the "status of combatants," leading to the creation of the National Defense Force.[32] The BLTP was able to help contribute to this breakthrough in Burundi's war-to-peace transition because of strong informal local accountability routines that it had created with the participants in its initial leadership training sessions. This presented the feedback necessary for the organization to identify a new opportunity in Burundi's context. It was able to act on this opportunity, or learn, because a new peacebuilding-focused donor – the United Kingdom's Department for International Development (DFID) – stepped in to provide crucial peacebuilding funding, enabling the BLTP to sustain formal peacebuilding accountability during Phase III of Burundi's war-to-peace transition. This combination of informal local accountability and formal peacebuilding accountability enabled the BLTP to take actions to reduce the gap between its peacebuilding aims and outcomes, or learn, in Burundi's new post-2003 political context.

After completing the new BLTP trainings, the Burundian military was so convinced of the value of the BLTP's method that it asked the BLTP to design a curriculum that could be integrated into the National Defense Force's regular training offerings. Once the BLTP's new military training activities were under way, the BLTP continued to build strong informal local accountability routines with its new series of trainees and continued to take regular actions to reduce the gap between its peacebuilding aims and outcomes, or learn. Although the integration of the BLTP techniques into the new military training curriculum did not transform the entire force, it did seem to help improve communication within the newly integrated military, as exemplified in the words of one participant:

Before, we thought that the "other" was mean – bad – even though you had never actually talked to him. That it wasn't even worth approaching or talking with him. If we begin to talk and exchange and let people express themselves then you see that they also have ideas ... There is a way to come together and understand one another. The mistrust was replaced by confidence in one another.[33]

---

[31] Interview with military BLTP participant B2, Bujumbura, December 8, 2008.
[32] Uvin and Campbell, "The Burundi Leadership Training Programme," 33–4.
[33] Interview with military BLTP participant B3, Bujumbura, December 10, 2008.

As a result of the trust that the BLTP had created in the participants of its initial leadership workshops, through its informal local account-ability routines, the BLTP was offered an opportunity to help influ-ence change in a key Burundian institution. It vigorously seized this opportunity and contributed to the transformation of Burundi's armed forces, a pivotal institution in Burundi's peace process. According to one participant, "Even if the politicians played a role, it was the military that suffered the consequences of the war. The military understood the need to do [conflict resolution work] better than the politicians."[34] A BLTP staff member agreed that the military was the driver of Bur-undi's peace process and, thus, that the BLTP's work with the military was its most important:

The biggest result and impact of the BLTP was in the security sector. It was a surprising result because of the importance of this sector in the conflict overall. But you shouldn't be naive and think that the BLTP caused the reform of the sector, it contributed along with many other things.[35]

The BLTP's strong informal local accountability routines, combined with formal peacebuilding accountability, did not mean that the BLTP always achieved its peacebuilding aims, for in many cases it did not. It meant that the BLTP engaged in regular organizational learning. This simultaneous upward and downward accountability enabled the BLTP to recognize key opportunities in the context, act on these opportuni-ties, and ensure that the BLTP had the relationships necessary for local actors to invest in the BLTP's interventions. In several instances during Phases II and III, this peacebuilding learning behavior enabled the BLTP to help advance Burundi's transition out of war.

BLTP as a Micro-adaptor

In August 2005, Pierre Nkurunziza, the former leader of the CNDD-FDD, was elected as Burundi's first post-conflict president. The country had made it through the worst of the war and a complex four-year transitional period and had now elected a Hutu president in elections that were widely regarded as free and fair. Soon after he was elected, President Nkurunziza began to signal to the international community that the Burundian government would not respond positively to inter-national pressure or directives.

During this phase in Burundi's war-to-peace transition (Phase IV), the BLTP entered a period of relative stagnation. It became a micro-adaptor.

---

[34] Interview with military BLTP participant B3, Bujumbura, December 10, 2008.
[35] Interview with BLTP staff member B7, Bujumbura, February 2010.

It adjusted its activities in response to feedback from participants, but it did not question the overall relevance of its aims or approach to Burundi's new political context. The BLTP continued to work with the Burundian National Defense Force to develop its internal training package, but did not initiate new initiatives or alter its peacebuilding aims. It continued to try to train Burundi's top leadership even though they did not want the BLTP's training. The context had changed, but the BLTP had not.

One month after the election, President Nkurunziza, his two vice presidents, and all twenty members of his cabinet participated in a five-day BLTP workshop.[36] Nkurunziza had agreed to this workshop because Wolpe reminded him that he had fought hard, if unsuccessfully, to include the CNDD-FDD in the Arusha peace process.[37] Wolpe hoped that the training of Nkurunziza's cabinet – the BLTP's highest-level training to date – would set the stage for further workshops with the new government. He wanted to ensure that government representatives possessed the communication and conflict resolution skills necessary to govern peacefully and effectively. But after the initial workshop in the Autumn of 2005, Nkurunziza indicated that he did not want to be "trained" by anyone. He particularly did not want to be trained by Wolpe or his team, who Nkurunziza viewed as allied with FRODEBU, the other major Hutu political party with whom the CNDD-FDD had a tense relationship.[38]

Instead of identifying the ways in which the election of the new government could affect the BLTP's ability to achieve its aims, the BLTP charged ahead with its goal of training Burundi's leaders with little regard for the altered landscape. It tried to replicate the model that it had so successfully deployed during Burundi's transitional period, but it was continually rebuffed by Nkurunziza's government. The local actors and their preferences had changed, but the BLTP was not able to grasp the significance of this change.

The BLTP's previous successes and Wolpe's steadfast commitment to his vision contributed to a singular focus on its original peacebuilding aims and approach.[39] Even though the BLTP maintained many of its

---

[36] Interview with BLTP staff member B9, Washington, DC, October 14, 2008.

[37] The Arusha Agreement was signed by nineteen political parties, but not by the two main rebel groups, the CNDD-FDD and the FNL, which were excluded from the Arusha process.

[38] Interview with observer O7, by telephone, January 14, 2009; interview with observer O6, Bujumbura, December 1, 2008.

[39] Alnoor Ebrahim, "Accountability Myopia: Losing Sight of Organizational Learning," *Nonprofit and Voluntary Sector Quarterly* 34, no. 1 (2005): 56–87.

informal local accountability routines, had the same staff and leadership, continued to employ the same training methodologies, and pursued the same goals, its donors were no longer focused on funding INGOs to do peacebuilding; they wanted to fund the initiatives of the new Burundian government.

The main peacebuilding activities that the BLTP implemented during this phase were carried over from Burundi's previous phase, funded by DFID and the US Agency for International Development (USAID). These donors were no longer focused on INGO peacebuilding in Burundi; they just wanted the projects completed. No new donors emerged who were willing to fund INGO peacebuilding, which would have reinvigorated the BLTP's formal peacebuilding accountability. Consequently, during this period, the BLTP did not alter its goals or activities to reduce the gap between its peacebuilding aims and outcomes. It did not engage in peacebuilding learning. Relatedly, it did not contribute to the type of change in Burundi's governance institutions as it had in the past. The post-2005 period also revealed the limits of the BLTP's approach. First, the "leaders" that the BLTP worked with had to be willing to participate in the training. Second, the BLTP had trained ninety-five leaders at its initial workshops, but it had been unable to assess whether the participants had used the training, and the network the BLTP had created was largely dormant by 2006.[40] According to a BLTP staff member, "We have trained people, but we have not succeeded in following them to see how they have applied it."[41] The trainings that it conducted with the National Defense Force led to the BLTP's most concrete contribution to Burundi's war-to-peace transition. But even this went only so far. Once the BLTP trained people, it could not control or monitor what individuals did with their training.

The BLTP intervened at the individual level. In some instances, it supported individual-level change. The BLTP was founded on the concept that when several individuals within one organization were trained, a critical mass could reinforce the learned behavior.[42] But in truth, the BLTP's impact was determined by what individuals and groups did with the skills and awareness that the BLTP "experience" gave them.[43] Over time and as new actors who had not been through the BLTP training entered the scene, the application of the BLTP techniques began to

---

[40] Interview with BLTP staff member B12, Bujumbura, June 25, 2009.
[41] Interview with BLTP staff member B12, Bujumbura, June 25, 2009.
[42] Uvin and Campbell, "The Burundi Leadership Training Programme."
[43] Interview with military BLTP participant B2, Bujumbura, December 8, 2008; and Uvin and Campbell, "The Burundi Leadership Training Programme."

dissipate, and the BLTP was not willing or able to repeatedly "train" the same people; it had to continuously turn its attention to potential new groups of trainees.[44]

BLTP as a Peacebuilding Learner (Again)

During Phases V and VI, the BLTP again became a peacebuilding learner. It adapted its approach to Burundi's new environment, which was plagued by increasing tension between Burundi's political parties. During these phases, the BLTP found new projects that were funded by peacebuilding donors and, relatedly, had a new set formal peacebuilding accountability and informal local accountability routines. It took regular actions to reduce the gap between its peacebuilding aims and outcomes and, also, managed to contribute to a new breakthrough in Burundi's political process, helping Burundians once again to govern together more effectively.[45]

In 2008, the BLTP became a subcontractor for an innovative new project run by the Integrated UN Mission to Burundi (BINUB): the Cadre de Dialogue project (see Chapter 4 for further discussion). Participation in the Cadre de Dialogue project helped the BLTP create new relationships with top-level Burundian leadership, which had eluded the BLTP during the previous phase. This collaboration between the BLTP and BINUB also helped break a deadlock in Burundi's parliament and encouraged crucial dialogue between Burundi's political parties that had not seemed possible for several years beforehand (see Chapter 2).[46] The BLTP also created a new partnership with the Netherlands Institute for Multiparty Democracy and began to branch out through other partnerships with INGOs, including Dutch Cordaid.[47]

By this time, the BLTP had established itself as a national NGO, managed from Bujumbura instead of from Washington, DC. It would no longer be an INGO – with staff zipping in and out of Bujumbura to run trainings – but was now a hybrid organization: a national NGO

---

[44] Interviews with military BLTP participant B3, Bujumbura, December 10, 2008; military BLTP participant B2, Bujumbura, December 8, 2008; and military BLTP participant B6, Bujumbura, December 6, 2008.

[45] Interview with BLTP staff member B9, Washington, DC, October 14, 2008.

[46] Susanna P. Campbell, "Independent External Evaluation: Peacebuilding Fund Projects in Burundi," evaluation (Bujumbura: Integrated UN Mission to Burundi [BINUB], 2010), accessed December 21, 2017, http://goo.gl/0lAQwG.

[47] Tina Robiolle and Steve McDonald, "The Burundi Leadership Training Program" (Washington, DC: WWICS), accessed December 21, 2017, www.wilsoncenter.org/the-burundi-leadership-training-program.

that implemented projects in collaboration with INGOs and IOs.[48] Expanding beyond Wolpe's myopic focus on training Burundi's leadership, the BLTP began to partner with other international actors and initiate projects that addressed other levels and types of leadership such as community leaders and women.[49] This shift allowed the BLTP to alter its peacebuilding aims and its formal peacebuilding accountability routines. Each new project also enabled the BLTP to establish new informal local accountability routines that were appropriate for the project's particular local stakeholders. As a result, the BLTP once again became a peacebuilding learner, acting to reduce the gap between its peacebuilding aims and outcomes in Burundi's new political context.[50]

In its resurgence, the BLTP maintained its focus on leadership training, facilitation, and Harvard's Getting to Yes approach, but it began to significantly broaden its definition of a leader and its aim of working with leaders. In other words, to reduce the gap between its peacebuilding aims and outcomes, the BLTP changed its peacebuilding aims and approach and then sought to learn in relation to these new aims. Without the large grants that had been provided by the World Bank and DFID, the BLTP had to be more opportunistic and respond to new funding opportunities and the demands of IOs, INGOs, and bilateral donors.[51] It had less capacity to influence the decisions of the funders themselves, in part because it no longer had Wolpe at its helm. That said, the BLTP did not "just" respond to donor and partner requests, but it had its own agenda that it pursued in Burundi: to strengthen the capacity of Burundi's leaders at all levels to dialogue and resolve their conflicts peacefully.

During these phases, the BLTP did not stagnate. It cut its losses, abandoned fruitless efforts, and increased its work on two projects – the Community-Based Democracy project in collaboration with Netherlands Institute for Multiparty Democracy and a women's leadership project in collaboration with Cordaid.[52] The BLTP made significant efforts to conduct workshops with the FNL and the CNDD-FDD in 2009 after the FNL was reintegrated into the government and the

---

[48] This transition began in 2004, when the BLTP received NGO status in Burundi, but it took several years for the BLTP to operate more or less independently from the WWICS.

[49] Interview with BLTP staff member B12, Bujumbura, June 25, 2009.

[50] Interview with BLTP staff member B10, via telephone, November 16, 2011.

[51] Interview with BLTP staff member B10, via telephone, November 16, 2011.

[52] BLTP, "Note sur l'École de la democratie" (Bujumbura: Burundi Leadership Training Program, November 2011); and BLTP, "Note sur le projet 'Renforcement du Leadership Feminin'" (Bujumbura: November 2011).

military. In spite of getting the FNL to the table, the CNDD-FDD refused to fully engage in dialogue.[53] Likewise, after the sour turn of the 2010 election cycle, the BLTP met repeatedly, without success, with key political actors to try to find a solution to the standoff between the opposition and the CNDD-FDD.[54]

The BLTP continued to take action to reduce the gap between its peacebuilding aims and outcomes in response to Burundi's evolving political context. It maintained a broad network of relations and built several new networks for each of its projects, establishing clear informal local accountability routines. Collaborations with INGOs and IOs created new routines that prioritized formal peacebuilding accountability, requiring the BLTP to regularly examine whether or not its ongoing projects were having their intended effect on local institutions. At times, the BLTP was able to contribute to local change that aligned with its peacebuilding aims, and at times it was not. Sometimes the context was just too difficult, and sometimes the momentum created by the BLTP workshops dissipated quickly because the participants were unable to transfer the training to their daily lives. Nonetheless, even though Burundi's political climate became increasingly difficult during these two phases, the BLTP continued to play a crucial role in bringing the different political parties together and enabling them, at least temporarily, to govern more effectively together.

Explaining the BLTP's Behavior

Not all the BLTP's activities were successful. Not all BLTP participants were changed by the training. But at several points, the BLTP's well-targeted and politically sensitive trainings supported crucial changes in Burundi's political and security institutions. These changes focused on core priorities in the Arusha Agreement and were widely viewed as advancing Burundi's peacebuilding process.

The BLTP maintained strong informal local accountability routines throughout all its interventions, from 2002 to 2014. Only its formal accountability routines varied, explaining its movement between peacebuilding learner and micro-adaptor behaviors. The strong informal local accountability routines that the BLTP established were not alone sufficient for it to learn and maintain its relevance to Burundi's rapidly evolving peacebuilding context. The BLTP also needed formal peacebuilding accountability. Prior to 2005, the BLTP had strong and engaged

---

[53] Interview with BLTP staff member B10, via telephone, November 16, 2011.
[54] Interview with BLTP staff member B10, via telephone, November 16, 2011.

donors who prioritized peacebuilding, ensuring that the organization had formal accountability routines that provided it with the incentive to listen and respond to a breadth of perspectives about its impact on Burundi's evolving context. After 2005, however, the BLTP lost its formal peacebuilding accountability routines because donors were no longer interested in funding INGOs to do peacebuilding, leading the BLTP to become a micro-adaptor. After 2008, the BLTP reestablished formal peacebuilding accountability routines with a new set of donors and was able, once again, to be a peacebuilding learner.

Informal Local Accountability

The BLTP was capable of creating strong informal local accountability routines, in part, because of its historical relationships with key actors across Burundi's political spectrum. The BLTP capitalized on these relationships and also built new relationships with emerging political, military, civil society, and economic leaders as well as key international actors. Even before the BLTP launched its first activity in 2002, its team spent more than three months talking with a wide range of Burundian and international actors. The team used the information that it gathered during that time to design the BLTP's initial activities.[55] According to Uvin and Campbell:

Seldom in our careers have we seen a project for which the preparation was so complete and thorough, the buy-in so widespread, and the understanding of the challenge so nuanced. The project has a strong sense of how its contributions relate to the ongoing dynamics and to other donors' activities. It is very politically savvy in informing and including all possible parties, thus greatly helping its success.[56]

Once the BLTP's activities were under way, it maintained these relationships. BLTP team members talked to as many people as possible about the organization's activities.[57] They solicited regular feedback from participants about what was working and what was not working. They talked to donors and international observers about what they were doing and invited them to observe. They talked to government officials – to those included in the BLTP and those excluded from it – to keep them informed of the BLTP's work and its accomplishments. The BLTP created a network of the leaders that it had trained, delegating

---

[55] Chris Argyris and Donald A. Schon, *Organizational Learning: A Theory of Action Perspective* (Boston, MA: Addison-Wesley, 1978).
[56] Uvin and Campbell, "The Burundi Leadership Training Programme," 45.
[57] Uvin and Campbell, "The Burundi Leadership Training Programme," 45–6.

authority to former "beneficiaries" to help improve its activities and suggest future directions.

The BLTP did not have a sophisticated monitoring and evaluation system; it simply asked participants to fill out questionnaires after each training session. Through its informal local accountability routines – the authority it gave its trainees to give feedback on ongoing activities and advise on future directions as well as the relationships and trust it established with key actors across the political spectrum – the BLTP received critical inputs about how to adjust its approach. It also used these networks to build local interest in and ownership of its work, to identify new opportunities to help advance Burundi's war-to-peace transition, and to find new donors to support these efforts.

The BLTP processed the information that it received from ongoing consultations in an open, relatively nondefensive way, practicing what the BLTP promoted by instilling a culture of dialogue, consultation, and problem solving within its own institution.[58] Although there was not much willingness to question Wolpe's overall vision during the first few years of operation, the BLTP team was committed to altering the means by which the BLTP sought to achieve this vision.[59] Wolpe had argued that the BLTP needed to see whether the BLTP's vision worked before questioning it, a process that he said would take several years.[60] Within the boundaries of the existing vision, the BLTP regularly discussed its successes and failures and the feedback that it received from participants, observers, and external evaluations. During the initial leadership trainings, the BLTP team was very well informed, connected to people that it aimed to influence, and always trying to improve its capacity to achieve its broader vision of enabling reconciliation among Burundi's leaders:

The BLTP achieved great relevance, contextual coherence, and flexibility with little in the way of conflict-sensitive systems. Indeed, it did not conduct cutting-edge conflict assessments; it did not systematically question and evaluate the relevance of its approach; and it did not produce good monitoring data at all – its written reports were relentlessly upbeat and un-self-critical. And yet, its organizational systems clearly worked well, suggesting that a clear vision

---

[58] Interview with BLTP staff member B9, Washington, DC, October 14, 2008. This approach is identified in the literature as being a core component of double-loop learning. See Chris Argyris, *On Organizational Learning* (Cambridge, MA: Blackwell, 1992).

[59] Interview with BLTP staff member B4, February 24, 2009.

[60] Interviews with BLTP staff member B8, Bujumbura, March 6, 2009; BLTP staff member B4, February 24, 2009; BLTP staff member B7, Washington, DC, October 29, 2008; and BLTP staff member B9, Washington, DC, October 14, 2008.

and willingness to adapt to reach this vision, rather than highly-developed organizational systems, explains its success.[61]

The lack of sophisticated monitoring systems employed by the BLTP challenges thinking on peacebuilding best practices, which calls for the development of increasingly sophisticated monitoring and evaluation systems.[62] This best practice often ignores the importance of consultation, discussion, relationships, and trust. In other words, it ignores the importance of informal local accountability necessary to solicit information, develop understanding, build knowledge, and engage in the type of organizational learning that monitoring and evaluation aim to support.

The BLTP's highly consultative approach enabled it to stay informed and to respond to Burundi's evolving political context at the same time that it influenced the evolution of this context. The highly transparent and consultative process also helped the BLTP reduce the number of people who could attempt to sabotage leadership training sessions and increased the number of stakeholders willing to support the BLTP's efforts. The BLTP also kept potential donors informed about its work and successes, setting the stage for new funding opportunities. These broad informal local accountability routines, with a wide range of stakeholders, ensured that the BLTP was informed of new opportunities envisioned by its participants, such as those presented by several military attendees of the initial leadership training workshops. One BLTP staff member noted, "One of the keys to whatever success we enjoy anywhere has been our capacity to be flexible and opportunistic."[63]

The BLTP team argued that its informal local accountability routines and workshop methodology enabled it to create new opportunities, not just take advantage of existing ones. Referring to the concept of "ripeness," which the conflict resolution literature describes as the points in time when conflicts are ready for resolution, one BLTP staff member commented:[64]

It is fine if you have it, but there are many situations where it is not ripe, but the alternative is too ghastly to contemplate. I think there are times when you need

---

[61] Uvin and Campbell, "The Burundi Leadership Training Programme," 18.

[62] Cheyanne Church and Mark Rogers, *Designing for Results: Integrating Monitoring and Evaluation in Conflict Transformation Programs* (Washington, DC: Search for Common Ground, 2006).

[63] Interview with BLTP staff member B7, Washington, DC, October 29, 2008.

[64] William I. Zartman, "Ripeness: The Hurting Stalemate and Beyond," in *International Conflict Resolution after the Cold War* (Washington, DC: National Academy Press, 2000), 225–50.

the push, and it depends on who is doing the pushing. If you just wait for the situation to be ripe, it might never totally become ripe.[65]

A participant in the BLTP's military workshops echoed this sentiment:

The willingness [to change] will not come directly [from the individual]. Even with people who do want to change, being forced to dialogue and change will help them to understand and have the willingness [to change]. Their willingness to change will evolve.[66]

The BLTP's opportunity to work closely with the Burundian military emerged from the experience of military officers in the BLTP's initial leadership training workshops. It occurred because of changes in the political context and the trust that the BLTP built with military leaders during these initial workshops. The BLTP's training methodology and informal local accountability routines helped it create this opportunity, and its formal peacebuilding accountability routines incentivized and enabled the BLTP to act quickly to take advantage of this crucial opportunity.

Formal Accountability Routines

The BLTP's lines of formal accountability ran to WWICS headquarters in Washington, DC, and to the BLTP's donors: primarily the World Bank and the UK Department for International Development in Phases II and III. At WWICS headquarters, the BLTP was primarily accountable to Howard Wolpe, who also ran the BLTP at the country level, leaving most of the formal accountability focused on the BLTP's donors. When the BLTP transitioned to becoming a national NGO, its formal accountability routines were responsive only to its donors.

Prior to 2005, the BLTP's formal peacebuilding accountability routines incentivized BLTP staff members to listen to the conflict- and peace-related information coming from their informal local accountability routines, abandon unsuccessful initiatives, and take advantage of new opportunities. The BLTP's clear vision, the international credibility of its staff, and regular briefing sessions with a broad range of stakeholders enabled the organization to establish a strategy that its donors followed. Instead of being a pawn of its donors' preferences, as implied by INGO literature, the BLTP compensated for its dependence on grants by advocating with donors to support the BLTP's approach. The BLTP spoke to many different donors and did all that it could to convince these donors of the BLTP's contribution, such that donors

---

[65] Interview with BLTP staff member B9, Washington, DC, October 14, 2008.
[66] Interview with military BLTP participant B3, Bujumbura, December 10, 2008.

were practically competing to fund the BLTP. In the end, the BLTP had enough funding to take on initiatives that it thought were important, rather than only responding to donor priorities.[67] This worked in all of the phases under study, except for the post-2005 election period (Phase IV), when donor interest in Burundi turned away from peacebuilding and toward supporting the government's development initiatives (see Chapters 2 and 5).

Between 2002 and 2005, the BLTP had two primary donors: the World Bank Post-Conflict Fund and the UK Department for International Development (DFID). Both of these donors funded the BLTP to work on peacebuilding and engaged in regular discussions with the BLTP about the effectiveness of its activities and how the activities might be adjusted in response to the context. The accountability mechanisms that these donors established for the BLTP were focused on accompanying the BLTP, prioritizing collaboration and joint decision making with the BLTP team and peacebuilding.

These formal accountability routines provided the BLTP with crucial information about its effectiveness and incentivized the organization to pay attention to this information. External evaluations, regular and clear feedback from donors, and their presence in several BLTP training sessions forced the BLTP to see flaws in its approach that it might have been unwilling or unable to address otherwise.[68]

Success can breed myopia and tunnel vision more often than failure.[69] For example, after the 2004 external evaluation commissioned by the World Bank Post-Conflict Fund, the BLTP largely dropped its initial focus on trying to get its trainees to initiate economic development projects and instead focused its leadership training on specific Burundian institutions, such as the military. As one BLTP staff member commented, "Self-evaluation is fine, but sometimes you have your own blinders on so that you don't see that it's not working. Sometimes you don't interpret the information correctly and you don't see what you need to see. That's why having an external evaluator is very important."[70]

The BLTP's formal peacebuilding accountability routines incentivized the organization to listen to the information it received from its informal local accountability routines and provided additional sources of information in the form of external evaluations. It is highly unlikely that the BLTP's formal peacebuilding accountability routines, including external

---

[67] One of the BLTP's key donors during this period was DFID.
[68] Interview with observer O7, by telephone, January 14, 2009.
[69] Ebrahim, "Accountability Myopia."
[70] Interview with BLTP staff member B4, February 24, 2009.

evaluations, would have been sufficient to ensure that the BLTP learned in relation to its peacebuilding aims or identified new opportunities in the context. Evaluations took place at the end of the project and were effective only in the sense that they provided the BLTP an opportunity for reflection. Without the BLTP's own informal local accountability routines, and the knowledge that they generated from them, it is unlikely that this opportunity for reflection would have delivered sustained action by the BLTP to reduce the gap between its peacebuilding aims and outcomes, or learn.

The BLTP's formal accountability routines shifted after 2005 (Phase IV), when the funding from DFID and the World Bank Post-Conflict Fund dried up and the BLTP was not able to find new donors that would give large grants. Donors were shifting their focus away from peacebuilding and toward development funding that supported the new government's priorities. At the same time, the funds that the BLTP received from DFID and others were not accompanied by strong formal accountability routines that forced the BLTP to engage in the type of critical reflection that would have been necessary for it to shift its approach.

By Phases V and VI (2009–2014), the BLTP had succeeded in building strong relationships with new donors – IOs and INGOs with whom the BLTP directly collaborated in the design and implementation of its new projects. Through strong formal peacebuilding accountability routines with these donors and the resulting collaborative relationships, the BLTP was able to influence key institutions in Burundi's peacebuilding process. The BLTP's contributions after 2008 were arguably less significant than its contributions during Burundi's transitional period (Phases II and III), in part because there were fewer peacebuilding opportunities within Burundi's broader political and security context. The political parties were increasingly polarized, most opposition parties were excluded from government after the 2010 elections, and the Nkurunziza's government used increasingly authoritarian and violent tactics to remain in power.

Throughout its existence, the BLTP faced the challenge of trying to create long-term change in Burundian society through short-term projects. It was subject to the same short-term contracts that plague many INGOs.[71] Prior to 2005, the BLTP was able to set its own agenda and successfully advocate with donors to support this agenda, which matched donors' own interests. But after 2005, fewer donors were interested in the BLTP's approach, and the BLTP was, at first, unwilling to adjust

---

[71] Cooley and Ron, "The NGO Scramble."

its approach to fit the new reality. BLTP staff and participants argued that the BLTP approach needed to be reinforced and sustained over a long time.[72] Change takes time.[73] And yet, the BLTP operated from project to project, grant to grant, an important manifestation of its formal accountability and dependence on grants, which BLTP staff saw as constraining their effectiveness.[74]

The BLTP case shows that donor formal accountability routines influence INGO country-office behavior. But it also shows that these donor preferences alone do not determine an INGO's behavior. Innovative country-office staff have a lot of room to maneuver within and outside of the existing formal accountability routines. Innovative country-office staff can influence donor preferences, leading to the revision of formal accountability routines. Innovative country-office staff can create a demand among donors for their organization's services, altering the traditional donor-driven relationship. And, at times, innovative country-office staff can bypass formal accountability routines to create informal local accountability that is not incentivized by these formal accountability routines.

Individual Country-Office Staff and Leadership

Rather than simply responding to donor demands, and their related formal accountability routines, the BLTP staff created the type of organization that they thought would help to build peace in Burundi. To do so, the BLTP country office steeped itself in informal local accountability. Informal local accountability was so ingrained in the BLTP's approach that its staff did not view it as "bad behavior." Nonetheless, informal local accountability was not required or incentivized by the BLTP donors and the BLTP had to repeatedly convince its donors of its importance, or just do it whether donors liked it or not.

As an INGO with few constraints other than satisfying the mandate of its headquarters and fulfilling the reporting requirements of its donors, the BLTP country-office staff had a lot of potential agency, which they readily employed. The BLTP country-office leadership and staff used their agency to create informal local accountability routines, find new donors and partners, and, relatedly, alter the focus of their formal

---

[72] Interviews with BLTP military participant B2, Bujumbura, December 8, 2008; BLTP military participant B3, Bujumbura, December 10, 2008; BLTP staff member B4, February 24, 2009; BLTP military participant B5, Bujumbura, December 10, 2008; BLTP military participant B6, Bujumbura, December 6, 2008; BLTP staff member B7, Washington, DC, October 28, 2008; BLTP staff member B9, Washington, DC, October 14, 2008; and BLTP staff member B10, via telephone, November 16, 2011.

[73] Interview with BLTP staff member B12, Bujumbura, June 25, 2009.

[74] Interview with BLTP staff member B12, Bujumbura, June 25, 2009.

accountability routines. The organization was, in turn, able to engage in regular peacebuilding learning, navigating the numerous changes in Burundi's political and security situation between 2002 and 2014.

The BLTP's country-office leadership took its role very seriously. Not only did Howard Wolpe have political clout and knowledge, but he was also a tireless advocate for his vision. At the same time, he sought to enable his Burundian colleagues to be leaders in their particular domains. Wolpe was highly responsive to the micro-level evolution of Burundi's political context while simultaneously believing that he could shape this context. He ensured that the BLTP had strong informal local accountability routines and also engaged in regular discussions with its donors. Wolpe's visionary leadership drove the organization forward and convinced donors and Burundi's leaders to follow, at least for a time. However, this vision also created myopia, blinding the organization to its irrelevance after 2005. Fabien Nsengimana, the director of the BLTP after 2006, was able to establish a slightly different vision for the organization, helping it focus on Burundi's new reality and find donors and partners that could support the BLTP's altered approach.

In sum, the BLTP's individual country-office staff were essential to the BLTP's successes, and failures, in Burundi. BLTP staff created the informal local accountability routines that grounded the BLTP's activities in the Burundian context. They convinced donors to fund the BLTP, providing essential financing and leading the formal peacebuilding accountability routines that provided the organization with the opportunity for self-reflection. Their mastery of donor formal accountability routines, in fact, helped them to figure out how to sidestep or bypass them when necessary to achieve their country-level peacebuilding aims. As the case of CARE Burundi confirms, the initiative of individual country-office staff largely determines whether or not an INGO is an empowered agent or a disempowered pawn.

CARE Burundi

CARE Burundi is part of CARE International, a decentralized international federation of INGOs with country offices managed by three primary headquarters offices: CARE USA, CARE Canada, and CARE Austria.[75] CARE International's mandate is to fight global poverty

---

[75] Most CARE country offices are managed by CARE USA, CARE Canada, or CARE Australia. As a confederation, CARE is composed of CARE Australia, CARE Canada, CARE Denmark, CARE Germany-Luxembourg, CARE France, CARE Japan, CARE Netherlands, CARE Norway, CARE Austria, CARE Thailand, CARE UK, and CARE

through humanitarian relief and development work. Each member of the CARE International federation adopts the same general approach, aims, and methods, but has different leadership, staff, and budgets and operates in accordance with the rules of its particular headquarters office. CARE Burundi is formally accountable to its primary headquarters and to the bilateral and multilateral donors who fund it to implement specific projects or initiatives. It is also accountable to the host government in the sense that the host government grants it permission to operate in the country and CARE Burundi did not want to get kicked out of the country.

CARE International established its office in Burundi in 1994. Its staff of about two hundred was 97 percent Burundian. There were only three or four international staff members at any one time: the country director; the assistant country director; the learning coordinator; and, later on, an advocacy coordinator. Over the next twenty years, CARE Burundi significantly shifted its approach and transformed its office, largely in response to changes in the Burundian context. In the next section, I discuss CARE Burundi's trajectory from 1999 to 2014, how and why it changed its behavior over this period, and the effect of these changes on the achievement of its peacebuilding outcomes.

CARE Burundi's Trajectory

As depicted in Table 3.3, during Phases I and II, CARE Burundi was a stagnant player. It was a humanitarian organization that was largely disconnected from those it claimed to serve, simply delivering humanitarian goods to Burundian communities. It did not have informal local accountability, or really much interaction at all with the communities, nor did it have formal peacebuilding accountability. This shifted during Phase III when CARE Burundi received a new country director and its headquarters management was transferred from CARE Canada to CARE USA. This set the stage for a thorough organizational change process that led to the creation of strong informal local accountability routines and formal peacebuilding accountability in Phase IV, making CARE Burundi a peacebuilding learner. In Phases V and VI, CARE Burundi maintained its strong informal local accountability routines, but its donors and headquarters shifted

---

USA. In addition to being in charge of specific CARE country offices where they implement programs, CARE members also collaborate with other CARE offices through supporting specific programs.

Table 3.3. *CARE Burundi*

	Informal Local Accountability	Formal Peacebuilding Accountability	Country Office Type	Result
CARE Phase I: Jan. 1999– Oct. 2001	No	No	Stagnant Player	Actions without consideration of effect on conflict dynamics
CARE Phase II: Nov. 2001– Nov. 2003	No	No	Stagnant Player	Actions without consideration of effect on conflict dynamics
CARE Phase III: Dec. 2003– Aug. 2005	No	No	Stagnant Player	Actions without consideration of effect on conflict dynamics
CARE Phase IV: Sept. 2005– Apr. 2009	Yes	Yes	Peacebuilding Learner	Actions to reduce gap between peacebuilding aims and outcomes
CARE Phase V: May 2009– May 2010	Yes	No	Micro-adaptor	Actions to reduce gap between *non*-peacebuilding aims and outcomes
CARE Phase VI: June 2010– Apr. 2014	Yes	No	Micro-adaptor	Actions to reduce gap between *non*-peacebuilding aims and outcomes

away from peacebuilding and, instead, focused on more traditional development aims. As a result, CARE Burundi was a micro-adaptor during these two final phases.

The CARE Burundi case demonstrates the importance of formal peacebuilding accountability in enabling country offices to learn in relation to their peacebuilding aims. Between 2004 and 2014, CARE Burundi's country program plans maintained conflict-sensitivity and peacebuilding as cross-cutting themes in all its projects.[76] CARE Burundi had strong informal local accountability routines throughout this

---

[76] Interviews with CARE staff member C2, Bujumbura, March 24, 2009; CARE staff member C3, Bujumbura, June 9, 2009; CARE staff member C4, Bujumbura, June 25, 2009.

time, demonstrating a real commitment to receiving regular feedback from stakeholders in each of its projects for the sake of learning, research, self-reflection, and continuous improvement of its activities.[77] In spite of these strong informal local accountability routines, the absence of consistent formal peacebuilding accountability meant that CARE Burundi did fulfill its aim of integrating peacebuilding throughout its activities. Given multiple competing priorities, when peacebuilding was no longer a priority for CARE Burundi's formal accountability routines, it was no longer a priority for all of its activities.

CARE Burundi as a Stagnant Player

During Phases I and II, CARE Burundi was a stagnant player. From 1994 to 2002, CARE Burundi operated as a standard humanitarian INGO: "CARE Burundi worked in spite of the conflict, not on it. We ignored the context and tried to deliver food."[78] Like most INGOs operating in Burundi at the time, CARE focused on delivering quick, short-term assistance for refugees, internally displaced people, and children without a home or family able to support them. CARE Burundi did not create informal local accountability, nor did it have formal peacebuilding accountability. It was accountable for the delivery of humanitarian aid, particularly food assistance. It did not attempt to influence Burundi's rapidly changing political context, nor did it attempt respond to the specific needs of the vulnerable populations that it aimed to help. It did not even consult much with the people it attempted to help. Instead, it focused on the logistics of food delivery: procuring, transporting, and distributing bags of grain and other nonperishable food.

During these early phases, CARE Burundi did initiate a couple of pilot peacebuilding projects in a northern province that was relatively prosperous and peaceful compared to Burundi's war-torn provinces.[79] Here, CARE implemented a peace education project that used theater performances to help Burundians resolve interpersonal and community-related conflicts, reportedly contributing to the resolution of several

---

[77] CARE Burundi, "A Journey of Empowerment: CARE Burundi's Rights-Based Learning Program Approach" (Bujumbura: CARE, 2010); CARE Burundi, "Analysing the Causes of Poverty: A Process and Change of Attitudes: CARE Burundi's Story" (Bujumbura: CARE Burundi, 2008); CARE International–Burundi, "Strategic Journey 2007–2011" (Bujumbura: CARE International, November 2006); and interviews with CARE staff member C9, Bujumbura, March 20, 2009; CARE staff member C10, Bujumbura, March 10, 2009; CARE staff member C11, Bujumbura, June 8, 2009.

[78] Interview with CARE staff member C11, Bujumbura, June 8, 2009.

[79] Mark Turner, "FT.com; Special Reports/Responsible Business 2001" (October 23, 2001), http://goo.gl/bS0CG0.

community-level conflicts.[80] It also began a pilot project that aimed to help rebuild the conflict resolution role of Burundi's traditional elders, the *bashingantahe*. These projects were disconnected from the vast majority of CARE Burundi's activities, however, and CARE Burundi did not take action to reduce the gap between these peacebuilding aims and outcomes to address the local implications of the larger shifts in Burundi's political and security context. In other words, during Phases I and II, in the absence of informal local accountability and formal peacebuilding accountability, CARE Burundi did not engage in organizational learning in relation to its peacebuilding aims.

CARE Burundi's formal accountability routines prioritized the delivery of humanitarian assistance, not peacebuilding. Like many INGOs, CARE country offices "live" from grant to grant, primarily from bilateral donors.[81] Between 1999 and 2003, the vast majority of donors gave only humanitarian funding, waiting until fighting stopped to provide development assistance.[82] Donors' focus on short-term humanitarian funding prevented CARE Burundi from doing "reasonably long-term rehabilitation and development programming."[83] CARE Burundi declared that it had no choice but to align its "priorities with the donor funding reality."[84] CARE Burundi's focus on humanitarian programming reflects the overall approach of CARE Canada, which managed the office until 2000. Unlike CARE USA, which took over management of the office in 2001, CARE Canada did not prioritize peacebuilding or conflict sensitivity, providing few incentives for staff to focus on these priorities.[85]

CARE Burundi's staff composition reflected the broader hierarchy in Burundian society at the time, with unequal power relations that had been a root cause of the conflict. How could CARE Burundi effectively work on peacebuilding if the composition of its staff paralleled some of the causes of the conflict? Burundian staff in senior positions were primarily male and Tutsi:[86]

---

[80] By creating a fictional reality that mirrored their real lives, the plays helped people understand their adversaries' perspective and allowed them to discuss the origins and acts of violent conflict. A similar peacebuilding strategy was being tried at the time through the development of radio soap operas by Search for Common Ground's Studio Ijambo. Julie Abbass, "Peace Education Project: Grassroots Community Research, Final Summary" (CARE Burundi, Bujumbura, June 10, 2001); Interview with CARE staff member C5, Bujumbura, March 25, 2009.

[81] Interview with CARE staff member C9, Bujumbura, March 20, 2009.

[82] ICG, "A Framework for Responsible Aid to Burundi."

[83] CARE Burundi, "CARE International in Burundi Strategic Plan Document, 2002–2005" (Bujumbura: CARE Burundi, 2001), 13.

[84] CARE Burundi, "Analysing the Causes of Poverty," 1.

[85] Interview with CARE staff member C6, Bujumbura, June 2, 2009.

[86] CARE Burundi, "A Journey of Empowerment," 2.

In this hierarchical society of Burundi, decades of conflict have occurred so that a few small elite can hold the power and all that comes with it. This system of governance has seeped into all walks of life. CARE Burundi senior staff mirrored this as well, information was not shared, advantages were hoarded and decision-making was confined to a small elite. This worked its way down through the organization and its projects with the bottom of the pile being the "beneficiaries" who were referred to as "simple" people because they were uneducated.[87]

According to an organizational climate survey conducted in 2002, most Hutu and female staff reported feeling marginalized and unrepresented:[88]

It was a horrible time to come to the [Burundi] office . . . a highly stressful time. In the international community, you had a lot of rejects from somewhere else. Everyone talked about Burundi as if it was a hell hole. There were a lot of part time and acting people because no one wanted to come to Burundi.[89]

Between 1999 and 2003, CARE Burundi also lacked consistent leadership. It had temporary country directors but no country director of a normal two- or three-year duration for conflict-affected countries.[90] Without stable and innovative leadership, CARE Burundi was not able to address poor staff morale or establish a different country strategy than the one imposed by its donors and headquarters. In the absence of entre-preneurial country-office leadership, country-office staff were not able to take advantage of the potential agency available to them. In the absence of formal peacebuilding accountability from its headquarters or donors, CARE Burundi was not able to effectively pursue its peacebuilding aims. This changed during Phase III with the arrival of a new country director and transformation of CARE Burundi's aims, approach, and staff com-position. The effect of this change was only visible in Phase IV, when CARE Burundi became a peacebuilding learner.

CARE Burundi as a Peacebuilding Learner

In 2004, in the midst of Phase III and soon after the arrival of country director Kassie McIlvaine, CARE Burundi began what it called its "jour-ney." It had taken a while for Care USA to find a permanent country director for Burundi in part because of the poor reputation of the office. The organizational change process that McIlvaine initiated transformed CARE Burundi from an office that reinforced the root causes of Bur-undi's conflict to one that embodied the openness and the ethnic and gender equality of the Arusha Agreement. CARE Burundi shifted away

---

[87] CARE Burundi, "Analysing the Causes of Poverty," 1.
[88] CARE Burundi, "Analysing the Causes of Poverty," 6.
[89] CARE Burundi, "Analysing the Causes of Poverty," 3.
[90] Interview with CARE staff member C11, Bujumbura, June 8, 2009.

from humanitarian assistance to focus on CARE USA's core priority: poverty reduction. CARE Burundi decided that, in Burundi, it was necessary to address the symbiotic relationship between the conflict and poverty. It convinced CARE USA and several donors that this focus on poverty reduction through peacebuilding was necessary in Burundi, creating formal accountability routines for CARE Burundi. The importance of a peacebuilding approach was expressed by a CARE staff member:

Programming needed to improve so as to get at what had torn this country apart for years – the conflict that was keeping the majority of the population in poverty. This is different from development in a country that has not experienced conflict at all. There, the field is free – you still need to pay attention to not do harm. But, in a post-conflict country there is always potential for conflict. The situation can change and explode and you have to really pay attention to what is going on [at the community level].[91]

CARE Burundi found that people's capacity to take care of themselves was strongly diminished by the war: "After ten years of civil war, people have really been affected in terms of their degree of poverty and their mentality. They have been traumatized. It is not the same as in a non-conflict context."[92] CARE also found that communities were dependent on handouts, and people did not trust that they could do things for themselves: "It takes time to build trust within the community and convince people that they have experience and that they can do something together and make a contribution."[93]

To make a real contribution to poverty reduction in Burundi, CARE had to address both the causes and the manifestations of the conflict. But before it could do this, it had to address how its own practices mirrored these conflict dynamics. According to CARE Burundi's own analysis:

In a society where ethnic and social divisions reigned for years, it is understandable that people do not want to dig deep to understand the tensions and their causes. Each person, and that included CARE staff, had their own personal wounds and memories. CARE had to find a way to create a supportive working environment so that staff and our partners were able and willing to start to dig deeper into what were the structural conditions that were holding this fertile country in poverty.[94]

CARE Burundi began an extensive organizational change process intended to alter the way that CARE staff interacted with the

[91] Interview with CARE staff member C5, Bujumbura, March 5, 2009.
[92] Interview with CARE staff member C5, Bujumbura, March 5, 2009.
[93] CARE Burundi, "Analysing the Causes of Poverty," 2.
[94] CARE Burundi, "Analysing the Causes of Poverty," 2.

communities they aimed to help: "Office decision-making, recruitment, management, assessment, and training were restructured to increase the transparency and inclusiveness of diverse staff – with a conscious effort to raise the voices and positions of women, Hutu, and Batwa across the organization."[95] Staff went out to the various rural communities that they worked in to try to understand the community members and their needs, hopes, and aspirations: "There was a collective understanding that we, the educated staff of CARE had no idea of the realities in the field, we did not truly understand the lives of our beneficiaries and what strengths and skills they had and what the true barriers to their development were."[96]

To better understand its relationship with the communities it aimed to help, CARE Burundi experimented with new types of interventions and brought in researchers to help CARE staff with their analysis and reflection.[97] CARE Burundi asked its partners to evaluate CARE's work.[98] No other CARE office had gone through this type of process before; CARE Burundi invented it.[99] This thorough and intensely personal process seemed to deeply affect CARE Burundi's staff and organizational culture. In the words of one CARE Burundi staff member:

Bit by bit, there were women and people from all ethnicities who occupied posts of responsibility. After having lived an ethnic war and losing members of our family, people learned how to live together and collaborate. That continues to be really good.[100]

To sustain its high degree of introspection and self-reflection, CARE Burundi began to develop a strong "learning culture," encouraging open discussion among staff and regular interaction with the communities that it aimed to help, which it now called "neighbors" rather than "beneficiaries."[101] CARE Burundi moved one staff person from each project team to live in the communities that they were working with. All staff members had previously been based in Bujumbura or suboffices in the smaller cities of Gitega, Muyinga, Ngozi, and Ruyigi. CARE Burundi argued that this shift was crucial for understanding the communities they worked with:

Our procedures and our way of working result in us spending less time with our neighbors. The fact that we arrive in our fancy 4×4 or motorcycles or

[95] CARE Burundi, "Journey of Empowerment," 3.
[96] CARE Burundi, "Analysing the Causes of Poverty," 3.
[97] CARE Burundi, "Analysing the Causes of Poverty," 4.
[98] CARE Burundi, "Analysing the Causes of Poverty," 6.
[99] Interview with CARE staff member C11, Bujumbura, June 8, 2009.
[100] CARE Burundi, "Analysing the Causes of Poverty," 6.
[101] CARE Burundi, "A Journey of Empowerment," 5.

with mobile telephones and radios and that we never have the time to stay and speak with them or spend the night makes it impossible to understand the life of our neighbors.[102]

By relocating staff to live in the communities that they worked with, CARE Burundi built strong informal local accountability routines. It delegated authority to local community groups to assess the effectiveness of CARE Burundi's work and to help decide on the future direction of the projects based in their communities.

By 2006, CARE Burundi's rigorous self-reflective process resulted in a new strategic plan and guide for its work. CARE's projects were now focused in three areas: empowerment of women, empowerment of youth, and empowerment of the marginalized.[103] Conflict sensitivity and peacebuilding were supposed to be integrated across all these areas to "promote and support reconciliation efforts through conflict sensitive interventions and analysis at different levels (local, national, and regional) and accompany the formal and informal structures in reinforcing good governance."[104] Through intense advocacy conducted by McIlvaine and the excellent reputation that CARE Burundi's organizational change process had built among donors in Burundi, CARE Burundi was able to find donors willing to fund projects in each of these focus areas.[105]

Burundi's 2005 elections ushered in a new period of hope. Average Burundians were hopeful that their politicians had finally put an end to the political antics that had caused so much death and trauma. The newly elected politicians were hopeful that they would finally get their share of wealth and prosperity. Donors were hopeful that Burundi's peace process would be an unequivocal success – partly their success – and that Burundi could now transition toward development. CARE Burundi positioned itself to be able to capitalize on this hope and deliver "empowering" programming to Burundians who had suffered from so many years of war and violence.[106]

---

[102] CARE Burundi, "Analysing the Causes of Poverty," 6.
[103] CARE Burundi, "Analysing the Causes of Poverty."
[104] CARE Burundi, "Analysing the Causes of Poverty," 16.
[105] Interview with CARE staff member C10, Bujumbura, March 10, 2009.
[106] CARE International–Burundi, "Strategic Journey 2007–2011," 15. For CARE Burundi, empowerment meant: "In all of our activities, we and our partners will take into account discrimination. Together with the concerned people, we will work for the adoption of attitudes, behaviors, and structures that promote the empowerment of marginalized people and the reduction of all forms of discrimination."

CARE Burundi actively positioned itself to receive the increased local-level peacebuilding and community-development funding that it anticipated would arrive after the 2005 elections. The accompanying formal peacebuilding accountability routines, combined with CARE Burundi's strong informal local accountability, enabled CARE Burundi to learn in relation to its peacebuilding aims. It did this first by realigning its peacebuilding aims and outcomes in response to the new post-2005 climate, which also required that it anticipate how Burundi's political and security situation, and associated donor funding opportunities, would evolve. After the 2005 elections, CARE Burundi continued to learn in relation to its peacebuilding aims, and implemented locally grounded and conflict-sensitive programs that adapted in response to the needs of the communities that CARE Burundi aimed to serve.

After 2004, CARE Burundi began empowering its own staff and then moved to work with and empower communities affected by the war. CARE Burundi's organizational change process was, in itself, a peacebuilding intervention that effectively altered the mindset of many of its staff and the way in which they interacted with one another, CARE Burundi's partners, and their target communities. CARE Burundi was widely regarded as an effective community-based peacebuilding organization in the immediate post-election period. Its sensitivity and responsiveness both to the evolving broader political context and to the needs of the communities that it served, enabled by its informal local accountability and formal peacebuilding accountability, made it an ideal peacebuilding learner.

CARE Burundi as a Micro-adaptor

In Phases V and VI, CARE Burundi was a micro-adaptor. Its focus on peacebuilding in Phase IV gradually transitioned into a focus on community-based development interventions, in line with the priorities of CARE USA and CARE Burundi's new crop of donors. CARE Burundi maintained its strong informal accountability routines with local communities, but it did not learn in relation to peacebuilding outcomes. Instead, it took regular actions to reduce the gap between its overall women and youth empowerment and poverty-reduction aims with changes in its women and youth empowerment outcomes, with little consideration for their relevance to conflict and peace related outcomes.

By 2009, CARE Burundi had ten ongoing projects, most of which provided empowerment training and income-generating activities for women and their communities, aiming to increase their family income, prevent sexual violence, and resolve interpersonal and community conflicts.[107] These community-level activities seemed to have had an important effect on the communities that CARE worked with, helping CARE Burundi build an excellent reputation among development actors in Burundi and within CARE International more broadly.[108] As a CARE staff member expressed:

> I have really been blown away by CARE Burundi's program when I hear people actually give testimonials about how their lives have changed. When I go and talk to a woman's group and can really sense the positive energy and their vision for a more positive future. They will continue whether CARE's project is there or not.[109]

In spite of the overall success of CARE's community projects, CARE did not focus directly on conflict, but implemented projects in communities that were ravaged by conflict. Aside from two small peacebuilding projects, CARE's projects did not have an explicit peacebuilding aim and did not consider peacebuilding as a core component.[110] As one CARE staff member commented: "They don't think it is very important. I think that the first reason is that they are preoccupied with other things in their projects. Second, they don't understand the [peacebuilding] effects."[111] CARE was now a micro-adaptor. It implemented projects that were grounded in the communities it worked with but detached from the conflict dynamics in those communities and within Burundi generally.

CARE Burundi's women's empowerment programming brought a lot of attention to the office. CARE USA's formal accountability routines – funding opportunities, headquarters visits, reporting requests and requirements – that prioritized women's empowerment were used to convey support to CARE Burundi for this type of intervention. CARE USA and other CARE country offices viewed CARE Burundi's women's empowerment program as exemplary and were interested in learning from its successes. This attention and support reinforced and strengthened CARE Burundi's work in this area, which in turn increased the attention that this work received.

---

[107] CARE Burundi, "Burundi – Country Profile," accessed December 21, 2017, www.care.org/country/burundi.

[108] Babu Ayindo, "Demystifying Theory of Social Change: Reflections on the Praxis of Select CARE Programs in Burundi" (Bujumbura: CARE Burundi, July 26, 2008); and interview with CARE staff member C16, Bujumbura, March 8, 2009.

[109] Interview with CARE staff member C9, Bujumbura, March 20, 2009.

[110] Ayindo, "Demystifying Theory of Social Change"; and Interview with CARE staff member C15, Bujumbura, March 26, 2009.

[111] Interview with CARE staff member C15, Bujumbura, March 26, 2009.

As one CARE Burundi staff member reported: "Within CARE Burundi, we have put some intrinsic reward around women's empowerment. It is trendy now. There is donor interest."[112] Of course, Burundian women were badly in need of empowerment. They were considered by many to be second-class citizens and were subject to high levels of domestic abuse, rape, and violence. Gradually, the increased support and encouragement from CARE USA, increased support and funding from new donors, and a preference from CARE Burundi's leadership for women's empowerment interventions made this CARE Burundi's new top priority. Its formal accountability routines now prioritized women's empowerment specifically, and poverty reduction initiatives in general, over peacebuilding or humanitarian intervention.

As women's empowerment became an increasingly important aspect of CARE Burundi's programming, peacebuilding and conflict sensitivity receded into the background. In reality, though, CARE Burundi had never fully integrated peacebuilding or conflict sensitivity across its projects, even though this was a core aspect of its strategic plan. CARE USA was increasingly focusing on women's empowerment – conducting rigorous studies of its work in this area and investing time in developing best practices in women's empowerment programming.[113] Several Scandinavian donors were also interested in supporting women's empowerment programming and enthusiastically funded CARE Burundi's emerging work in this area.[114] In other words, by 2008 CARE Burundi's formal accountability routines were increasingly focused on community-based development and women's empowerment, not on peacebuilding. The strong interest of its country director in promoting and pursuing women's empowerment work removed country-office resistance to this focus.

Even though CARE's own analysis indicated that "the conflict is caused by politicians holding on to power, it is about access and control over resources," CARE's programming did not attempt to directly address power relations in Burundi or enable local administrators to better serve their communities. It paid little attention to governance, policy, government, or politics.[115] Many of its program documents indicated that it would operate at the provincial, regional, and national level, but it largely did not.[116]

[112] Interview with CARE staff member C9, Bujumbura, March 20, 2009.
[113] Interview with CARE staff member C3, Bujumbura, June 9, 2009.
[114] Interview with CARE staff member C3, Bujumbura, June 9, 2009.
[115] O. Tankari, "Projet Sasagaza Amahoro: Repandre la paix—Evaluation Finale" (Bujumbura: CARE Burundi; and Washington, DC: USAID, March 2010).
[116] Tankari, "Projet Sasagaza Amahoro: Repandre la paix."

The narrow focus of CARE's projects on the community level was partly because of the short-term nature of its funding. Donors funded projects for only one or two years. CARE's projects took time to initiate because CARE started by building trust and relationships with communities (through informal local accountability), leaving little time to work with the administration and government.[117] "The impact depends on the investment," suggested one CARE staff member.[118] Short-term investment leads to short-term impact:[119]

> If it is a short-term project, then we can't work with the political structures or the structures of the state … In general, the administration is there and they are just informed about what we are doing, but nothing else. The structures of the state have much more influence than CARE. When we work together we have much more of a chance of impact than CARE does alone. When CARE leaves, the administration should continue to support what we have done.[120]

Although many of the groups and associations that CARE projects helped form continued to function after the CARE project finished, it is unclear what effect they had. These groups were now "empowered," but they lacked resources, skills, and opportunities.[121] The investment was short-term. CARE Burundi learned in relation to these short-term goals, but it did not address the larger political, security, and economic issues that affected Burundians' livelihood. This major weakness in CARE's empowerment approach was mentioned by many CARE Burundian staff members.[122] They wondered how they could help alter the structural causes of conflict and poverty that left so many Burundians, and so many Burundian women, disempowered?[123]

To at least some degree, the absence of formal peacebuilding accountability routines inhibited CARE Burundi from making a larger contribution to these structural and political issues. That said, as the BLTP case demonstrated, even with both formal peacebuilding accountability and informal local accountability routines, no intervening organization is ever

---

[117] Interviews with CARE staff member C5, Bujumbura, March 25, 2009; and CARE staff member C1, Bujumbura, June 8, 2009.

[118] Interview with CARE staff member C16, Bujumbura, March 8, 2009.

[119] Interview with CARE staff member C16, Bujumbura, March 8, 2009.

[120] Interview with CARE staff member C1, Bujumbura, June 8, 2009.

[121] Ayindo, "Demystifying Theory of Social Change"; interviews with CARE staff members C16, Bujumbura, March 8, 2009, and C1, Bujumbura, June 8, 2009; Lukas van Trier, "Lessons Learned and Challenges Faced in Community-Based Peacebuilding in Burundi" (CARE Nederland: The Hague, October 2010).

[122] Interviews with CARE staff member C18, Bujumbura, June 16, 2009; CARE staff member C16, Bujumbura, March 8, 2009; and CARE staff member C23, Bujumbura, June 5, 2009.

[123] Interview with CARE staff member C15, Bujumbura, March 26, 2009.

guaranteed to achieve its peacebuilding aims in a highly dynamic and complex context such as Burundi. Furthermore, even if a peacebuilding intervention achieves its aims, the broader political and security context in which they take place can change very quickly, instantly undermining the project's gains.

Explaining CARE Burundi's Behavior

CARE Burundi underwent an intensive organizational change process that enabled it to better understand, empower, and support the Burundian communities in which it worked. In so doing, it developed strong informal local accountability routines. Nonetheless, CARE Burundi's commitment to engage directly with these communities was in constant tension with its formal accountability to its donors and headquarters.

Even though CARE USA and CARE Burundi's donors readily capitalized on the information and relationships created through this informal local accountability, their numerous reporting, fundraising, communication, and information requests (through formal accountability routines) meant that country-office staff were unable to pay attention to much of the information they received. In this sense, CARE Burundi's strong informal local accountability was not considered "bad behavior" by CARE USA and CARE Burundi. After all, like many INGOs, CARE Burundi was highly decentralized and its country-office staff had a lot of leeway to create new initiatives, as long as they could find the money to support these initiatives and properly account for their time and resources. In other words, CARE Burundi could create and support informal local accountability as long as it was also able to effectively carry out all of the other tasks and deliverables required by its formal accountability routines.

But CARE USA and CARE Burundi's donors did not directly incentivize informal local accountability, either. In fact, these principals seem to have reduced the potential effectiveness of CARE Burundi's informal local accountability by continuously placing demands and requirements on the country office (through formal accountability routines), greatly reducing the time country-office staff had to spend with the Burundian communities that they aimed to serve.

Informal Local Accountability

After 2004, CARE Burundi had a high degree of informal local accountability. It solicited regular input from the various stakeholders in its projects – partners, community members, and donors – and involved these actors in decision-making about its projects. Even though its donors required only superficial reporting on project outputs, CARE Burundi developed its own project monitoring system outside of its formal accountability routines to try to account for change that it observed.[124]

In spite of the high degree of feedback that CARE Burundi received from communities, partners, and other stakeholders, its staff members were unable to pay attention to much of it.[125] They were overwhelmed by the amount of information that they received. Staff received reports about their own projects, other projects, CARE USA priorities, and CARE International strategies and approaches.[126] Staff complained that they could not manage all this information and did not have enough time to think about the implications for their projects in the communities they worked with.[127] Much of the information within CARE Burundi was communicated via email, leaving little time for teams to openly discuss it.[128] According to one CARE Burundi report, "While project teams have monthly obligations to report their work and pursue their learning agenda questions, most information is collected to inform donors whose reporting requirements tend to favor output tracking [of what they deliver], and not dig deeper to question the program logic, or the meanings and implications of what is seen on the ground."[129]

When CARE's generally overworked staff had to choose what to do with their time, many prioritized spending time in the office writing reports to headquarters and donors, a key formal accountability routine, over field visits and discussions with beneficiaries and partners.[130] The people who spent the most time with the communities that CARE worked with tended to be the lowest staff on the totem pole. In other words, the people who had the most direct influence on the quality of a project and its impact on the Burundian population had the least authority in the organization. Several of these field coordinators – staff

---

[124] Interviews with CARE staff members C2, Bujumbura, March 24, 2009; and C3, Bujumbura, June 9, 2009. Project outputs refer to the actual things that a project does – train people, distribute supplies, build things – not the outcome or effect of these activities.

[125] Interviews with CARE staff member C2, Bujumbura, March 24, 2009; CARE staff member C24, June 10, 2009; CARE staff member C1, Bujumbura, June 8, 2009; and CARE staff member C5, Bujumbura, March 25, 2009.

[126] Interview with CARE staff member C2, Bujumbura, March 24, 2009.

[127] Interview with CARE staff member C4, Bujumbura, June 25, 2009.

[128] Interview with CARE staff member C4, Bujumbura, June 25, 2009.

[129] CARE Burundi, "A Journey of Empowerment," 8.

[130] Interviews with CARE staff members C24, Bujumbura, June 10, 2009; C18, Bujumbura, June 16, 2009; and C3, Bujumbura, June 9, 2009.

who were relocated to live directly with communities – complained that their managers were too preoccupied with writing reports and proposals to visit the field and see what was happening with the projects. In the words of one field coordinator:

When you ask how many field visits [our supervisors] make, they will say that they are too busy to come to the field. This really affects the work on the ground because people don't know what is happening and they don't understand what we are doing. We feel abandoned. It affects us psychologically. Theoretically, we are supposed to come to Bujumbura every Friday afternoon, but many people don't want to come because their supervisors never visit them and after a full week in the field they are exhausted and just want to go home.[131]

In spite of CARE Burundi's strong informal local accountability routines, country-office staff focused on responding to the formal accountability routines of their headquarters and donors. When the informal and formal accountability routines aligned, learning occurred. When they did not, formal accountability won out over informal local accountability. Country-office staff argued that any additional "learning" was the responsibility of CARE Burundi's Learning Team, not of each project.[132] A self-assessment of CARE Burundi's learning practices supported this conclusion:

The demands of CARE's projects and contractual obligations to donors do not leave much time for critical reflection. While CARE has made a concerted effort to embed learning into project agendas ... there are not yet clear and systematic policies and incentives that mandate staff to make time for analysis, sharing and learning. Without clear policies and an understanding of why reflective learning is essential, staff tend to leave responsibility for learning and reflection on the learning team.[133]

In spite of the challenges the office faced processing information that it received about its projects, its focus after 2003 on increased informal local accountability did make it a more effective organization.[134] According to one CARE Burundi staff member, "The difference between this office and other [CARE] offices is that it faces the normal challenges of any office – monitoring and evaluation, developing real partnerships – but instead of getting stuck in them, the office is able to address the challenges and move beyond them. It recognizes the pain and addresses it and then moves on."[135]

---

[131] Interview with CARE staff member C26, Bujumbura, June 4, 2009.
[132] Interview with CARE staff member C4, Bujumbura, June 25, 2009.
[133] CARE Burundi, "A Journey of Empowerment," 8.
[134] Interview with CARE staff member C1, Bujumbura, June 8, 2009.
[135] Interview with CARE staff member C10, Bujumbura, March 10, 2009.

Although CARE Burundi's emphasis on informal local accountability made it relatively effective at community-based empowerment, it did not make it an effective peacebuilder. Given limited time and resources, CARE Burundi's staff focused on the priorities of CARE USA, its donors, and the leadership of its office. Although these different actors prioritized peacebuilding for a short time after 2005, prioritization shifted to a focus on women's empowerment and community-based income-generating activities. This shift incentivized CARE Burundi's staff to pay attention to information that aligned with these formal accountability routines and discard the rest.

Formal Accountability Routines

In spite of CARE Burundi's strong investment in informal local accountability, its formal accountability routines always predominated, determining which informal information was listened to or discarded.

CARE Burundi depended primarily on short-term grants from donors to fund its projects. Unlike the BLTP, which had only two or three donors at a time, CARE Burundi often had many donors, and their associated formal accountability routines, to manage. CARE's dependence on grants led it to prioritize interaction with donors and headquarters over interaction with communities. Each donor had its own reporting requirements that it wanted CARE Burundi to fulfill and reports that it wanted CARE Burundi to write to show that it was doing so. To ensure that it had enough projects ongoing at any one time, CARE Burundi had to continuously prepare new project proposals. The office was also responsible for producing increasingly frequent, time-consuming reports to CARE USA to ensure compliance with its accounting standards.

CARE's dependence on grants, and the arduous formal accountability routines this dependence created, diminished the organization's capacity to adapt to the evolving context, supporting a key claim in the INGO literature.[136] According to one CARE Burundi staff person: "We are not very flexible because we live from grant to grant."[137] CARE Burundi could respond to a new context only if the funding was available; the organization became more focused on sustaining its existing projects, and the salaries of the staff they employed, than on responding to Burundi's evolving political and security context. One CARE Burundi staff member commented as follows:

---

[136] Cooley and Ron, "The NGO Scramble."
[137] Interview with CARE staff member C11, Bujumbura, June 8, 2009.

More time on downward accountability would ... allow the learning behavior to be more productive. We have tons of data but we can't process it. I don't have a work–life balance. No one who works for this organization in a senior position has. Downward accountability gives back more. It's more satisfying. The more we have upward accountability, the more burnout there is because it gives back less. Upward accountability is counterintuitive. Its purpose is downward accountability, possibly, but it actually creates less of that.[138]

CARE Burundi's formal accountability routines were determined both by CARE USA, which managed CARE Burundi from 2003 onward, and bilateral donors that gave CARE Burundi grants for specific projects. Unlike the BLTP, whose formal accountability prioritized peacebuilding, most of CARE Burundi's formal accountability routines prioritized poverty reduction and women's empowerment. Although McIlvaine established both peacebuilding and empowerment as the core priorities of CARE Burundi and succeeded in getting donors to fund a few specific peacebuilding projects, the peacebuilding focus quickly dissipated. CARE USA gave more attention to CARE Burundi's women's empowerment projects, providing technical assistance, training, and global publicity, and directing donors toward CARE Burundi to support their work in this area. The community-based empowerment focus won out, and CARE Burundi shifted its energy away from peacebuilding.[139]

One problem facing CARE Burundi was that CARE International was a multimandate organization. Stated one CARE staff member, "There is an identity issue for CARE. We think we can do anything and everything well. Because we are decentralized, we look more like a quilt."[140] Each CARE office selects its main area of focus. CARE Burundi was primarily focused on the development of women through community-based empowerment processes. It believed that it could "mainstream" peacebuilding throughout its activities, but it created few incentives for staff to do so.[141] Organizations learn and act in relation to targets, and peacebuilding and conflict sensitivity were not the main target for the majority of CARE Burundi's projects.[142] They were not the focus of CARE Burundi's formal accountability routines.

---

[138] Interview with CARE staff member C4, Bujumbura, June 25, 2009.

[139] Interviews with CARE staff members C10, Bujumbura, March 10, 2009; and C11, Bujumbura, June 8, 2009.

[140] Interview with CARE staff member C9, Bujumbura, March 20, 2009.

[141] International Alert, Saferworld, and FEWER, "Conflict Sensitive Approaches to Development, Humanitarian Assistance and Peacebuilding: A Resource Pack" (Africa Peace Forum/CECORE/CHA/FEWER/International Alert and Saferworld) (London: International Alert, Saferworld, and FEWER, 2004).

[142] Barbara Levitt and James G. March, "Organizational Learning," *Annual Review of Sociology* vol. 14, no. 1 (1988): 319–40.

Most CARE Burundi staff felt that conflict sensitivity and peace-building were in the realm of CARE Burundi's conflict advisor, not in their realm.[143] Project teams focused on achieving specific community development or empowerment aims, not on conducting conflict analysis in addition to everything else on their plate.[144] Most CARE staff and senior leadership did not really understand what conflict sensitivity or peacebuilding were.[145] If a project's donor did not prioritize conflict sensitivity or peacebuilding, the project team did not prioritize it.[146] The staff person assigned to help mainstream conflict sensitivity within CARE Burundi wielded little power and depended on the willingness of the project managers and staff to examine the conflict dimensions of programming.[147]

CARE UK is the office within CARE International mandated to support conflict sensitivity and peacebuilding throughout the federation.[148] In response to a request from the Burundi office, CARE UK provided funding and technical support to help CARE Burundi increase the conflict sensitivity of its programming and develop effective peacebuilding programming.[149] This support helped projects avoid creating conflict by applying the "Do No Harm" approach, but it did not turn these projects into peacebuilding projects that affected the conflict dynamics.[150] It was not enough to counterbalance the pull of CARE Burundi's formal accountability routines. After CARE UK withdrew most of its support from the Burundi office in 2009, any remnants of a peacebuilding focus left along with it. Mainstreaming conflict sensitivity and peacebuilding would have required support from CARE Burundi senior leadership to help create the institutional incentives for staff to integrate yet another priority into their projects. This type of buy-in of senior leadership would have also required support from CARE USA and key donors, prioritizing formal peacebuilding accountability that would incentivize CARE Burundi's leadership to focus on peacebuilding above other aims.

---

[143] Interview with CARE staff member C16, Bujumbura, June 8, 2009.
[144] CARE Burundi, "Learning from Peace and Conflict Monitoring (LCPM) Bi-Annual Narrative Report, November 2007–April 2008" (Bujumbura: CARE Burundi, April 2008).
[145] Interviews with CARE staff members C11, Bujumbura, June 8, 2009; and C16, Bujumbura, June 8, 2009.
[146] Interview with CARE staff member C16, Bujumbura, June 8, 2009.
[147] CARE Burundi, "Learning from Peace and Conflict Monitoring."
[148] CARE Burundi, "Learning from Peace and Conflict Monitoring."
[149] Interview with CARE staff member C2, Bujumbura, March 24, 2009.
[150] Interview with CARE staff member C8, Bujumbura, March 23, 2009.

Individual Country-Office Staff and Leadership

CARE Burundi's leadership and key country-office staff played a crucial role in the prioritization and focus of the office. Even though CARE Burundi depended on grants and was formally accountable to its headquarters and donors, its country-level leadership played a key role in determining how the office responded to and interpreted these formal accountability routines. The agency and influence of country-office leadership and staff are largely absent from most accounts of INGO behavior.[151]

CARE Burundi became a revered office within CARE International and among INGOs in Burundi in large part because of the leadership of Kassie McIlvaine, her successor, Michelle Carter, and key CARE Burundi staff.[152] Because CARE International is such a decentralized organization, country directors and senior staff have a great deal of freedom to shape the priorities of their office.[153] The freedom that CARE International's structure and approach gives to its country directors can lead to excellent or to highly flawed outcomes. The success and failure of these country offices, thus, relies on the capacity and vision of a handful of senior country-office leadership.[154]

The organizational change process that Kassie McIlvaine initiated in 2003 enabled CARE Burundi to articulate a new peacebuilding agenda for the organization that donors were eager to support. The intense organizational change process that the office underwent allowed it to question its overall approach, capacity, knowledge, and even the makeup of its staff and to alter these factors to more effectively pursue its new aims. In other words, the change process enabled the organization to undergo a high degree of organizational learning, or actions to reduce the gap between the country office's aims and outcomes. After this organizational change process, CARE Burundi maintained a relatively consistent approach until the arrival of a new country director in 2009, when the office underwent a different organizational change process.

CARE Burundi's staff played a crucial role in framing and shaping how the organization responded to Burundi's evolving context, the priorities of its headquarters, and the incentives offered by donors. Its senior staff prevented CARE Burundi from being a mere pawn of the preferences of donors and headquarters, as described by one of CARE Burundi's donors:

---

[151] Cooley and Ron, "The NGO Scramble."
[152] Interview with CARE staff member C10, Bujumbura, March 10, 2009.
[153] Interview with CARE staff member C10, Bujumbura, March 10, 2009.
[154] Interview with CARE staff member C12, via telephone, June 6, 2009.

CARE Burundi is one of the best offices that I have seen in CARE. There are challenges, but they have been smart in selecting donors. They have been smart in cultivating the relationships to certain donors and CARE International members, so they are now in a much better position to select or decide what kind of donors they want to collaborate with. You have probably met Kassie – she was very deliberate in doing this. She did this on purpose.[155]

These key senior staff individuals shaped how the office responded to formal accountability routines and even helped alter them, if only temporarily.

Conclusion

The behavior of the BLTP and CARE Burundi was almost perfectly juxtaposed. The BLTP was a peacebuilding learner for all but one phase under study and made important contributions to the transformation of Burundian institutions in each of these periods. CARE shifted from a stagnant player organization to a peacebuilding learner for only one phase, and then became a micro-adaptor. What explains the difference in the country-office behavior of these two INGOs?

The literature on INGOs focuses on the role played by formal accountability routines in determining INGO behavior. The predominant theories argue that because INGOs are dependent on donor funds, they are continuously running after donors and are subject to donor preferences.[156] As a result, the literature argues, INGOs are unable to set their own agenda or respond to the population. Instead, they are focused on the needs and preferences of their donors.[157] The behavior of the BLTP and CARE Burundi both supports and contradicts this theory. These INGOs were subject to the whims of donors at times, but they were able to shape donors' behavior and set an agenda that donors were eager to support at other times. In addition to adding much-needed nuance to existing theories of INGO behavior, these case studies demonstrate the importance of three additional factors in determining INGO behavior: the focus of formal accountability routines, informal local accountability routines, and the agency of key country-office staff.

Both the BLTP and CARE Burundi had atypical informal local accountability mechanisms for much of the period under study. Both of these organizations went beyond donor requirements to create informal local accountability routines, complementing what they viewed as

---

[155] Interview with CARE Burundi donor C12, Bujumbura, June 6, 2009.
[156] Cooley and Ron, "The NGO Scramble."
[157] Cooley and Ron, "The NGO Scramble."

the shallow downward accountability requirements of their funders. These informal processes enabled the BLTP and CARE Burundi to receive regular feedback and buy-in from the people they aimed to affect, the donors they wanted to fund them, and the politicians and other actors who could undermine or support their activities.

The major difference between the BLTP and CARE Burundi was the focus of their formal accountability routines. The BLTP consistently prioritized peacebuilding, whereas CARE Burundi, as a multimandate organization, iterated among humanitarian aid, peacebuilding, and development. Most analyses of INGOs paint formal accountability as destructive to the performance of INGOs. The BLTP case, however, shows that formal accountability can play an important role for INGOs by providing an external check on their work and enabling organizations to undergo a process of double-loop learning. Through this double-loop learning, which enables an organization to question its underlying assumptions, INGOs can question whether their country-level aims and activities remain relevant to the changing context.[158]

The CARE Burundi case shows that formal accountability routines can play an important role in determining the lessons that the organization learns from external assessments. Because CARE Burundi's formal accountability emphasized community-based development and women's empowerment, external assessments by headquarters and donors encouraged CARE to alter its behavior to more effectively pursue these development aims rather than peacebuilding aims.

The crucial role played by formal accountability in the behavior of both INGOs challenges the notion that one can mainstream "peacebuilding" or "gender," enabling the organization to address the causes of conflict or gender equality in all its activities. These cases show that mainstreaming succeeds only when the thing being mainstreamed is the organization's priority and is supported by its formal accountability routines.[159] In the end, staff must make choices about which information to pay attention to and which actions to take. The cases discussed in this chapter show that staff tend to focus on the priorities of their donors, their headquarters, and the country-level leadership. To mainstream a concept throughout an organization's activities, staff need to view the concept as the organization's top priority over other potential priorities.

---

[158] Argyris, *On Organizational Learning.*

[159] See also Mark A. Pollack and Emilie M. Hafner-Burton, "Mainstreaming International Governance: The Environment, Gender, and IO Performance in the European Union," *Review of International Organizations* 5, no. 3 (July 2010): 285–313.

Thus, it may be very difficult for an organization to function effectively as a truly multimandate organization.

The BLTP and CARE Burundi cases also show the crucial importance of country-level leadership in determining the behavior and performance of INGOs. Both organizations were led by entrepreneurial leaders who set the vision and direction for their organization. These leaders established strong informal local accountability systems to ensure that their organizations were grounded in the context that they sought to affect. These leaders were able to have a large impact on their organizations in part because both organizations were highly decentralized, as INGOs often are.

Rather than being pawns of donors, these leaders used their informal local accountability mechanisms and high-quality performance to position themselves as the best providers of key services that the donors wanted to support. Their investment in organizational change and high-quality programming, even if not incentivized by donors, encouraged donors to fund them. After 2005, donors in Burundi quickly shifted from focusing on peacebuilding to focusing on development, encouraging CARE Burundi to shift its focus toward development and leaving the BLTP without much funding for its peacebuilding efforts.

Scholarship on the INGO role in global governance views INGOs as less accountable than IOs, states, and firms.[160] The absence of formal ties to states, populations, or shareholders makes INGOs potentially more flexible and responsive to local institutions than other actors in global governance, however. INGOs have the potential to shift their approach in response to new funding opportunities and changes in the country environment. Contrary to the literature's claims, this flexibility is not always hijacked by donor interests and priorities.[161] Key country-office staff can play a crucial role in determining how the country office responds to its incentive structure and the country context.

The BLTP and CARE Burundi case studies show that the formal accountability routines of INGOs, like those of IOs and bilateral donors, do inhibit the degree to which INGOs can respond to the needs of the local populations that they aim to serve. But these cases also show that informal local accountability routines and entrepreneurial country-office staff can help INGOs achieve a high degree of local relevance and performance, at least temporarily. Furthermore, the BLTP case shows that accountability to donors can play a constructive role when it incentivizes INGOs to listen to the feedback they receive from diverse local

[160] Grant and Keohane, "Accountability and Abuses of Power in World Politics."
[161] Cooley and Ron, "The NGO Scramble"; and Ebrahim, "Accountability Myopia."

stakeholders and investigate their continued relevance to the country's changing context. By examining the behavior of two INGOs over time in one country, this chapter has provided a nuanced explanation for the variation in INGO performance, with significance for scholars and policy makers alike.

4 International Organizations in Peacebuilding: Globally Accountable, Locally Constrained

Nestled on the vast shores of Lake Tanganyika, the United Nations (UN) compound on the edge of Bujumbura, called Guantanamo by Burundians, was surrounded by high walls rimmed with razor wire. Armed guards were placed at each entrance. These seemingly impenetrable walls and guards kept out most Burundians and kept in most UN staff. With this degree of security, I expected to find a palace inside the gates. After making my way through multiple security checks, I saw rows of silver shipping containers, each one with a letter, a number, and a UN logo. There were hundreds of them. But these containers did not hold cars, supplies, or some illicitly trafficked good. They held UN staff and their desks, lamps, chairs, and filing cabinets. Hidden away behind the high walls, cut off from the hustle and bustle of Burundian life, were the UN staff members charged with reforming the country's political and security institutions in hopes of preventing Burundi from backsliding into war.

This chapter tells the story of two International Organizations (IOs) operating in Burundi between 1999 and 2014: the UN Development Programme's (UNDP) country office in Burundi, which I refer to as UNDP Burundi, and the four UN political and peacekeeping missions mandated by the UN Security Council, which I refer to collectively as UN Missions. Compared to the INGOs discussed in Chapter 3 that were able to create and sustain strong informal local accountability routines, the IO country offices discussed in this chapter were constrained by their formal accountability to UN member states, including to the Burundian government. While formal accountability to states may make IOs more globally accountable, it also makes it more difficult for them to be locally accountable to stakeholders beyond the central government.

I will refer to the four UN political and peacekeeping missions reviewed in this chapter interchangeably as UN peace operations and UN Missions. UN political missions are "United Nations civilian missions that are deployed for a limited duration to support Member States in good offices, conflict prevention, peacemaking and peacebuilding."[1] UN peacekeeping missions include both peacekeeping soldiers and UN civilian staff and are mandated to use force to keep a peace that has been agreed upon by political parties, or enforce peace that the warring parties are not yet willing to keep.[2] *Peace operation* is a term used to refer to the broad range of UN peacekeeping and political missions mandated by the UN Security Council. Even though UNDP Burundi and the four UN Missions are all part of the broader UN system, they have different accountability structures, bureaucratic routines, and mandates.

UNDP is directly accountable to the General Assembly through UNDP's executive board. The executive board is made up of thirty-six member states that serve on a rotating basis, overseeing the organization's global policy work and its country offices in more than 170 countries.[3] UNDP is funded entirely from voluntary contributions – funding provided solely on a voluntary, as opposed to a mandatory, basis by UN member states and other multilateral organizations.[4]

UN political and peacekeeping missions are part of the UN Secretariat. They are mandated by the UN Security Council and managed by the Department of Peacekeeping Operations (DPKO), the Department of Field Support, and the Department of Political Affairs (DPA).[5] They are financed by the mandatory contributions that each UN member state is required to give to the organization, known as assessed contributions. Although the UN Security Council mandates UN political and peacekeeping missions, the UN General Assembly finances them based on recommendations of the Advisory Committee on Administrative and Budgetary Questions and the Fifth Committee of the General Assembly.[6]

By comparing two separate organizations within a broader IO – the United Nations – this chapter reveals the diversity that exists in IO

---

[1] UN Secretary-General, "United Nations Political Missions: Report of the Secretary-General" (New York: United Nations, 2014), 2, accessed December 21, 2017, http://goo.gl/gRgzbr.

[2] "What Is Peacekeeping?" UN peacekeeping website, accessed November 9, 2015, http://goo.gl/qYc29.

[3] "Executive Board," UN Development Programme (UNDP) website, accessed November 9, 2015, http://goo.gl/0zmGkp.

[4] "Income and Expenditures," UNDP website, accessed November 9, 2015, http://goo.gl/rF81HA.

[5] "Department of Field Support," UN peacekeeping website, accessed November 9, 2015, http://goo.gl/q1srq; and "Overview," UN Department of Political Affairs website, accessed November 9, 2015, http://goo.gl/OmMgwi.

[6] "About the Fifth Committee," UN General Assembly website, accessed November 9, 2015, http://goo.gl/U17h3p; and "Peacekeeping Budgets," UN website, accessed November 9, 2015, http://goo.gl/2PyMI9.

Table 4.1. *UN Missions and UNDP Country-Office Behavior*

	Phase I: Jan. 1999– Oct. 2001	Phase II: Nov. 2001– Nov. 2003	Phase III: Dec. 2003– Aug. 2005	Phase IV: Sept. 2005– Apr. 2009	Phase V: May 2009– May 2010	Phase VI: June 2010– Apr. 2014
UN Missions	Peacebuilding Learner	Sovereignty Reinforcer	Peacebuilding Learner	Sovereignty Reinforcer	Sovereignty Reinforcer	Sovereignty Reinforcer
UNDP	Stagnant Player	Stagnant Player	Stagnant Player	Sovereignty Reinforcer	Sovereignty Reinforcer	Stagnant Player

country-office behavior, even among country offices that are part of the same overall IO and operating in the same country (as is depicted in Table 4.1). Even though their behavior varies, the UN Missions to Burundi and UNDP Burundi share a similar constraint that is a result of the broader structure of the UN: the Burundian government, as a UN member state, is one of the principals to whom the country offices are accountable. This formal accountability to the Burundian government pre-positioned these two organizations to be sovereignty reinforcers. At several points in time, however, the UN Missions became peacebuilding learners because innovative country-level staff created informal local accountability routines that grounded their interventions in the needs of a broader group of Burundian stakeholders beyond the Burundian government. UN Missions are mandated to protect international peace and security and, thus, always have peacebuilding, in the broadest sense of the term, as their top priority. UNDP Burundi, on the other hand, prioritized formal accountability for development for all but two phases and lacked informal local accountability for the entire period under study. It iterated between stagnant player and sovereignty reinforcer behavior.

This chapter starts with a synthesis of the scholarship on IO country-office performance, highlighting its focus on the preferences of principals and organizational pathologies. Although this literature explains some of the factors that determine the country-office behavior of IOs, the two case studies presented here show that this literature does not fully explain this behavior. Both rationalist and constructivist scholars underestimate the amount of independent decision-making power that an IO country office holds.

IO Behavior: Rationalist and Constructivist Explanations

Most studies of international institutions have focused on IOs, as opposed to INGOs or bilateral aid agencies. Because of the role that

IOs play in furthering and moderating state interests, IOs have served as fertile ground for academic and policy debates about the evolving nature of international relations. Scholars argue that IOs are the most account-able organizations in world politics because they are directly accountable to states.[7] States establish and design IOs.[8] They sit on IO governing boards and make decisions about IO goals, budgets, staffing, and change processes.[9] The analysis has been limited, however, to IO headquarters-level behaviors and processes, without an examination of the potential for differentiated outcomes at the IO country-office level.

The rationalist IO scholarship assumes that the preferences of IO member states determine the behavior of the entire IO bureaucracy, including country offices. This scholarship describes the member state (s) as the principal(s) to whom the IO, or agent, is accountable.[10] In these principal–agent relationships, the "principal" temporarily delegates authority to an "agent" to act on her behalf.[11] "Delegation is a condi-tional grant of authority from a *principal* to an *agent* that empowers the latter to act on the behalf of the former."[12] The principal holds the agent accountable through a delegation chain. The delegation chain describes the link between the original principal and the number of levels down in the IO bureaucracy to which authority is delegated. The core require-ment of principal–agent theory is that the principal possesses information about the agent's behavior and mechanisms to control this behavior. In the terminology used here, this information is transferred through formal accountability routines.

Principal–agent scholarship posits that the longer the delegation chain – for example, between UN headquarters in New York and a country office in Bujumbura – the more difficult it is for states to control the behavior of IO bureaucrats.[13] But even in cases of long delegation chains, rationalist scholars argue, IO member states will seek to use their authority to ensure that staff within the IO bureaucracy do not behave in

---

[7] Ruth W. Grant and Robert O. Keohane, "Accountability and Abuses of Power in World Politics." *American Political Science Review* 99, no. 1 (April 4, 2005): 29–43.

[8] Barbara Koremenos, Charles Lipson, and Duncan Snidal, "The Rational Design of International Institutions," *International Organization*, vol. 55, no. 4 (2001): 761–99.

[9] Daniel L. Nielson, Michael J. Tierney, and Catherine E. Weaver, "Bridging the Rationalist–Constructivist Divide: Re-Engineering the Culture of the World Bank," *Journal of International Relations and Development* 9, no. 2 (2006): 107–39.

[10] Darren Hawkins, David Lake, Daniel Nielson, and Michael Tierney (eds.) *Delegation and Agency in International Organizations*, (Cambridge, UK: Cambridge University Press, 2006).

[11] David A. Lake, "Delegating Divisible Sovereignty: Sweeping a Conceptual Minefield," *Review of International Organizations* 2, no. 3 (2007): 219–37.

[12] Hawkins et al., *Delegation and Agency*, 7.

[13] Lake, "Delegating Divisible Sovereignty."

ways that member states do not condone.[14] According to David Lake, "It is precisely because bureaucrats are self-seeking with guile and often possess hidden information or take hidden actions that principals will seek to design carefully oversight and control mechanisms to limit opportunism by their agents."[15]

This scholarship seems to overlook some of the implications of power in world politics. All states do not wield the same power, and many disenfranchised populations are completely unrepresented in IOs by states or by civil society advocates.[16] According to Grant and Keohane:

Accountability in world politics is inextricably entangled with power relationships ... Those who would hold power-wielders to account need power themselves. Weak actors – including small, poor countries in the Global South and, more, their often disenfranchised publics – lack the capacity systematically to hold powerful actors accountable.[17]

For IOs engaged in international peacebuilding, these power relations present tensions among the three main sources of legitimacy for IOs: "whether they serve the interests of their member states, the purposes for which they were established, and evolving standards of benefits and harms."[18] Serving the (often competing) interests of its member states may not enable the IO to fulfill its original purpose (be it international peace and security, development, or humanitarian aid) or the evolving best practice (for example, conflict sensitivity). IO scholarship does not explain how IO accountability and legitimacy affect IO country-office behavior or outcomes.

Constructivist scholars posit that bureaucratic dysfunction, practices, and shared cultural frames determine IO country-office behavior.[19] These scholars argue that IOs will become swept up in organizational pathologies that inhibit them from efficiently fulfilling their mandates.[20] Path dependency, even if it is the wrong path, is much less costly in terms of people's time and possibly their careers than attempting to alter

---

[14] Hawkins et al., *Delegation and Agency*.

[15] Lake, "Delegating Divisible Sovereignty," 222.

[16] Grant and Keohane, "Accountability and Abuses of Power in World Politics," 37.

[17] Grant and Keohane, "Accountability and Abuses of Power in World Politics," 40.

[18] Grant and Keohane, "Accountability and Abuses of Power in World Politics," 37.

[19] Michael Barnett and Martha Finnemore, *Rules for the World: International Organizations in Global Politics* (Ithaca, NY: Cornell University Press, 2004); and Séverine Autesserre, *Peaceland: Conflict Resolution and the Everyday Politics of International Intervention* (Cambridge, UK: Cambridge University Press, 2014).

[20] Michael Barnett and Martha Finnemore, "The Politics, Power, and Pathologies of International Organizations," *International Organization* 53, no. 4 (1999): 699–732; and Barnett and Finnemore, *Rules for the World*.

the behavior of these bureaucratic behemoths.[21] At the country level, scholars argue, IOs have organizational practices and cultures that inhibit IOs, and other international actors, from building local-level peace.[22]

Considered together, rationalist and constructivist theories of IO behavior present a picture of IOs as puppets of their principals, cultures, and bureaucratic pathologies with little capacity to circumvent these constraints or alter their behavior.[23] The two IO cases discussed in this chapter show that bureaucratic pathologies, organizational culture, and the preferences of principals play a role in country-office behavior but do not determine it. Instead, the behavior of IO country offices is explained by the interaction between the accountability routines created by their principals and headquarters-level bureaucrats, and the way in which IO country-office staff navigate, interpret, and circumvent these routines.

UN Political and Peacekeeping Missions to Burundi

This section focuses on four consecutive UN peace operations in Burundi deployed between 1999 and 2014: the UN Office in Burundi (UNOB), the UN Operation in Burundi (ONUB), the UN Integrated Office in Burundi (BINUB), and the UN Office in Burundi (BNUB). These missions moved between sovereignty reinforcer and peacebuilding learner behavior, as depicted in Table 4.2.

The Trajectory of UN Peace Operations in Burundi

UN Missions are mandated to protect international peace and security, which means that peacebuilding is always their priority, giving them formal peacebuilding accountability. The UN Missions discussed here show that even though UN Missions tend to exhibit sovereignty reinforcer behavior, innovative country-office staff can, at times, establish

---

[21] Barnett and Finnemore, *Rules for the World*; and Paul DiMaggio and Walter Powell, "The Iron Cage Revisited: Institutional Isomorphism and Collective Rationality in Organizational Fields," in *The New Institutionalism in Organizational Analysis*, ed. Paul DiMaggio and Walter Powell (Chicago: Chicago University Press, 1991), 64–5.

[22] Séverine Autesserre, "Hobbes and the Congo: Frames, Local Violence, and International Intervention," *International Organization* 63, no. 2 (2009): 249–80; Autesserre, *Peaceland* ; and Séverine Autesserre, *The Trouble with the Congo: Local Violence and the Failure of International Peacebuilding* (Cambridge, UK: Cambridge University Press, 2010).

[23] Tana Johnson's work, which examines the role of international bureaucrats in IO design, presents an exception to this trend. See Tana Johnson and Johannes Urpelainen, "International Bureaucrats and the Formation of Intergovernmental Organizations: Institutional Design Discretion Sweetens the Pot," *International Organization* 68, no. 1 (2014): 177–209.

Table 4.2. *United Nations Missions to Burundi (UNOB, ONUB, BINUB, BNUB)*

	Informal Local Accountability	Formal Peacebuilding Accountability	Country Office Type	Result
UN Missions Phase I: Jan. 1999– Oct. 2001 **(UNOB)**	Yes	Yes	Peacebuilding Learner	Actions to reduce gap between peacebuilding aims and outcomes
UN Missions Phase II: Nov. 2001– Nov. 2003 **(UNOB)**	No	Yes	Sovereignty Reinforcer	Actions to align with peacebuilding preferences of principals
UN Missions Phase III: Dec. 2003– Aug. 2005 **(UNOB and ONUB)**	Yes	Yes	Peacebuilding Learner	Actions to reduce gap between peacebuilding aims and outcomes
UN Missions Phase IV: Sept. 2005– Apr. 2009 **(ONUB and BINUB)**	No	Yes	Sovereignty Reinforcer	Actions to align with peacebuilding preferences of principals
UN Missions Phase V: May 2009– May 2010 **(BINUB)**	No	Yes	Sovereignty Reinforcer	Actions to align with peacebuilding preferences of principals
UN Missions Phase VI: June 2010– Apr. 2014 **(BNUB)**	No	Yes	Sovereignty Reinforcer	Actions to align with peacebuilding preferences of principals

informal local accountability routines that help the UN Mission to overcome its allegiance to the host government and enable it to respond to
the broader interests of the state and society. The UN Mission's vacilla-
tion between sovereignty reinforcer and peacebuilding learner behavior
points to, on the one hand, the influence that Mission leadership and key

staff can have on the performance of UN political and peace operations and, on the other hand, to the difficulties faced by even the most innovative staff in creating sustainable change in the UN's slow and unwieldy bureaucracy.

Peacebuilding was a top priority for the UN Missions in Burundi. Between 2007 and 2014, two UN Missions – BINUB and BNUB – received funding from the UN Peacebuilding Fund (PBF). In fact, compared to other recipient countries, Burundi was one of the top recipients of funding from the PBF, with contributions amounting to over US $55 million. Burundi was also a top priority country of the UN Peacebuilding Architecture.

The UN Peacebuilding Architecture was established in 2005 and comprises the UN Peacebuilding Commission (PBC), the PBF, and the Peacebuilding Support Office (PBSO). It aims to promote a coherent international approach to peacebuilding by focusing the efforts of all UN organizations and member states toward a country's peacebuilding priorities under the leadership of the Special Representative of the Secretary-General (SRSG) and his or her national counterparts. The UN Peacebuilding Fund provides an important source of support for UN peace operations to implement peacebuilding activities, which are mandated by the UN Security Council but are not covered by the assessed contributions provided to the UN Mission by the UN General Assembly.

UN peace operations have three primary lines of accountability. The first is to the UN Security Council, which mandates the peace operation and requires regular reports from the peace operation. The second is to either DPKO or DPA at headquarters, depending on whether or not the peace operation is a peacekeeping or a political mission, respectively. The third is to the government of the country to which the peace operation is deployed, often termed the "host government." The host government must grant its consent for the deployment of peace operations that are Chapter VI½ and below, which included UNOB, BINUB, and BNUB but not ONUB, which was Chapter VII. The host government can declare UN personnel persona non grata, requiring them to leave the country.

UN Missions benefit from organizational change that happens through the creation of each new mission. Ideally, a peace operation is designed and created for a particular moment in a country's war-to-peace trajectory, providing the opportunity to start off locally relevant. But goals and mandates that are developed via consensus among UN Security Council members and UN bureaucrats at headquarters are inevitably partly irrelevant to the needs of a specific country, particularly one undergoing a high degree of instability and change. Furthermore, an assessment of Security Council mandates for UN peacekeeping operations shows that missions are given the same general mandate, challenging the assumption that each mission is targeted toward the specific needs and capacities of a conflict-affected country.[24] As discussed in this chapter, the degree to which a UN peace operation achieves its Security Council mandate is not systematically monitored by the UN Security Council or even DPA or DPKO.

These factors – the vague mandate, the lack of performance measures, and the potentially competing interests among Security Council members – combine to give a UN peace operation a great degree of autonomy. Contrary to many critiques of UN peace operations as being highly rigid organizations, the accountability structure of these organizations leaves a great deal of potential authority for the head of the peace operation – the SRSG or the ERSG and her or his key staff – to influence the behavior and peacebuilding effectiveness of the peace operation. This section considers the different behaviors of the UN peace operations in Burundi and then assesses the role that informal local accountability, formal accountability, and key peace operation staff played in the behavior of the peace operation and its achievement of its peacebuilding aims.

UNOB: From Peacebuilding Learner to Sovereignty Reinforcer
The UN Office in Burundi (UNOB) was a political mission. It was active in Burundi during Phases I, II, and part of III, although the analysis here focuses on Phases I and II. UNOB did not have peacekeepers but was, instead, mandated to use its diplomatic capacity to help create the political framework for peace in Burundi. UNOB was established in November 1993 to support peace and reconciliation after the assassination of Burundi's first democratically elected president on October 21, 1993. The Security Council had called for the establishment of UNOB "as a confidence-building measure, to facilitate the restoration of constitutional rule, and to promote peace and reconciliation."[25] In 2004, UNOB's mandate was ended to make way for the deployment of a long-awaited UN peacekeeping mission, the Organization of the United Nations Operation in Burundi (ONUB).

Between 1993 and 2004, UNOB transitioned from a small but effective political office to a slightly larger office that was unable to carry out

---

[24] Charles Petrie and Adrian Morrice, "Scrambling and Pulling Together the UN's Civilian Capacities in Conflict-Prone States," in *Peacebuilding Challenges for the UN Development System*, ed. Stephen Browne and Thomas G. Weiss (New York: Future United Nations Development System, 2015), 39–52.

[25] UN Secretary-General, "Letter Dated 2 November 1999 from the Secretary-General Addressed to the President of the Security Council," UN Security Council, S/1999/1138 (November 5, 1999), accessed December 21, 2017, http://goo.gl/qyTSCs.

the most basic tasks necessary to oversee the implementation of Burundi's Arusha Agreement. UNOB transitioned from peacebuilding learner in Phase I to sovereignty reinforcer in Phase II. During this entire time, UNOB had formal peacebuilding accountability routines; its whole purpose was to advance the peace process. What changed over time was UNOB's leadership and staff. UNOB's leadership determined whether or not it had informal local accountability routines and, in turn, whether or not it took regular actions to reduce the gap between its peacebuilding aims and outcomes, or learn. In the subsequent paragraphs, I discuss these changes in UNOB's behavior, beginning in 1999.

After the regional embargo on Burundi was lifted in January 1999, the UN Secretary-General indicated that because Burundi's peace process had entered a "critical stage," he would upgrade the level of the UNOB by appointing the head of the office, Cheikh Tidiane Sy, as his representative in Burundi. Sy was subsequently replaced by Jean Arnault in May 2000.[26] Both Sy and Arnault followed Burundi's peace process closely and conducted informal negotiations with the various parties. To support their negotiations, Sy and Arnault created strong informal local accountability routines with key political actors and observers across the political spectrum.

These diplomatic efforts were the extent of UNOB's activities at the time, and Jean Arnault, in particular, was a highly engaged and effective interlocutor with the FNL rebel group.[27] Within his limited diplomatic means, Arnault took regular actions to reduce the gap between his aim of facilitating a peace agreement with the FNL and the actual incremental outcomes of his negotiation efforts. He and his staff made UNOB a peacebuilding learner. Nonetheless, UNOB did not succeed in integrating the FNL into the peace process, which depended on many factors beyond its control.

After the inauguration of Burundi's transitional government on November 1, 2001, the UN Secretary-General again increased the size and standing of the UNOB to support the important mandate of its new head of office, SRSG Berhanu Dinka. The UNOB and SRSG Dinka were mandated to lead the Implementation Monitoring Commission (IMC) of the Arusha Agreement. As discussed in Chapter 2, the IMC was a central mechanism in Burundi's Arusha peace agreement with a

---

[26] Secretary-General, "Letter Dated 12 April 1999 from the Secretary-General Addressed to the President of the Security Council," United Nations Security Council S/1999/426, April 15, 1999, accessed December 14, 2011, http://daccess-ods.un.org/access.nsf/Get? Open&DS=S/1999/426&Lang=E&Area=UNDOC.

[27] Interviews with UNOB staff and observers, Bujumbura, 2000 and 2001.

far-reaching mandate: "Follow up, monitor, supervise, coordinate, and ensure the effective implementation of all of the provisions of the Agreement."[28] Because the Arusha Agreement left many crucial issues unresolved, such as a ceasefire agreement with the rebel groups and the exact organization of the new armed forces, the IMC was charged with addressing the most difficult issues that years of peace talks had been unable to resolve.

Unfortunately, by most accounts, Dinka was not up to the task of leading this important body.[29] He convened meetings, but did not attempt to wield political pressure or even produce a clear scorecard of which aspects of the Arusha Agreement were implemented. Most international and Burundian observers felt that Dinka was more concerned with his upcoming retirement than with engaging in the proactive diplomacy required to facilitate the implementation of the Arusha Agreement.[30] As IMC meetings dragged on with little real progress, it was seen as another venue for Burundian politicians to collect per diems.[31] According to a UN staff member, the "IMC was supposed to govern the government, but instead has fallen into the same political games as the government."[32]

Under SRSG Dinka's leadership, UNOB became a sovereignty reinforcer. It responded to the preferences of its principals at UN headquarters and in the Burundian government by organizing meetings. However, it did not create strong informal local accountability with the diverse stakeholders in the IMC or take clear actions to reduce the gap between its ambitious mandate and its actual outcomes, or learn. The absence of informal local accountability meant that UNOB had little real information about its actual outcomes with which to learn.

Of course, even if UNOB under SRSG Dinka had been a peacebuilding learner, there is no guarantee that the IMC would have fulfilled its mandate. But, most observers argued that SRSG Dinka did not try. He did not take significant actions to attempt to reduce the gap between UNOB's aims and outcomes. The UNOB case, therefore, points to the crucial role played by a UN peace operation's SRSG and other senior staff in determining whether a peace operation will simply carry out its

---

[28] Parties to the Arusha Agreement, "Arusha Peace and Reconciliation Agreement for Burundi" (Arusha, Tanzania, August 28, 2000), 88–9.

[29] Interviews with international and UN staff members, Bujumbura, July 2002.

[30] Interview with diplomat, Bujumbura, August 7, 2002; and informal discussions, Bujumbura, August–October 2002.

[31] Interview with observer Bujumbura, August 1, 2002.

[32] Interview with UN staff member, Bujumbura, August 8, 2002.

preplanned tasks or whether it will innovate and learn, attempting to make the UN's ambitions of global peace and security into a local reality.

ONUB: Peacebuilding Learner

On May 21, 2004, Security Council Resolution 1545 mandated a Chapter VII peacekeeping mission in Burundi: the United Nations Operation in Burundi (ONUB). ONUB was deployed the following month. Its SRSG, Carolyn McAskie, arrived in Bujumbura on June 25, 2004, less than five months before the scheduled end of Burundi's transitional phase. Before the scheduled date of the end of the transition phase – October 31, 2004 – Burundians, with ONUB's support, were supposed to accept a new constitution, organize elections at six different levels, disarm and reintegrate ex-combatants into society, and implement key judicial and security reforms.[33]

Even though a UN peacekeeping mission was called for in the Arusha Agreement, the Security Council had been reluctant to deploy the mission without a ceasefire.[34] It had taken over three years of advocacy by the Burundian government, rebel groups, and international actors to convince the Security Council to mandate a UN peacekeeping operation in Burundi. In 2004, UN Secretary-General Kofi Annan commented that ONUB "opened a new chapter in the Burundi peace process."[35]

ONUB was a peacebuilding learner. It created strong informal local accountability routines, had strong formal peacebuilding accountability, and took regular actions to reduce the gap between its peacebuilding aims and outcomes. These efforts delivered clear dividends. ONUB succeeded in pushing Burundians to end the transitional phase, albeit a year later than planned, and helped to organize Burundi's first post-conflict elections, ushering in a new period of hope for most Burundians and observers.

By the time ONUB arrived, Burundians, international donors, and key regional states were eager for a forceful UN presence. They argued that they needed international political leadership that could unite the plethora of fragmented international actors operating in Burundi, help

---

[33] See ICG, "Elections in Burundi: The Peace Wager," Africa Briefing series, no. 20 (Brussels: ICG, December 9, 2004), accessed December 20, 2017, www.crisisgroup .org/africa/central-africa/burundi/elections-burundi-peace-wager.

[34] Parties to the Arusha Agreement, "Arusha Peace and Reconciliation Agreement for Burundi" (Arusha, Tanzania, August 28, 2000), 94.

[35] UN Department of Public Information, Peace and Security Section, "ONUB: United Nations Operation in Burundi" (New York: United Nations, 2006), http://goo.gl/ vAUlha.

advance Arusha's stagnating institutional reforms, and negotiate an ever-elusive ceasefire with the remaining rebel groups.[36] ONUB did not disappoint.[37]

ONUB's leadership team brought continuity with the previous UN and African Union missions, strong relationships with UN headquarters and with the South African mediation team, and a deep knowledge of Burundi's history and political actors.[38] The well-selected leadership team helped the mission start off with a high degree of understanding of the context. SRSG McAskie was a former Canadian government official with an impressive UN pedigree who had also served as a member of the facilitation team for the Arusha peace process.[39] McAskie and her deputies used their background knowledge and connections to establish strong informal local accountability with diverse

[36] Conversations with members of Burundian civil society and members of the international community, Bujumbura, June 2004.

[37] ONUB was given a Chapter VII mandate, permitting it to use "all necessary means" to fulfill its mandate, which had three broad strands. First, ONUB was to support the organization of democratic elections prior to the deadline for the end of the transitional government, October 31, 2004. The Security Council deemed the legislative elections to be the most crucial. Second, ONUB was to support security sector reform, including disarmament and demobilization of former combatants who would not be integrated into the armed forces, and support for the reestablishment of confidence among the former rebels and members of the Burundian Army that would be integrated into a new, combined National Defense Force. Third, ONUB was given the general Chapter VII peacekeeping tasks of enabling humanitarian access, protecting civilians, returning refugees and IDPs, and ensuring the protection of UN staff and assets. See UN Security Council, "Resolution 1545 (2004) Adopted by the Security Council at Its 4975th Meeting, on 21 May 2004" (New York: United Nations, May 21, 2004), para. 5, accessed December 21, 2017, http://unscr.com/en/resolutions/1545.

[38] McAskie was given two deputies. The Principal Deputy Special Representative of the Secretary-General (PDSRSG) position went to Nureldin Satti, who had been the deputy SRSG to Berhanu Dinka since 2002. Satti brought significant knowledge of the political context and created continuity between UNOB and ONUB. Ibrahima D. Fall, formerly with UNICEF, became the quadruple-hatted deputy SRSG, with responsibility for the development and humanitarian communities as Resident Coordinator, Humanitarian Coordinator, and Resident Representative of UNDP. In addition, Welile Nhalpo was made the head of ONUB's Political Section. Nhalpo had been working on the Arusha peace process on the behalf of South Africa since the mid-1990s, and brought to the mission not only close ties with South Africa but a wealth of knowledge and relationships with Burundi's political actors. This relationship between South Africa and the UN was further strengthened by the continuation of the African Mission in Burundi (AMIB) Force Commander Major-General Derrick Mgwebi as ONUB's force commander. See Stephen Jackson, "The United Nations Operation in Burundi (ONUB): Political and Strategic Lessons Learned" (New York: United Nations, 2006), 8.

[39] Trudeau Foundation, "Carolyn McAskie," accessed December 21, 2017, www.trudeau foundation.ca/fr/communaute/carolyn-mcaskie; United Nations, "Carolyn McAskie Appointed Special Representative of Secretary-General for Burundi," press release (New York: United Nations, May 26, 2004), accessed December 21, 2017, http://goo.gl/3dSWfC.

stakeholders on Burundi's political scene, ensuring that they were able to take the pulse on the rapidly evolving context and find inroads for political compromise.

Through these diplomatic efforts, ONUB helped to ensure the appointment of the National Independent Electoral Commission in August 2004, the adoption of an electoral calendar, the drafting of an interim constitution, and on October 20, 2004, the acceptance of a law declaring that the draft constitution was the interim constitution until a constitutional referendum took place.[40] Once the final timetable for the elections was established, ONUB deployed all its relevant resources to support the organization of Burundi's first post-conflict elections, managing to help organize six rounds of elections in a six-month period. Stephen Jackson reports that ONUB's electoral unit was under intense pressure from various political actors to either speed up or slow down the electoral process, which he said ONUB resisted deftly, focusing on the "technical" nature of its work.[41] In all his interviews, Jackson wrote, "the single point of agreement from all was that ONUB's role in the conduct of elections in Burundi has been 'unimpeachable' and an 'immeasurable contribution' to the cause of peace."[42]

ONUB played a crucial role in advancing Burundi's war-to-peace transition through Phase III, in large part because of its senior leadership's focus on maintaining strong informal networks that provided regular feedback on the environment and the effectiveness of efforts. In other words, the leadership established strong informal local accountability routines with key politicians and civil society actors and kept strong connections to key regional and Western states that were closely involved in Burundi's transition. The support of the Security Council and DPKO, the section of the UN bureaucracy that managed ONUB, helped. The Security Council and DPKO were both focused on ensuring a smooth end to Burundi's transitional period, which helped to create the formal peacebuilding accountability to headquarters and member states necessary to support McAskie and her team's political maneuvering. These factors enabled ONUB to take regular actions to reduce the gap between their peacebuilding aims and outcomes, or learn, in a highly complex political context and even organize the 2005 elections, signaling the success of the Arusha peace process.

[40] UN Security Council, "Second Report of the Secretary-General on the United Nations Operation in Burundi" (New York: United Nations, November 15, 2004), 1–3, accessed December 21, 2017, http://goo.gl/lSwHFK.
[41] Jackson, "The United Nations Operation in Burundi (ONUB)," 18.
[42] Jackson, "The United Nations Operation in Burundi (ONUB)," 19.

BINUB and BNUB: Sovereignty Reinforcers with Pockets of Learning

The UN Integrated Office in Burundi (BINUB) – deployed in Phase IV and V – and the UN Office in Burundi (BNUB) – deployed in Phase V and VI – were sovereignty reinforcers with pockets of learning.[43] They had formal peacebuilding accountability but were unable to establish informal local accountability across their organizations. BINUB, in particular, was nonetheless able to establish several pockets of informal local accountability within several key peacebuilding projects.

BINUB's informal local accountability, combined with its formal peacebuilding accountability, led key peacebuilding project teams to take regular actions to reduce the gap between their peacebuilding aims and outcomes, or learn. Several of these projects, in turn, made clear and important contributions to achieving their peacebuilding aims. As I discuss in more detail in the subsequent sections, BINUB and BNUB were able to establish these pockets of learning because of the initiative of key staff and the support of the Secretary-General's country representatives, who were willing to break or bend formal accountability routines to enable peacebuilding learning.

After August 2005, ONUB had little time to bask in the glory of Burundi's successful elections. Soon after President Pierre Nkurunziza's inauguration, his government began to try to weaken the international community's influence on Burundian politics. The new Burundian government made the argument that peace had already been built in Burundi and that the election of Nkurunziza as the first postwar president proved this.[44] Now it was time for the Burundian government to consolidate this peace with the support of development assistance from donors. The new government perceived ONUB as a threat to its sovereignty. It believed that McAskie and her deputies favored Burundi's former political leadership, specifically FRODEBU, with which ONUB had worked closely since its deployment.[45]

---

[43] The data for this analysis are drawn from interviews and archival document review conducted explicitly for this book as well as from interviews, participant observation, and review of internal documents conducted for two large evaluations that this book's author conducted for the UN Peacebuilding Fund of BINUB's and BNUB's peacebuilding interventions. For more information, see Susanna P. Campbell, "Independent External Evaluation: Peacebuilding Fund Projects in Burundi" (Bujumbura: Integrated UN Mission to Burundi, 2010), accessed December 21, 2017, http://goo.gl/0lAQwG; Susanna P. Campbell et al., "Independent External Evaluation: UN Peacebuilding Fund Project Portfolio in Burundi, 2007–2013" (New York: UN Peacebuilding Support Office, 2014).

[44] Interview with UN staff member U01, Bujumbura, June 6, 2009.

[45] Jackson, "The United Nations Operation in Burundi (ONUB)," 23.

On January 1, 2007, BINUB was deployed. The UN Secretariat and the Burundian government had agreed to establish BINUB after prolonged negotiations in which the Burundian government insisted that BINUB be a political mission, without any peacekeeping troops.[46] The government also wanted McAskie out as SRSG. To avoid being formally declared persona non grata, McAskie left Burundi before the mission ended. Her deputy, Nureldin Satti, took over as acting SRSG until the mission closed on December 31, 2006.[47] Satti was subsequently declared persona non grata before the end of his term. This experience led the mission leadership to recommend that, "when a transition comes to an end, it may be prudent to consider replacing the entire echelon of top UN Mission management in order to promote the confidence of the post-transition government that it is dealing with an entirely new dispensation."[48]

BINUB was unique in several respects.[49] BINUB was charged with supporting and empowering the Burundian government to build strong and just postwar institutions, responding to the Burundian government's request for the UN to play a less intrusive role. In Resolution 1719 establishing BINUB, the Security Council reaffirmed its "strong commitment to the sovereignty, independence, territorial integrity and unity of Burundi," and emphasized "the importance of Burundian ownership of peacebuilding, security and long-term development."[50] BINUB largely refused to take credit for its own actions but ensured that the government and other Burundian partners received accolades.[51] In fact, BINUB

---

[46] Gilbert Fossoun Houngbo and Ramadhan Karenga, "Consultations between the Government of Burundi and the United Nations on the Post-ONUB Period, Bujumbura, 21–24 May 2006" (Bujumbura: United Nations, May 24, 2006), 21–4.

[47] Peace and Security Section of the Department of Public Information, "ONUB: United Nations Operation in Burundi – Facts and Figures" (New York: United Nations, 2007), accessed December 21, 2017, https://peacekeeping.un.org/mission/past/onub/facts.html.

[48] Jackson, "The United Nations Operation in Burundi (ONUB)," 10.

[49] The Security Council mandate gave BINUB the responsibility to strengthen national capacity to mitigate conflict, strengthen good governance, promote freedom of the press, consolidate the rule of law, support the implementation of the comprehensive ceasefire agreement, help develop a plan for security sector reform, help demobilize and reintegrate former combatants, reduce the proliferation of small arms and light weapons, promote and protect human rights, help establish transitional justice mechanisms, and increase coordination by the government and within the international community, particularly for the fulfillment of the Poverty Reduction Strategic Plan. See UN Security Council, "Resolution 1719 (2006) Adopted by the Security Council at Its 5554th Meeting, on 25 October 2006" (New York: United Nations, October 25, 2006), 2–4, accessed December 21, 2017, http://unscr.com/en/resolutions/1719.

[50] UN Security Council, "Resolution 1719 (2006)," 1.

[51] Youssef Mahmoud, "Partnerships for Peacebuilding in Burundi: Some Lessons Learned," unpublished paper, October 15, 2009; and interviews with UN staff members 1.36, Bujumbura, June 25, 2009; 1.70, Bujumbura, March 19, 2009; and 1.20, Bujumbura, June 22, 2009.

played such a "supportive" role that many UN member states and Burundian civil society wondered what BINUB actually did.[52]

BINUB was one of the first two UN Missions to receive funding from the PBF, which is the first and only financing source in the UN solely designated to fund peacebuilding activities. Burundi was selected as one of the first two countries on the UN Peacebuilding Commission's agenda, largely due to the urging of McAskie, who became the head of the UN's new Peacebuilding Support Office after she left ONUB. The PBF resources enabled BINUB to implement a range of peacebuilding tasks that were outlined in its Security Council mandate, but for which it did not receive funding from the Fifth Committee of the General Assembly, the body responsible for allocating UN assessed contributions to peace operations. These assessed contributions normally funded aspects of peace operations concerned with advising the government, deploying and maintaining peacekeepers, offering short-term training, or implementing short-term, quick impact projects, not the implementation of more complex peacebuilding projects.

BINUB was an integrated mission, which meant that the entire UN presence in the country came under the direct authority of the representative of the Secretary-General to Burundi. Youssef Mahmoud was given the title of Executive Representative of the Secretary-General (ERSG), signaling that he was the Resident Coordinator of the UN development agencies in Burundi, the Humanitarian Coordinator of all humanitarian efforts in the country, and the Secretary-General's representative in the country.

The integration of the UN system at the country level was held up by the UN Secretariat as an organizational ideal in post-conflict contexts where both the UN country team (UNCT) – composed of all UN development and humanitarian agencies operating in that country – and a peace operation were present. The UN argued that integration of the UN at the country level enabled it "to maximize the individual and collective impact of the UN's response, concentrating on those activities required to consolidate peace."[53] In fact, BINUB was viewed by many in UN headquarters as the perfect manifestation of this new policy, leading to numerous study missions from UN headquarters.[54] The Burundian government supported this approach, arguing that the integration of the

---

[52] Interviews with UN staff, donors and civil society members, including 1.10, New York, May 6, 2009; UO2, Bujumbura, March 24, 2009; and 1.33, Bujumbura, June 18, 2009.

[53] UN Secretary-General, "Decision of the Secretary-General: 25 June Meeting of the Policy Committee" (New York: United Nations, 2008), 1.

[54] Interviews with UN staff members: 1.12, Bujumbura, June 24, 2009; 1.15, Bujumbura, June 9, 2009.

UN into one structure would reduce the leverage that the UN had over the government as well as the number of actors that the government had to manage.[55] Paradoxically, it seems to have had the opposite effect.

The integrated structure of BINUB and its focus on peacebuilding, backed by PBF funding, enabled ERSG Mahmoud to wield a high degree of political power with UN staff in Burundi, international donors there, and the Burundian government.[56] Using the political networks of key staff members who had also worked for UNOB and ONUB, Mahmoud was able to gather excellent intelligence about the evolving political situation and relay messages to key political actors.[57] He established strong informal local accountability with a broad range of key Burundian and international actors. One international observer commented that Mahmoud was always better informed than other international actors and that BINUB was a powerful force with which to contend: "Mahmoud is the director of the orchestra."[58]

Out of the eighteen peacebuilding projects that BINUB implemented, however, only seven helped to transform local Burundian institutions in line with the projects' peacebuilding aims.[59] The other eleven projects failed to contribute to their peacebuilding aims, instead largely strengthening the capacity of a Burundian state that was increasingly authoritarian, corrupt, and engaged in extrajudicial killings.[60] The seven projects that made a clear and important contribution to their peacebuilding aims were unique in three respects.

First, each project established its own informal local accountability routines, forming strong relationships with key stakeholders across the government, in civil society, and in the international donor community. For example, the Cadre de Dialogue Project, on which the Burundi Leadership Training Program (BLTP) was a subcontractor, created strong informal local accountability routines. The Cadre de Dialogue project facilitated dialogue sessions between Burundi's political parties and civil society

[55] Interview with UN staff member UO1, Bujumbura, June 6, 2009.
[56] Interviews with key BINUB staff members and members of the international community, Bujumbura, 2009.
[57] Interview with BINUB staff member 1.12, Bujumbura, May 31, 2009.
[58] Interview with observer O17, Bujumbura, June 16, 2009.
[59] Susanna P. Campbell, "Independent External Evaluation: Peacebuilding Fund Projects in Burundi" (Bujumbura: Integrated UN Mission to Burundi, 2010), accessed December 21, 2017, http://goo.gl/0lAQwG.
[60] Human Rights Watch, *Pursuit of Power: Political Violence and Repression in Burundi.* New York, NY 2009; International Crisis Group (ICG), "Burundi: Ensuring Credible Elections," *Africa Report* (Brussels: International Crisis Group, February 17, 2010), accessed December 21, 2017, www.crisisgroup.org/africa/central-africa/burundi/burundi-ensuring-credible-elections.

during a tense period in which the political parties were at a deadlock in parliament. The Cadre de Dialogue created an internal evaluation group made up of members of its dialogue sessions. After each dialogue session, this group would assess the effectiveness of the session and advise BINUB staff on how to address deficiencies and build on strengths.[61] The Cadre de Dialogue project was housed in the Ministry of Good Governance and was co-run by a director from the UN and a director from the ministry. This allowed its staff to escape BINUB's razor-wire-rimmed compound and relate on a daily basis to a wide range of stakeholders in the Burundian government, civil society, and to other international and national actors who were unwilling or unable to take the time to enter BINUB's fortress or to pay the taxi fare required to get there.[62]

Second, each of BINUB's successful peacebuilding projects was led by individual staff members who were committed to achieving the peace-building aims and willing to work around the barriers in the UN system and the Burundian government. These staff did not share any particular type of training or background, but they did share a commitment to persevering through numerous organizational and environmental bar-riers in the pursuit of peacebuilding. They were willing, moreover, to break or bend rules within the UN in order to get things done.

Third, each of these projects received strong support from ERSG Mahmoud and his top deputies, giving project staff freedom to take risks and navigate the UN's unyielding bureaucratic procedures and create pockets of learning where effective peacebuilding projects could be implemented. With the support of the ERSG and his core staff, the successful peacebuilding projects were altered and adapted to ensure that they maintained their relevance to the changing context. They were jointly conceived, designed, implemented, and monitored by BINUB and the Burundian government. There was a high degree of ownership and buy-in from all sides. These projects were not without fault – they could have been much more cost-effective, but, compared to others, they did create noticeable and important changes in Burundian institutions.[63] For example, the projects helped improve the relationship between the general population and the military, unblock deadlocks in the parliament, and increase accountability for perpetrators of human rights abuses.[64]

In January 2010, the Burundian government requested that Mahmoud leave the country on the grounds that he was biased in favor of the

---

[61] Interview with UN staff member, 1.42, June 17, 2009.
[62] Interview with UN staff member, 1.42, June 17, 2009.
[63] Campbell, "Independent External Evaluation: Peacebuilding Fund Projects in Burundi."
[64] Campbell, "Independent External Evaluation: Peacebuilding Fund Projects in Burundi."

National Independent Electoral Commission and against the government. The government apparently wanted a weaker UN presence during the 2010 election cycle. Burundi's 2010 elections led to the withdrawal of almost all the opposition political parties and the almost complete domination of the CNDD-FDD at all levels and sectors of government. A UN Security Council press release that month summarized the situation: "Despite the deep divide among political actors over the elections and the fact that a single party will dominate the political landscape for the next five years, it is remarkable that neither of those factors has led to the return of large-scale violence, as has been widely feared."[65] As Chapter 2 explained even if there was not an immediate outbreak of violence after the 2010 elections, the political and security situation was tense and many politicians from opposition parties fled the country.

At the beginning of 2011, even though the political and security situation in Burundi was steadily deteriorating, and in response to pressure from the Burundian government, the Security Council downgraded the UN peace operation presence, this time to a small political mission called Office of the UN in Burundi, known by its French acronym, BNUB. BNUB was mandated by the Security Council to strengthen judicial independence, promote inclusive political dialogue, support the establishment of transitional justice mechanisms, promote and protect human rights, ensure that all economic strategies in Burundi had a focus on peacebuilding and equitable growth, and support Burundi's chairmanship of the East African community.[66] Unlike its predecessor, BNUB was not programmatically integrated with UNDP Burundi. Its SRSG was in charge of the political process, and the deputy SRSG was focused on development and humanitarian programming with a relatively apolitical lens.

BNUB implemented a series of community-level peacebuilding activities, but many of these activities were largely detached from the broader political context. They resembled the standard development and humanitarian activities that the UNDP, UN High Commissioner for Refugees (UNHCR), the Food and Agriculture Organization (FAO), and other UN specialized agencies implemented in each country where they worked. Even though these activities were funded by the UN PBF and given the overall label of peacebuilding projects, they did not lead to

[65] UN News Centre, "Burundi Outlook Good 'in Many Regards' as It Turns to Economic Development – UN," December 9, 2010, accessed December 21, 2017, http://goo.gl/88WWu8.
[66] UN Security Council, "UN Security Council Resolution 1959," December 6, 2010, accessed December 21, 2017, www.un.org/en/ga/search/view_doc.asp?symbol=S/RES/1959(2010).

clear changes in local institutions or behaviors.[67] They did not target key political institutions nor did they have a clear sustainable positive effect on the lives of Burundians most affected by the violent conflict. In the words of one beneficiary of BNUB's peacebuilding activities: "I do not see how giving goats to this avenue can consolidate peace in Burundi."[68]

BNUB's peacebuilding activities had a positive effect on the relationship between some former combatants and their communities, but most beneficiaries questioned the reach and sustainability of this effect. Furthermore, like some of the unsuccessful peacebuilding activities implemented by BINUB, several of BNUB's peacebuilding projects actually did harm, increasing conflict between local members of the FNL and CNDD-FDD and further isolating some of the most vulnerable Burundians whom the programs were designed to help. Unlike BINUB, BNUB did not benefit from the integration of the mission under the political leadership of the ERSG. As a result, the peacebuilding projects that the members of the UNCT implemented lacked formal peacebuilding accountability and were instead focused primarily on fulfilling each UNCT member's humanitarian or development mandate.

Unlike BINUB's successful peacebuilding projects, which were built on strong informal networks and innovative informal local accountability approaches, BNUB's peacebuilding projects lacked strong feedback from the populations and communities that they aimed to serve, focusing instead on the opinions of the government ministries with whom they worked. This led the associated UN staff to take actions to reduce the gap between their aims and activities with the preferences of their principals, both at headquarters and their interlocutors in the Burundian government, rather than with the preferences of the broader group of Burundians that their peacebuilding projects aimed to serve.

Explaining UN Mission Behavior

The four UN peace operations described here had formal accountability that prioritized peacebuilding, broadly defined, as articulated in their Security Council mandates. These peace operations varied, however, in the degree to which their head of office – the SRSG or ERSG – embraced

---

[67] For a full description and assessment of BNUB's peacebuilding projects, see Susanna P. Campbell et al., "Independent External Evaluation: UN Peacebuilding Fund Project Portfolio in Burundi, 2007–2013" (New York: UN Peacebuilding Support Office, 2014).

[68] Interview with Burundian community member 3g, December 3, 2013, cited in Campbell et al., "Independent External Evaluation: UN Peacebuilding Fund Project Portfolio in Burundi, 2007–2013," 28.

and proactively pursued this mandate. The peace operations also varied in the degree to which the SRSG or ERSG supported the creation of informal local accountability routines that enabled the organization to receive regular feedback on its peacebuilding activities. The variation in the approach of the peace operation leadership and the presence or absence of informal local accountability routines influenced the degree to which a particular operation was able to take regular actions to reduce the gap between its peacebuilding aims and outcomes and, as a corollary, the likelihood that it would achieve its peacebuilding aims.

Informal Local Accountability

The four UN peace operations discussed in this section had varying degrees of informal local accountability. UNOB initially had strong informal local accountability, but this dissipated under the leadership of SRSG Dinka. ONUB had strong informal local accountability throughout most of the mission, during which it focused on achieving a peaceful end to Burundi's transition period. BINUB had some pockets of informal local accountability, but was unable to instill this approach in all its activities. BNUB established informal local accountability only in relation to its diplomatic initiatives, not in relation to the community-based peacebuilding projects that it implemented.

Among the four peace operations, the activities that contributed to their peacebuilding aims in Burundi had one common feature: strong informal local accountability routines that ensured that the operation received regular feedback from a broad range of Burundian and international stakeholders. These informal local accountability routines also enabled the UN to delegate informal authority to a representative group of Burundian stakeholders to advise the operation during the implementation process.

For example, BINUB's Cadre de Dialogue project brought together Burundi's political parties for a dialogue process that would have been impossible in parliament because of political jockeying and deadlock. The staff of the Cadre de Dialogue project regularly consulted with the full spectrum of political actors both within and outside government to ensure buy-in for their project and to adapt it to the current political dynamics. Cadre de Dialogue staff did not confine themselves to interfacing with their government counterparts; they included civil society and opposition parties in their dialogue sessions and gave participants the power to influence the future direction of these sessions.

Informal local accountability routines for other BINUB projects included subcontracting a local human rights NGO to regularly assess the reform of Burundi's National Intelligence Services, the chief architect of torture and extrajudicial killings in Burundi. The continued funding for BINUB's reform project with the National Intelligence Services was contingent on a positive report from this local human rights NGO. Other successful construction-focused projects, such as in the rehabilitation of the army barracks, established more direct feedback from participants who were directly involved in the implementation of the project. In these ways, BINUB involved local stakeholders in the implementation of peacebuilding projects and gave these local actors the authority to incrementally assess the success of a project and influence its implementation.

These informal local accountability routines, however, were not directly compatible with the formal procedures that governed the UN bureaucracy, including those of UNDP and DPKO. For example, BINUB staff members who wanted to create informal local accountability routines had to figure out workarounds, often with high transaction costs. It would have been easier and less time consuming for staff simply to implement their projects as designed and follow existing procedures without having to develop informal local accountability mechanisms. This is what most of BINUB's projects did. Nonetheless, the pockets of learning created through strong informal local accountability, formal peacebuilding accountability, and the support from the ERSG and his core team enabled some of BINUB's peacebuilding projects to contribute to key changes in Burundi's political and security institutions.

One BINUB staff member summarized the challenges that the UN faced when trying to innovate in this way:

When you see how many people in New York are aggressive about Mahmoud and anyone who tries to do things differently, you see that we kill our own innovators. So, we end up being a very routine-based organization. I mean, look at Mahmoud. He is the SRSG, and he has a lot of latitude to do things differently. But imagine if you were a national staff or lower-level UN manager. You try and do something innovative and you are out. Making a career in the UN is not necessarily about performing better or having a better impact on the issues you are supposed to work on, it is mingling and fitting into the minimum standard established by the organization.[69]

Formal Accountability Routines

As discussed earlier, there are three primary lines of formal accountability for UN peace operations: (1) accountability to the Security Council for fulfilling the mandate of a peace operation; (2) accountability to the UN bureaucracy in New York; and (3) accountability to the host

---

[69] Interview with UN staff member 1.14, Bujumbura, 2009.

government. Each of these accountability lines influenced the behavior of the UN peace operations deployed in Burundi.

The formal peacebuilding accountability routines to the UN bureaucracy in New York – reporting practices, communication with supervisors or desk officers, and procurement practices – connected each mission with the UN Security Council, DPKO, and DPA and incentivized each operation to prioritize peacebuilding in Burundi in line with its Security Council mandate. But neither the Security Council, the UN Peacebuilding Support Office that oversaw the PBF, nor the DPA or DPKO ensured that BINUB implemented high-quality peacebuilding activities. These headquarters entities conducted general conflict analyses of Burundi's evolving context and selected peacebuilding activities that corresponded to the needs identified in the analysis, but they did not pay attention to how the activities were implemented.[70] As one UN staff member commented:

We are accountable to the United Nations organization not to the people we are supposed to serve. That's the thing. A doctor or a physician is evaluated based on the number of people he or she helps recover. Us, you could work in Afghanistan and people continue to die and you get promoted.[71]

The four UN Missions' formal accountability routines incentivized country-office staff to focus on whether or not project money was spent, not whether activities contributed to the type of change the missions sought in Burundi's institutions. The formal routines and procedures that governed people's day-to-day behavior discouraged staff from leaving their compound to meet with key partners in government, much less civil society members or the people whom their activities would affect.[72] UN staff spent most of their time writing reports or updates for headquarters and coordinating with other UN entities or international donors.[73] BINUB, for example, monitored the implementation of different projects according to a long, color-coded list of percentages of funds that each project had spent, with no indication of which funds had been

---

[70] Interviews with UN staff members: 1.28, Bujumbura, June 25, 2009; 1.37, New York, May 5, 2009; 1.40, Bujumbura, June 19, 2009; 1.41, Bujumbura, June 31, 2009.

[71] Interview with UN staff member 1.14, Bujumbura, June 2009.

[72] Interviews with UN staff members: 1.20, Bujumbura, June 22, 2009; 1.41, Bujumbura, June 24, 2009; 1.20, Bujumbura, June 22, 2009; 1.45, Bujumbura, November 29, 2009; October–November 2009 interviews for Campbell, "Independent External Evaluation: Peacebuilding Fund Projects in Burundi."

[73] Interviews with UN staff: 1.44, Bujumbura, November 3, 2009; 1.45, Bujumbura, November 29, 2009; 1.40, Bujumbura, June 19, 2009; 1.70, Bujumbura, March 19, 2009; 1.71, Bujumbura, March 25, 2009; 1.41, Bujumbura, May 31, 2009.

spent or whether the activities had achieved their intended outcome.[74] As one UN staff member described, the UN peace operations did not track or measure their success:

We don't measure our success. People report project results, or outputs, not outcomes or impact. They do not even know what an outcome or impact is. They do not know the difference. And they have no real information. They say what they hope for, but not what they actually achieve, and with no real data.[75]

Another UN staff person expressed understanding about the reluctance of peace operations to monitor their outcomes and assess their successes and failures, particularly when their mandates were so ambitious:

[We] need to maintain member state support. We do not openly criticize because it has grave consequences. For example, if BINUB were to say that they could not achieve their very complicated mandate, then posts could be cut. If BINUB could not deliver on a specific piece of its mandate, posts could be cut by results-based budgeting process. Then, BINUB would lose that capacity and couldn't work in that area.[76]

UN peace operation staff prepared inputs for the Secretary-General's reports that listed the contribution of the different activities they implemented, but often without any evidence to justify the extent of the mission's contribution.[77] Most staff implementing peacebuilding projects funded by the UN PBF simply implemented the projects as designed.[78] Once the Burundian government and the UN Secretariat had approved each peacebuilding project, the UN largely viewed implementation as a technical activity that did not require political oversight or adaptation to an evolving context. One person who designed projects commented that the people implementing BINUB's less successful projects, those without pockets of learning, did not realize that they had to make these projects their own and alter them in response to the evolving context.[79] Without the realization that a project might need to be adapted, organizational learning is not possible.

It took BINUB two years to staff its Joint Monitoring and Evaluation Unit, and the staff were mostly junior and had little experience with monitoring and evaluation for peacebuilding or conflict-sensitive

---

[74] Participant observation of UN meeting, Bujumbura, November 6, 2009.
[75] Interview UN staff member 1.12, Bujumbura, May 5, 2009.
[76] Interview with UN staff member 1.9, New York, May 6, 2009.
[77] Interviews with UN staff members: 1.37, New York, May 5, 2009; 1.41, Bujumbura, May 31, 2009.
[78] Campbell, "Independent External Evaluation: Peacebuilding Fund Projects in Burundi."
[79] Interviews with UN staff members: 1.20, Bujumbura, March 22, 2009; 1.45, Bujumbura, November 29, 2009; 1.44, Bujumbura, November 3, 2009.

programming.[80] As a result, for the vast majority of their work, BINUB and BNUB lacked systematically valid data about outcomes, preventing them from even attempting to learn from successes and failures. Projects monitored the goods bought, the meetings and trainings organized, and the money spent, assuming that these outputs would have an impact on Burundi's institutions.[81]

For UNOB and ONUB, the outcomes sought had been so clear and information about them so widely available – the Arusha Agreement signed or not, the constitution revised or not, peaceful elections held or not – that the organizations had plenty of data about whether or not they had achieved their goals. BINUB and BNUB, however, aimed to achieve much more incremental change in Burundi's institutions, calling for a higher degree of monitoring and more widespread informal local accountability routines to determine whether or not these outcomes were being achieved.

The reports and code cables that UN Mission staff wrote to the Secretary-General and the Security Council were rarely examined or mapped against the operations' Security Council mandate.[82] Instead, the majority of the interactions between UN headquarters and the peace operation were made up of day-to-day communication between the SRSG or ERSG and the country desk officer at DPA or DPKO. The desk officer for a particular country occupies a much lower staff rank than the SRSG or ERSG, which created the potential for tension when the desk officer attempted to tell the SRSG or ERSG what to do.[83]

The integration of the UN system in Burundi under the ERSG during BINUB further complicated BINUB's accountability routines.[84] Even though the various UN organizations in Burundi were integrated under the ERSG's overall leadership, the accountability routines and incentive mechanisms remained separate.[85] The various UN organizations in Burundi – UNDP; the UN International Children's Emergency Fund (UNICEF); the UN High Commissioner for Refugees (UNHCR); the World Health Organization (WHO); FAO; the World Food Program

[80] Interviews with UN staff members: 1.17, Bujumbura, June 7, 2009; 1.40, Bujumbura, June 19, 2009.
[81] Interview with UN staff member 1.41, Bujumbura, May 31, 2009.
[82] Interviews with UN staff members: 1.46, New York, February 26, 2010; 1.37, New York, May 5, 2009; 1.47, New York, October 26, 2010; 1.14, Bujumbura, June 3, 2009; 1.11, New York, May 6, 2009.
[83] Interviews with UN staff members: 1.28, Bujumbura, June 25, 2009; 1.71, Bujumbura, March 25, 2009.
[84] Interviews with UN staff members, including UO3, Bujumbura, June 1, 2009.
[85] Interviews with UN staff members, including 1.15, Bujumbura, June 9, 2009; 1.18, Bujumbura, June 11, 2009; 1.16, Bujumbura, June 7, 2009.

(WFP); the UN Population Fund, the UN Development Fund for Women; United Nations Educational, Scientific and Cultural Organization (UNESCO); the Joint United Nations Programme on HIV/AIDS (UNAIDS); the Office of the High Commissioner for Human Rights (OHCHR); the Office for the Coordination of Humanitarian Affairs (OCHA); International Labor Organization (ILO); UN-Habitat – were all primarily accountable to their separate governing boards at headquarters, not to the ERSG.[86] The three integrated sections (Security Sector Reform and Small Arms, Justice and Human Rights, and Peace and Governance) were made up of staff from the different UN entities – DPKO, DPA, UNDP, and OHCHR. Even though they were housed in the same office and worked to implement the same operational plans, these staff held contracts with their parent organizations and were, consequently, also accountable to separate entities. The aims of the separate entities that made up BINUB's integrated mission were often incompatible with BINUB's aims.

At their best, the integrated units in BINUB helped to bridge the knowledge gap among those who were mandated to prevent the reemergence of violent conflict in Burundi (i.e., DPKO), those who had been working on the political dimensions of the Burundian peace process for more than a decade (i.e., DPA), and those who had the operational capacity to implement projects (i.e., UNDP, UNHCR, OHCHR).[87] At their worst, the integrated units were consumed by multiple different requirements of the different headquarters entities that they reported to and undermined by the reluctance of the Burundian government to support their efforts.

BINUB's ERSG and his senior leadership team lacked both the time and the institutional incentives to ensure that the entire integrated mission worked toward shared peacebuilding priorities.[88] Several staff commented that BINUB's integration and the resulting collaboration among staff from different UN agencies, funds, programs, departments, and offices were highly tenuous and seemed like they might unravel at any moment.[89]

---

[86] BINUB, "Stratégie intégrée d'appui des Nations Unies à la consolidation de la paix au Burundi: 2007–2008" (Bujumbura: United Nations, 2006); and UN Peacebuilding Commission, "Strategic Framework for Peacebuilding in Burundi" (New York: United Nations, July 30, 2007).

[87] Interviews with UN staff, including UO3, Bujumbura, June 1, 2009; 1.17, Bujumbura, June 7, 2009; 1.23, Bujumbura, June 19, 2009; 1.32, Bujumbura, November 18, 2009; 1.44, Bujumbura, November 3, 2009.

[88] Campbell, "Independent External Evaluation: Peacebuilding Fund Projects in Burundi."

[89] Interviews with UN staff, including 1.17, Bujumbura, June 7, 2009; 1.15, Bujumbura, June 9, 2009; UO3, Bujumbura, June 1, 2009.

The relationship between the UN Missions and the Burundian government also influenced the peace operations' behavior. Burundi's post-2005 government was willing to use its status as a UN member state to attempt to control the UN peace operations deployed on its territory. By asking three subsequent representatives of the Secretary-General to leave – McAskie, Satti, and then Mahmoud – the Burundian government signaled that it was willing to use the levers at its disposal to ensure that the UN Missions did not pose too great a threat to its interests.

The government's formal leverage was relatively blunt. It could threaten to kick out the head of the peace operation, or it could advocate for the closure of the mission. More informally, however, the Burundian government could refuse to work with the UN, collaborate on activities, or advance the joint agenda. The UN Missions in Burundi could not carry out their work without the direct cooperation of the Burundian government, which was a necessary partner in the implementation of most aspects of the mandates.

The authority that the Burundian government held over BINUB and BNUB, in particular, led these UN Missions to focus an enormous amount of energy on maintaining good relations with the Burundian government, at times to the detriment of their relations with civil society, opposition leaders, and international actors. The high degree of collaboration between BINUB and the Burundian government contributed to BINUB's unwillingness to openly and honestly examine the contribution that it was making to Burundi's evolving war-to-peace transition. The Burundian government was allergic to critique, and BINUB was adamant that it should be perceived as supporting the government, not imposing anything on it.[90] For example, BINUB sought to couch the results of a 2009 external evaluation of BINUB's peacebuilding projects commissioned by the PBF in soft language that would be more palatable to its government counterparts.[91] BINUB feared that overt criticism would create more tension in an already fraught UN–government relationship.

In sum, in a bureaucracy where staff are assessed on the basis of how much money they spend, there was little direct incentive to do the time-consuming work of developing the informal local accountability routines that would have helped a project achieve the intended effect on the evolving context. And yet, UNOB, ONUB, and BINUB developed these routines, although BINUB only developed pockets of informal local accountability. These UN Missions were able to create this informal

---

[90] Interviews with UN staff, including 1.71, Bujumbura, May 25, 2009; 1.36, Bujumbura, June 25, 2009.
[91] Participant observation, Bujumbura, November 2009.

local accountability when key staff, with the support of the mission leadership, circumvented the formal accountability routines that stood in the way.

Individual Country-Office Staff and Leadership

The leadership of each UN peace operation in Burundi played a crucial role in the operation's behavior, its organizational learning, and the degree to which it contributed to its peacebuilding aims. According to a former UN SRSG:

> Diplomatic representatives [of states] have a lot more constraints than we do. They have a very clear policy that they have to follow. With the UN, the policy directives are not nearly as clear and, on the ground, you have an enormous amount of freedom to determine what you do and what you focus on.[92]

Each representative of the Secretary-General deployed to lead a peace operation in Burundi helped determine the priorities of the operation, picking among a long list of relatively vague tasks in the Security Council mandate.[93] In the absence of strict performance measures from headquarters, each SRSG or ERSG could choose how to "spin" his or her successes and failures in the draft reports her or his staff prepared for the Secretary-General. These same draft reports were used as the basis for the reports that the Secretary-General released about each country in which its peace operations were deployed, meaning that the SRSG or ERSG could decide what to include and exclude in the Secretary-General's reports about the missions they ran. Consequently, it mattered a lot where and how the SRSG's or ERSG's energy and resources were directed. The SRSG's or ERSG's priorities and approach greatly influenced the politics, policy, and contribution of the peace operation.

In the UNOB case, SRSG Dinka's seeming unwillingness to push Burundian parties to implement the most feasible aspects of the Arusha Agreement may have helped prolong Burundi's transitional period. Dinka's passive approach is in contrast to the proactive efforts of his predecessor, SRSG Arnault, and his successor, SRSG McAskie. Both Arnault and McAskie actively negotiated with Burundi's political parties, and Arnault also engaged with its rebel groups. McAskie developed such strong relationships with key players in Burundi's transitional government that once Nkurunziza was elected, he deemed her to be too close to his political competitors and requested that she leave her post.

---

[92] Interview with former UN SRSG, Brussels, 2015.
[93] Interviews with UN staff members, including 1.60, via telephone, March 11, 2009; 1.14, Bujumbura, June 3, 2009; 1.71, Bujumbura, March 25, 2009; O25, Geneva, July 2008.

ERSG Mahmoud took a very different approach than McAskie had taken. Mahmoud required his staff change the way the UN related to the Burundian government to be more respectful of their sovereign authority to govern.[94] BINUB's approach was to facilitate action by the government and to refuse to take credit for it, which left many observers questioning what BINUB was doing with all of the resources it received from UN headquarters.

As the head of BINUB, Mahmoud was also in charge of overseeing the projects funded by the PBF, as well as the political leadership and coordination of the entire UN system operating in Burundi. Given the large number of staff he had to manage and the ongoing negotiations he was engaged in with the FNL, Mahmoud had limited resources to dedicate to overseeing BINUB's peacebuilding projects or to encouraging projects to develop informal local accountability. He focused much of his energy on the Cadre de Dialogue project, specifically by talking to high-level political figures; showing his commitment to the overall process; and helping unblock barriers within the UN bureaucracy, which resisted such a project. Most of the rest of BINUB's projects were implemented as designed, with neither informal local accountability nor regular action by the project staff to reduce the gap between their peacebuilding aims and their intermediary outcomes, or learn.

Mahmoud's expulsion by the Burundian government in 2010 influenced the staff morale at BINUB and reduced staff willingness to take risks. They no longer had a champion, nor were they enthusiastic about working with a government that had been so disrespectful to their boss, particularly when he had been so deferential to the government.[95] After Mahmoud left, BINUB staff began to leave gradually, searching for their next posting before the inevitable closure of BINUB.[96] BNUB's subsequent SRSGs controlled significantly fewer resources than Mahmoud or McAskie had, and they were no longer in charge of the UN specialized agencies in Burundi, but only of the steadily downsized UN political mission, BNUB. BNUB's SRSGs focused their attention on maintaining their relationships with the Burundian government and attempting to facilitate dialogue among Burundian political parties, to which the government was increasingly hostile. BNUB's SRSGs discouraged any innovations, including informal local accountability, by staff that might undermine its fragile relationship with the Burundian government.

---

[94] Interviews with UN staff members, including 1.36, Bujumbura, June 25, 2009.
[95] Interviews with UN staff members, including O22, 2010.
[96] Interviews with observer O23, 2011.

Burundi's UN peace operations show that attention of senior mission leadership is necessary to help staff bypass potential organizational and bureaucratic barriers to the achievement of their peacebuilding aims. When achievement of a peacebuilding aim required that the peace operation create informal local accountability, work faster than usual, collaborate more than usual, or take more politically informed action than usual, the intervention of senior leadership was necessary to show the bureaucrats in the peace operation, headquarters staff, and other UN organizations that these exceptions had the leadership's approval and were, indeed, worthy priorities.

Intervention by senior leadership was necessary not only to remove potential bureaucratic roadblocks, but also to provide incentives and accountability to the staff implementing these initiatives. This speaks to the UN's incentive structure, where positive visibility is an important indicator of success in an organization that does not have other clear measures of success.[97] In this large, impersonal bureaucracy, personal relationships and connections are an important determinant of individual success.[98] The senior leadership of UNOB, ONUB, and BINUB who were committed to peacebuilding helped encourage and reward innovative peacebuilding programming by their staff, reinforcing formal peacebuilding accountability. Those who were not committed to innovative peacebuilding and informal local accountability, or who could not demonstrate this commitment across all peacebuilding activities, reduced the incentives for positive peacebuilding performance.

The time and energy of the senior leadership of a UN peace operation are naturally limited. There are often many more activities than a peace operation's SRSG or ERSG or his or her deputies are able or willing to oversee. "Forgotten" projects may be more likely to veer off target, do harm, or, at least, not have a positive impact. The senior leadership of UN peace operations plays a crucial role in conveying the importance of formal peacebuilding accountability routines and in incentivizing country-office staff to create the informal local accountability routines necessary to learn in a changing context. Given that the time of a peace operation's senior leadership is limited, it is likely that even some of the best UN Missions will be sovereignty reinforcers with only pockets of learning.

---

[97] Interviews with UN staff members, including 1.10, New York, May 6, 2009; 1.90, New York, March 12, 2009; 1.71, Bujumbura, March 25, 2009.

[98] Interviews with key UN staff members, including 1.71, Bujumbura, March 25, 2009.

Conclusion: UN Political and Peacekeeping Missions to Burundi

The UN peace operations deployed to Burundi made crucial contributions to the country's war-to-peace transition. They facilitated vital changes in Burundi's political and security institutions that enabled its war-to-peace transition to advance. In spite of these successes, the UN peace operations also had multiple peacebuilding failures in Burundi. They failed to carry out the tasks delegated to them. They implemented peacebuilding projects that did harm to Burundians. In their rush to spend the money allocated to them, they failed to learn and wasted precious resources. Even within one peace operation, such as BINUB, there was a high degree of variation in peacebuilding success and failure. Pockets of learning contributed to positive peacebuilding performance, while "business as usual" contributed to wasteful and irrelevant interventions.

When UN peace operations contributed to their peacebuilding aims, they possessed the two characteristics described in Chapter 1: informal local accountability and formal peacebuilding accountability. The leadership of the UN peace operation played a crucial role in interpreting this formal accountability and incentivizing informal local accountability. Like in INGOs, the role of country-office leadership seems to be particularly crucial in UN peace operations. Because of the relatively broad mandates provided by the UN Security Council and the fact that a peace operation's contribution to this mandate is not closely monitored, the SRSG or ERSG has leeway to decide on the trajectory and priorities of the peace operation. Rather than being one of the most constrained actors in global governance because of their allegiance to states, as the IO literature claims, the ambiguity inherent in IO mandates that are agreed upon by multilateral bodies, such as the Security Council, give individual country-office leadership and senior staff a high degree of potential agency to influence how the IO responds to the country context.

UNDP in Burundi

The United Nations Development Programme (UNDP) is a prominent actor in conflict-ridden countries. In most cases, it is in a country before violence erupts and will be there after it dissipates.[99] In 2001, the UNDP

---

[99] In addition to the research that I did in Burundi, the findings presented in this chapter are supported by the research and interviews that I did in 2012 for an internal review of UNDP's peacebuilding strategy; see Susanna P. Campbell and Lisa Schirch, "UNDP's Role in Peacebuilding: Issues and Strategies," Internal UNDP Report, September 17, 2012.

Executive Board transformed the Emergency Response Division into the Bureau of Crisis Prevention and Recovery (BCPR) with the mandate: "To enhance UNDP's efforts for sustainable development, working with partners to reduce the incidence and impact of disasters and violent conflicts, and to establish the solid foundations for peace and recovery from crisis, thereby advancing the UN Millennium Development Goals (MDGs) on poverty reduction."[100] The establishment of BCPR was spurred in part by the release of the "Report of the Panel on United Nations Peace Operations," or the Brahimi Report, which specifically identified UNDP as "best placed to take the lead on implementing peace-building activities."[101] Prior to this time, UNDP's board had been reluctant to link its development work and violent conflict, partly because it wanted "to protect the integrity of development programs and insulate them from more controversial issues."[102] But the UNDP board insisted that UNDP Burundi "develop new methodologies and tools to integrate concern for prevention of violent conflict into its programming and measure the impact of development strategies and different types of projects on the risk of conflict."[103] What was unclear at the time and remains so today is whether UNDP would be able to transform itself from a traditional apolitical development organization into a nimble conflict prevention and peacebuilding organization.

UNDP establishes four-year country program agreements with a host government that are approved by UNDP's governing board. In particularly unstable contexts, these country program agreements often cover only two-year periods, as was the case with several of UNDP Burundi's country program agreements. These country program agreements contain a situation analysis, lessons learned from UNDP's past cooperation with the country, the proposed new program's goals and activities, and a description of how the program will be monitored and evaluated.

UNDP country offices' direct cooperation with host governments in developing and implementing its country programs encourages its

---

[100] Executive Boards of the UN Development Programme and of the UN Population Fund, "Role of UNDP in Crisis and Post-Conflict Situations" (New York: United Nations, 2000), http://goo.gl/ANRbNS; and quotes from the UNDP Bureau for Crisis Prevention and Recovery (BCPR), "Bureau Strategy 2007–2011" (New York: United Nations, January 2007), 8, http://goo.gl/q5lHCP.

[101] UN General Assembly Security Council, "Report of the Panel on United Nations Peace Operations" (New York, November 13, 2000), para. 46, accessed December 21, 2017, www.un.org/en/ga/search/view_doc.asp?symbol=A/55/305.

[102] Executive Boards of the UNDP and UN Population Fund (UNPF), "Role of UNDP in Crisis and Post-Conflict Situations," 6.

[103] Executive Boards of the UNDP and UN Population Fund (UNPF), "Role of UNDP in Crisis and Post-Conflict Situations," 6.

country offices to maintain strong relationships with the host government. The organization views the fact that it maintains these strong relationships with the host government before, during, and after the outbreak of violent conflict as one of its major comparative advantages. Like UN peace operations, this allegiance to the host government pre-positions UNDP country offices to be either stagnant players, if they do not prioritize peacebuilding, or sovereignty reinforcers, if they do. UNDP's need to maintain strong relationships with the host government can make it difficult for the organization to reach beyond its relationship with the host government and create informal local accountability routines with a broad representative group of local stakeholders.

The case study of UNDP in Burundi shows that the country office's allegiance to the Burundian government and reliance on two- to four-year planning horizons, which did not align with events on the ground in Burundi, inhibited it from taking regular actions to reduce the gap between its broad peacebuilding aims and outcomes in Burundi's changing political and security context. In spite of UNDP Burundi's commitment to helping to build peace in Burundi, the country office's predominance of formal accountability for development aims, as opposed to peacebuilding aims, also inhibited it from directly addressing Burundi's evolving conflict dynamics.

The Trajectory of UNDP Burundi

This section describes UNDP Burundi's behavior between 1999 and 2014 (see Table 4.3). During most of this period, UNDP Burundi was a stagnant player, implementing largely the same country program during the entire period, except for several pockets of learning. UNDP Burundi's integration into two UN Missions helped alter its behavior in Phases III, IV, and V, however. When integrated under ONUB in Phase III, UNDP Burundi became a stagnant player with pockets of learning. UNDP Burundi's integration under ONUB was much less complete than its integration under BINUB, affecting the degree to which the UN Mission and its formal peacebuilding accountability influenced UNDP Burundi's activities. When more fully integrated under BINUB in Phases IV and V, UNDP Burundi became a sovereignty reinforcer with pockets of learning. Even during the phases when UNDP Burundi worked closely with a UN Mission, UNDP's rigid bureaucratic rules and the dominance of formal accountability throughout the organization inhibited the Burundi country office from taking regular actions to reduce the gap between its peacebuilding aims and outcomes.

Table 4.3. *United Nations Development Programme in Burundi*

	Informal Local Accountability	Formal Peacebuilding Accountability	Country Office Type	Result
UNDP Phase I: Jan. 1999– Oct. 2001	No	No	Stagnant Player	Actions without consideration of effect on conflict dynamics
UNDP Phase II: Nov. 2001– Nov. 2003	No	No	Stagnant Player	Actions without consideration of effect on conflict dynamics
UNDP Phase III: Dec. 2003– Aug. 2005	No	No	Stagnant Player	Actions without consideration of effect on conflict dynamics
UNDP Phase IV: Sept. 2005– Apr. 2009	No	Yes	Sovereignty Reinforcer	Actions to align with peacebuilding preferences of principals
UNDP Phase V: May 2009– May 2010	No	Yes	Sovereignty Reinforcer	Actions to align with peacebuilding preferences of principals
UNDP Phase VI: June 2010– Apr. 2014	No	No	Stagnant Player	Actions without consideration of conflict dynamics

UNDP Burundi as a Stagnant Player

Between 1999 and 2005 (Phases I, II, and III), with the exception of its election unit discussed in the next section, UNDP Burundi's projects remained largely the same in spite of the fact that the organization openly advocated for the UN to adapt to Burundi's changing context. After the removal of regional sanctions in 1999, UNDP "engaged in relentless advocacy" for resumed development cooperation by international donors even before complete security had returned to Burundi.[104] UNDP

---

[104] Executive Boards of the UNDP and UNPF, "Second Country Cooperation Framework for Burundi (2002–2004)" (New York: United Nations, July 24, 2001), para. 16, http://goo.gl/3uZ4xQ.

argued that development and expanded humanitarian aid would "help to consolidate the restoration of peace."[105] At the time, most donors believed that security was a precondition for the resumption of development aid.[106]

Since the outbreak of Burundi's war in 1993, donors had given primarily humanitarian assistance to Burundi. UNDP Burundi, as a development organization, was poorly funded during this period.[107] UNDP Burundi viewed the suspension of the embargo in 1999 as an opportunity to increase the amount of money it received from development donors. The incentives for UNDP to raise development funds were strong. UNDP is the lead agency for the UN development community and is responsible for organizing donor roundtables to raise development funds for specific countries.[108] The head of UNDP at the country level, its Resident Representative, is rewarded by the organization for "the volume of resources" that it raises in the country.[109] UNDP's fundraising efforts for its Burundi Country Program had been generally successful. On December 12, 2001, donors pledged $440 million for humanitarian, reconstruction, and development aid.[110]

At several points between 1999 and 2005, UNDP Burundi wrote analyses and policy statements that advocated for the UN and donors to adapt to Burundi's changing context. Yet during this period, UNDP Burundi failed to take regular actions to reduce the gap between its own peacebuilding aims and outcomes. In the UN's Common Country Assessment, the guiding analysis for UN development operations in a particular country, UNDP Burundi wrote that the integration of Nkurunziza into the transitional government in November 2003 marked

[105] Executive Boards of the UNDP and UNPF, "Second Country Cooperation Framework for Burundi (2002–2004)," para. 16.

[106] ICG, "A Framework for Responsible Aid to Burundi," Africa Report Number 57 (Brussels, Belgium: International Crisis Group, February 21, 2003). www.crisisgroup .org/africa/central-africa/burundi/framework-responsible-aid-burundi.

[107] Executive Boards of the UNDP and UNPF, "Extension of the First Country Cooperation Framework for Burundi," note by the administrator (New York: United Nations, December 20, 2000), accessed December 21, 2017 http://web.undp.org/ execbrd/pdf/bdiextI.pdf.

[108] UN Development Group, "UN Resident Coordinator Generic Job Description," January 29, 2009, accessed December 21, 2017, https://undg.org/document/un-resident-coordinator-generic-job-description/.

[109] Craig Murphy, The United Nations Development Programme: A Better Way? (Cambridge, UK: Cambridge University Press, 2006), 295.

[110] "Burundi: Donors Pledge $440 Mn," Africa Recovery, United Nations 14, no. 4 (January 2011), accessed December 15, 2017, www.un.org/en/africarenewal///subjindx/144 aidf.htm.

the beginning of Burundi's post-conflict transition, which would end when the country began a "true process of sustainable development."[111]

In spite of the UN's own claim that it should alter its approach in response to the November 2003 event, UNDP Burundi did not alter its activities. Instead, it extended its 2002–2004 country program plan for a year so that the plan could align with the planning cycles of the other UN development organizations and the UN in Burundi to develop a joint UN Development Assistance Framework (UNDAF).[112] The UNDAF was a core part of the reform agenda that the UN Secretary-General outlined for the United Nations in 1999. He believed that the UNDAF would enable the UN development community in each country to work toward the same overall objectives and, ideally, to advance the Millennium Development Goals (MDGs).

UNDP's Burundi country program focused on implementing democratic and economic governance, combating poverty, and preventing HIV/AIDS. These activities could have been designed and implemented through a peacebuilding lens, but UNDP Burundi chose not to do so. Instead, in its 2002–2004 program, UNDP Burundi removed the goal of mainstreaming peacebuilding and conflict prevention that had appeared in its earlier program documents.[113] A 2004 evaluation of UNDP Burundi's Democratic Governance project – a continuation of the project included in its 1999–2001 country program – found that the project was not focused on the specific needs and capacities of the transitional government at that point in time.[114] The evaluation argued that the project's activities were more appropriate for a democratically elected government, not a transitional government.[115]

The evaluation noted that the Democratic Governance project was ill-prepared for predictable challenges in Burundi's context: changes of staff in key government positions and the preoccupation of government officials with political maneuvering.[116] As a result, the project started late

[111] UN Country Team Burundi, "Burundi: Les défis du processus de transition," bilan commun de pays [common country assessment (CCA)] (Bujumbura, February 2004), 69, accessed December 15, 2017, http://goo.gl/zpaUFR.

[112] Because of the unstable context in Burundi at the time, UNDP's 2002 country plan was only for a two-year period, 2002–2004.

[113] Executive Boards of the UNDP and UNPF, "Second Country Cooperation Framework for Burundi" (New York: United Nations), para. 26.

[114] Stanislas Makoroka and Oliver Le Brun, "La révue du projet d'appui au programme national de gouvernance démocratique," Evaluation Report (Bujumbura: UNDP, February 2004), para. 30, accessed December 21, 2017, http://goo.gl/VklqKT.

[115] Makoroka and Le Brun, "La révue du projet d'appui au programme national de gouvernance démocratique," para. 30.

[116] Makoroka and Le Brun, "La révue du projet d'appui au programme national de gouvernance démocratique," para. 11.

and was unable to achieve many of its ambitious objectives. The evaluators argued that once the project was off the ground, the UNDP Burundi staff who ran it erroneously believed that their role was to implement the project as planned, not to alter it to fit the particular circumstances in Burundi.[117] UNDP and the rest of the UN Country Team (UNCT) – the group of all UN development and humanitarian agencies operating in that country – in Burundi blamed the poor impact of this project and other projects during this period on the fact that Burundian beneficiaries were unable to sustain results, rather than on the possibility that their activities may have been poorly designed and poorly adapted to Burundi's transitional phase.[118]

Even though UNDP Burundi implemented peacebuilding activities throughout the period of study, UNDP Burundi saw itself as a development organization that worked in and around conflict, not on it. This was reflective of UNDP headquarters' general prioritization of development above all other aims, creating formal accountability routines for its country offices that prioritized development. Consequently, it pursued a phased approach to intervention in Burundi, as elsewhere, treating humanitarian assistance and development as occurring in a linear sequence with a seamless transition in between.[119] UNDP's advocacy efforts in Burundi aimed to encourage donors to initiate the development phase as soon as possible, enabling UNDP Burundi to transition to full development programming, its core mandate, and receive more funding.[120]

The reality in Burundi was much less linear and much more complex. Even in the most intense phases of the war, some provinces were largely peaceful. These provinces were ready for development projects that aimed to build people's capacity to improve their livelihoods, rather than humanitarian programming that focused on distributing food, seeds, plastic sheeting, buckets for water, and other "life-saving" goods.[121] A 2002 review of the role of UNDP Burundi in reintegration and reconstruction programs reiterated this lesson: "Humanitarian assistance and development cooperation do not follow a consecutive linear progression but rather should be viewed in the totality of a given situation.

---

[117] Makoroka and Le Brun, "La révue du projet d'appui au programme national de gouvernance démocratique," para. 11–12.

[118] UN Country Team Burundi, "Burundi: Les défis du processus de transition," para. 70.

[119] UNDP, "Evaluation of UNDP Support to Conflict-Affected Countries" (New York: Evaluation Office, 2006), 28, accessed December 21, 2017, http://goo.gl/QfIuyT.

[120] Makoroka and Le Brun, "La révue du projet d'appui au programme national de gouvernance démocratique."

[121] ICG, "A Framework for Responsible Aid to Burundi."

Peace, reintegration, and development should all be considered as critical components and objectives of post-conflict management, coexisting synergistically."[122]

UNDP Burundi's effort to encourage donors to give more development funding to Burundi led it to downplay the complex political dynamics and the violence that continued in Burundi. For example, in November 2001, the representative of the World Health Organization in Burundi was murdered, found floating in Lake Tanganyika. With the donor conference on Burundi planned for the next month in Paris, UNDP downplayed the murder and the overall trend of escalating violence, which it feared would discourage donors from committing development funds to Burundi.[123]

UNDP as a Stagnant Player with Pockets of Learning

The deployment of ONUB to Burundi in 2004 (at the end of Phase III) brought a new political awareness and focus on peacebuilding to UNDP. UNDP Burundi was integrated under the political leadership of ONUB, and Ibrahima D. Fall became the quadruple-hatted deputy SRSG, with responsibility for both the development and humanitarian communities as Resident Coordinator, the Humanitarian Coordinator, and the Resident Representative of UNDP Burundi. UNDP Burundi's new partnership with ONUB and new Resident Representative, the head of the UNDP country office, contributed to its success in supporting Burundi's 2005 democratic elections, creating a pocket of peacebuilding learning.[124]

In spite of its integration under ONUB for part of its 2005–2007 country program, the rest of UNDP Burundi's program maintained largely the same focus for this two-year period as it had previously: good governance, rehabilitation, and the fight against HIV/AIDS. UNDP Burundi updated its country plan slightly to focus on elections and the reintegration of ex-combatants.[125] But the rest of UNDP Burundi's projects remained largely the same as they had during the preceding six years.

---

[122] UN Country Team Burundi, "Burundi: Les défis du processus de transition," para. 115.

[123] Participant observation as UN staff member, Bujumbura, 2001.

[124] Jackson, "The United Nations Operation in Burundi (ONUB)," 23–4; and United Nations System in Burundi, "Lettre de présentation de l'équipe de pays," Resident Coordinator Annual Report Introductory Letter (Bujumbura, 2005), http://goo.gl/jDnPvW.

[125] UNDP and the Republic of Burundi, "Plan d'action du programme de pays 2005–2007" (Bujumbura, May 2005).

During Phase III, UNDP Burundi was still a stagnant player; its formal accountability routines did not prioritize peacebuilding nor did it have informal local accountability across its activities. As a result, UNDP Burundi did not take regular actions to reduce the gap between its peacebuilding aims and outcomes. Instead, it largely implemented the same activities it had been implementing for the previous two phases without adapting them to macro- or micro-level changes in Burundi's political or security situation. The pocket of learning that UNDP Burundi established in its election-focused activities was made possible by two factors. First, SRSG McAskie and UNDP headquarters were focused on the successful organization of the elections, creating formal peacebuilding accountability for UNDP's election unit. Second, the election unit worked with ONUB's networks to create strong informal local accountability routines to enable it to navigate the complex political climate around the elections.

UNDP Burundi had also benefited from foresight in planning for its election support. It had included its support for the elections in its 2005–2007 country program and in the UN's 2005–2007 UN Development Assistance Framework (UNDAF), fulfilling UNDP's global commitment to be "the major implementing body for UN electoral support."[126] Supporting the elections was, thus, something that UNDP had planned for. UNDP Burundi's approach to the 2005 elections was different from its approach to the inauguration of Burundi's transitional government in 2001 (initiating Phase II) or the implementation of the comprehensive ceasefire agreement with the CNDD-FDD in 2003 (initiating Phase III). In response to these two phases, UNDP did not take actions to reduce the gap between its peacebuilding aims and outcomes in response these critical turning points in Burundi's war-to-peace transition. The importance of electoral support to UNDP headquarters meant that UNDP Burundi made sure to integrate the 2005 elections into its 2005–2007 country program plan. This made it much easier for UNDP Burundi to mobilize quickly to support the organization of the 2005 elections once its assistance was needed.

A 2008 evaluation of UNDP Burundi's 2005–2007 support for the reintegration of internally displaced persons and refugees provides a window into the effectiveness of its other activities between 2005 and

---

[126] UN Department of Political Affairs, "UN Entities" (New York: UN Department of Political Affairs, 2011), accessed December 21, 2017, www.un.org/ruleoflaw/un-and-the-rule-of-law/department-of-political-affairs/; UNDP, "UNDP and Electoral Assistance: Ten Years of Experience" (New York: United Nations, 2000), http://goo.gl/Xt68ok; UNDP and the Republic of Burundi, "Plan d'action du programme de pays 2005–2007" (Bujumbura, May 2005), 1.

2007. The evaluation found that the project made an important contribution through the construction of basic social service infrastructure and the distribution of farming supplies.[127] Nonetheless, the evaluators found that the project's overall performance was very poor.[128] It suffered from poor leadership, insufficient staff capacity, and poor communication within UNDP Burundi.

Even though it had included a specific reference to coordination with the effort supporting the Disarmament, Demobilization, and Reintegration (DDR) of former combatants in its country program document, the reintegration project failed to do so or to take advantage of other opportunities to adjust to related changes in the Burundian context that arose during its implementation (i.e., the repatriation of refugees and early harvests).[129] In addition, the evaluation found that the project's objectives were overly ambitious and did not respond to real reintegration needs. It argued that the project lacked measurable qualitative or quantitative indicators, and that both the reintegration project and UNDP Burundi lost credibility because the project was consistently late in delivering on its promises.[130]

UNDP Burundi as a Sovereignty Reinforcer with Pockets of Learning

The deployment of BINUB in 2007 significantly altered UNDP Burundi's leadership, program, and structure. With the integration of UNDP Burundi under BINUB, ERSG Mahmoud became the new UNDP Resident Representative. This meant that one individual was in charge of both the political and the development components of the mission. The main elements of UNDP's 2005–2007 program were subsumed within the UN's Integrated Peacebuilding Support Strategy for Burundi. UNDP contributed core staff to BINUB's three integrated sections: the Human Rights and Justice section, the Democratic Peace and Governance section, and the Security Sector Reform and Small Arms section.[131]

---

[127] UNDP, "Évaluation du programme d'appui à la réhabilitation, réintégration des sinistrés et de lutte contre la pauvreté" (Bujumbura, September 2009), accessed December 21, 2017, http://goo.gl/4MAsPW.

[128] UNDP, "Évaluation du programme d'appui à la réhabilitation, réintégration des sinistrés et de lutte contre la pauvretee," 29.

[129] UNDP, "Évaluation du programme d'appui à la réhabilitation, réintégration des sinistrés et de lutte contre la pauvreté," 5–7, 31.

[130] UNDP, "Évaluation du programme d'appui à la réhabilitation, réintégration des sinistrés et de lutte contre la pauvreté," 5–7.

[131] BINUB, "UN Integration in Burundi in the Context of a Peacebuilding Office BINUB: Lessons Learned from June 2006 to Oct 2007" (Bujumbura: United Nations, February 2008), accessed December 21, 2017, http://goo.gl/mxKonC.

UNDP Burundi was made responsible for managing the US $35 million given to Burundi by the UN PBF in 2007, discussed previously, and for procuring all related goods.

Once subsumed under BINUB, UNDP Burundi's integrated sections were focused on BINUB's priorities and peacebuilding approach. The rest of UNDP Burundi functioned much as it had prior to its integration under BINUB, however, UNDP Burundi was now focused on aligning with the priorities of Burundi's democratic government rather than simply implementing its two- or four-year country program without adapting to the evolving preferences of the government, as it had in the past. In spite of the overall focus on the preferences of the Burundian state, UNDP Burundi and BINUB initiated several peacebuilding activities that took regular actions to reduce the gap between their peacebuilding aims and outcomes and helped advance Burundi's war-to-peace transition. During this phase, UNDP Burundi was a sovereignty reinforce with pockets of learning.

Because of existing disagreements between the FNL and the Burundian government, the FNL did not begin to disarm its combatants until April 2009, as mandated by the comprehensive ceasefire agreement signed by the FNL and CNDD-FDD on September 7, 2006.[132] The full demobilization of the FNL's twenty-one thousand combatants would constitute the separation of its political and military capacities, a prerequisite for the FNL's participation in the 2010 elections. Unfortunately, the Multi-Donor Reintegration Program that had funded the CNDD-FDD's DDR had closed in 2008, and no money was set aside to fund the demobilization of the FNL, particularly the demobilization of the eleven thousand non-combatants whom the FNL argued were an integral part of their organization.

BINUB and UNDP Burundi responded quickly – taking action to reduce the gap between their peacebuilding aims and outcomes – to ensure that the FNL combatants received the same reintegration assistance as the CNDD-FDD had received, allowing the FNL to transform into a political party prior to the 2010 elections. The Joint UNDP-BINUB Security Sector Reform and Small Arms section distributed the first payment, funded by the PBF emergency fund, to the eleven thousand associated adults;[133] UNDP's Bureau for Crisis Prevention

---

[132] Mahmoud, "Partnerships for Peacebuilding in Burundi," 11.

[133] UN Security Council, "Sixth Report of the Secretary-General on the United Nations Integrated Office in Burundi" (New York: United Nations, November 30, 2009), 38, accessed December 21, 2017, www.un.org/en/ga/search/view_doc.asp?symbol=S/2009/611.

and Recovery (BCPR) provided additional funding for the cantonment of the FNL and to supplement the PBF's funding for the demobilization of the eleven thousand associated adults.[134] UNDP's Early Recovery Unit followed up with a second tranche that was given to the former combatants once the people returned to their towns of residence.[135] Finally, UNDP Burundi targeted its community development programming in the provinces and areas where the majority of FNL combatants returned.[136]

Several other projects that UNDP Burundi implemented in collaboration with BINUB also made an important contribution to Burundi's peacebuilding process: the Cadre de Dialogue project that was mentioned in the previous section, the projects with the Burundian National Defense Force, and the local public service project.[137] But the majority of projects that UNDP Burundi and BINUB implemented together were not of high quality, did not sustain their relevance during Burundi's war-to-peace trajectory, and did not make a clear contribution to their specific project aims or to the general peacebuilding aims of UNDP.[138]

For example, UNDP Burundi/BINUB supported the reconstruction of local tribunals, but failed to consult with the population or monitor contractors, leading to shoddy work that did not meet the needs of the local judiciary.[139] It procured police uniforms for the newly created Burundian National Police, intending to improve the perceived

---

[134] Interviews with UN staff members, including 1.44, Bujumbura, November 4, 2009. The associated adults constituted a group of men and women who were not normal combatants, but who were part of the FNL's broader force. They were verified on the FNL's list, but they were not likely to be reintegrated into the Burundian Army or police and they still needed to be demobilized and reintegrated into society.

[135] The term "early recovery" is the development community's word for peacebuilding. It aims to enable a quicker and more effective response by the international community to the foggy phases of war-to-peace transitions that do not easily correspond to strict humanitarian, peacekeeping, or development definitions. "Early recovery is guided by development principles that seek to build on humanitarian programs and catalyze sustainable development opportunities. It aims to generate self-sustaining, nationally owned, resilient processes for post crisis recovery." See Cluster Working Group on Early Recovery and UNDG-ECHA Working Group on Transition, "Guidance Note on Early Recovery" (Geneva: UNDP, BCPR, April 2008), 6, accessed December 21, 2017, www.humanitarianlibrary.org/resource/guidance-note-early-recovery-2008-0.

[136] UNDP Burundi, "Appui à la réintégration durable des ex-combattants," accessed September 30, 2011, http://goo.gl/iw6FTu.

[137] Campbell, "Independent External Evaluation: Peacebuilding Fund Projects in Burundi."

[138] Campbell, "Independent External Evaluation: Peacebuilding Fund Projects in Burundi."

[139] Campbell, "Independent External Evaluation: Peacebuilding Fund Projects in Burundi."

professionalism of the police. But within a week or two, the dark blue uniforms faded to pink and purple, leading to public ridicule of the new police force rather than an improved perception of its professionalism.[140]

Many other members of the UN development community in Burundi had similar problems designing, implementing, and monitoring peacebuilding projects. The UN Population Fund implemented a youth peacebuilding project that was plagued by local corruption.[141] Other organizations, such as UNICEF, focused on their core mandate of helping vulnerable children in Burundi without asking how Burundi's peacebuilding dynamics related to children's vulnerability or how UNICEF's programming might influence these dynamics.[142] In fact, few UN staff regularly visited or talked to their beneficiaries to gain a better understand how the conflict affected them.[143] According to one UN staff person:

The opportunity cost of being targeted and specific to meet peacebuilding priorities is very high because of the extent to which we have standardized programming implementation. The fact that Burundi has innovative [peacebuilding] programming is 80 to 90 percent due to Youssef [Mahmoud]. Youssef had a knack for using [PBF funding] for his own purposes.[144]

Unlike most of the other UN development organizations, UNDP had a special mandate to engage in conflict prevention and peacebuilding programming. Why was it not able to fulfill this mandate during this period in Burundi? Why was UNDP able to respond so quickly to the opportunity presented by the demobilization of the FNL, but not able to align the rest of its programming with Burundi's evolving context? I argue that this failure was because of the predominance of formal accountability for development, not for peacebuilding, and because of the general absence of informal local accountability across most of its projects.

UNDP Burundi as a Stagnant Player

In May 2010, after a tumultuous preelection period, Burundi's communal elections took place. The CNDD-FDD won 64 percent of the vote. Claiming fraud, the opposition parties withdrew from the subsequent elections. The UN did not attempt to facilitate a dialogue between the

---

[140] Campbell, "Independent External Evaluation: Peacebuilding Fund Projects in Burundi," 189–92.
[141] Campbell, "Independent External Evaluation: Peacebuilding Fund Projects in Burundi."
[142] Interview with UN staff member 1.18, Bujumbura, June 11, 2009.
[143] Interview with UN staff member 1.30, Bujumbura, June 15, 2009.
[144] Interview with UN staff member O25, Geneva, July 2008.

opposition parties and the CNDD-FDD, nor did it encourage multiparty democracy in Burundi. It continued to declare the elections legitimate and pressured the opposition to agree. The presidential elections were held on June 28, 2010, with Pierre Nkurunziza as the only candidate. Once the electoral period was over, Burundi had essentially become a one-party state that increasingly used violence and intimidation to consolidate its power.

Unlike the 2005 elections, where the president had been appointed by the parliament, the Burundian people directly elected the president in 2010. For both Burundians and international actors, this round of elections marked Burundi's real transition to democracy. For UNDP Burundi, it marked the transition toward relatively normal development cooperation between UNDP Burundi and the government of Burundi and a chance to move out from the shadow of BINUB.[145] For the previous three years, UNDP Burundi's country program had been subsumed within BINUB. UNDP Burundi did not even have its own country program document from 2007 to 2009. UNDP Burundi now had its own country program document (2010–2014) and it was no longer integrated under BINUB, which had been replaced by a much smaller, political mission: BNUB. UNDP Burundi and BNUB operated according to the UN's standard division between the political actors – DPA and DPKO – and the development actors – UNDP and the other members of the UNCT.

UNDP Burundi played an important role in the 2010 elections by providing technical support to the National Independent Electoral Commission, procuring ballots and other supplies, managing the US $46.5 million election trust fund, and running a civic education campaign.[146] The UN reported that technical failures caused the postponement of the first round of elections by three days, from May 21, 2010, to May 24, 2010.[147] In reality, UNDP Burundi had failed to adequately check the ballots and distributed ballots that did not contain all the parties that were supposed to be on them, creating speculation of fraud in an already politically charged environment.[148] As mentioned

---

[145] Executive Representative of the Secretary-General, "2010 Resident Coordinator Annual Report - Burundi" (New York: UNDP Group, 2010), 2, http://goo.gl/IFsgqp.

[146] UNDP, "UNDP to Support Burundi Elections" (September 23, 2009), accessed December 21, 2017, www.undp.org/content/undp/en/home/presscenter/articles/2009/09/23/undp-to-manage-usd-44-million-fund-for-burundi-elections.html; and UN Secretary-General, "Seventh Report of the Secretary-General on the United Nations Integrated Office in Burundi" (New York: UN Security Council), 2, accessed September 19, 2011, http://goo.gl/wNAe30.

[147] UN Secretary-General, "Seventh Report of the Secretary-General," 2.

[148] Interview with observer O22, 2010.

previously, UNDP Burundi had made a similar procurement mistake in relation to police uniforms in 2009.[149] Although DPKO mobilized United Nations Mission in the Democratic Republic of the Congo (MONUC) resources to reprint the ballots and distribute them by the May 24 elections, the rumors about fraudulent elections had already spread.[150]

After the 2010 elections resulted in a single-party state and increased political violence, UNDP Burundi continued implementing its country program largely as if nothing had changed. The UN Secretary-General visited Burundi during the election period and declared: "It is imperative that these elections be a success. Burundi has an opportunity to become a success story and a model for the continent."[151] After the elections, the UN and much of the international community acted as if the elections helped to consolidate democracy in Burundi.

UNDP Burundi's 2010–2014 country program contained the same aims and projects that the country office had implemented from 2007 to 2009, with the exception of a new focus on tourism and infrastructure development.[152] The new program did not focus much on peacebuilding in spite of an increasingly polarized political environment. UNDP Burundi had "moved on" and believed that peacebuilding was a symbol of its past program under BINUB, but was not important for its present and future work in Burundi.[153]

UNDP Burundi had designed its new program on the assumption that the 2010 elections would be successful. The result of the elections technically supported this definition because they were declared free, fair, and mostly peaceful by international observers. But, in reality, Burundi's government was growing increasingly authoritarian. Nonetheless, UNDP Burundi continued implementing its country program as designed for successful elections. Much of the rest of the international community initially echoed UNDP's approach. For international actors, regional heads of state, and many Burundians, fatigue with Burundi's peacebuilding process had set in.[154] They believed that the 2010 elections would mark a successful culmination of years of peacebuilding, not the

[149] Campbell, "Independent External Evaluation: Peacebuilding Fund Projects in Burundi."
[150] Interview with observer O22, 2010.
[151] UN News Centre, "Ban Lauds Burundians for Gains in Consolidating Peace," June 9, 2010, accessed December 21, 2017, http://goo.gl/I4WK7a.
[152] UNDP, "Programme de pays pour le Burundi (2010–2014)" (Bujumbura, August 2009), http://goo.gl/75NcC8.
[153] Interview with UN staff member UP2, Bujumbura, June 24, 2009.
[154] Interview with observer O12, via telephone, May 4, 2010; and interview with international donor O16, November 7, 2011.

beginning of an entirely new peacemaking process. They were unprepared and unwilling to change their plans.

Explaining UNDP Burundi's Behavior

A key component of UNDP's approach, and its related formal accountability, is the idea that UNDP is in a country for the long haul and will have a long-term impact on its development.[155] In Burundi, this long-term perspective led to path dependency. UNDP Burundi implemented largely the same activities during a fifteen-year period without taking regular actions to reduce the gap between its peacebuilding aims and outcomes, even in the face of large critical shifts in Burundi's war-to-peace transition that UNDP Burundi itself identified as meriting a change in program strategy.

UNDP Burundi was not a peacebuilding learner for any of the periods under study. The peacebuilding contributions that UNDP Burundi did achieve were due to the on-the-job innovation of staff, who created informal local accountability; their capacity to bypass bureaucratic barriers; and the peacebuilding prioritization and monitoring mechanisms put in place by UN Headquarters, ONUB, and BINUB for UNDP's election support and PBF-funded projects.[156]

Informal Local Accountability

UNDP Burundi developed several informal local accountability mechanisms in the projects that it jointly implemented with ONUB and BINUB, but otherwise it had very poor feedback from national actors other than the Burundian government.[157] UNDP staff tended to stay in Bujumbura, not traveling to the countryside to talk with their "beneficiaries."[158] Local staff were predominantly Tutsi and were reportedly reticent to go out to the countryside and talk to poor Hutu.[159] Many international staff, consumed by meetings and report writing, were also reluctant to leave the capital. One staff member commented, "Burundi is not a place where you see suffering people everywhere," making it easy for people to focus on high-level discussions with government officials

---

[155] Campbell and Schirch, "UNDP's Role in Peacebuilding."

[156] Campbell, "Independent External Evaluation: Peacebuilding Fund Projects in Burundi."

[157] Interviews with key UN staff members and observers, including O28, Bujumbura, November 2009.

[158] Interview with UN staff member UP1, Bujumbura, June 19, 2009.

[159] Interviews with UN staff member UP1, Bujumbura, June 19, 2009, and observer O4, Bujumbura, June 26, 2009.

and other international actors and forget about the poverty and violence facing people outside of Bujumbura.[160]

Formal Accountability Routines

UNDP country offices are accountable to their headquarters, their donors who give country-focused contributions, and the host government that gives the UNDP country office permission to operate in the country. UNDP country offices are primarily evaluated on the amount of money they raise from donors based in the country and for spending this money in line with their planned country programs.[161] In line with this focus, UNDP has become the main administrator of UN trust funds, including the PBF, of which UNDP takes a 7 percent overhead.[162]

UNDP argues that its comparative advantage in conflict-affected countries lies in the fact that it is in the country before, during, and after violent conflict.[163] To sustain its presence in a country over the long haul and raise funds from donors present in the country, UNDP has attempted to become a jack-of-all-trades, implementing activities that it may not have an explicit mandate or capacity to implement. According to a 2011 review of UNDP by the UK government, "UNDP's near universal mandate means its technical resources are spread very thinly."[164] UNDP has built its reputation as a financial and project management organization, but its staff may not have the skills to manage the different types of projects that the organization takes on. "UNDP's results framework, Human Resources, and prioritization on areas where it can add most value are all weak and reduce its impact."[165] A 2005 review of UNDP's capacity warned that if UNDP continued to serve as the administrator for the UN system and fill programming gaps left by other UN agencies, its focus on administration would "detract UNDP from its core development mandate and divert human resources that could be used to further develop UNDP's lead role in development."[166]

[160] Interview with UN staff member UP1, Bujumbura, June 19, 2009.
[161] UNDP Evaluation Office, "Evaluation of Results-Based Management at UNDP" (New York: United Nations, December 2007), 37, accessed December 21, 2017, http://goo.gl/6JovPS.
[162] Campbell et al., "Independent External Evaluation: UN Peacebuilding Fund Project Portfolio in Burundi, 2007–2013."
[163] Campbell and Schirch, "UNDP's Role in Peacebuilding: Issues and Strategies."
[164] Department for International Development, "Multilateral Aid Review: United Nations Development Programme (Including the Bureau for Crisis Prevention and Recovery)" (London: UK Aid, March 2011), 4, accessed December 21, 2017, http://goo.gl/fU4sbz.
[165] Department for International Development, "Multilateral Aid Review."
[166] UNDP, "Evaluation of UNDP Support to Conflict-Affected Countries," 41.

In Burundi, UNDP's focus on raising funds, spending funds, and administering funds – all within a one-year budget cycle – seemed to be a much higher priority for the organization than the goal of achieving peacebuilding or development outcomes. UNDP Burundi tracked the success of its projects based on whether they delivered what they said they would deliver – number of people trained, number of houses rebuilt, and the like – not the impact or outcome of these efforts.[167] UNDP Burundi failed to ask or answer basic questions about its projects, for example: Were the houses that were built constructed of the appropriate quality? Were they used by the people who were supposed to use them? Did training lead to changes in individual behavior or institutions?[168] According to a 2007 evaluation of UNDP's monitoring and evaluation systems, this lack of reflection is a function of the organization's broader incentive structure:

Staff contracts and the tenure of office of the Resident Representative/Country Director are both shorter than the period of the CPD [country program document] and not necessarily in phase with the CPD. Hence accountability for results implicitly concerns only short-term targets – such as resource mobilization, delivery and project outputs – rather than longer-term development outcomes. Since programme staff in many offices are funded from extra-budgetary resources, their accountability for results is aligned more to outputs of projects as opposed to delivering at outcome level.[169]

Even more than focusing on specific deliverables, UNDP Burundi tracked money: money spent, money raised, money not spent.[170] At each UNDP Burundi coordination meeting for PBF-funded projects, the leadership of UNDP Burundi held up a color-coded sheet that listed how much money had been spent on each project.[171] The goal was to pressure staff members to spend the money allocated to them. UNDP leadership did not assess the degree to which a project had contributed to the desired change in Burundi's institutions, or even if the planned

[167] Campbell, "Independent External Evaluation: Peacebuilding Fund Projects in Burundi"; Campbell et al., "Independent External Evaluation: UN Peacebuilding Fund Project Portfolio in Burundi, 2007–2013."
[168] Campbell, "Independent External Evaluation: Peacebuilding Fund Projects in Burundi"; Campbell et al., "Independent External Evaluation: UN Peacebuilding Fund Project Portfolio in Burundi, 2007–2013."
[169] UNDP Evaluation Office, "Evaluation of Results-Based Management at UNDP" (New York: United Nations, December 2007), 37, accessed February 15, 2018, http://web.undp.org/execbrd/pdf/RBM_Evaluation.pdf.
[170] Campbell, "Independent External Evaluation: Peacebuilding Fund Projects in Burundi."
[171] Participant observation, UNDP Coordination Meetings, Bujumbura, Burundi, November 6, 2009; Campbell, "Independent External Evaluation: Peacebuilding Fund Projects in Burundi."

expenditures made sense in Burundi's rapidly evolving context.[172] In other words, there was no incentive to create informal local account-ability that would have provided feedback and understanding about intermediary outcomes, nor was there the incentive to take action to improve projects where some type of feedback was available.[173] This pattern is found in UNDP more broadly.[174] According to a 2012 review of UNDP's conflict prevention and crisis response capacity: "BCPR's focus on projects as outputs, varied interpretations of outcomes, and a lack of clarity regarding how to measure BCPR's indirect role, specific contributions, and added value within a given context, have contributed to a tendency to focus on activities rather than outcomes or tangible results."[175]

Without feedback on the outcomes of its projects, UNDP Burundi could not take informed actions to reduce the gap between its aims and outcomes, or learn. When high-level UNDP staff made trips to see UNDP projects being implemented, open and reflective discussion often took place and actions were taken to reduce the gap between the project goals and outcomes, or learn, but these field trips were few and far between.[176] In most cases, however, UNDP Burundi did not aim to better understand or reflect on its impact or improve its programming. This characteristic was also found in other UNDP offices.[177] According to another evaluation of UNDP's interventions in conflict-affected coun-tries: "Both national and international staff need a more supportive and stimulating environment in which time and effort is [sic] devoted to reflection and analysis, to developing a culture in which local concerns take priority over UN concerns, and to the needs and wishes of those on a career path."[178] Multiple UN staff interviewed for this book, both

---

[172] Interview with UN staff person U01, Bujumbura, November 6, 2009.

[173] Campbell, "Independent External Evaluation: Peacebuilding Fund Projects in Burundi"; Campbell et al., "Independent External Evaluation: UN Peacebuilding Fund Project Portfolio in Burundi, 2007–2013."

[174] Rafeeudin Ahmed, Manfred Kulessa, and Khalid Malik, "Lessons Learned in Crises and Post-Conflcit Situations: The Role of UNDP in Reintegration and Reconstruction Programmes" (New York: UNDP Evaluation Office, 2002), 20, accessed December 21, 2017, www.researchgate.net/publication/44832533_Lessons_learned_in_crises_and_post-conflict_situations_the_role_of_UNDP_in_reintegration_and_reconstruction_programmes; and UNDP, "Rapport de la mission d'évaluation externe du PCAC II," Evaluation Report (Bujumbura, January 30, 2005), accessed December 21, 2017, http://goo.gl/tLo1OG.

[175] UNDP, "Strategic Review of the Bureau for Crisis Prevention and Recovery," final report (New York: United Nations, March 10, 2010), iv.

[176] Interview with UN staff member UP1, Bujumbura, June 19, 2009.

[177] Department for International Development, "Multilateral Aid Review: United Nations Development Programme (Including the Bureau for Crisis Prevention and Recovery)," 4.

[178] UNDP, "Evaluation of UNDP Support to Conflict-Affected Countries," 46.

from UN Missions and from UNDP Burundi, argued that they had no time to think.[179] The push to deliver, without feedback about their outcomes or constructive interaction with their intended beneficiaries, left them without the chance to reflect on their actions or their contribution to Burundi's war-to-peace transition.

Rather than focusing on understanding the broader Burundian context, UNDP Burundi largely focused on its relationships with the Burundian government and relied on the government to inform it about the evolution of joint activities.[180] As a UN member state, the government of Burundi was both the recipient of UNDP's projects and one of its bosses, or principals. To operate in Burundi, UNDP had to agree upon and sign a country program with the government of Burundi. "UNDP generally considers governments and government institutions as its major partners."[181] One UNDP Burundi staff person commented that, as a result, UNDP "had difficulty being up-to-date with all of the [other UN] agencies because we did not have anyone in the field."[182]

Thus, UNDP Burundi lacked the information and incentives to pressure the Burundian government to alter policies, particularly in politically sensitive areas such as governance or security sector reform. UNDP Burundi's partnership with DPKO under ONUB and BINUB helped it implement more politically sensitive programming than it had previously pursued in Burundi, making formal peacebuilding accountability a priority for the projects on which they collaborated. In several instances, these projects also developed informal local accountability routines and, as a result, made important contributions to their peacebuilding aims. But once BINUB withdrew from Burundi, UNDP's capacity and willingness to engage in politically sensitive conversations with the government significantly decreased.

UNDP Burundi's allegiance to the Burundian government mirrored its relationships with the rest of the UN system in Burundi. It prioritized coordination and coherence with the rest of the UN system over its alignment with the Burundian context.[183] For example, in spite of the fact that its own conflict analysis identified 2003 as a critical turning point in Burundi that required an entirely new approach by the

[179] Interviews with UN staff members, including 1.41, Bujumbura, May 31, 2009; 1.71, Bujumbura, March 25, 2009; 1.45, Bujumbura, October 29, 2009; 1.44, Bujumbura, November 3, 2009.

[180] Interviews with UN staff members, including UP1, Bujumbura, June 19, 2009; and UP3, New York, 2009.

[181] UNDP, "Evaluation of UNDP Support to Conflict-Affected Countries," 54.

[182] Interview with UNDP staff member UP1, Bujumbura, June 19, 2009.

[183] Interviews with key UN staff members, including 1.43, Bujumbura, November 12, 2009.

international community, UNDP Burundi waited two years to change its approach because it wanted to be aligned with the other UN agencies in a common UNDAF, which was finalized in 2005. This behavior reflects an overall pattern in UNDP: "there is a "tendency for staff to get caught up in inter-agency preoccupations rather than the needs of beneficiaries."[184]

Although BINUB's joint programs with UNDP Burundi enabled the creation of teams that combined political, local, and peacebuilding programming knowledge, they further decreased the efficiency of the UN. Staff had to navigate at least two sets of bureaucratic procedures, learning both systems in what staff reported as a steep learning curve.[185] Contradictory messages were coming from the ERSG's office and from UNDP's leadership: the ERSG was focused on the relevance of programming to peace consolidation, while the UNDP Burundi was focused on spending the funds allocated to each project.[186] Staff were confused as to the true organizational priorities.

A 2004 review of UNDP found that "integrated institutional arrangements can also limit the range of flexibility and speed required of one actor," with serious implications for the ability of actors to respond to complex and fluid post-conflict dynamics.[187] The challenge, the review notes, is finding a balance between flexibility and coherence. Too much flexibility can "serve as an invitation to strategic incoherence and lack of accountability," whereas too much coherence can lead to alignment with other international actors at the expense of alignment with the changing context.[188] The review found that UNDP is at the coherence-heavy end of the spectrum, with "real implications for its ability to achieve its goals on the basis of a flexible response."[189]

Underlying UNDP Burundi's focus on spending money, raising money, and aligning with the policies of the government and other UN organizations was a cumbersome bureaucracy. UNDP's procedures were

---

[184] UNDP, "Evaluation of UNDP Support to Conflict-Affected Countries," 57.
[185] Interviews with UN staff member UO3, Bujumbura, June 1, 2009.
[186] Interviews with UN staff member UO3, Bujumbura, June 1, 2009. The joint steering and monitoring committees for the PBF projects regularly requested information about outcomes, but in most cases staff did not deliver this information. These consultative bodies had no direct sanctions or incentives that they could mobilize to encourage the production of such information.
[187] Ken Menkhaus and Ben K. Fred-Mensah, "Institutional Flexibility in Crises and Post-Conflict Situations: Best Practices from the Field" (New York: UNDP Evaluation Office, December 2004), 15, accessed December 21, 2017, http://web.undp.org/evaluation/evaluations/documents/CPC_evaluation_2004.pdf.
[188] Menkhaus and Fred-Mensah, "Institutional Flexibility in Crises and Post-Conflict Situations," 15.
[189] Menkhaus and Fred-Mensah, "Institutional Flexibility in Crises and Post-Conflict Situations," 15.

notoriously slow, bureaucratic, and insensitive to the requirements of Burundi's dynamic context and the PBF funds that UNDP Burundi was charged with administering.[190] UNDP Burundi staff argued that UNDP was the "most bureaucratic organization" partly because it did "a lot of the procedural work for the whole [UN] system."[191]

For the PBF projects, UNDP's bureaucratic procedures had a negative effect on Burundi's war-to-peace transition in at least two instances, mentioned earlier.[192] One was the instance of the procurement of cheap and embarrassing police uniforms.[193] The other was another UNDP procurement office mistake of procuring faulty ballots for the 2010 elections, leading to the postponement of the elections by several days.[194]

Even UNDP's more successful peacebuilding projects had to contend with very slow procedures and planning cycles that were ill-suited to the fast pace and unpredictable nature of events in Burundi. Staff prided themselves on finding ways of working around UNDP's arduous procedures and caging their requests in bureaucratic language that would ensure easy approval.[195] UNDP's formal accountability routines, which prioritized spending money, not returning it, required staff to follow procedures that many considered to be irrelevant or counterproductive.[196] Project planning had to take place so far in advance that it inevitably included activities that were no longer appropriate, leaving little space for project teams to take actions to reduce the gap between a project's aims and intermediary outcomes during the implementation phase. Still, staff had to implement the projects so that the money could be spent as planned.

In spite of UNDP headquarters' expressed commitment to peacebuilding and conflict-sensitive development, UNDP's primary corporate focus is on development.[197] In other words, UNDP's formal

---

[190] Campbell, "Independent External Evaluation: Peacebuilding Fund Projects in Burundi."

[191] Interview with UN staff member UP1, Bujumbura, June 19, 2009.

[192] Campbell, "Independent External Evaluation: Peacebuilding Fund Projects in Burundi."

[193] Campbell, "Independent External Evaluation: Peacebuilding Fund Projects in Burundi."

[194] Interview with observer O22, 2010.

[195] Interview with observer UO2, Bujumbura, 2009.

[196] Interviews with UN staff members, including UO2, Bujumbura, March 24, 2009; 1.19, Bujumbura, June 15, 2009; 1.32, Bujumbura, November 18, 2009; 1.44, Bujumbura, November 3, 2009.

[197] See Campbell and Schirch, "UNDP's Role in Peacebuilding: Issues and Strategies." Conflict-sensitive development refers to development programming that does not exacerbate the drivers of conflict and, ideally, contributes to the drivers of peace in a particular country.

accountability routines most often prioritized development, and only in certain exceptions could country offices adopt formal peacebuilding accountability routines. UNDP Burundi staff commented repeatedly that the peacebuilding focus of UNDP Burundi when it was integrated with BINUB was one of these exceptions, and that it was only temporary; they were anxious to get out from under BINUB to do real development activities.[198] Development activities are funded from core UNDP funding; conflict prevention and peacebuilding work is not.[199] Conflict analysis is not systematically done or integrated into programming, even in conflict-affected countries.[200] According to a 2009 assessment of UNDP's peacebuilding capacity:

UN staff that are not working directly or explicitly on conflict issues do not want to hear about conflict or its relation to their work. For instance, governance staff do not see the relevance of conflict prevention tools and approaches, because they are not framed in terms that they understand or accept.[201]

BINUB and UNDP Burundi staff repeatedly expressed the desire for more training in peacebuilding design and project implementation, which they felt they had been thrust into without a proper induction phase.[202] UNDP Burundi's monitoring and evaluation advisor had no specific monitoring or peacebuilding training.[203] Without monitoring their activities or seeking feedback from a representative group of stakeholders through informal local accountability, few UNDP Burundi projects were able to understand or improve their contribution to Burundi's war-to-peace transition. Instead, they simply assumed that they had an impact. Mary Kaldor's 2005 study of UNDP's work in post-conflict countries found this trend across many UNDP offices.[204]

Individual Country-Office Staff and Leadership
In UNDP broadly, much decision-making power is given to the UNDP Resident Representative. Not only is this individual often given the Resident Coordinator position, making him or her responsible for

---

[198] Interviews with UN staff members, including 1.15, Bujumbura, June 9, 2009; UP2, Bujumbura, June 24, 2009; UO3, Bujumbura, June 1, 2009.

[199] Interview with UN staff member UP3, New York, 2009.

[200] UNDP, "Evaluation of UNDP Support to Conflict-Affected Countries," 57.

[201] Diana Chigas and Peter Woodrow, "Assessment of BCPR-Supported Conflict Prevention Initiatives" (Cambridge, MA: CDA Collaborative Learning Projects, December 9, 2009), 10.

[202] Campbell, "Independent External Evaluation: Peacebuilding Fund Projects in Burundi."

[203] Interviews with UN staff members and participant observation, Bujumbura, November 2009.

[204] UNDP, "Evaluation of UNDP Support to Conflict-Affected Countries," 40.

coordinating all UN development and humanitarian organizations operating in the country (i.e., the UNCT), but the UNDP Resident Representative is responsible for raising funds from donors at the country level and for working with the host government to develop UNDP's country program. As a result, the approach of the UNDP Resident Representative can have an important influence on how the UNDP country office responds to the evolving country context.

A study of UNDP peacebuilding capacity discussed the particular role of the UNDP Resident Representatives in peacebuilding:

> Mainstreaming [peacebuilding] depends a lot on management and leadership at the country level because it is so decentralized. If you work with countries that are on the brink ... leadership is absolutely crucial. You can do lots of workshops with program staff, but without the leadership buy-in then it doesn't work.[205]

When UNDP Burundi was integrated within ONUB and BINUB, its Resident Representative helped establish formal peacebuilding accountability for specific peacebuilding-focused projects. Under this arrangement, UNDP Burundi still had a country director who ran the organization on a daily basis, but the organization was under the overall political leadership of the deputy SRSG for ONUB and the ERSG for BINUB. The difference between the two arrangements was that ERSG Mahmoud had significant influence over the actions of UNDP, not just those of DPKO staff, as had been the case with SRSG McAskie. Because the heads of the three integrated sections reported directly to Mahmoud, he was able to influence the direction and focus of their programs. Partly because of the historical relationships that several key UN staff members had with Burundian politicians, the ERSG and his team had excellent access to information and analysis about the evolution of negotiations, which created informal local accountability for their dialogue efforts, and were well-prepared to capitalize on new opportunities to influence the trajectory of Burundi's war-to-peace transition.[206]

Nonetheless, the ERSG was not able to influence the interventions of much of the rest of the UN system, including those UNDP Burundi projects outside of his direct control. Although ERSG Mahmoud was technically the boss of UNDP, the day-to-day operations were managed by the UNDP country director and his deputies, all of whom came from more classic development backgrounds. In addition, UNDP Burundi

---

[205] Interview with UN staff member UP5, New York, March 1, 2010.
[206] Interviews with UN staff members and observers, including 1.50, Bujumbura, June 20, 2009; and 1.35, Bujumbura, June 15, 2009.

had developed a bad reputation because of its pre-2007 performance and weak capacity.[207] In an effort to improve capacity to manage successfully the US $35 million provided by the PBF, UNDP headquarters had significantly upgraded the quality and quantity of UNDP Burundi staff.[208]

But the new leadership and staff brought into UNDP Burundi were relatively insensitive to Burundi's political context. During the 2010 election period, the UNDP Burundi country director went on vacation.[209] He was thus not around to ensure that the election ballots were correctly printed and distributed. Although misprinted ballots may have seemed like a simple technical issue, the repercussions of the ballot blunder were significant for Burundians and for the tone of the election cycle, creating speculation of fraud in an already politically charged environment.[210] The expulsion of ERSG Mahmoud in 2010 left a large void in BINUB and UNDP, enabling UNDP to reclaim its position as the coordinator of the UN development system in Burundi and to switch to a more traditional development approach, focusing on implementing development projects rather than working on conflict.[211]

UNDP's incentive mechanisms were designed for a predictable development context where the organization could directly support, rather than challenge, the policies of the government.[212] UNDP country representatives are incentivized to stay in the country so that they can implement country programs before, during, and after conflict. Challenging the government's policies could lead the government to kick a UNDP country representative out of the country, potentially inhibiting their promotion within the organization. Although some UNDP country directors have reportedly been willing to take this risk, none of the UNDP Burundi country directors fit in this category. In fact, UNDP Burundi's staff openly expressed their fear of alienating the Burundian government if they were to adopt a more overt peacebuilding approach.[213]

---

[207] Interview with UN staff member O26, 2010.

[208] Interview with UN staff members, including UP2, Bujumbura, June 24, 2009.

[209] Interviews with observers O23, Bujumbura, 2011; and O12, via telephone, May 4, 2010.

[210] Interview with observer O22, Bujumbura, 2010.

[211] Campbell et al., "Independent External Evaluation: UN Peacebuilding Fund Project Portfolio in Burundi, 2007–2013."

[212] This paragraph synthesizes key findings from Campbell and Schirch, "UNDP's Role in Peacebuilding: Issues and Strategies."

[213] Interviews with UN staff, New York, October 2012.

UNDP Burundi, the Challenge of Conflict-Sensitive Development

In spite of UNDP's commitment to conflict-sensitive development work, its corporate prioritization of development, which prioritized formal development accountability routines, and focus on raising and spending money generally inhibited UNDP Burundi from learning in relation to its peacebuilding or conflict-sensitive aims and from making a positive contribution to Burundi's war-to-peace transition. Left on their own, UNDP Burundi's senior leadership seemed unable or unwilling to alter these broader institutional incentives. As a result, for much of the time under study, UNDP Burundi was a stagnant player. It simply implemented its activities as planned without adapting to changes in the political and security dynamics or to the preferences of the Burundian government.

The UNDP Burundi case study also points to the difficulty that development organizations face when trying to pursue peacebuilding "on the side." Without formal peacebuilding accountability routines at both the headquarters and the country-office level, development organizations may not be able to infuse their organizations with an awareness of conflict dynamics and the potential negative and positive impact of development activities on them. Even when they do manage to create formal peacebuilding accountability for a few projects, as UNDP Burundi did in collaboration with ONUB and BINUB, this focus is likely to be temporary and require a high degree of rule-breaking or rule-bending behavior by individual staff to circumvent formal accountability routines intended to incentivize other outcomes. Development organizations are likely, instead, to view a big shift in a country's war-to-peace transition as an opportunity to engage in "normal" apolitical development programming, rather than as an opportunity to continue to implement development activities that aim to address the root causes of violent conflict.[214]

Conclusion: Understanding the Decentralized Behavior of International Organizations

As discussed at the beginning of this chapter, the scholarly literature argues that IOs are the most accountable of the global governors because of their allegiance to states. From a rationalist perspective, this accountability translates into a strong agreement between the principals, or IO

---

[214] World Bank, *World Development Report 2011: Conflict, Security, and Development* (Washington, DC: World Bank, 2011).

member states, and the agent, its country offices. From a constructivist perspective, accountability is distorted by organizational pathologies that inhibit the organization from achieving the goals of its principals. For UNDP and the four UN peace operations in Burundi, these assumptions do not fully hold.

The case studies do show that the principal–agent relationship between UN country offices and their governing boards plays a crucial role in determining the formal accountability routines and organizational targets to which these organizations are bound at the country level. They also show that the UN bureaucracy and its related pathologies create a set of heavy bureaucratic constraints that UN country offices must contend with. Although these two theoretical perspectives help explain the basic structural factors that influence UNDP and UN peace-operation behavior at the country level, they do not explain what country-office staff do with these structural constraints.

This chapter shows that preferences of UN principals and bureaucratic routines, alone, are likely to lead to failed peacebuilding performance at the country level. Combined, these UN formal accountability routines can incentivize country offices to be static, making it difficult for them to exhibit organizational learning behavior in response to the rapidly changing dynamics of a conflict-affected country. For IOs, these formal routines prioritize allegiance to the host government, sovereignty reinforcing behavior, simple path dependency grounded in implementing two- to four-year plans, or stagnant player behavior.

In spite of the strong constraints from formal accountability routines facing UNDP country offices and UN peace operations, this chapter shows that important pockets of learning and positive peacebuilding performance can emerge. These exceptions surfaced because of the initiative of the country-office leadership and key country-office staff that circumvented existing formal accountability routines to enable the project or organization to fit the conflict-affected context. Senior country-office leaders leveraged their political power and institutional weight to empower key staff to create informal local accountability routines that delegated authority to a representative group of local stakeholders, which in turn held the project or organization accountable for achieving its peacebuilding aims.

The formal accountability routines in the UN peace operations, and in UNDP under ONUB and BINUB, incentivized action on the information coming from these informal local accountability routines by prioritizing peacebuilding above development or humanitarian aims. When formal accountability routines prioritize peacebuilding, they incentivize country-office staff to pay attention to the peacebuilding-related information coming from their informal local accountability routines, enabling the project or organization to take actions to reduce the gap between its peacebuilding aims and outcomes, and increasing the likelihood that the organization will contribute to its local peacebuilding aims.

For the UN in Burundi, however, positive peacebuilding performance came with very high transaction costs, as staff attempted to make the risk-averse UN system function like a lithe political organization. As one UN staff person in Burundi commented:

I think that all UN involvement has had an impact. If you go into depth, you say there, there, and there something has happened. The other question is whether the impact has been cost-worthy. Shouldn't it have had a larger impact? This is where the UN has gone wrong.[215]

While IOs may be the most accountable organizations at the global level, they have a high degree of difficulty being locally accountable because of their formal accountability routines. Compared to the INGO case studies in Chapter 3, the IO country offices in this chapter had much greater difficulty establishing and maintaining informal local accountability. Like the INGOs, however, the initiative of country-office staff and leadership were necessary for the country office or specific projects to create and sustain informal local accountability. But, unlike INGOs, IO country-office staff may have much greater barriers to circumvent. Rule-breaking or rule-bending behavior may be more necessary in IOs than INGOs whose formal accountability routines can vary depending on their donor and context.

In general, this chapter also points to the importance of studying the country-office behavior of IOs and the behavior of individual IO bureaucrats, rather than assuming that IO behavior conforms with the governance and accountability structures visible at headquarters. IOs, and particularly the UN, are complex organizations with multiple principals, multiple mandates, and multiple organizations. Within these complex organizations, individual staff can play a crucial role in navigating complexity and influencing the direction of organizational behavior, particularly at the decentralized level. The role of individual agents, as shown in this chapter, thus points to a crucial omitted variable in most studies of IO behavior and an important area for future research.

---

[215] Interview with former UN staff member in Burundi, 1.48, via telephone, June 1, 2015.

5   Bilateral Development Donors: Accountable for Global Targets, Not Local Change

A red velvet rope guided us to the room where four government officials were seated on a dais raised two feet above the ground. Donors sat in long rows of chairs facing the dais. It was 2009, and the relationship between international donors and the Burundian government was tumultuous. Donors wanted to give Burundi money that would enable the government to achieve the donors' aims, namely the Millennium Development Goals (MDGs) and other targets outlined in Burundi's donor-facilitated Poverty Reduction Strategic Plan (PRSP). But the Burundian government was uninterested in having donors impose policies or an agenda. The government wanted money, but it did not want advice or funding that was conditional on changes in the government's behavior. The purpose of this meeting was to coordinate funding.

The United Kingdom's Department for International Development (DFID), although not a historical donor to Burundi like Belgium or Germany, played a crucial role in the donor community at that time in large part because of the personality and political savvy of its staff. They were known to be smart, innovative, and well informed about cutting-edge strategies for effective aid in conflict-affected contexts. Throughout its operation in Burundi, DFID was committed to conflict-sensitive development, a form of peacebuilding that meant that its development activities would not reinforce the causes of conflict and would, ideally, help to mitigate them.

At the global level, DFID had spearheaded efforts among Organization for Economic Cooperation and Development (OECD) countries to improve the effectiveness of aid to conflict-affected and fragile states.[1] Soon after it was established in 1997, DFID had produced two white papers that committed the organization to mitigating violent conflict so that development could take place, rather than waiting for the

---

[1] Organisation for Economic Cooperation and Development (OECD), "United Kingdom Development Assistance Committee (DAC) Peer Review, Peer Review" (2010), 13, accessed December 22, 2017, http://goo.gl/M4mrYD.

establishment of peace before providing development aid.[2] According to the OECD, "The UK government sees security and stability as preconditions for development and for achieving the MDGs. Thus, DFID is strongly committed to increasing its aid to fragile countries and conflict zones, where the MDGs are most vulnerable to derailment."[3] DFID was one of the first donors to follow through on its commitment to the MDGs by allocating the majority of its aid to the poorest countries.[4]

Over the next decade, DFID progressively increased its capacity for engagement with fragile and conflict-affected states, producing numerous policy documents and guidelines and investing substantial resources in augmenting its own capacity in this area. For example, DFID created a Conflict, Humanitarian, and Security Department; an Africa Conflict Group; a Post-Conflict Reconstruction Unit; Global and Africa Conflict Prevention Pools; fragile states country teams; and a joint DFID–Foreign Commonwealth Office–Ministry of Defence Stabilization Unit; among other initiatives.[5] With its 2009 white paper, DFID moved "to put unprecedented emphasis on conflict and on politics as key determinants of the prospects of success in development and development assistance... Never before... has an institution with the weight of DFID set out the arguments so clearly."[6] In spite of its pledge to work toward peace and development in conflict-affected countries, however, during much of the period under study, DFID implemented a relatively standard development program in one of the poorest, most conflict-ridden countries in the world: Burundi.

This chapter discusses the evolution of DFID's support to Burundi and the factors that influenced its behavior during the different phases of Burundi's transition (as depicted in Table 5.1). First, however, it discusses the existing literature's explanations for the country-level behavior of bilateral donors.

Bilateral Donor Performance

Scholars have viewed the country-level performance of bilateral donors from several different perspectives, but they have not examined in detail

---

[2] Dan Smith, "Towards a Strategic Framework for Peacebuilding: Getting Their Act Together: Overview Report of the Joint *Utstein* Study of Peacebuilding" (Brattvaag, Norway: Royal Norwegian Ministry of Foreign Affairs, April 2004), 36–7, accessed December 22, 2017, http://goo.gl/UOGdhm; and Simon Lawry-White, "Review of the UK Government Approach to Peacebuilding and Synthesis of Lessons Learned from UK Government Funded Peacebuilding Projects 1997–2001" (London: DFID, 2003), accessed December 22, 2017, https://goo.gl/SMO4Qg.

[3] OECD, UK DAC Peer Review, 2010," 30,

[4] Bob Baulch, "Aid Distribution and the MDGs," *World Development* 34, no. 6 (June 2006): 933–50.

[5] See OECD, "United Kingdom DAC Peer Review" (2006), 43, accessed December 22, 2017, http://goo.gl/M4mrYD.

[6] Dan Smith, "Development Thinking Develops: DFID's White Paper and What Comes Next," *Dan Smith's Blog* (August 21, 2009), accessed December 22, 2017, http://goo.gl/3YIQdy.

Table 5.1. *DFID Country-Office Behavior*

	Phase I: Jan. 1999– Oct. 2001	**Phase II:** Nov. 2001– Nov. 2003	**Phase III:** Dec. 2003– Aug. 2005	**Phase IV:** Sept. 2005– Apr. 2009	**Phase V:** May 2009– May 2010	**Phase VI:** June 2010– Apr. 2014
DFID	n/a	Peacebuilding learner	Peacebuilding learner	Stagnant player	Stagnant player	Stagnant player

the factors that enable or inhibit bilateral donors from achieving their country-level aims, particularly in conflict-affected countries. The scholarship on international aid has tended to focus on donors' initial aid allocation decisions to a particular country. Building on data collected and disseminated by the OECD Development Assistance Committee (OECD-DAC), this scholarship argues that donor strategic interest, rather than humanitarian need within the recipient country, motivates donor aid allocation.[7] The research says little, however, about the behavior of donors once they make their initial aid allocation decisions.

Scholars have also focused on the institutional incentives at play in international aid. They have highlighted the consequences of the broken feedback loop between the recipient and the donor (discussed in Chapter 1) and the tendency of bilateral donors to be consumed by their own policies to the detriment of their understanding of the particular country context.[8] This literature analyzes the patterns of behavior at donor headquarters level without investigating how these incentive structures manifest at the country level. Although more detailed country-level accounts are widespread in literature on the ethnography of aid, this scholarship does not investigate the relationships between headquarters and country offices or examine variation in donor behavior, particularly in fragile and conflict-affected countries.[9]

By investigating the behavior of one donor over a fifteen-year period in one country, this chapter fills several important gaps in the existing literature. In particular, it shows that alterations in the focus of a donor's formal accountability routines can significantly change how this

---

[7] Alberto Alesina and David Dollar, "Who Gives Foreign Aid to Whom and Why?" *Journal of Economic Growth* 5, no. 1 (March 1, 2000): 33–63.

[8] Clark C. Gibson et al., *The Samaritan's Dilemma: The Political Economy of Development Aid* (Oxford, UK: Oxford University Press, 2005); and Bertin Martens et al., *The Institutional Economics of Foreign Aid* (Cambridge, UK: Cambridge University Press, 2002).

[9] James Ferguson, *The Anti-Politics Machine: "Development," Depoliticization, and Bureaucratic Power in Lesotho* (Minneapolis: University of Minnesota Press, 1994); David Mosse, *Adventures in Aidland: The Anthropology of Professionals in International Development* (New York: Berghahn, 2011); and Todd Moss, Gunilla Pettersson, and Nicolas van de Walle, "An Aid-Institutions Paradox? A Review Essay on Aid Dependency and State Building in Sub-Saharan Africa," Working Paper no. 74 (Washington, DC: Center for Global Development, January 2006).

donor engages with the country context. It also shows the important role that donor participation in informal local accountability can play in facilitating the establishment of these informal routines and in enabling their effectiveness.[10]

DFID Burundi

In 2002, DFID opened its office in Burundi and focused almost solely on peacebuilding. As depicted in Table 5.2, DFID Burundi had informal local accountability and formal peacebuilding accountability during Phases II and III and was a peacebuilding learner. In 2005, after the election of Pierre Nkurunziza as Burundi's new president, DFID Burundi shifted to a focus on development, the MDGs, and the aid effectiveness agenda, which emphasized aligning with government development priorities. From 2005 to 2010 (Phases IV and V), even though DFID Burundi was led by a highly skilled and politically knowledgeable leader and supplied with conflict analyses and conflict advisors, its interventions were largely insensitive to Burundi's conflict dynamics and did not seek to have a peacebuilding effect. During this period, DFID Burundi did not have informal local accountability or formal peacebuilding accountability routines. In 2011 (Phase VI), DFID headquarters announced that it would close its Burundi office and stop all bilateral assistance to Burundi. It argued that Burundi was now ready to stand on its own without DFID's development assistance. How did a bilateral donor that made such strong commitments to conflict-sensitive development and peacebuilding fail to continue to pursue these goals in Burundi – one of the poorest and most fragile states in the world?

DFID as a Peacebuilding Learner

Between 1999 and 2004, DFID Burundi went from being a detached humanitarian donor to one that was highly engaged in peacebuilding and that supported some of the most innovative peacebuilding projects in Burundi.[11] Before 1999, DFID viewed Burundi as a humanitarian situation and provided some humanitarian assistance. DFID's funding

---

[10] For an example of this phenomena in relation to the UN PBF, see Campbell et al., "Independent External Evaluation: UN Peacebuilding Fund Project Portfolio in Burundi, 2007–2013."

[11] In addition to the documents and interviews cited, the analysis of DFID's behavior in Phase I is informed by research that I conducted for a report that I wrote for the International Crisis Group (ICG) on aid to Burundi; see ICG, "A Framework for Responsible Aid to Burundi."

Table 5.2. *DFID Burundi*

	Informal Local Accountability	Formal Peacebuilding Accountability	Country Office Type	Result
DFID Phase I: Jan. 1999– Oct. 2001	n/a	n/a	n/a	n/a
DFID Phase II: Nov. 2001– Nov. 2003	Yes	Yes	Peacebuilding Learner	Actions to reduce gap between peacebuilding aims and outcomes
DFID Phase III: Dec. 2003– Aug. 2005	Yes	Yes	Peacebuilding Learner	Actions to reduce gap between peacebuilding aims and outcomes
DFID Phase IV: Sept. 2005– Apr. 2009	No	No	Stagnant Player	Actions without consideration of effect on conflict dynamics
DFID Phase V: May 2009– May 2010	No	No	Stagnant Player	Actions without consideration of effect on conflict dynamics
DFID Phase VI: June 2010– Apr. 2014	No	No	Stagnant Player	Actions without consideration of effect on conflict dynamics

approach to Burundi did not change when the Arusha Agreement was signed in August 2000. Along with many other donors who had withdrawn aid in response to the regional embargo against Burundi (1996–1999), DFID wanted evidence that the peace process was really on track before reengaging as a development partner.[12]

Initially, DFID had followed the lead of other donors and Julius Nyerere, the mediator of Burundi's Arusha peace talks until late 1999 and held back aid from Burundi. Clare Short, the head of DFID in London, said that Nyerere believed that regional sanctions, in spite of

---

[12] Statements by Clare Short, Secretary of State for International Development, *House of Commons Hansard Written Answers for 18 Dec 2002*, pt. 14 (London, 2002), accessed December 22, 2017, http://goo.gl/Gg99zB.

the humanitarian cost, encouraged President Buyoya to commit to the Arusha peace talks.[13] In this sense, DFID's peacebuilding strategy at the time was to withhold aid. After the Arusha Agreement was signed, however, DFID and other donors continued to apply this tactic, reneging on their promises to reward Burundian politicians' efforts.[14]

In February 2002 (Phase II), Short and her fellow development ministers from Norway and the Netherlands visited the countries of the Great Lakes region, including Burundi. This trip changed Short's perspective on Burundi.[15] In December 2002, she confirmed DFID's commitment "to an increasing effort to bring peace and help restart efforts to develop Burundi's full potential," and advocated that other donors do the same.[16] In so doing, Short established formal peacebuilding accountability that would guide DFID's renewed engagement with Burundi. Shortly thereafter, DFID established an office in Burundi to "see what was going on, engage and report back, play a role."[17] The office consisted of one international staff member and two Burundian staff members and focused almost exclusively on peacebuilding, with the aim of establishing peace before DFID Burundi made the transition to typical development assistance:[18] As one DFID staff member said, "We were there to support the peace process."[19]

DFID Burundi's commitment to peacebuilding between 2002 and 2004 (Phases II and III) was unique not only in comparison to many other bilateral donors in Burundi, but also in comparison to other DFID country programs:

> DFID [in Burundi] did everything but the standard development program. They hired conflict advisors to sit in the country. They wanted to work with demobilized soldiers. They were doing stuff that no other donor was doing. They broke so much ground based directly on policies coming out of London... It was one our best examples ever of taking on board conflict policies [developed at DFID headquarters].[20]

---

[13] ICG, "A Framework for Responsible Aid to Burundi."

[14] ICG, "A Framework for Responsible Aid to Burundi."

[15] Interview with DFID staff member D10, Bujumbura, July 16, 2002.

[16] Statements by Clare Short, Secretary of State for International Development, *House of Commons Hansard Written Answers for 4 Nov 2002*, pt. 8 (London, 2002), accessed December 22, 2017, http://goo.gl/LH8J52; and statements by Clare Short, Secretary of State for International Development, *House of Commons Hansard Written Answers for 17 Dec 2002*, pt. 8 (London, 2002), accessed December 22, 2017, http://goo.gl/COUFV8.

[17] Interview with DFID staff member D3, via telephone, October 12, 2011; and interview with DFID staff member D10, Bujumbura, July 16, 2002.

[18] Interview with DFID staff member D10, Bujumbura, July 16, 2002.

[19] Interview by DFID staff member D3, via telephone, October 12, 2011.

[20] Interview with DFID staff member D2, via telephone, May 20, 2010.

Initially, the office had an annual budget of UK £2 million, which increased to UK £5 million a year by 2004. DFID used the money to fund new projects and opportunities as they emerged.[21] It did not have a predetermined set of activities or goals; it sought to fund projects that would contribute to momentum in Burundi's peacebuilding process.[22]

Along with the US Agency for International Development's (USAID) Greater Horn of Africa Initiative, USAID's Office of Transition Initiatives, and the World Bank Post-Conflict Fund and Multi-Country Demobilization and Reintegration Program, DFID Burundi's support for peacebuilding activities helped a community of peacebuilding NGOs and civil society organizations flourish in Burundi.[23] Most other donors to Burundi at the time gave only humanitarian funding.[24]

Although the amount of money that DFID Burundi gave paled in comparison to that of many other donors in Burundi, DFID Burundi's support was strategically targeted toward core priorities in Burundi's peacebuilding process. DFID Burundi also established informal local accountability routines that provided regular feedback about its outcomes, so that the office could take regular action to reduce the gap between its peacebuilding aims and outcomes, including by encouraging its grantees to adapt to the evolving conflict dynamics. During Phases II and III, DFID Burundi was a peacebuilding learner.

DFID as a Stagnant Player: Development and the Fragile State

With the August 2005 inauguration of Pierre Nkurunziza as president of Burundi, DFID Burundi's formal accountability routines shifted to prioritize development. Its new approach, now for Phase IV, aimed "to support the new government in delivering an early peace dividend to the population, building an effective state with better governance, and starting to make progress toward the MDGs."[25] DFID believed that the inauguration of Burundi's first democratically elected government in

---

[21] The recipients of these funds included the BLTP, International Alert, the Jan van Eck of the Center for Conflict Resolution in Cape Town, Action Aid, Accord in South Africa, and the United Nations. Based on interviews with DFID staff members D10, Bujumbura, July 16, 2002; and D3, via telephone, October 12, 2011.

[22] Interview with DFID staff member D3, via telephone, October 12, 2011.

[23] See Larry Beyna et al., "Greater Horn of Africa Peace Building Project – the Effectiveness of Civil Society Initiatives in Controlling Violent Conflicts and Building Peace: A Study of Three Approaches in the Greater Horn of Africa," evaluation (Washington, DC: Management Systems International, June 2001).

[24] ICG, "A Framework for Responsible Aid to Burundi."

[25] DFID, "DfID Burundi, 2009–2011: Issues and Choices Paper: Burundi's Options for 2009–11" (Bujumbura, 2009), 4.

twelve years required an approach that aimed to strengthen the capacity of the state to deliver basic social services, namely health, education, and justice.[26] Since health and education were two of DFID's top development priorities, this new focus fit nicely with the push from DFID headquarters to achieve progress in these areas.

In 2005, DFID appointed Sue Hogwood, the former UK ambassador to Rwanda and Burundi, as the director of its Burundi office. In so doing, it devolved the management of the office from London to the country-office level. Two program officers, a Foreign Commonwealth Office (FCO) representative, and Burundian support staff were appointed to the office, bringing the total number of staff to seven. The integration of the FCO and DFID into one office was a unique structure for DFID, intended to give its development work a political focus.[27]

DFID Burundi's new program strategy was a response to priorities articulated by the Burundian government. In his inaugural speech, President Nkurunziza announced that there would be free primary education for all Burundians.[28] The next year, he declared that there would be free maternal health care.[29] The Burundian government had failed to budget for either of these initiatives or to warn donors that the initiatives were coming down the pike. Nonetheless, DFID Burundi and other donors rallied to support the government in achieving these aims by including them as priorities in the donors' development cooperation plans with Burundi.[30]

After the 2005 elections, there was a sense of euphoria in Burundi. The government, international actors, and average Burundians all hoped that the country was entering a new period of peace and progress.[31] The design of DFID's post-2005 Burundi program was partly a response to this hopefulness. DFID Burundi wanted to make sure that the Burundian government could deliver its promises to the Burundian people, namely free primary education and maternal health care. DFID Burundi argued that if the government could not significantly improve its health and education systems, "how stable would [Burundi] have been?"[32]

DFID Burundi gradually phased out the thirty-odd projects that it had inherited from its 2002–2004 plan, including the Burundi Leadership

---

[26] DFID, "DfID Burundi, 2009–2011," 1.

[27] Interview with DFID staff member D11, Bujumbura, June 26, 2009.

[28] IRIN, "Burundi: Free Schooling Starts with Huge Logistical Problems," September 19, 2005, accessed December 22, 2017, http://goo.gl/guDtF2.

[29] IRIN, "Burundi: Nkurunziza Announces Free Maternal Healthcare, Pay Rise for Workers," May 1, 2006, accessed December 22, 2017, http://goo.gl/bbdz9z.

[30] DFID, "DfID Burundi, 2009–2011," 9.

[31] Interviews with observer O4, Bujumbura, June 26, 2009, and DFID staff member D1, Bujumbura, June 1, 2009.

[32] Interview with DFID staff member D6, Bujumbura, June 6, 2009.

Training Program (BLTP), and adopted a program-based approach in which DFID Burundi collaborated directly with the government to develop and fulfill sectorial policies in the areas of health, education, and justice.[33] Because of well-documented corruption in the government and ongoing scandals, DFID Burundi did not provide funding directly to the government.[34] Instead, it collaborated with other donors to manage funds and give money to the government in increments for agreed-upon activities.[35]

DFID Burundi's program complied with its corporate prioritization of health and education and its commitment to aligning its approach with the government's policies, as outlined in the Paris Declaration for Aid Effectiveness.[36] DFID's headquarter-based leadership had made a commitment to health and education as part of the MDGs and through other key commitments, such as the International Health Partnership.[37] As a development agency, DFID was eager to focus on core development priorities and to provide its offices with budgets to spend on development.

In spite of the strong commitment that DFID headquarters had also made to carry out politically sensitive development, DFID's program in Burundi from 2005 through 2009 (Phase IV) existed on two parallel and largely disconnected tracks: a development track and a diplomatic track. The development track aimed to increase the capacity of the state to deliver education and health care. According to DFID Burundi's own reports, DFID Burundi made an important contribution in each of these areas.[38] Its justice and governance programming was based on a development model and aimed foremost to strengthen the capacity of the Burundian government to ensure justice and the rule

---

[33] DFID, "DfID Burundi, 2009–2011," 10.

[34] DFID, "DfID Burundi, 2009–2011," 11.

[35] DFID, "The Closure of DFID's Aid Programme in Burundi: Written Evidence Submitted by the Department for International Development" (London: UK Parliament–International Development Committee, 2011), para. 26, accessed December 22, 2017, http://goo.gl/G6kD7s.

[36] The Paris Declaration on Aid Effectiveness outlines five principles: *ownership* by developing countries of their own poverty reduction strategies and objectives; *alignment* of donor countries behind these strategies and objectives and use of local systems to deliver aid; *harmonization* and coordination of donor approaches and modalities; a focus on achieving and measuring *results* of development cooperation; and the creation of *mutual accountability* between donors and recipient countries.

[37] DFID, "DfID Burundi, 2009–2011," 9; and interview with DFID staff member D6.

[38] International Development Committee (IDC), "The Closure of DFID's Bilateral Aid Programme in Burundi: Tenth Report of Session 2010–12," House of Commons report (London: House of Commons, October 28, 2012), accessed December 22, 2017, http://goo.gl/gwBIwv.

of law.[39] The Ministry of Justice and the Burundian National Police, two of the most corrupt and dysfunctional ministries, repeatedly stalled DFID Burundi's efforts to strengthen the justice system, leading DFID Burundi eventually to abandon the aspect of its program that funded the Ministry of Justice.[40]

The approach that DFID had taken in Rwanda influenced its approach in Burundi. The DFID office in Rwanda oversaw DFID's Burundi program. Hogwood reported directly to the Rwanda office. Furthermore, several of the DFID Burundi staff had worked in the DFID Rwanda office. Hogwood had been the ambassador to Rwanda and Burundi from 2001 until she took the DFID post in 2005. Soon after the 1994 Rwandan genocide, DFID had invested heavily in Rwanda and had prioritized pursuit of the MDGs above pursuit of peace, justice, human rights, and governance.[41] It had been committed to increasing the capacity of the state to deliver services, not to strengthening state–society relations.[42] Even though Burundi was different from Rwanda in many ways, DFID applied a similar approach to its work in Burundi.

The leadership of DFID based in Rwanda and London saw the 2005 elections as a trigger for DFID to move from a peacebuilding focus (2002–2004) to a core development focus.[43] In fact, it argued that DFID should provide direct aid to the Burundian budget (i.e., budgetary aid), even though there would be no way to monitor the use of the funds.[44] Although the DFID Burundi office successfully convinced its superiors that budgetary aid was not appropriate, the rest of the program went ahead.

DFID Burundi's political and peacebuilding activities were mainly confined to the diplomacy and reporting work of Hogwood and the FCO liaison officer. Their analyses and diplomatic actions were not integrated into DFID Burundi's development cooperation programming, or vice versa. DFID Burundi's development projects were not based on an analysis of their relationship to the conflict environment, and development assistance was not used directly to influence political outcomes.

---

[39] Communication with DFID staff member D12 via email, February 17, 2012.

[40] DFID, "The Closure of DFID's Aid Programme in Burundi," para. 26.

[41] IDC, "House of Commons Oral Evidence Taken Before the International Development Committee: Working with Fragile and Conflict-Affected States: DRC, Rwanda and Burundi" (London: UK Parliament, 2011), 12–13 [hereafter, IDC, "Working with Fragile and Conflict-Affected States"], accessed December 22, 2017, http://goo.gl/jnDQ4V.

[42] IDC, "Working with Fragile and Conflict-Affected States."

[43] Interview with DFID staff member D13, via telephone, October 12, 2011.

[44] Interview with DFID staff member D13, via telephone, October 12, 2011.

Hogwood was very well informed about Burundian politics and a vocal advocate for high-quality peacebuilding by international actors and the Burundian government alike. Said one observer, "Sue Hogwood was amazing. There was no way to keep up with her."[45] As the UK ambassador to Rwanda and Burundi from 2001 to 2004, she had followed the politics of Burundi and collaborated closely with Georgina Yates, the director of DFID's Burundi office at the time. In addition to her own capacity and network, Hogwood benefited from the UK's position on the UN Security Council and the strong knowledge base about Burundi that existed within DFID more broadly.[46] Most of her staff were also well respected and influential; they were not afraid to speak up and try to hold the international community and Burundians to a higher standard.

In spite of DFID's small program in Burundi, Hogwood and her team's excellent reputation with Burundians and foreigners alike and Hogwood's determination enabled the office "to punch above its weight."[47] She pressured the UN and other international actors to harmonize their approaches and align with the government's priorities as they had agreed to in the Paris Declaration for Aid Effectiveness. She also helped the UN improve the quality of its peacebuilding programming. As an observer at the regular meetings of the Joint Steering Committee for the UN PBF, she ensured that there was some degree of programmatic oversight of PBF security-sector activities by supporting the creation of informal local accountability routines for several key projects, such as the project with the Burundian intelligence service (SNR).[48]

The DFID Burundi office provided the following self-assessment:

We have been able to play an influential role. The government sees us as a partner with whom they can do business (we come with no baggage and no hidden agenda), and partners see us as leaders ... This places us in an influential position, and DFID can – and does – play a strong advocacy role, including on best practice and conflict transformation, and on political and security issues.[49]

Yet, in spite of Hogwood's political astuteness and the conflict analysis performed by the DFID Burundi office, DFID Burundi's programming was not sensitive or adapted to the conflict dynamics. DFID was thus a stagnant player, working around the political and security dynamics rather than trying to influence them directly. DFID Burundi's

---

[45] Communication with observer O17, Bujumbura, June 16, 2009.
[46] Communication with observer O17, Bujumbura, June 16, 2009.
[47] DFID, "DfID Burundi, 2009–2011," 4.
[48] Interviews with key informants, Bujumbura, 2009.
[49] DFID, "DfID Burundi, 2009–2011," 5.

strong informal local accountability routines with other political and international actors in Bujumbura supported DFID Burundi's diplomatic efforts, but did not translate into strong informal local accountability for DFID Burundi's development activities. DFID Burundi's formal accountability for development predominated, making development outcomes and indicators the primary target of DFID Burundi's interventions, in spite of DFID's overall commitment to implementing conflict-sensitive development activities.

DFID Burundi's health, education, governance, and justice activities were largely detached from the causes of Burundi's conflict and its manifestations, even though Burundi's health, education, governance, and justice systems had been heavily affected by the war. In fact, exclusionary education policies in particular had played a role in perpetuating Burundi's war.[50] Education in Burundi had long been used as a tool of oppression by the state. Hutu were systematically excluded from primary and secondary education, and more than one hundred thousand Hutu intellectuals had been massacred in 1972.[51] Burundi's health system, for its part, had been complicit in corruption schemes and preferential treatment and was reported to be connected to the murder of the head of the World Health Organization in Burundi who had uncovered high-level corruption within the Burundian government involving antimalarial drugs.[52]

In spite of the legacy of violence and conflict in Burundi's education and health institutions, DFID Burundi treated its education and health programs as apolitical development projects.[53] DFID Burundi had a regional conflict advisor who commissioned a thorough conflict analysis of the political situation in 2009 and met regularly with DFID Burundi staff, but neither the conflict advisor nor DFID Burundi tried to integrate his analysis into DFID Burundi's health or education programs or any of DFID Burundi's other ongoing activities.[54] This pattern reflects a broader organizational trend with DFID offices in other countries as well: "DFID country teams in most insecure countries assess the extent

---

[50] Tony Jackson, "Equal Access to Education a Peace Imperative for Burundi" (London: International Alert, June 2000), accessed December 22, 2017, http://goo.gl/6W2NVT.

[51] Jackson, "Equal Access to Education a Peace Imperative for Burundi," 2.

[52] "Burundi Spy Chief Found Guilty of WHO Director's Murder," *New Zealand Herald*, May 31, 2013, accessed December 22, 2017, www.nzherald.co.nz/world/news/article.cfm?c_id=2&objectid=10123996.

[53] IDC, "Working with Fragile and Conflict-Affected States."

[54] Interviews with DFID staff member D5, Bujumbura, June 18, 2009; and DFID staff member D8, in Bujumbura, June 15, 2009.

and nature of conflict, but these assessments rarely make explicit links to program choices and management."[55]

DFID Burundi's work in the justice sector was more sensitive to Burundi's political and security context because it was based on an understanding of the role of access to justice in the conflict. Nonetheless, DFID Burundi took the relatively standard development approach of trying to directly strengthen the Ministry of Justice. DFID Burundi lacked a fine-grained analysis of the actors and issues preventing progress from taking place in the justice sector and could therefore not develop a more nuanced program.[56] The Minister of Justice was notoriously uncooperative with donors and other international actors and repeatedly stonewalled DFID Burundi, eventually leading DFID Burundi to abandon its efforts.[57]

DFID Burundi argued that its post-2005 approach played "a strong role in reinforcing state capability, responsiveness, and accountability" through its support for an international NGO-run communication campaign "to promote dialogue between the citizens and the state" and its work to create the Burundi Revenue Authority.[58] In fact, DFID Burundi's programs focused more on strengthening top-down state capacity than on the responsiveness of the state to its population. The communication campaign that it supported intended to increase state–society interaction but was largely deemed to be unsuccessful.

DFID Burundi's post-2005 support to Burundi contradicted DFID's own policy papers on state-building. "State-building is not a technical process of strengthening government institutions – this is more accurately described as 'institution building.' In all contexts, state-building is principally about strengthening the relationship between the state and society, and developing effective ways to mediate this relationship."[59]

DFID's efforts to create the Burundi Revenue Authority focused on increasing the capacity of the state to collect, and extract, taxes from the population, but not on the responsiveness of the state to the population's needs or demands. According to a UK parliamentarian who visited the Burundi project:

[55] Interviews with DFID staff members D5 and D8; and National Audit Office, "Department for International Development: Operating in Insecure Environments– National Audit Office" (London: National Audit Office, October 16, 2008), para. 26, accessed December 22, 2017, http://goo.gl/wMCWHg.
[56] Interview with DFID staff member D1, Bujumbura, June 1, 2009.
[57] DFID, "The Closure of DFID's Aid Programme in Burundi," para. 26.
[58] DFID, "The Closure of DFID's Aid Programme in Burundi," para. 26; and interview with DFID staff member D1, Bujumbura, June 1, 2009.
[59] DFID, "Building the State and Securing the Peace," Emerging Policy Paper (London: DFID, June 2009), paras. 10–11, accessed December 22, 2017, http://goo.gl/jo7nO3.

The tax authority stuff is purely national budget stuff; there is no way of making it local or giving any form of accountability other than through the Government ... In Burundi it could quite clearly be argued that all we are doing is raising money to go into the President's pocket, because it goes into the budget pot and we have absolutely no control whatsoever of the budget pot, which as an aid community we are contributing half to anyway.[60]

A study by a local corruption watchdog found that half of the Burundian government's 2006 and 2007 budget was embezzled.[61]

In response to the results of Burundi's 2010 elections, DFID did not attempt to address the increasing likelihood of armed violence or the growing authoritarianism of the Burundian government. Instead, DFID painted these fraught elections as a sign that Burundi was ready to begin its "transition from a fragile state to a more stable and prosperous future."[62] In spite of numerous objections within and outside the UK government, DFID closed its bilateral program with Burundi in 2012.[63] It justified this decision partly based on the program's purported contribution to state-building: "The [DFID Burundi Country] programme has also invested strongly in building government capacity to deliver basic services (including access to justice), in line with DFID's fragile states principles on state-building. This approach has prepared the ground for a responsible exit, as sustainability has been built into most of DFID's programme."[64]

The decision to stop DFID's development cooperation with Burundi seems to have been largely political.[65] Although the relative unimportance of Burundi may have given the DFID Burundi office some autonomy in earlier years, it now made the DFID Burundi program an easy target for DFID's downsizing efforts.[66] With the departure of Hogwood in 2010, the Burundi office also lacked a strong advocate in favor of DFID's Burundi program.

Explaining DFID Burundi's Behavior

In the 2000s and 2010s, DFID had become a "leading proponent of engagement in fragile states," conflict-sensitive development, and

[60] IDC, "Working with Fragile and Conflict-Affected States."
[61] Burundi Réalités, "Burundi: Half of the National Budget Embezzled Within Two Years," *AllAfrica* (February 2, 2008), accessed December 22, 2017, http://goo.gl/FVrY9b.
[62] Interview with DFID staff member D5, Bujumbura, June 18, 2009.
[63] International Alert, "The Closure of DFID's Aid Programme in Burundi" (London: UK Parliament), accessed December 22, 2017, http://goo.gl/d183kA.
[64] DFID, "The Closure of DFID's Aid Programme in Burundi," 9.
[65] Interview with DFID staff member D2, via telephone, May 20, 2010.
[66] Interview with DFID staff member D2, via telephone, May 20, 2010.

peacebuilding.[67] It committed to allocating 30 percent of its aid to fragile and conflict-affected states by 2014. It amassed an impressive cadre of conflict advisors across the organization. It spent millions on research into improving the impact of development in fragile and conflict-affected states. It continued to push multilateral organizations to be more conflict sensitive and engage in more effective conflict prevention, peacebuilding, and state-building.[68] Since 2001, it has produced several white papers and policy documents that have established new standards for engagement with fragile and conflict-affected states, for both DFID and the rest of the international community.

In spite of DFID's intense investment in improving aid to conflict-affected and fragile states, its country program in Burundi was unable to maintain a focus on conflict-sensitive development or take regular actions to reduce the gap between its peacebuilding (conflict-sensitive development) aims and outcomes after critical turning points in Burundi's evolving war-to-peace transition. From 2002 to 2004, DFID's support to Burundi was primarily focused on peacebuilding. Because of the intervention of DFID's Director, Clare Short, DFID Burundi was focused solely on peacebuilding during this period and was accountable for funding peacebuilding activities. As a result, it could take advantage of new opportunities in Burundi's peacebuilding process and support new initiatives by INGOs and multilateral organizations. This case shows that even development donors can adopt peacebuilding as the priority for a country office for a period of time.

During this period, between 2002 and 2004 (Phases II and III), DFID Burundi supported several innovative peacebuilding activities, some of which engendered crucial changes in Burundian institutions. DFID Burundi's peacebuilding achievements were not due to the provision of large amounts of money – DFID Burundi's budget from 2002 to 2004 paled in comparison to its post-2005 budget. Instead, DFID Burundi's peacebuilding achievements were due to formal peacebuilding accountability and informal local accountability. Between 2002 and 2004, DFID Burundi focused on supporting Burundi's peace process and responding to the specific peacebuilding needs and opportunities that appeared in this context, incentivized by the formal peacebuilding accountability that Short created for the Burundi office. To identify key peacebuilders and key opportunities to support them, DFID Burundi established strong

---

[67] OECD, "United Kingdom DAC Peer Review" (2010), accessed February 15, 2018, www.oecd.org/dac/peer-reviews/45519815.pdf; OECD, "United Kingdom DAC Peer Review" (2006).

[68] OECD, "United Kingdom Development DAC Peer Review" (2006), 35.

informal local accountability routines. In addition, DFID Burundi incentivized its grantees to establish and sustain informal local accountability routines, if they did not already have them.

After 2005, DFID Burundi changed its approach. It moved to formal accountability for standard development targets, not peacebuilding (inclusive of conflict-sensitive development). It directed most of its resources through the Burundian government and focused on core development priorities: health, education, and governance. Even though the peace process was ongoing, DFID Burundi's programs largely lacked a conflict-sensitive lens and did not explicitly aim to reduce the recurrence of violence in Burundi. Furthermore, the office failed to respond to key peacebuilding opportunities and new trends in Burundi's peacebuilding process in 2009 and 2010. In fact, just as Burundi seemed to be descending toward renewed conflict, DFID declared its program in Burundi a success and closed its office there.

During Phases III, IV, and V (2005–2011), DFID Burundi had most of the trappings of a conflict-sensitive development actor, but these characteristics did not make a difference in the way it implemented its activities. Formal development accountability predominated and determined how the office related to Burundi's evolving war-to-peace transition. DFID Burundi's director was a skilled political operative with in-depth knowledge of Burundi and the Great Lakes region. The FCO and DFID were integrated into one office in DFID Burundi, supposedly ensuring that the political and development arms of the UK government were also integrated. A regional conflict advisor supported the office. Its staff went to trainings on improving programming in fragile states. It conducted regular in-house conflict analyses and brought in external analysts to do more conflict analysis. Its staff regularly and openly discussed the conflict environment and their programming approaches. They were all well read and well informed about Burundi's political and security context and DFID's conflict-related policies. The programs that DFID Burundi supported were based on deep analysis and an intensive planning process. DFID Burundi's director had a great deal of autonomy and decision-making power.

Yet, DFID's program in Burundi between 2005 and 2011 failed to respond to the particular nature of Burundi's institutions. This was in large part because of the shift to formal accountability for development, not peacebuilding. Implicit in DFID Burundi's development focus was the assumption that the Burundian state represented the Burundian people and was carrying out policies that would not foster renewed violent conflict. Implicit in DFID's broader commitment to the aid effectiveness agenda and the MDGs is the idea that if the government also commits itself to the MDGs and if donors help finance these commitments, then they will be achieved. But in a country rife with exclusionary practices and corruption, direct support for the government's policies did not lead to the desired change in Burundi's social services. DFID's focus on the MDGs supported quick, easily measurable results rather than riskier, but possibly much more important, conflict-sensitive programming with potentially more ambiguous results. The decision to close the Burundi program in 2012 seems to have been made on a whim by UK politicians, not unlike the decision to open the office in 2002.

Informal Local Accountability

After 2005, DFID Burundi did not have strong informal local accountability routines. DFID Burundi regularly exchanged information with the international community in Burundi and with key government partners to support its diplomatic activities and to influence the behavior of the broader community of donors in Burundi. DFID had little contact, however, with the beneficiaries and most of the other stakeholders in the development programs that it funded.

By all accounts, DFID Burundi had a high degree of open and transparent information sharing within its small office.[69] Staff openly discussed issues that arose in their activites and in Burundian politics. They shared information with their head office in Kigali and headquarters in London, but they resolved most problems locally. Bucking the trend in much of the aid industry, DFID Burundi staff read a lot: keeping up on the latest local news, political analyses, relevant guidance and reports from headquarters, and reports from their projects. They had access to a wealth of resources about best practices, thematic strategies, and DFID's particular approach. Members of the international community reported that Hogwood was always on top of the latest information about both Burundi's evolving peace process and the international community's response.[70] When the office received negative information about programs or projects, staff discussed it openly and decided what to do.[71] They resolved issues at the country-office level and in consultation with the Kigali office and took issues to headquarters only when necessary.[72]

[69] Interviews with DFID staff member D1, Bujumbura, June 1, 2009; DFID staff member D3, via telephone, October 12, 2011; DFID staff member D6, Bujumbura, June 6, 2009; DFID staff member D5, Bujumbura, June 18, 2009; and DFID staff member D7, Bujumbura, June 4, 2009.

[70] Communication with observer O17, Bujumbura, June 16, 2009.

[71] Interviews with DFID staff members D1, Bujumbura, June 1, 2009; D5, Bujumbura, June 18, 2008; and D7, Bujumbura, June 4, 2009.

[72] Interview with DFID staff member D6, Bujumbura, June 6, 2009.

However, DFID Burundi did not have sufficient data on whether it was achieving its desired outcomes in relation to Burundi's conflict dynamics, partly because these types of data were not regularly collected by the Burundian government and partly because DFID Burundi did not collect these data.[73] In other words, DFID Burundi did not have information on the potential gap between its peacebuilding (or conflict-sensitive development) aims and outcomes.

DFID Burundi staff spent most of their time in Bujumbura interacting with their counterparts there. They relied on partners' quarterly reports about project outputs and on conversations with partners and observers in Bujumbura to understand their grantees progress, both within and outside of Bujumbura.[74] DFID Burundi project staff conducted a minimum of two field visits a year per project.[75] They did not believe it was their role to systematically monitor the implementation of their programs and projects outside of Bujumbura. Instead, they focused on policy-level engagement, discussion, and reform with government officials and international partners. The FCO staff person regularly visited the countryside to assess the situation, but he did not collect information about DFID's development or justice interventions.[76] An evaluation report of DFID's programs in fragile states found that other country offices were also generally unable to monitor and evaluate the outcomes of their activities in fragile states.[77]

Donors tend to have influence over a project when deciding whether to fund it or whether to renew its funding. But donor influence tends to dramatically decline once the donor gives money to a grantee. At this point, it is up to the implementing partner to ensure the relevance of the project to the context. DFID Burundi could only support, advise, and assist in this effort. Once the money was committed, DFID Burundi staff were incentivized by DFID headquarters to ensure that money was spent, not to return the money to headquarters and possibly lead headquarters to diminish DFID Burundi's future budgets.[78] Like the INGO country offices discussed in Chapter 3 and the IO country offices discussed in Chapter 4, DFID's country offices are also most accountable for spending the money that is allocated to them to spend. This sets up a

---

[73] Interview with DFID staff member D5, Bujumbura, June 18, 2009.
[74] Interview with DFID staff member D5, Bujumbura, June 18, 2009.
[75] Interview with DFID staff member D7, Bujumbura, June 4, 2009.
[76] Interview with DFID staff member D4, Bujumbura, March 20, 2009.
[77] Nick Chapman and Charlotte Vaillant, "Synthesis of Country Programme Evaluations Conducted in Fragile States," evaluation report (London: DFID, February 2010), accessed December 22, 2017, http://goo.gl/L7Avr7.
[78] Interview with DFID staff member D2, via telephone, May 20, 2010.

disincentive for bilateral country offices to create time-consuming informal local accountability routines that they are not staffed to maintain. It
incentivizes bilateral donor country offices to receive reports from
grantees and ensure that grantees have spent their money as planned
rather than investigating for themselves whether activities are having the
desired effect.

Based on the information that DFID Burundi received from its grantees, its levers to influence their behavior were restricted to relatively
blunt instruments. DFID could disburse funds, postpone the disbursement of funds, and stop the disbursement of funds. In the absence of
these formal legal actions, donors can attempt to influence grantee activities through dialogue. Most of DFID Burundi's attempts to influence
the direction of the projects that it funded took the form of dialogue –
informing, advocating, persuading, and discussing. If, after discussions,
DFID Burundi believed that a project was not successful, DFID Burundi
had to negotiate with the DFID Kigali and London offices – informing,
advocating, persuading, and discussing its approach in Burundi; why
things were not proceeding according to plan; and determining what
the office wanted to do about it.

DFID partners were not made aware of DFID's broader commitment
to conflict-sensitive development. DFID Burundi did not train its partners in the "DFID approach" or share policy papers or guidelines with
partners. It provided technical support during discussions, drafted program documents, and appointed technical assistants to serve in different
ministries or intervening organizations.[79] But DFID did not invest serious time or energy in building the capacity of its partners to implement
effective programs, whether conflict-sensitive or not, or monitor and
evaluate these programs. This light touch further reduced the capacity
of DFID Burundi to influence the outcomes of the activities that it
funded. It largely relied on the capacity, knowledge, and will of its
partners to achieve outcomes. It did not have the staff to facilitate greater
monitoring of its projects or the inclination to establish informal local
accountability mechanisms.[80]

DFID headquarters' decision to assign a small number of staff to its
Burundi office followed the logic that a small pot of money required a
small number of people to manage it. But in fragile and conflict-affected
states, this approach may not be the right one.[81] The OECD-DAC's

[79] Interviews with DFID staff members D1, Bujumbura, June 1, 2009; and D5,
   Bujumbura, June 18, 2009.
[80] Interview with DFID staff member D1, Bujumbura, June 1, 2009.
[81] Chapman and Vaillant, "Synthesis of Country Programme Evaluations."

"Supporting State-building in Situations of Conflict and Fragility: Policy Guidance" recommends that donors increase the "staff-to-aid spending ratio" to take into account the investment needed by staff to understand local networks of power and to develop appropriate approaches for engaging with them.[82] DFID's "Synthesis of Country Programme Evaluations Conducted in Fragile States" makes a similar recommendation, commenting that "operating in a fragile state is typically more labor-intensive and expensive than elsewhere for a variety of reasons including the weakness of host governments, a risky operating environment, difficult communications, and ill-adapted internal procedures and regulations."[83]

All of this contributed to DFID Burundi being a stagnant player, implementing activities that were largely detached from Burundi's macro- and micro-level political and security situation. DFID Burundi was also unable to take action to reduce the gap between its peacebuilding (i.e., conflict-sensitive development) aims and the outcomes of its grantees' activities. DFID Burundi lacked information about the relationship between its grantees' activities and the micro- or macro-level political and security dynamics that would have come through informal local accountability. It also lacked the incentive that formal peacebuilding accountability would have provided to respond to this information.

Formal Accountability Routines

As an organization, DFID is "completely focused on MDGs and aid effectiveness," not on politics.[84] In spite of the cutting-edge policies and publications that DFID has released on conflict prevention, peacebuilding, and state-building, DFID is primarily focused on development and pursuing the Aid Effectiveness Agenda, outlined in the Paris and Accra agreements.[85] In DFID, "anything against Paris is bad."[86] The Aid Effectiveness Agenda aims to reduce the duplication of donor efforts, lessen the administrative burden that donors place on recipient countries, and improve the sustainability of the results of aid interventions.

---

[82] OECD-DAC, "Supporting State-building in Situations of Conflict and Fragility: Policy Guidance," DAC Guidelines and Reference Series (Paris: OECD, February 28, 2011), 90, accessed December 22, 2017, http://goo.gl/LNKjkv.

[83] Chapman and Vaillant, "Synthesis of Country Programme Evaluations."

[84] Interview with DFID staff member D9, via telephone, February 12, 2009.

[85] OECD-DAC, "Paris Declaration and Accra Agenda for Action," accessed December 22, 2017, http://goo.gl/mvd33W.

[86] Interview with DFID staff member D2, via telephone, May 20, 2010; and observer O3, via telephone, March 10, 2010.

The core aid effectiveness principles – national ownership, alignment of donor governments behind host government policies, harmonization of aid modalities among donors, a focus on results, and the creation of mutual accountability – were designed for donors intervening in "normal" developing countries, not in conflict-affected countries.[87] By applying the aid effectiveness principles to its Burundi program from 2005 onward, DFID's incentive structures and related formal accountability routines acted as if Burundi were a well-developed democratic country that was relatively free of conflict or violence. One DFID staff person commented that it is easier to do development cooperation when "the government and the state are one [and] the same," meaning that the government actually represents the interests of the people.[88]

Much of Burundi's political leadership was more focused on its own enrichment than on developing and implementing policies that would benefit its people:

People like the president of Burundi "could not care less about human rights; they have no interest at all. We have no leverage whatsoever on them, because they are quite happy for us to do whatever aid we want" presumably because they get their cut in different ways through budget support and everything like that – "and we have to work around it."[89]

Although the difficulty of implementing the aid effectiveness principles in fragile and conflict-affected states is well known, DFID did not provide its Burundi country office with tools for managing these challenges.[90] An audit of DFID's capacity to operate in insecure environments found that DFID, in general, does not have sufficient guidance for how staff should operate or design programs in insecure environments, and it had "no operational guidance on how to ensure that aid is conflict-sensitive."[91]

DFID Burundi staff attended workshops on fragile states, but the workshops concentrated more on relatively general academic literature and failed to provide specific guidance on what to do differently in Burundi or how to do it.[92] The regional conflict advisor was focused

[87] OECD-DAC, "Paris Declaration and Accra Agenda for Action."
[88] Interview with DFID staff member D8, Bujumbura, June 15, 2009.
[89] Minister Richard Harrington citing a conversation that he had with the EU Ambassador to Burundi. See IDC, "Working with Fragile and Conflict-Affected States," 10.
[90] Stephen Jones, Katarina Kotoglou, and Taylor Brown, "The Applicability of the Paris Declaration in Fragile and Conflict-Affected Situations," evaluation of the Implementation of the Paris Declaration (Paris: OECD, August 2008), accessed December 22, 2017, http://goo.gl/AJCGH2.
[91] National Audit Office, "Department for International Development: Operating in Insecure Environments – National Audit Office," 5, 26.
[92] Interviews with DFID staff members D1, Bujumbura, June 1, 2009; and D5, Bujumbura, June 18, 2009.

on his own initiatives, like the 2009 strategic conflict assessment.[93] He did not help the Burundi office make its programs conflict sensitive or encourage the pursuit of development strategies that were appropriate to a state emerging from civil war.[94]

It was not that the DFID Burundi staff did not know that Burundi was in a different situation than other countries. They were aware of this fact as well as of the complexities and nuances of Burundian politics. But they had a limited menu of options for engagement. DFID's institutional imperatives to transition to full development mode as quickly as possible, to make measurable progress toward the MDGs, and to abide by the principles of aid effectiveness predominated. The formal accountability routines associated with these priorities governed the behavior of DFID's Burundi country office and its cooperation program from 2005 onward.

DFID Burundi argued that by supporting the Burundian government's development priorities and engaging with it in a respectful way, DFID Burundi gained its trust and had greater influence in political discussions.[95] But there is little evidence that the provision of health and education funds gave DFID Burundi more influence on the behavior of the Burundian government. DFID's commitment to the Paris Declaration and the overall aid effectiveness agenda privileges a strong relationship with the recipient government and discourages activities that challenge the authority of the government or build the capacity of the population and civil society to hold the government accountable. Nonetheless, unlike with UN peace operations and other sovereignty reinforcers, the aid effectiveness agenda does not incentivize country offices to respond directly to the political and security preferences of the government, or work directly on these conflict dynamics. Stagnant players, like DFID Burundi after 2005, implement activities that are largely disconnected from the political and security climate and aim to work *in spite* of the conflict dynamics, not *on* the conflict dynamics.

DFID Burundi's focus on education and health corresponded to DFID's corporate priorities and policies, creating formal accountability for DFID country offices to deliver results in these areas. DFID headquarters leadership made a strong commitment to health and education as part of the MDGs and through other key DFID commitments, such as the International Health Partnership.[96] In addition, when DFID

---

[93] Interviews with DFID staff members D5, Bujumbura, June 18, 2009; and D8, Bujumbura, June 15, 2009.
[94] Interviews with DFID staff members D5, Bujumbura, June 18, 2009; and D8, Bujumbura, June 15, 2009.
[95] Interview with DFID staff member D7, Bujumbura, June 4, 2009.
[96] Interview with DFID staff member D6, Bujumbura, June 6, 2009.

Burundi surveyed the field of donors in Burundi in 2005 and 2006, it found that health, education, and justice lacked leadership and investment from other donors. To avoid duplication of efforts and support the Nkurunziza's new priorities, DFID focused on these areas.[97]

DFID country offices are rewarded primarily for spending the money that they are allocated and for delivering tangible results that provide success stories.[98] In fact, DFID ministers used several anecdotes from DFID Burundi's health and education work in Burundi to illustrate the overall value of DFID's work.[99]

Although formal development accountability routines to headquarters predominated, DFID's relationship to the recipient government was also important and in line with the principle of ownership in the Paris Declaration. In DFID, being branded as "difficult" by the recipient government can be harmful. For a DFID country director, it is better "if you don't rock the boat."[100] Although Hogwood was an outspoken member of the international community, not afraid to hold the Burundian government and other international and regional actors to account, she maintained a good relationship with the Burundian government.[101]

The focus of DFID's accountability mechanisms on demonstrating tangible results toward the MDGs encouraged DFID to focus on Burundi's less difficult problems. DFID Burundi's interventions in health and education delivered quicker and more tangible results than efforts in justice and led to much more positive attention from DFID's headquarters.[102] Pursuit of the MDGs privileges simple, easily measurable results. The MDGs fail to measure the complex peacebuilding or statebuilding that is necessary for fragile and conflict-affected countries to make progress toward the MDGs.[103]

DFID has strong policy guidance for actions in fragile and conflict-affected states, but it lacks the formal accountability routines necessary to

---

[97] DFID, "DfID Burundi, 2009–2011," 9; and interview with DFID staff member D6, Bujumbura.

[98] Interviews with DFID staff members D1, Bujumbura, June 1, 2009; via telephone, May 20, 2010; D6, Bujumbura, June 6, 2009; and D7, Bujumbura, June 4, 2009; and with DFID staff member D2, by telephone, May 20, 2010.

[99] Testimony by Hilary Benn on DFID's support for education in Burundi, *House of Commons Hansard Written Answers for 23 May 2007*, pt. 0012 (2007), accessed December 22, 2017, http://goo.gl/CwoMHV; and DFID, *House of Commons: International Development – Fifth Special Report* (2008), accessed December 22, 2017, http://goo.gl/qWpcdL.

[100] Interview with DFID staff member D1, Bujumbura, June 1, 2009.

[101] Interview with DFID staff member D7, Bujumbura, June 4, 2009.

[102] Interviews with DFID staff members D1, Bujumbura, June 1, 2009; D5, Bujumbura, June 18, 2009; and D6, Bujumbura, June 6, 2009, Bujumbura.

[103] IDC, "Working with Fragile and Conflict-Affected States," 6.

implement this guidance.[104] Although DFID's country director possesses
a high degree of autonomy in designing a country program, DFID's
formal accountability routines prioritize a pure development focus and
quick, tangible results.[105] DFID offices can include less conventional
programming, as DFID Burundi did with its governance and justice
program and with its peacebuilding-focused support from 2002 to
2004. But, given the limited time and difficulties faced in conflict-
affected states, DFID's formal accountability structures seem to discourage innovative and time-consuming peacebuilding and state-building
programming, or the informal local accountability routines necessary
for peacebuilding performance.

With formal accountability primarily for development and without
informal local accountability, DFID Burundi had neither the information or the incentives to take regular actions to reduce the gap between
its peacebuilding (i.e., conflict sensitive development) aims and outcomes. From 2005 onward, DFID Burundi was a stagnant player. It
implemented development interventions that were largely detached from
and irrelevant to Burundi's evolving conflict dynamics, and did not
alter this approach in response to critical turning points in Burundi's
war-to-peace transition.

Individual Country-Office Staff and Leadership
Leadership made a big difference in DFID's approach in Burundi,
although not in the way one might suspect. Georgina Yates, the head
of DFID Burundi from 2002 to 2004, was instrumental in finding and
supporting key peacebuilding actors in Burundi and in supporting their
informal local accountability routines. She did not have to use rule
breaking or bad behavior to create these informal local accountability
routines because she already had high-level headquarters permission –
from Clare Short – to circumvent DFID's standard development
accountability routines. Sue Hogwood was DFID Burundi's country
director from 2005 to 2009. Hogwood was well respected by the international community and by many in the Burundian government. She
brought to DFID Burundi an intense commitment to the country and
knowledge of the broader Great Lakes region. She influenced not only
DFID's approach in Burundi, but also the general approach of the

---

[104] Interviews with DFID staff member D8, Bujumbura, June 15, 2009; and DFID staff
member D2, via telephone, May 20, 2010; and National Audit Office, "Department for
International Development: Operating in Insecure Environments: National Audit
Office."
[105] Interviews with DFID staff member D2, via telephone, May 20, 2010; and with DFID
staff member D8, Bujumbura, June 15, 2009.

international community. She was transferred to a DFID West Africa office in mid-2009, less than a year before the Burundi 2010 elections.

After Hogwood's departure, the DFID office shifted even further away from a political focus, and in 2011, its closure was announced. Hogwood enabled DFID Burundi to be much more politically relevant than it may have been otherwise; she served as a strong advocate for DFID's cooperation with Burundi. With her absence, an asset for DFID and Burundi was lost.

Hogwood used her political perspective and high degree of local knowledge of Burundi and the region to negotiate DFID's politically sensitive program agreements and conditions with the government, to encourage the government to take certain types of actions in relation to the ongoing peace process, and to influence and inform the broader international community in Burundi. But her political knowledge was not employed to implement or design conflict-sensitive development or peacebuilding interventions, to respond programmatically to key peace-building opportunities, or to prioritize the serious involvement of communities or civil society in DFID's state-building efforts.[106]

Although DFID's conflict advisors helped the Burundi office select projects and influenced the design of other projects and initiatives, they were not able systematically to help ensure the relevance of the projects that DFID funded.[107] Because DFID did not implement its own projects but funded projects implemented by NGOs and IOs, it did not have the capacity to alter the way projects were implemented. It could recommend certain changes, but its tools for enforcing these recommendations were blunt: give money or withdraw money. It could advise and assist its grantees, but it could not control their actions, nor could a small staff closely monitor thirty-odd projects.

DFID headquarters has amassed an impressive cadre of very smart, well-trained, and innovative staff. But there were few incentives for staff to take posts in fragile and conflict-affected countries.[108] According to a 2008 audit of DFID's work in insecure environments, 70 percent of staff surveyed thought that working in an insecure environment would positively impact their careers, but only 30 percent reported that taking these positions actually had a positive impact.[109] When combined with the

---

[106] Interview with DFID staff member D4, Bujumbura, March 20, 2009; and IDC, "Working with Fragile and Conflict-Affected States."

[107] Interview with DFID staff member D3, via telephone, October 12, 2011.

[108] National Audit Office, "Department for International Development: Operating in Insecure Environments: National Audit Office," 28.

[109] National Audit Office, "Department for International Development: Operating in Insecure Environments."

organization's focus on development, the lack of incentives for staff to work in fragile and conflict-affected countries discourages individuals from taking these difficult posts and, once in these posts, from challenging the predominant organizational frames and status quo.

Conclusion

DFID Burundi is a crucial case of an international donor because of DFID's position as a proponent of conflict-sensitive development and its strong commitment to doing development in fragile and conflict-affected states. DFID's own policy documents and other literature, including the 2011 *World Development Report*, indicate that effective aid to fragile and conflict-affected states is different from aid to more stable countries. Instead of simply working through existing state institutions, DFID's policy documents state that aid should build stronger state–society relations, and thus more accountable state institutions.[110] In spite of these findings, from 2005 onwards, DFID's development support to Burundi largely ignored the reality of the Burundian institutions that it funded, simply reinforcing the state's existing policies and structures rather than attempting to transform them or make them more accountable to Burundians.

This case sheds important light on the existing literature on international aid. It demonstrates that there is heterogeneity in donor behavior, even within one donor in one country over time, that has important implications for our understanding of the peacebuilding performance of bilateral donors. It also supports general patterns found in the literature, such as the broken feedback loop between bilateral donors and the population that they aim to serve.[111]

The DFID Burundi case confirms the critical role played by formal accountability routines in donor organizations. It shows that development organizations that focus solely on accountability for development outcomes may be highly ineffective at doing conflict-sensitive development in fragile or conflict-affected states. Unless donors adapt their standard development approaches to the particular political and institutional dynamics of conflict-affected countries, they are unlikely to intentionally influence these institutions.

So long as political analysis is seen as an optional add-on rather than as central to the whole development process, agencies will not make the

---

[110] DFID, "Building the State and Securing the Peace."

[111] Martens et al., *The Institutional Economics of Foreign Aid*; and Bernhard Reinsberg, "Foreign Aid Responses to Political Liberalization," *World Development* 75 (2015): 45–61.

necessary investment in understanding the political dynamics at work in the countries in which they operate, or make fundamental changes in their own organization, values, attitudes and behavior ... the temptation to revert to technocratic, supply driven approaches will be hard to resist, and opportunities will be missed.[112]

The DFID Burundi case study also provides insights into the role of informal local accountability in donor organizations. Unlike INGOs or IOs that design and implement many of their projects themselves, bilateral donor organizations work primarily through partners and depend on partners' capacity to design and implement the projects. Once DFID Burundi committed money to a project or program, it largely lost the ability to influence the direction of that project or program. In response to new information about an activity's achievement of its objectives, DFID had a limited repertoire of possible actions. It could provide technical assistance, which entailed sitting down with the partner and discussing the problem and providing some kind of advice. Or it could stop the flow of the money, which it would do only as a last resort. In the end, DFID was highly dependent on the partner organization's willingness and capacity to implement a program. DFID Burundi did not train its partners. It did not analyze its partners' capacity to achieve its goals.

The DFID Burundi case shows that the capacity of a donor to support informal local accountability depends on (1) its ability to influence and support informal local accountability routines established by grantees, and (2) its ability to create its own informal local accountability routines that provide additional feedback about the broader context that it aims to influence. This implies that donors should focus on training their staff in a skill set that includes knowledge of organizational change processes, management, facilitation, joint monitoring, and mutual capacity building. The more that they can accompany and support the informal local accountability efforts of their grantees, the more likely their grantees may be to implement locally grounded interventions. Engaging in more active collaboration with grantees would also require a greater number of field-level staff per donor, enabling staff to collaborate directly with partners, and helping to establish and reinforce strong informal local accountability mechanisms.

The DFID Burundi case also demonstrates that regardless of the political skills of the country-office leadership and the number of conflict advisors and policy papers, formal accountability routines play an

---

[112] Sue Unsworth, "Is Political Analysis Changing Donor Behavior?" (London: Conference of the Development Studies Association, 2008), accessed December 22, 2017, http://goo.gl/vui28P.

essential role in determining the country-level behavior of international donors. If the country office prioritizes development, then it will support relatively apolitical development activities. If it prioritizes conflict-sensitive development or peacebuilding, then it is more likely to support activities that are focused on addressing the causes of conflict in a particular country. If its grantees also establish informal local account-ability mechanisms, then they are more likely to contribute to changes in local institutions that mitigate violence.

This chapter points to a broader problem within the international development industry. States and IOs have increasingly pushed for the establishment of global standards and targets as well as streamlined international development efforts.[113] The MDGs, the Post-2015 Sustainable Development Goals, and the New Deal on Peacebuilding and State-building are all examples of this trend. Although such international efforts to harmonize state behavior are a crucial aspect of today's efforts at global development governance, they contribute to perverse effects of international development aid, particularly in fragile and conflict-affected countries.[114]

By focusing donor country-office attention on achieving global targets and demonstrating their achievement to their headquarters, these global standards can undermine the local relevance and effectiveness of inter-national aid. This is likely to occur in conflict-affected and fragile coun-tries where the government – the main interlocutor for these global targets – may not have the capacity or will to ensure that international standards are responsive to the needs of their population. DFID Bur-undi, like other donors, focused on strengthening the state, not on strengthening the state's responsiveness to its population.[115] As other scholars have argued, the focus of bilateral development donors on shoring up state institutions in conflict-affected countries is likely to also undermine these states' responsiveness and accountability to their populations.[116]

---

[113] Stephen Knack, "Building or Bypassing Recipient Country Systems: Are Donors Defying the Paris Declaration?" *Journal of Development Studies* 50, no. 6 (June 3, 2014): 839–54.

[114] Judith Kelley and Beth A. Simmons, "Politics by Number: Indicators as Social Pressure in International Relations," *American Journal of Political Science* 59, no. 1 (2015): 55–70.

[115] William Brown, "Sovereignty Matters: Africa, Donors, and the Aid Relationship," *African Affairs* 112, no. 447 (April 2013): 262–82.

[116] Gibson et al., *The Samaritan's Dilemma: The Political Economy of Development Aid*; and Moss, Pettersson, and van de Walle, "An Aid-Institutions Paradox?"

Conclusion

> Many people make the mistake of confusing information with knowledge. They are not the same thing. Knowledge involves the interpretation of information. Knowledge involves listening.[1]
>
> Mankell, 2011

Global governors are structured to serve the interests of the global elite, not the disenfranchised populations in conflict-affected countries.[2] They are accountable to states and powerful individuals, even though they often claim to serve the interests of the most impoverished and vulnerable populations. How, then, can global governors serve the local interests of conflict-affected populations? In countries where the government is strong, represents the majority of the population, and governs a state that can deliver social services throughout its territory, the government could represent local-level interests. But strong democratic states are not where the majority of peacebuilding happens. Peacebuilding most often takes place in countries experiencing violent contestation of political authority precisely because the government is not able to serve the interests of its population. In these contexts, global governors need to develop local accountability beyond the host government so that they can gain knowledge of the needs, capacity, and preferences of the specific local institutions they aim to transform.

Informal local accountability permits IO, INGO, and bilateral donor country offices to build knowledge about the broader population that is affected by their activities. Informal local accountability helps create knowledge because it builds relationships between country-office staff and local actors who represent the diversity in society. The organizations' formal peacebuilding accountability, in turn, incentivizes country offices

---

[1] Henning Mankell, "The Art of Listening," *New York Times* (December 10, 2011), sec. Opinion, accessed December 23, 2017, www.nytimes.com/2011/12/11/opinion/sunday/in-africa-the-art-of-listening.html?src=me&ref=general.

[2] For a discussion of the elite focus of global governance, see Jeff Colgan and Robert Keohane, "The Liberal Order Is Rigged," *Foreign Affairs*, April/May 2017.

to pay attention to knowledge about conflict dynamics and attempt to narrow the gap between peacebuilding aims and outcomes, or learn. This positive peacebuilding performance increases the likelihood that country offices will capitalize on opportunities to achieve their peacebuilding aims.

Delegating authority to local stakeholders inevitably requires that individual staff bypass or bend the standard operating procedures that were created to ensure the country office's accountability to the organization's headquarters and donors. Thus, seemingly bad behavior is necessary for good performance.

Formal accountability of a country office to its headquarters or donors is important because the organization needs to track whether or not it is meeting its aims, provide necessary technical and financial support, and ensure that the organization's resources are used efficiently and effectively. But formal accountability routines can also incentivize country offices to respond to the preferences of international stakeholders, not local stakeholders, potentially undermining the local relevance and impact of the country office's activities.

I derive the findings presented in this book from field research that I conducted over a fifteen-year period into twenty-eight cases of organizational behavior in five diverse intervening organizations in Burundi. They draw on more than three hundred interviews in Burundi during and after the country's civil war, as well as additional fieldwork with a broad range of IOs, INGOs, and bilateral donors in the Democratic Republic of the Congo (DRC), Nepal, South Sudan, and Sudan.

By drawing on these rich data to explain variation in the subnational behavior and performance of IOs, INGOs, and bilateral donors, the previous chapters help to clear up the murkiness of existing scholarship, which until now has not examined variation in country-level performance. The case studies show why some country offices perform poorly, supporting many of the bureaucratic, cultural, and normative explanations in the literature. They also clarify why these same organizations sometimes achieve positive performance, supporting the claims of the resource- and learning-focused explanations.

This book also identifies a crucial variable omitted from previous studies: the agency of individual country-office staff who sidestep bureaucratic, cultural, and formal accountability systems to create informal local accountability mechanisms. Contrary to claims in the literature, "agency slack" is not necessarily a bad thing for the organization's principals.[3] Positive peacebuilding performance requires that individual

---

[3] For a discussion of agency and agency slack in International Organizations, see Darren G. Hawkins, David A. Lake, Daniel L. Nielson, and Michael J. Tierney, *Delegation and*

staff deviate from the accountability systems put in place by their principals.[4] Far from being an infrequent occurrence, this type of individual agency is a relatively common phenomenon. Bad behavior, thus, may not be viewed as so bad by many within these organizations, even if it is not formally rewarded by the organizations' principals and their established accountability mechanisms.

By comparing IO, INGO, and bilateral donor country offices, this book deviates from much of the global governance literature, which tends to analyze IOs, INGOs, and states separately. At the country-office level, IOs, INGOs, and states can behave in very similar ways, even though there are important differences among them that influence their engagement with the country environment. For example, IOs may be more likely to align with state preferences. Nonetheless, the crucial role of individual agency and informal local accountability in peacebuilding performance makes it difficult to predict, ex ante, which IO, INGO, or bilateral donor country offices will perform and which ones will not.

The findings also challenge assumptions about the relative value of IOs, INGOs, and states in the international system. Because most literature on global governance views accountability to states as most important, states and IOs are considered to be better at global governance than INGOs.[5] I have argued, however, that INGOs may have the greatest potential for positive peacebuilding performance because of their smaller size and relative independence from state authority. IOs may be second in line because their country-office leadership seems to have room to permit or support the creation of informal local accountability, while bilateral donor country offices may have the least room to maneuver because of potentially strict formal accountability routines and targets from headquarters.

Because organizational performance is increasingly important for legitimacy, there is an emergent paradox: the legitimacy of IOs, INGOs, and state aid agencies may be increasingly dependent on their willingness

Agency in International Organizations (Cambridge, UK: Cambridge University Press, 2006).

[4] This conceptualization of innovative staff is similar to William Easterly's classification of "Searchers": people who seek out solutions, adapt to local circumstances, and require local-level feedback to figure out if what they are doing is working. For discussion of the difference between "Searchers" and "Planners," see William Easterly, "Planners versus Searchers in Foreign Aid," *Asian Development Review* 23, no. 2 (2006): 1–35; and William Easterly, *White Man's Burden: Why the West's Efforts to Aid the Rest Have Done So Much Ill and So Little Good* (Oxford, UK: Oxford University Press, 2006).

[5] For discussion of accountability in global governance, see Ruth Grant and Robert Keohane, "Accountability and Abuses of Power in World Politics," *American Political Science Review* 99, no. 1 (2005): 29–43.

to delegate their authority to local actors that are unrepresented by the institutions of global governance. Legitimate global governance in peace-building is likely to require improved local, not global, accountability.

Implications for Peacebuilding Policy and Practice

This book has important implications for policy and practice. The con-texts is familiar to people who have worked in conflict zones, where what they *have to do* often inhibits them from doing what they *should do*. The formal accountability requirements placed on a country office by donors, headquarters, or governing boards are extractive in nature. They are intended to make the country office accountable to external actors that do not have the time or resources to follow the day-to-day implementation of activities. The basic assumption is that formal accountability mechan-isms will improve the ability of country offices to achieve their aims. Many country-office staff, however, find that numerous requirements and requests from headquarters and donors diminish their ability to engage with the conflict-affected contexts they are supposed to be helping.

The list of formal accountability tasks is long: write donor proposals; read and write donor and headquarters reports, emails, and cables to and from headquarters; coordinate within the organization and with other international actors; establish agreements with procurement services and subcontractors; ensure that money is spent on schedule and according to prescribed objectives; monitor progress toward global indicators ... The list goes on; but the effect is simple. Country-office staff often function in a manner similar to that of headquarters-based bureaucrats. They spend long hours in the office, socializing mostly with other international actors, largely detached from the people and context they aim to trans-form.[6] Security measures instituted over the past decade have made it even more difficult for staff to escape the confines of their offices or the walled compounds in which they live.[7]

---

[6] For discussion of how the incentive structure of country offices influences the behavior of their staff, see Susanna P. Campbell, "Organizational Barriers to Peace: Agency and Structure in International Peacebuilding" (PhD Dissertation, Tufts University, 2012); Campbell, "Routine Learning? How Peacebuilding Organizations Prevent Liberal Peace," in *A Liberal Peace? The Problems and Practices of Peacebuilding*, ed. Susanna P. Campbell, David Chandler, and Meera Sabaratnam (London: Zed, 2011), 89–105. For discussion of the organizational culture and practices of international peacebuilders, see Séverine Autesserre, *Peaceland: Conflict Resolution and the Everyday Politics of International Intervention* (Cambridge, UK: Cambridge University Press, 2014).

[7] For discussion of how increased security provision has altered the behavior of aid workers, see Sarah Collinson and Mark Duffield with Carol Berger, Diana Felix da Costa, and Karl Sandstrom, "Paradoxes of Presence: Risk Management and Aid Culture in

Country offices can mitigate the potentially perverse effect of these formal accountability routines by creating informal local accountability, giving local actors the authority to influence the way the organization's activities are conceived and implemented. Informal local accountability in turn, requires innovation by individual country-office staff that is not incentivized by their organization's formal accountability routines. These findings have five important implications for peacebuilding policy and practice.

(1) It is difficult to incentivize informal local accountability through top-down formal accountability requirements. If an intervening organization were to require its country offices to establish informal local accountability, then informal local accountability would be transformed into a top-down formal accountability requirement. Informal local accountability would likely be subject to the same constraints as formal accountability requirements, which are focused on checking boxes, spending money, complying with accounting procedures, and writing reports to headquarters and donors. Thus, the accountability mechanism would still create a formal feedback loop with the organization's headquarters, donors, and other principals, and not with the diverse local stakeholders whom the country office aims to affect.

If informal local accountability were to become a formal requirement, tracked through standard formal accountability routines, there would be no guarantee that the informal mechanisms would include a representative group of stakeholders, that they would contribute to building trust and a relationship between the country office and the stakeholders, or that the country-office leadership would integrate local feedback into decision-making about the project. There is no guarantee that a formal requirement for local accountability would actually delegate authority to a representative group of local stakeholders or, as a corollary, lead to the creation of the type of local accountability mechanisms that support peacebuilding performance. Informal local accountability could easily become just another item on the country-office checklist, along with gender sensitivity, conflict sensitivity, human rights–based approaches to programming, and other attempts to alter country-office behavior without altering the underlying incentive structure (formal accountability) of the country office.

CARE Burundi was supported by two headquarters-level efforts related to informal local accountability: one to increase the responsiveness of the office to its target communities, and one to increase conflict sensitivity. In addition, CARE Burundi was one of CARE International's learning offices, meaning that it was committed to employing best practices in learning and had a learning and conflict-sensitivity unit. CARE Burundi volunteered to participate in these processes and, in return, it received support from headquarters for these efforts. The support from headquarters *helped* committed country-office staff develop innovative informal local accountability mechanisms, but it did not *require* informal local accountability nor did it furnish the majority of ideas that made it possible; these came from country-office staff. If country-office staff had not been interested in creating informal local accountability, the efforts of headquarters would have had little traction. Furthermore, headquarters did not alter the formal accountability routines that disincentivized informal local accountability. Instead, it simply put more, largely voluntary, requirements on CARE Burundi's already full agenda.

Additional interviews that I conducted with the United States Agency for International Development (USAID) and its partners also demonstrate the challenge of formalizing local accountability. USAID headquarters has adopted policies to encourage learning, local-level feedback, and conflict sensitivity.[8] However, its country offices and partners indicate that they have difficulty implementing these policies because of the number of formal accountability requirements and restrictions placed on them. For example, in the DRC, one USAID partner argued that there is no time to learn or reflect because of the pressure to comply with contractual regulations and deliver quickly.

There is so much pressure to be accountable. You feel that you are one step away from having the rug yanked out from under you. By accountable, I mean complying with the rules and regulations and not having any corruption or fraud. There is not much appetite for failure. We get a grant and we have to hit the ground running. You often have problems because you don't have time to train people. We don't even have any reflection time. This is a big complaint. If an activity is not a big failure, we just go onto the next thing.[9]

As this quote shows, intervening organizations would likely first need to reduce the constraints on learning and innovation created by the

---

[8] Valerie Haugen and Nina Papadopoulos, "Checklist for Conflict Sensitivity in Education Programs," United States Agency for International Development, Office of Conflict Management and Mitigation, November 2013, accessed December 23, 2017, www.usaid.gov/sites/default/files/documents/1865/USAID_Checklist_Conflict_Sensitivity_14FEB27_cm.pdf; and United States Agency for International Development, "What Difference Does Collaborating, Learning, and Adapting Make to Development? Key Findings from our Literature Review," April 2017, USAID Learning Lab Website, accessed April 2017, https://usaidlearninglab.org/lab-notes/what-difference-does-collaborating-learning-and-adapting-make-development-key-findings.

[9] Interview with INGO staff member 129.2, Kinshasa, DRC, May 23, 2015.

existing formal accountability routines before they could incentivize informal local accountability.

(2) Because informal local accountability is not directly incentivized by formal accountability, it is often transaction intensive and difficult to sustain. Creating and sustaining informal local accountability routines often overtaxes country-office staff who are already spread thin. CARE Burundi created strong informal local accountability routines during several periods, relocated staff to live in the communities where they worked, and appointed a monitoring and evaluation officer to each of its programs. But the community-based staff reported feeling abandoned by the rest of the country office. Their managers in the main country office found themselves overstretched and unable to process much of the local feedback that they received through this informal local accountability. One CARE Burundi staff member described the counterintuitive relationship between formal accountability (upward accountability) and informal local accountability (downward accountability):

We have tons of data but we can't process it. I don't have a work–life balance. No one who works for this organization in a senior position has. Downward accountability gives back more. It's more satisfying. The more we have upward accountability [to donors and headquarters], the more burnout there is because it gives back less. Upward accountability is counterintuitive. Its purpose is downward accountability, possibly, but it actually creates less of that.[10]

It is difficult for the INGOs, IOs, and bilateral donors alike to sustain informal local accountability because of the additional work required to create it and because their bureaucracies seem to default to their normal way of operating, guided by formal accountability routines.[11]

(3) The solution may be to foster a conducive environment for individual entrepreneurship at the country level rather than focusing on country-office accountability. The basic assumption behind reform efforts in IOs, INGOs, and bilateral aid agencies is that

---

[10] Interview with CARE staff member C4, Bujumbura, June 25, 2009.
[11] For discussion of these patterns within the UN, see Susanna P. Campbell, "Independent External Evaluation: Peacebuilding Fund Projects in Burundi," evaluation (Bujumbura: BINUB, 2010), accessed December 23, 2017, www.unpbf.org/wp-content/uploads/Independent-Evaluation-Burundi.pdf; Susanna P. Campbell, Tracy Dexter, Michael G. Findley, Stephanie Hofmann, Josiah Marineau, and Daniel Walker, "Independent External Evaluation: UN Peacebuilding Fund Project Portfolio in Burundi, 2007–2013" (New York: United Nations Peacebuilding Support Office, 2014), accessed December 23, 2017, www.unpbf.org/wp-content/uploads/FINAL-Independent-External-Evaluation-PBF-Burundi_English-version_March2014.pdf.

improved organizational performance results from curtailing the bad behaviors of individual staff members.[12] To this end, these organizations have created best practice guides, programming policies, questionnaires, evaluation procedures, program support units, and compliance procedures to help guide the behavior of country-office staff and ensure that they design, implement, monitor, and evaluate their activities in the appropriate way. To ensure that country-office staff comply with these guidelines, country offices must report back (through formal accountability routines) indicating that they have followed the rules, best practices, or compliance procedures.

One of the most resounding complaints from country-office staff interviewed for this book was that they did not have the time to think about what they were doing, much less innovate. They were so busy implementing, reporting, coordinating, and administering – fulfilling the accountability requirements put in place by donors and headquarters – that they did not have time to think about whether all these activities might have the desired effect on the conflict-affected country. As one UN staff member put it:

> Our work is exhausting. We have no time to think and read. You need to be physically and mentally detached from your daily routine in order to really think about it.[13]

This problem is not reserved for country offices or even global governance institutions. The challenge of fostering innovation has been the subject of numerous business books and self-help guides. For example, Peter Senge's *The Fifth Discipline* builds on the same research on organizational learning as I have built on in this book.[14] This research by Chris Argyris and Donald Schon argues that for organizations to learn continuously, they need to process real-time feedback about their outcomes in an open and non-defensive way that allows them to "think" critically about

---

[12] For further discussion of the problems facing approaches to reform of IOs and bilateral donors, in particular, see Michael Lipson, "Peacekeeping Reform: Managing Change in an Organized Anarchy," *Journal of Intervention and Statebuilding* 6, no. 3 (2010): 279–98; Andrew Natsios, "The Clash of Counter-Bureaucracy and Development," (Washington, DC, Center for Global Development, 2010); Report of the High-Level Independent Panel on United Nations Peace Operations, *United Our Strengths for Peace: Politics, Partnership, and People* (New York: United Nations, June 16, 2015); and United Nations Development Program, "Evaluation of Results-Based Management at UNDP" (New York: Evaluation Office, December 2007).

[13] Interview with UN staff member 1.12, Bujumbura, June 24, 2009.

[14] Peter Senge, *The Fifth Discipline* (New York: Doubleday, 1990).

whether they have found the right solution to the right problem.[15] This type of learning requires that people think in new ways that do not conform to standard operating procedures and existing organizational knowledge.

This type of critical thinking and organizational learning is particularly important for peacebuilding outcomes. The organizations engaged in international peacebuilding are not structured to receive feedback about their outcomes. The beneficiaries of their services – impoverished and often disenfranchised populations – do not have formal authority to sanction or incentivize behavior within the intervening organization. There is no buyer of the goods or services, other than the host government, who can use its purchasing power to signal satisfaction or dissatisfaction.[16] In international peacebuilding, as well as in development and humanitarian intervention, the service is simply delivered to the population rather than demanded or bought by the population.

Headquarters and donors attempt to correct for this inherently broken feedback loop by implementing monitoring and evaluation plans, another type of formal accountability routine. But even these plans often measure service delivery rather than outcomes or impact.[17] When evaluations do focus on impact, they rarely provide real-time feedback and may or may not be used by the organization to alter its behavior. Many evaluations are treated simply as a box-checking exercise and are shelved as soon as they are completed. At other times, intervening organizations may use evaluations to improve a particular program or project, but such action is rarely required and, if it is, the focus is often on whether or not

---

[15] Chris Argyris, *On Organizational Learning* (Boston: Blackwell, 1992); and Chris Argyris and Donald A. Schon, *Organizational Learning: A Theory of Action Perspective* (Boston: Addison-Wesley, 1978).

[16] For discussion of the nature of the state in conflict-affected countries and the implications for international intervention, see Naazneen Barma, *The Peacebuilding Puzzle: Political Order in Post-Conflict States* (Cambridge, UK: Cambridge University Press, 2016); Alex de Waal, "Mission without End? Peacekeeping in the African Political Marketplace," *International Affairs* 85, no. 1 (2009): 99–113; Alex de Waal, *The Real Politics of the Horn of Africa: Money, War, and the Business of Power* (Cambridge, UK: Polity Press, 2015); Jeffrey Herbst, *States and Power in Africa: Comparative Lessons in Authority and Control* (Princeton, NJ: Princeton University Press, 2000); Dipali Mukhopadhyay, *Warlords, Strongman Governors, and the State of Afghanistan* (Cambridge, UK: Cambridge University Press, 2014); and William Reno, *Warlord Politics and African States* (Boulder, CO: Lynne Rienner, 1998).

[17] For elaboration of the type of information that is gathered about projects and programs, see Collaborative Learning Project, *Time to Listen: Hearing People on the Receiving End of International Aid* (Cambridge, MA: CDA Collaborative Learning Projects, 2012); Natsios, "The Clash of Counter-Bureaucracy and Development"; and UNDP, "Evaluation of Results-Based Management at UNDP."

to continue to fund a project or program, rather than improving the project during the implementation process.

An INGO staff person in South Sudan described how donors and INGOs tend to deal with feedback that they receive from evaluations or reports that they commission: "The people who commission research reports don't read them. They spend money on the contextual analysis, but then they bury it."[18] Other interviewees in Burundi, Nepal, South Sudan, and Sudan shared similar complaints. In spite of the tendency of many country offices to ignore or hide negative feedback, there are times when individual staff choose to use reports and evaluations to alter their overall policies or specific activities. For example, the UN Peacebuilding Support Office significantly altered its overall policies and approach based on several external evaluations, although these evaluations came too late to spur alterations in the actual activities that they evaluated.[19] Individual staff often have a lot of discretion about whether evaluations or reports are used to improve future activities or whether they simply "sit on the shelf."

Peacebuilding is fundamentally experimental. No one knows whether or not it will work. Even if a particular project or activity worked in another country or in the same country at a different time, there is no guarantee that it will work in the current context at the current point in time. To understand whether their peacebuilding activities are working or not, country offices need feedback. To evaluate whether country offices are implementing the right peacebuilding activities or have designed them in the right way, country offices need time to process feedback about their activities and to think critically about what changes might need to be made or whether they may need to stop what they are doing altogether. This type of learning and innovation requires entrepreneurial individuals within the country office who are familiar enough with the country context to identify a truly representative group of stakeholders and who are able and willing to delegate authority to this group. These may be individuals with a long history in the country and country office, or they may be individuals who have recently arrived and are able to work with knowledgeable people who can help them to understand the conflict dynamics and its cleavages.

(4) A country office may not be able to achieve positive peacebuilding performance and positive development or humanitarian performance at the same time. The sectoral focus of formal

---

[18] Interview, INGO staff member 212, Juba, South Sudan, January 28, 2016.
[19] Communication from UN staff person, 2014, referring to influence of this evaluation: Campbell et al., "Independent External Evaluation: UN Peacebuilding Fund Project Portfolio in Burundi, 2007–2013."

accountability matters. If a country office thinks that it will be assessed primarily on whether or not it advances peacebuilding aims, it will focus on peacebuilding aims. Likewise, if a country office thinks it will be assessed on whether or not it advances humanitarian or development aims, it will focus on humanitarian or development aims. The primary focus of formal accountability helps to determine the worldview of the country office, the particular information it pays attention to about the country context, and how it responds to this information.[20] As a result, a single country office may not be able simultaneously to prioritize positive performance in relation to peacebuilding, development, and humanitarian aims.

Peacebuilding, development, and humanitarian relief, and associated ways of engaging with the country context, are not always compatible. Peacebuilding is a highly complex and transaction-intensive task that requires the support of country-level leadership to help overcome bureaucratic barriers, provide political support for potentially vulnerable staff, and engage in complex negotiations with the host government that may directly challenge the host government's political behavior.[21] Development cooperation relies on maintaining long-term relations with the host government and focuses on the achievement of long-term health, education, child mortality reductions, and other development goals, rather than trying to directly alter the conflict dynamics that may undermine these goals.[22] Humanitarian aid often aims to maintain its political neutrality so that it can focus on the humanitarian imperative of supplying life-saving services to people in need, regardless of their political affiliation. The likelihood of a country office successfully pursuing peacebuilding, development, and humanitarian aims at the same time is slim. But many country offices still attempt to pursue all three broad aims, without openly acknowledging that it might not be possible to do them all equally well.

[20] This claim is based in part on the work of Lynn Eden; see Lynn Eden, "'Getting It Right or Wrong': Organizational Learning about the Physical World," in *Organizational Learning in the Global Context*, ed. M. Leann Brown, Michael Kenney, and Michael Zarkin (Aldershot, UK: Ashgate, 2006), 197–216; and Eden, *Whole World on Fire: Organizations, Knowledge, and Nuclear Weapons Devastation* (Ithaca, NY: Cornell University Press, 2004).

[21] For the particular challenges of transaction-intensive development work, see Lant Pritchett and Michael Woolcock, "Solutions When the Solution Is the Problem: Arraying the Disarray in Development," *World Development* 32, no. 2, (2004): 191–212.

[22] For example, see the Millennium Development Goals (MDGs) and Sustainable Development Goals (SDGs). The adoption of SDG 16 – focused on the equal provision of peace, justice, and strong institutions – in 2015 is the first set of global development goals that also aims to simultaneously address the determinants of peace and justice.

(5) Less may be more. Increasing the proportion of funding available for peacebuilding may increase the likelihood of higher levels of peacebuilding performance because more country offices may be able to focus on peacebuilding as their primary aim. Nonetheless, more resources are unlikely, on their own, to lead to improved peacebuilding performance. In order to achieve positive peacebuilding performance, informal local accountability routines are also necessary. The creation and maintenance of these routines is time intensive, both because of the transaction costs of navigating around bureaucratic barriers to them and because designing and participating in informal local accountability takes time. In spite of many donors' push to spend more money in conflict-affected and fragile countries, one lesson from this book is: less may well be more. By focusing on just a few key priority interventions and doing them well, global governors may be more likely to achieve their peacebuilding aims at the local level.

An INGO staff member in Juba, South Sudan, described the problematic attitude of many INGOs that the pressure to spend money creates:

People focus on spending. They have so much to spend and so little time. People spend 40 percent of their time talking about their burn rate (the rate at which they spend their money). They want to keep the burn rate up so that they don't lose profit. You could spend a million more effectively, rather than 40 million and not be effective at all. You could be a lot more effective with less money.[23]

An INGO staff member in Nepal echoed this concern:

This rush to spend at the end of every fiscal year. There is no way you can keep tabs on that money. It fuels corruption at a rate that nothing else does. Back in their capitals, it is higher risk for donors not to spend.[24]

The argument to focus less on spending money and more on engaging directly with ongoing activities runs counter not only to policy documents and advocacy campaigns that call for increased aid to conflict-affected countries, but also to organizations' own predisposition to grow and expand.[25] It contradicts donors' increasing emphasis on reducing the amount of money allocated for donor staffing and increasing the amount allocated for projects. Because their country offices often have few staff, donors tend to try to reduce their transaction costs by allocating large grants to international actors that can manage money in a way that

---

[23] Interview, INGO staff member 212, Juba, South Sudan, January 28, 2016.
[24] Interview, INGO staff member 323, Kathmandu, Nepal, April 18, 2016.
[25] For discussion of the role of bureaucrats in organizational expansion, particularly in IOs, see Tana Johnson, *Organizational Progeny* (Oxford, UK: Oxford University Press, 2014).

complies with donor standards. Thus, organizations such as PricewaterhouseCoopers has become engaged in peacebuilding and development, making it difficult for small national or international NGOs to receive crucial funding.[26]

The focus on spending money seems to decrease the opportunities for country-office organizational learning. With more money to spend, country-office staff spend even more of their time administering grants and ensuring compliance with the organization's standards, leaving little time to establish or incentivize informal local accountability routines. The donor's incentive structure is passed down to its subcontractors, whether INGOs, IOs, private companies, national NGOs, or host government agencies. Instead of simply allocating more money in the hope that the money will fix the problem, global governors should consider how they can engage more effectively with the local context and give their staff the time necessary to think and learn.

Recommendations for Improved Peacebuilding Performance

Given that global governors are not structured for local-level learning and that top-down efforts to improve the effectiveness of these organizations through increased formal accountability may have a perverse effect, what can these organizations do to create a conducive environment for individual entrepreneurship and organizational learning at the country level?

Standard solutions employed to improve peacebuilding performance include conducting conflict analysis, appointing conflict advisors or units, providing training in conflict analysis and conflict-sensitive programming, and developing and monitoring evaluation plans that integrate peacebuilding indicators. Increasingly, policy and practice literature in the peacebuilding and development communities has also identified the importance of country-level organizational learning and adaptive management in facilitating country-level outcomes.[27] However, these

---

[26] Interview with donor staff person 101-1, Kinshasa, DRC, April 15, 2015.

[27] See also other important work on the role of organizational learning in peacebuilding and development performance: CDA Collaborative Learning Projects, *Reflecting on Peace Practice (RPP): Participant Training Manual* (Cambridge, MA: CDA Collaborative Learning Projects, 2008); Cheyanne Church and Mark Rogers, *Designing for Results: Integrating Monitoring and Evaluation in Conflict Transformation Programs* (Washington, DC: Search for Common Ground, 2006); Lise Morjé Howard, *UN Peacekeeping in Civil Wars*, (Cambridge, UK: Cambridge University Press, 2008); Annika Schlingheider, Erica Pellfolk, Gabriele Maneo, and Harsh Desai, "Managing to Adapt: Analyzing Adaptive Management for Planning, Monitoring, Evaluation, and Learning" (London: London School of Economics and Political Science, April 2017).

policy prescriptions seldom address the numerous barriers to learning and the possibility that staff may circumvent these obstacles, nor do they test which best practices are, in fact, necessary for improved performance.[28]

Recommendations for improved peacebuilding policy and practice are a form of inquiry in and of themselves. Country-office staff are often overwhelmed by a long list of best practices and recommendations that may or may not make a difference in a particular context or in relation to particular organizational constraints and opportunities. In crafting the recommendations that follow, I focused on solutions that seem to make a difference even in the face of the numerous barriers to performance that I outlined in this book. Adding layers of bureaucracy, analytical frameworks, or reporting requirements is unlikely to significantly improve the peacebuilding performance of country offices. Organizations need to build new routines and processes that enable them to engage more effectively with dynamic conflict environments and to recognize when they cannot achieve their desired outcomes in these contexts.

I have argued that improved peacebuilding performance requires that country offices (1) have formal accountability routines that prioritize peacebuilding above other priorities, and (2) create informal local accountability that empowers a representative group of local actors to influence the trajectory of its peacebuilding activities. Although creating both of these types of accountability faces significant obstacles, country offices may be able to overcome these barriers, at least temporarily, and improve the likelihood that their country offices contribute to achieving their peacebuilding aims.

(1) To the extent possible, organizations should employ accompaniment-focused accountability rather than compliance-focused accountability. *Accompaniment-focused accountability* is grounded in the belief that a project's aims, inputs, and outputs should be adapted in response to changes in the context, and that formal accountability routines should facilitate this contextual relevance. To implement accompaniment-focused accountability, the donor or headquarters should engage in regular discussions with implementing staff as to whether the project is, in fact, having the desired effect and how

---

[28] For an exception to this trend, see my earlier work that discusses the importance of organizational learning for peacebuilding performance as well the barriers to organizational learning: Susanna P. Campbell, "When Process Matters: The Potential Implications of Organizational Learning for Peacebuilding Success," *Journal of Peacebuilding and Development* 4, no. 2 (2008): 20–32.

it might need to be adjusted to improve its effect on the evolving context.[29]

Compliance-focused accountability assesses inputs (what goes into the organization in terms of money, supplies, and staff) and outputs (what comes out of the organization in terms of the money it spends, the things it buys, and the activities it implements). In spite of many donors increasing focus on monitoring results, compliance-focused accountability still seems predominant. It measures the degree to which inputs and outputs correspond to the donor's original country strategy and project aims.[30] It does not focus on the overall impact of the project or its relevance to the evolving country context. Compliance-focused accountability generally assumes that the project aims and approach are relevant to the context and that the country office simply needs to implement the activities.

Every intervening organization is likely to have significant compliance requirements, which are motivated by the need to reduce corruption and ensure that money is spent in the way that taxpayers and other contributors intend. Nonetheless, there may still be opportunities for accompaniment-focused accountability alongside compliance-focused accountability. For example, one of CARE Burundi's main donors traveled to Burundi for several weeks and worked with the CARE Burundi team to establish the aims and design of the programs that it would fund.[31] This same donor made several additional visits during the program implementation process to see whether or not the aims and design were still relevant and to discuss how they might need to change.

By visiting programs and, even better, participating in informal local accountability processes, headquarters and donors may incentivize the creation of high-quality informal local accountability processes. If donors and headquarters are open to receiving information about both success and failure as well as to supporting processes to address their deficiencies

---

[29] The importance of this type of open and nondefensive approach to processing both positive and negative information about outcomes is based on the research of Argyris and Schon (1989). The importance of engaging in this type of reflective adaptation in highly dynamic contexts where the project seeks to alter behaviors is outlined in the work of Pressman and Wildavsky (1984). See Chris Argyris and Donald A. Schon, "Participatory Action Research and Action Science Compared," *American Behavioral Scientist* 32, no. 5 (1989): 612–23; and Jeffrey Pressman and Aaron Wildavsky, *Implementation: How Great Expectations in Washington Are Dashed in Oakland* (Berkeley: University of California Press, 1984).

[30] For the principles behind this type of efficiency auditing, see Vaughan S. Radcliffe, "Knowing Efficiency: The Enactment of Efficiency in Efficiency Auditing," *Accounting, Organizations and Society* 24, no. 4 (May 1999): 333–62.

[31] Interview with donor to Care Burundi, C12, Bujumbura, June 6, 2009.

and augment their strengths, then country offices may be incentivized to do the same.

A donor representative in the DRC articulated the value of this accompaniment-focused approach:

Our organization, at the moment, has a very strong emphasis on having an open relationship and expressing when things aren't going right. You see this in how we spend the funding. It is a difficult environment and no one knows what will and will not work. We say, let's be realistic and let's have a partnership and dialogue around it. When our partners see that this space is created then they have a dialogue around it. We don't just want a glossy report. We will not condition their funding on whether they admit failure or not.[32]

The degree to which donors or headquarters can engage in accompaniment-focused accountability will depend, in part, on the rigidity of their compliance-focused accountability routines and, as a corollary, the agency possessed by individual staff. But it is also likely to depend on the willingness of donor, headquarters, and/or country-office staff to travel to the places where peacebuilding activities are being implemented and to take time to understand what is and is not working. Donors, headquarters staff, and even country-office staff are unlikely to build this type of knowledge by simply receiving or reading reports. They are likely to build the greatest understanding of the relevance of peacebuilding interventions to the local contexts by seeing the local contexts in which peacebuilding takes place.

(2) Identify and foster skill sets that enable entrepreneurship and learning. If the solution to the peacebuilding problem is to foster entrepreneurship and learning, then organizations engaged in peacebuilding should hire and train staff in these skills. Skills and personality traits that encourage learning and entrepreneurship include having a growth mindset rather than a fixed mindset, nondefensiveness as opposed to defensiveness, comfort with not knowing the answers, and the ability to function in a complex environment.[33] Because managing open discussions about success and failure often requires facility with conflict resolution and dialogue facilitation, it may be helpful for staff to understand the basic principles of this field. But there is also some indication that teams made up of only people who have this particular skill set will be hampered in the peacebuilding field. In a 2010 evaluation of UN

---

[32] Interview with bilateral donor staff member 144, Goma, DRC, April 27, 2016.

[33] Argyris and Schon, *Organizational Learning*; and United States Agency for International Development, "Evidence Base for Collaborating, Learning, and Adapting," August 2016, 19–22.

peacebuilding activities, I found that project teams that were associated with successful outcomes were made up of staff with technical expertise in a certain type of program (e.g., security sector reform or political dialogue processes), expertise in the particular local institution with which they were working, expertise in dialogue and learning, and expertise in the routines and procedures of their own organization.[34] There is an important opportunity for further research on the specific personality characteristics and skill sets that may enable staff to be entrepreneurs and contribute to learning in IOs, INGOs, and bilateral donors and, specifically, to create and learn from informal local accountability routines.

(3) Increase funding for peacebuilding. If formal peacebuilding accountability is necessary for peacebuilding performance, then increased funding for peacebuilding would likely lead to more peacebuilding, and more effective peacebuilding, as long as it is accompanied by informal local accountability. In international intervention, the type of resource – whether humanitarian, development, peacebuilding, or some other type of transitional aid – influences the focus of formal accountability routines. If a country office is funded primarily to implement development activities, then it will implement development activities. If a country office is funded primarily to implement peacebuilding activities, it will implement peacebuilding activities. One challenge facing international peacebuilding efforts is that funding for intervention still falls within very distinct silos, with the vast majority of funds going to humanitarian and development interventions and much less going toward peacebuilding.[35] To alter the focus of formal accountability routines, the sources of funding also have to be altered. This does not mean that simply providing peacebuilding funding will solve all problems, but that altering the ratios of funding among peacebuilding, humanitarian, and development aid will enable more peacebuilding to occur. Once available, this funding should be allocated in a way that ensures that staff have the time to engage in and incentivize country-office organizational learning: ensuring that there are enough staff to monitor and support accompaniment-focused accountability and giving country-office staff the training and support necessary to develop high-quality peacebuilding interventions and related informal local accountability routines.

---

[34] Campbell, "Independent External Evaluation: Peacebuilding Fund Projects in Burundi."

[35] For a discussion of the patterns and silos of humanitarian and development financing, see High-Level Panel on Humanitarian Financing Report to the General, "Too Important to Fail: Addressing the Humanitarian Financing Gap" (Istanbul: World Humanitarian Summit, January 2016).

Beyond Burundi and Peacebuilding

Intervening organizations engaged in peacebuilding tend to replicate their formal accountability routines from one country office to the next to ensure that all country offices comply with the same standards.[36] For this reason, although most of my findings are derived from research conducted in Burundi, they have implications for these same kinds of organizations operating in conflict-affected countries around the world. Formal accountability routines, by definition, are replicated, with some variation, from one office to the next, holding each country office accountable for complying with the organization's global targets and standards. Over time, through institutional isomorphism, the formal accountability routines of different organizations operating within the same organizational field come to resemble one another.[37] Numerous studies of INGOs, IOs, and bilateral aid agencies point to similar formal accountability routines of country offices operating in other countries. These formal accountability routines also emphasize the delivery of goods and services, compliance with spending requirements set by internal accountants and global accounting firms, and regular reporting to headquarters and donors.[38]

My research in Burundi is supported by field research that I conducted in the DRC, South Sudan, and Sudan in 2015 and 2016. Interviews in these countries showed that informal local accountability routines also seem to be necessary for positive country-office performance.[39] They enable IOs, INGOs, and bilateral donors to reach beyond their standard interlocutors in government and the international community to better understand the local institutions they aim to influence. For these country offices to use the information provided through informal local

---

[36] For a discussion of the way that institutional isomorphism leads to the replication of organizational forms within a broader organizational "field," in part through organizational routines, see Paul DiMaggio and Walter Powell, "The Iron Cage Revisited: Institutional Isomorphism and Collective Rationality in Organizational Fields," in *The New Institutionalism in Organizational Analysis*, ed. Paul DiMaggio and Walter Powell (Chicago: Chicago University Press, 1991), 64–5.

[37] See, for example, William Easterly, *White Man's Burden: Why the West's Efforts to Aid the Rest Have Done So Much Ill and So Little Good* (Oxford, UK: Oxford University Press, 2006); Alnoor Ebrahim, *NGOs and Organizational Change: Discourse, Reporting, and Learning* (Cambridge, UK: Cambridge University Press, 2003); Bertin Martens et al., *The Institutional Economics of Foreign Aid* (Cambridge, UK: Cambridge University Press, 2002); and Natsios, "The Clash of Counter-Bureaucracy and Development."

[38] See, for example, Alexander Cooley and James Ron, "The NGO Scramble: Organizational Insecurity and the Political Economy of Transnational Action," *International Security* 27, no. 1 (2002): 5–39.

[39] For example, interview with INGO staff member 143-2, Goma, DRC, April 27, 2015.

accountability, their formal accountability routines also matter for the type of local information to which they are likely to respond. But there were two main differences between these countries and Burundi – differences that influenced country offices' formal and informal local accountability routines.

First, my research in Sudan and South Sudan showed that it is of course very difficult for country offices to establish informal local accountability routines when their access to diverse populations is restricted because of insecurity or other travel restrictions. Several INGOs, bilateral donors, and IO staff in South Sudan argued that the lack of access to the population only made country offices more rigid and more focused on spending money in line with their plans and indicators:

Donors are not very forgiving if their indicators are not met. The INGOs spend a lot of time manipulating reports. The donors can't actually monitor and go out there and see what is happening. Because the donors can't monitor, the INGOs have a lot of report manipulation going on.[40]

In Sudan, it is difficult for country offices to establish informal local accountability not just because of insecurity but also because the Sudanese government restricts the number and location of their visits outside of Khartoum.[41]

It is very difficult to do development here. There's a lot of blocking and obstruction. There's no access. There's no way of monitoring. You can't get travel permits. Monitoring is really restricted. National NGOs are often corrupt or have no capacity. We are trapped. There is no political engagement and backup. Why do rule of law when you don't have political engagement?[42]

In spite of these restrictions on country offices' ability to monitor their activities, many IOs, INGOs, and bilateral donors continue to spend money and implement activities, often with little real knowledge of the actual outcome.

Second, the singular focus of many international actors in Burundi on building peace was not present in the DRC, South Sudan, and Sudan. Thus, there were fewer opportunities for peacebuilding performance because fewer organizations had formal accountability routines that

---

[40] Interview with INGO staff member 212, Juba, South Sudan, January 28, 2016.

[41] The high level of regulation of INGOs also presents a problem for access and informal local accountability in South Sudan. See Lindsay Hamsik, "A Thousand Papercuts: The Impact of NGO Regulation in South Sudan," *Humanitarian Exchange*, Special Feature, The Crisis in South Sudan, No. 68 (January 2017), accessed December 23, 2017, http://odihpn.org/magazine/a-thousand-papercuts-the-impact-of-ngo-regulation-in-south-sudan/.

[42] Interview with donor staff member 415-1, Khartoum, Sudan, February 2, 2016.

prioritized peacebuilding. For example, even though the DRC has continued to suffer from violence and instability in its eastern provinces, most country offices are located in Kinshasa, approximately 1,700 miles away. In 2015, the majority of IO, INGO, and bilateral donor offices operating in Kinshasa prioritized development, not peacebuilding or humanitarian aid, even though the needs for both remained vast.

I was in South Sudan in 2016, at which point international donors, IOs, and INGOs were in a stage of crisis, unsure what they should do or how they should do it. The international community had engaged in an intense state-building effort after the signature of the Comprehensive Peace Agreement in 2005 and the establishment of South Sudan in 2011, but with the outbreak of war in 2013 and continued deterioration of the political and security situation, donors no longer believed that they could collaborate directly with the state. Instead, most donors decided to provide only humanitarian aid. In spite of the enormous need for peace in South Sudan, few actors felt that they could work directly on peacebuilding without a viable political agreement between the warring parties.

In Sudan in 2016, peacebuilding was not something that most intervenors felt that they could support either, in spite of the numerous ongoing conflicts on Sudan's territory. This was primarily because of the very poor relationship between most intervening actors and the Sudanese government. The Sudanese government viewed efforts to support civil society or build peace as direct challenges to its political authority and, thus, used many of the levers at its disposal to curtail these activities. In other words, without a commitment to prioritizing peacebuilding, or one of its variants, few actors carried out peacebuilding activities even in contexts that seemed to be in real need of peace.

The findings presented in this book have potentially important implications for humanitarian and development activities as well. Development and humanitarian tasks are implemented by many of the same IOs, INGOs, and bilateral donors that carry out peacebuilding tasks. As a result, although some development and humanitarian tasks are less complex than international peacebuilding, they may be subject to many of the same opportunities and constraints.[43] Simple development and humanitarian tasks – such as constructing roads and delivering emergency food and nutrition supplies – may require less learning because they do not aim to alter the behavior of individuals and institutions. Yet, as

---

[43] For a discussion of simple versus complex tasks in international state building, see Stephen D. Krasner and Thomas Risse, "External Actors, State-Building, and Service Provision in Areas of Limited Statehood: Introduction," *Governance* 27, no. 4 (October 2014): 545–67.

numerous studies of humanitarian and development aid have revealed, even very simple tasks can do harm if they are not adjusted to the reality of the context or if the people implementing them are not aware of their influence on the local political economy.[44] And many development and humanitarian interventions are highly complex, aiming to alter the governance frameworks and livelihood systems of the state and society.[45]

For the theory presented here to be relevant to humanitarian, development, and other organizational aims, one needs to adjust the focus of formal accountability. If the organization prioritizes accountability for development, then one would expect the organization to exhibit higher levels of development-related performance when it has corresponding informal local accountability routines. The same applies for humanitarian or other goals. Because many of the organizations intervening in conflict-affected countries aim to simultaneously achieve development, humanitarian, peacebuilding, stabilization, and other goals, the focus of formal accountability may not be obvious. It may shift based on changes in headquarters-level leadership in the organization, the pet project of a key donor or legislator, the focus of a particular bureaucrat, or a broad organizational change process that leads to the reformulation of organization-wide priorities. Understanding the particular prioritization that is conveyed by headquarters to the country office is, thus, important for understanding the behavior and performance of the country office. This concept is relevant for peacebuilding, humanitarian, and development.

Regardless of the organizational aim, intervention in non–conflict-affected countries is likely to be easier than in conflict-affected countries. Thus, intervening organizations working in these contexts may not need to establish such deep informal local accountability routines or engage in as much learning. Nonetheless, the development policy literature is increasingly calling for improved country-level organizational learning

---

[44] See, for example, Mary Anderson, *Do No Harm: How Aid Can Support Peace – or War* (Boulder, CO: Lynne Rienner, 2010); *International Alert*, Saferworld, and FEWER, "Conflict Sensitive Approaches to Development, Humanitarian Assistance and Peacebuilding: A Resource Pack" (London, 2004); de Waal, "Mission without End?" 99–113; and Fiona Terry, *Condemned to Repeat? The Paradox of Humanitarian Action* (Ithaca, NY: Cornell University Press, 2002).

[45] For examples of complex humanitarian and development interventions, see Matthew Andrews, Lant Pritchett, and Michael Woolcock, *Building State Capability: Evidence, Analysis, and Action* (Oxford, UK: Oxford University Press, 2017); Secure Livelihoods Research Consortium, Feinstein International Center, Tufts University, accessed December 23, 2017, http://fic.tufts.edu/research-item/secure-livelihoods-research-consortium/; and World Bank, *World Development Report 2011: Conflict, Security, and Development* (Washington, DC: World Bank, 2011).

and adaptation.[46] The logic is much the same as in the peacebuilding literature: country-office learning is necessary to ensure that interventions are relevant to the local context, do not exacerbate political and social tensions, and garner the support and investment of the local actors and institutions they aim to help.[47]

In sum, the relevance of this book beyond Burundi and peacebuilding is due, in part, to the relatively general nature of the theory presented. Accountability routines are a common feature of all hierarchical organizations, and informal local accountability is a challenge faced by most global governors intervening in another country. Because these two organizational features are the core components of the theory presented here, the theory should have resonance for other organizations operating in other countries, although the particular conditions and the particular organizational characteristics that determine performance may vary. The significance of the findings in this book is due in part to the dearth of systematic, cross-organizational comparative studies of the behavior of IO, INGO, and bilateral donor country offices. By presenting a relatively general theory of a phenomenon that has received little attention, this book aims to set the stage for further refinement of this theory across contexts, types of organizations, and issue areas.

Alternative Explanations

In peacebuilding literature, variation in the peacebuilding performance of IOs, INGOs, and bilateral donors is often traced to one or more of three different factors: the country environment, the organizational population, and the features of the particular intervening organization. Clearly these factors are important. Study of them provides crucial

---

[46] Ingie Hovland, "Knowledge Management and Organisational Learning: An International Development Perspective," Working Paper (London: Overseas Development Institute, August 2003); Ben Ramalingam, Miguel Laric, and John Primrose, "From Best Practice to Best Fit: Understanding and Navigating Wicked Problems in International Development" (London: Overseas Development Institute Report, September 2014); Laura Roper, Jethro Pettit, and Deborah Eade, eds., *Development and the Learning Organization* (Boulder, CO: Lynne Rienner, 2003); Craig Valters, Clare Cummings, and Hamish Nixon, "Putting Learning at the Centre" (London: Overseas Development Institute Report, March 2016); Dr. Gregory Wilson, "What Is Adaptive Management?" (Washington, DC: United States Agency for International Development Website, November 2016), accessed January 31, 2017, usaidlearninglab.org/lab-notes/what-adaptive-management.

[47] See, for example, Campbell, "When Process Matters"; CDA Collaborative Learning Projects, *Reflecting on Peace Practice (RPP)*; Howard, *UN Peacekeeping in Civil Wars*; and *International Alert, Saferworld*, and FEWER, "Conflict Sensitive Approaches to Development, Humanitarian Assistance and Peacebuilding."

insight into the nature of international peacebuilding and the behavior of global governors, but it does not fully explain variation in peacebuilding performance at the country level.

Country Environment Explanations

Doyle and Sambanis argue that the United Nations achieves negative, or sovereign, peace only when the country environment has a low level of open hostility between the parties and a strong local capacity, measured primarily in terms of electricity consumption and the rate of gross domestic product (GDP) change per capita.[48] My research indicates, however, that positive peacebuilding performance can take place even in the midst of high hostility and weak state capacity. For example, the Burundi Leadership Training Programme (BLTP) achieved positive peacebuilding performance and contributed to its peacebuilding aims during Burundi's transitional phases, times of high hostility and weak state capacity.[49] As the earlier discussion of South Sudan and Sudan reveals, however, what may matter most is whether the necessary conditions for positive performance can be met: informal local accountability and formal peacebuilding accountability. These can occur in both violent and nonviolent contexts, but they may not be able to occur in contexts where the host government and/or security constraints prevent country offices from accessing a diverse group of local actors or when donors are not able or willing to prioritize peacebuilding.

Organizational Population Explanations

Another strand of peacebuilding scholarship focuses on the shared culture of the broader organizational population of global governors engaged in peacebuilding, identifying the general culture of IO, INGO, and bilateral donor country offices, as well as other international actors operating in a country. Drawn from sociological institutionalism, this perspective views a single organization as part of a broader group of organizations that conform to similar patterns of behavior, which, over time, develop similar structures and practices.[50] This scholarship identifies three primary reasons why intervening organizations have not

---

[48] Michael Doyle and Nicholas Sambanis, *Making War and Building Peace: United Nations Peace Operations* (Princeton, NJ: Princeton University Press, 2006): 73–83.

[49] As discussed in Chapter 3, World Bank, "Data Catalog," World Bank Burundi Country Data, accessed September 1, 2014, http://data.worldbank.org/country/burundi.

[50] See DiMaggio and Powell, "The Iron Cage Revisited," 64–5.

transformed war-torn countries into liberal democratic states: the imposition of a standard Western template; a peacebuilding culture and organizational practices that isolate international actors from local perspectives; and the bureaucratic practices of intervening actors.

These scholars argue that international actors will never achieve their liberal peacebuilding aims because they impose a standard liberal democratic template – grounded in the rule of law, liberal democracy, and a market-based economy – that is mismatched with the institutional environment of war-torn countries.[51] They argue that international peacebuilding ignores the historical reality of countries' violent state formation process and the broader sources of global inequality that perpetuate this violence.[52] They also argue that it is implausible to expect countries to undergo extensive institutional transformation over a short period of time, or to attribute changes to international intervention that are often misguided and out of touch with the local reality.[53]

This scholarship critiques the standard template of peacebuilding strategies, programs, activities, and tasks that intervening organizations replicate from one country to the next.[54] The template approach

---

[51] For a synthesis of these arguments, see Susanna P. Campbell, David Chandler, and Meera Sabaratnam, eds. *A Liberal Peace? The Problems and Practices of Peacebuilding* (London and New York: Zed, 2011).

[52] See Mohammed Ayoob, "State Making, State Breaking, and State Failure," in ed. Chester A. Crocker, Fen Osler Hampson, and Pamela Aall, *Leashing the Dogs of War: Conflict Management in a Divided World* (Washington, DC: United States Institute of Peace, 2007), 95–114; Michael Barnett and Christoph Zürcher, "The Peacebuilder's Contract: How External State-Building Reinforces Weak Statehood," in ed. Timothy Sisk and Roland Paris, *The Dilemmas of Statebuilding: Confronting the Contradictions of Postwar Peace Operations*, (Abingdon, UK: Routledge, 2009), 23–52; David Chandler, "Back to the Future? The Limits of Neo-Wilsonian Ideals of Exporting Democracy," *Review of International Studies* 32, no. 3 (2006): 475–94; Pierre Englebert and Denis M. Tull, "Postconflict Reconstruction in Africa: Flawed Ideas about Failed States," *International Security*, 32 no. 4 (2008):106–39; Astri Suhrke, "Reconstruction as Modernization: The 'Post-Conflict' Project in Afghanistan," *Third World Quarterly* 28 no. 7(2007): 1291–1308.

[53] See Michael Barnett, "Building a Republican Peace: Stabilizing States after War," *International Security* 30, no. 4 (2006): 87–112; Stephan Haggard and Lydia Tiede, "The Rule of Law in Post-Conflict Settings: The Empirical Record," *International Studies Quarterly* 57, no. 4 (2013), 1–13; Astri Suhrke, *When More Is Less: The International Project in Afghanistan* (New York: Columbia University Press, 2011); Suhrke, "Reconstruction as Modernisation," 1291–1308.

[54] See PBPS, "United Nations Peacekeeping Operations: Principles and Guidelines" (New York: Peacekeeping Best Practices Section, Division of Policy, Evaluation and Training, Department of Peacekeeping Operations, UN Secretariat, 2008), 53; Daniel Serwer and Patricia Thomson, "A Framework for Success: International Intervention in Societies Emerging from Conflict," in ed. Chester A. Crocker, Fen Osler Hampson, and Pamela Aall, *Leashing the Dogs of War: Conflict Management in a Divided World* (Washington, DC: United States Institute of Peace Press, 2007), 369–88.

to peacebuilding is problematic, critics maintain, because a "mandate or doctrine that established fixed rules would either become out of sync with a complex reality or would dangerously shoehorn that reality so that it fit the rules. Either way, it could be fatal for the operation."[55] Supply-driven templates favor international legitimacy over national or local legitimacy, focusing on developing internationally legitimate institutions rather than those that are domestically legitimate.[56] These scholars argue that the wholesale application of this liberal peace agenda to countries emerging from conflict can stifle national peacebuilding capacity and local democratic processes, reducing the country's capacity to sustain peace.[57]

The evidence presented in this book does not contradict the claim that the supply-driven approach of international peacebuilders is ineffective and potentially harmful. Two of the types of country offices identified, in fact, exhibit this behavior: sovereignty reinforcers and stagnant players. Nonetheless, this book shows that some country offices can adapt their templates to particular local contexts. Country offices that were peacebuilding learners and micro-adaptors were able to use informal local accountability to adapt their international templates to local opportunities and perspectives.[58]

Furthermore, this book shows that global governors do not have the capacity to impose a wholesale liberal peace agenda on conflict-affected countries in part because they need the consent and buy-in of local actors to achieve their peacebuilding aims.[59] Global governors may not have the

---

[55] Barnett, "Building a Republican Peace," 91.

[56] Susan Woodward, "Do the Root Causes of Civil War Matter? On Using Knowledge to Improve Peacebuilding Interventions," *Journal of Intervention and Statebuilding* 1, no. 2 (2007): 143–70.

[57] Barnett and Zürcher, "The Peacebuilder's Contract;" Charles T. Call and Elizabeth M. Cousens, "Ending Wars and Building Peace: International Responses to War-Torn Societies," *International Studies Perspectives* 9 (2008): 1–21; Virginia Page Fortna, "Peacekeeping and Democratization," in ed. Anna Jarstad and Timothy Sisk, *From War to Democracy* (Cambridge, UK: Cambridge University Press, 2008), 39–70; Ashraf Ghani and Clare Lockhart, *Fixing Failed States: A Framework for Rebuilding a Fractured World* (Oxford, UK: Oxford University Press, 2008); Beatrice Pouligny, "Civil Society and Post-Conflict Peacebuilding: Ambiguities of International Programmes Aimed at Building 'New' Societies; *Security Dialogue* 36 (2005): 495–510; Oliver P. Richmond and Jason Franks, "Liberal Hubris? Virtual Peace in Cambodia," *Security Dialogue* 38, no. 1 (2007): 27–48; Astri Suhrke, "The Limits of Statebuilding: The Role of International Assistance in Afghanistan" (San Diego, CA: Chr. Michelsen Institute, 2006); Suhrke, "Reconstruction as Modernisation," 1291–1308.

[58] Roger Mac Ginty, in part in reaction to the liberal peace critique, refers to this as hybrid peace. For elaboration of this concept, see Roger Mac Ginty, "Hybrid Peace: The Interaction between Top-Down and Bottom-Up Peace," *Security Dialogue* 41, no. 4 (2010): 391–412;

[59] Campbell, "Routine Learning."

power or authority to impose norms on a conflict-affected country precisely because the localization of these norms involves adaptation, rejection, or cooptation by local actors.[60] Additionally, when a peacebuilding aim is implemented and localized through informal local accountability, it may no longer mirror the Western liberal institutions that may have been its inspiration. Instead, as Mac Ginty argues, it may be a hybrid of Western liberal institutions and local institutions.[61] Or, as Sabaratnam claims, the local actors may be more committed to creating liberal democratic institutions than their Western counterparts are, reversing the assumed liberal–local divide.[62]

Some scholars who focus on the behavior of the entire population of organizations engaged in peacebuilding claim that shared international culture and practices are the problem.[63] Autesserre argues that the focus of international intervenors on national-level (as opposed to local-level) manifestations of the conflict, and their related organizational practices, prevents them from understanding the local context and building local-level peace.[64] She describes a similarly bifurcated context to the one identified by critical ethnographers of international aid, where international aid actors are largely ignorant of the reality faced by the local actors they aim to help, with the two communities existing in separate social and cultural planes.[65] The consequences of this irrelevance may be

---

[60] Amitav Acharya, "How Ideas Spread: Whose Norms Matter? Norm Localization and Institutional Change in Asian Regionalism," *International Organization* 58, no. 02 (2004): 239–75; Barnett and Zürcher, "The Peacebuilder's Contract."

[61] Roger Mac Ginty, "Hybrid Peace: The Interaction between Top-Down and Bottom-Up Peace," *Security Dialogue* 41, no. 4 (2010): 391–412; Mac Ginty, "Hybrid Peace: How Does Hybrid Peace Come About?" in ed. Susanna P. Campbell, David Chandler, and Meera Sabaratnam, *A Liberal Peace? The Problems and Practices of Peacebuilding* (London: Zed, 2011), 209–25.

[62] Meera Sabaratnam, "The Liberal Peace? An Intellectual History of International Conflict Management, 1990–2010," in ed. Susanna P. Campbell, David Chandler, and Meera Sabaratnam, *A Liberal Peace? The Problems and Practices of Peacebuilding* (London: Zed, 2011), 13–30.

[63] Séverine Autesserre, "Hobbes and the Congo: Frames, Local Violence, and International Intervention," *International Organization* 63, no. 02 (2009): 249–80; Autesserre, *Peaceland;* Séverine Autesserre, *The Trouble with the Congo: Local Violence and the Failure of International Peacebuilding,* Vol. 115, (Cambridge, UK: Cambridge University Press, 2010); de Waal, "Mission without End?" 99–113; Kathleen Jennings, "Blue Helmet Havens: Peacekeeping as Bypassing in Liberia and the Democratic Republic of the Congo," *International Peacekeeping* 23, no. 2 (2016): 302–25; and Jennings, "Life in a 'Peace-Kept' City: Encounters with the Peacekeeping Economy," *Journal of Intervention and Statebuilding* 85, no. 1 (2015): 99–113.

[64] Autesserre, "Hobbes and the Congo;" Autesserre, *Peaceland;* DiMaggio and Powell, "The Iron Cage Revisited;" 64–5.

[65] See, for example, Bruce Berman, "Ethnicity, Patronage and the African State: The Politics of Uncivil Nationalism," *African Affairs* 97, no. 388 (1998): 305–41.

even greater for peacebuilding than for standard development aid. Rather than transforming the institutions that caused the war into ones that can sustain peace, aid that is blind to conflict dynamics can reinforce the status quo, potentially contributing to greater violence and conflict.[66] Although Autesserre provides insightful and important findings about the common cultures and practices within this broader organizational population, she does not describe the heterogeneity within this population or the causes of positive peacebuilding performance.

The evidence presented in this book shows that although the culture and practices of international peacebuilders may discourage country offices from engaging with local actors, they do not determine the behavior of country offices. The shared culture of international intervenors may influence their behavior, but this culture is rooted in formal accountability routines and can be altered through informal local accountability. Both peacebuilding learners and micro-adaptors are able to establish strong informal local accountability mechanisms, with key country-office staff building strong relationships with a variety of local actors. Autesserre acknowledges that there are exceptional individuals who do not abide by cultural constraints, but she argues that they are the exception, not the rule; does not explain the mechanisms by which these actors operate; and does not examine how their behavior might enable positive peacebuilding performance.[67]

IO bureaucracy scholarship argues that bureaucratic pathologies are at the root of the failure of international peacebuilding. Barnett and Finnemore explain that IOs, as bureaucracies, tend to reproduce themselves: "The result is that what began as a relatively narrow technical intervention (training police) expands into a package of reforms aimed at transforming non-Western societies (where most peacebuilding takes place) into Western societies."[68] Rather than build the capacity of local institutions to implement activities, international bureaucracies implement much of the activities themselves in a manner that fits with their standards and approach. The "same normative valuation on impersonal, generalized rules that defines bureaucracies and makes them powerful in

---

[66] Peter Uvin, *Aiding Violence: The Development Enterprise in Rwanda* (West Hartford, CT: Kumarian Press, 1998).

[67] For a discussion of the role of exceptional individuals in determining peacebuilding success, see Campbell, "Organizational Barriers to Peace." For Autesserre's discussion of exceptional individuals, see Séverine Autesserre, "International Peacebuilding and Local Success: Assumptions and Effectiveness," *International Studies Review* 19, no. 1 (2017): 114–32; and Autesserre, *Peaceland*, 273;

[68] Michael Barnett and Martha Finnemore, *Rules for the World: International Organizations in Global Politics* (Ithaca, NY: Cornell University Press, 2004), 34.

modern life can also make them unresponsive to their environments, obsessed with their own rules at the expense of primary missions, and ultimately lead to inefficient, self-defeating behavior."[69]

The case studies presented in this book show that accountability routines embedded in IO bureaucracies discourage local responsiveness to the context. But this does not mean that local responsiveness is impossible. In spite of bureaucratic "pathologies," some individual country-office staff are able to work around bureaucratic routines and establish informal local accountability that enables positive peacebuilding performance.

Organizational Explanations

To describe the behavior of a single organization, scholars put forward hypotheses related to the organizational characteristics, financial and material resources, procedures, and types of interventions implemented.

The literature on the rational design of IOs focuses on the scope of the issues covered by the organization; the degree of centralization of tasks; the degree of control exercised by the organization's principals; and the flexibility of the institution's rules and procedures to adapt to new situations.[70] Because these factors primarily address how states exercise their preferences when forming international institutions, not all are relevant to this analysis of how organizations respond to and influence the dynamics of a country's war-to-peace transition. Nonetheless, scholarship on organizational learning argues that several related factors may influence an organization's behavior and performance in complex, uncertain situations.[71] The degree of organizational hierarchy, the size of the organization, the profile of staff hired, and the degree of

---

[69] Michael Barnett and Martha Finnemore, "The Politics, Power, and Pathologies of International Organizations," *International Organization* 53, no. 4 (1999): 699–700.

[70] The most prominent work in this vein is Barbara Koremenos, Charles Lipson, and Duncan Snidal, "The Rational Design of International Institutions," *International Organization* 55, no. 4 (October 2001): 761–99.

[71] Ariane Berthoin-Antal, Uwe Lenhardt, and Rolf Rosenbrock. "Barriers to Organizational Learning," in ed. M. Dierkes, A. Berthoin-Antal, J. Child, and I. Nonaka, *Handbook of Organizational Learning and Knowledge* (Oxford, UK: Oxford University Press, 2000), 865–85; M. Leann Brown and Michael Kenney, "Organizational Learning: Theoretical and Methodological Considerations," in ed. M. Leann Brown, Michael Zarkin, and Michael Kenney, eds. *Organizational Learning in the Global Context* (Hampshire, UK: Ashgate, 2006): 1–20; and George Huber, "Organizational Learning: The Contributing Processes and the Literatures," *Organization Science* 2, no. 1 (1991): 88–115.

decentralized decision-making may influence whether or not an organization can achieve its aims in a highly dynamic context.[72]

The evidence presented in this book shows that although these organizational characteristics may influence the behavior of country offices, they do not determine country-office behavior or peacebuilding performance. For example, all the case study organizations had a relatively high degree of decentralized decision-making, but not all the organizations achieved positive performance all the time. The leadership and key staff of the smaller organizations did seem to find it easier to ensure that informal local accountability routines were created for all the different peacebuilding activities, but the larger hierarchical organizations, such as the United Nations, also managed to create informal local accountability routines and achieve positive peacebuilding performance at times. Moreover, in eleven out of sixteen cases, small organizations were not peacebuilding learners failing to meet this minimal measure of peacebuilding performance.

The literature on organizational frames argues that the founding mandate "imprints" the organization with cognitive, normative, and regulative structures that are difficult to change.[73] The cases discussed here show that while the founding mandate of the organization does seem to influence the organization's propensity to have formal peacebuilding accountability routines, there are organizations that were founded to do one thing, such as development, that still manage to adopt other priorities for specific country offices. For example, both CARE and the Department for International Development (DFID) prioritized peacebuilding for their Burundi-based country offices during one of Burundi's phases.

Given the role of individual staff in determining peacebuilding performance, hiring practices would seem to be important. But across the five case study organizations over fifteen years, there was a high degree of variation in the profile of staff hired, showing that the specific hiring practices of country-office staff were not necessary for informal local accountability or peacebuilding performance.

Recruitment, hiring, and training processes of global governors do not generally focus on supporting the type of political engagement and

---

[72] Berthoin-Antal et al., "Barriers to Organizational Learning," 865–85; Brown and Kenney, "Organizational Learning," 1–20; Eden, "Getting It Right or Wrong" 197–216; Eden, *Whole World on Fire*; David Lake, "Delegating Divisible Sovereignty: Sweeping a Conceptual Minefield," *Review of International Organizations* 2, no. 3 (2007): 219–37.

[73] For discussion of the role of founding mandates, see W. Richard Scott, *Institutions and Organizations, Foundations for Organizational Science* (Thousand Oaks, CA: Sage, 1995), p. 115.

learning behavior that seem to facilitate positive peacebuilding perform-ance. As one staff person from a bilateral donor in Sudan observed, the hiring practices of bilateral donors are determined by standard minimal criteria for foreign service appointments that do not focus on the political background or knowledge of these individuals or their openness to engagement with local actors.[74] The criteria for the appointment of UN staff are noncommittal about particular personality characteristics and indifferent to prior political or contextual knowledge.[75] In fact, prior to being deployed to a country office, UN staff are not expected to have knowledge of the country context and do not receive training about how to engage with this context or its populations.[76] Perhaps the BLTP was the most intentional in its staff appointments, selecting people with a strong background on Burundi and who were widely respected among diverse Burundian constituents. But even with this top-notch team, the BLTP did not consistently exhibit positive peacebuilding performance throughout the period under study.

Although the specific personality characteristics of country-office leadership matter, it is unclear exactly what characteristics these are. Informal local accountability could not exist without the explicit or implicit support of the country-office leadership. The country-office leadership had to endorse the rule breaking and bending behavior that informal local accountability required. In this sense, entrepreneurial country-office leadership is endogenous to informal local accountability. One does not exist without the other. But it is not clear that particular hiring practices lead to the appointment of individuals who are support-ive of informal local accountability or what specific personality charac-teristics are present in these leaders.

The literature on international peacebuilding argues that individual country offices must be well resourced in order to achieve their man-dates. Much of this literature focuses on UN peace operations and argues that if these operations have sufficient resources and soldiers that are deployed quickly enough, then they will have the desired peacebuilding effect.[77] The case studies presented here show that although resources

---

[74] Interview with donor staff member 420, Khartoum, Sudan, February 4, 2016.

[75] For discussion of the problems of ensuring that the right staff are deployed to conflict-affected countries, see Advisory Group of Experts, "The Challenge of Sustaining Peace Report of the Advisory Group of Experts for the 2015 Review of the United Nations Peacebuilding Architecture" (New York: United Nations, June 29, 2015).

[76] Campbell, "Independent External Evaluation: Peacebuilding Fund Projects in Burundi"; interview with UN staff person 1.23, Bujumubra, June 19, 2009.

[77] Doyle and Sambanis, *Making War and Building Peace*; United Nations General Assembly Security Council, "The Report of the Panel on United Nations Peace Operations: The

can be important, what matters most is how an organization uses the resources that it has. Both the United Nations and DFID in Burundi were very well resourced at points in time, but this did not correlate with their positive peacebuilding performance.

Much of the policy-focused peacebuilding scholarship argues that if international intervenors conduct better analysis, are better coordinated, have better headquarters leadership, and carry out better evaluations, they will have better peacebuilding results.[78] The evidence presented in this book shows, however, that such policy measures are insufficient for improved peacebuilding performance because organizations still employ accountability mechanisms that prioritize accountability to the organization's principals, not to the local population. All organizations doing peacebuilding have some policy rhetoric about creating "local ownership" for their activities, but their incentive mechanisms seldom facilitate ownership that extends beyond the host government.[79] In fact, by implementing such policy approaches, international institutions often act as if they are increasing their peacebuilding performance without actually altering their engagement with their strategic or operational environment, potentially discouraging reforms that may attempt to do so.

Finally, the breadth of peacebuilding activities implemented by the case study organizations, spanning economic, security, and socioeconomic domains, shows that the exact type of program or activity or the precise strategy adopted by a country office does not determine its performance. Instead, what matters is how a strategy is implemented and whether or not it is adapted to the local context.

Open Questions

This book's examination of the peacebuilding performance of IOs, INGOs, and bilateral donors in war-torn countries opens several new

Brahimi Report" (New York, November 13, 2000), accessed December 23, 2017, www.un.org/en/events/pastevents/brahimi_report.shtml.

[78] Charles T. Call and Vanessa Wyeth, *Building States to Build Peace* (Boulder, CO: Lynne Rienner, 2008); Roland Paris and Timothy D. Sisk, *Managing Contradictions: The Inherent Dilemmas of Postwar Statebuilding* (New York: International Peace Academy, 2007); OECD-DAC, *Principles for Good International Engagement in Fragile States and Situations* (Paris: Organization for Economic Cooperation and Development, 2007); OECD-DAC, *State Building in Situations of Fragility: Initial Findings* (Paris: Organization for Economic Cooperation and Development, August 30, 2008), accessed December 23, 2017, www.oecd.org/dac/conflict-fragility-resilience/docs/41212290.pdf.

[79] For an excellent discussion of the contradictions inherent in local ownership and its application in the UN, see Sarah B. K. von Billerbeck, *Whose Peace? Local Ownership and United Nations Peacekeeping* (Oxford, UK: Oxford University Press, 2016).

areas of inquiry with implications for theories of global governance and international peacebuilding and peacekeeping.

Who exhibits "bad behavior"? By circumventing or bending the standard operating procedures set up by headquarters, innovative staff are able to give authority to local stakeholders to hold the global governors accountable for local outcomes. Yet, not much is known about who these rule benders and breakers are and what enables them to build effective informal local accountability routines. Which type of rule-bending or -breaking behavior enables effective peacebuilding and which type undermines it? What leads individual staff to undermine or alter the formal accountability routines established by their principals? Are particular personalities more likely to innovate than others? Do social networks within the organization facilitate and/or undermine rule-bending or rule-breaking behavior? What degree of engagement by country-office leadership is necessary for effective "bad behavior"? Do the mandate or moral claims of the organization motivate these individual staff? Does the age or seniority of the rule-breaker matter? Do the in-country networks of the rule-breaker or rule-bender matter? Does informal local accountability require rule-breaking teams, or is one individual sufficient to create this routine? Do the motivations and characteristics of rule-breakers differ between IOs, donors, and INGOs? Do the motivations and characteristics of the rule-breakers differ depending on the geographic regions in which country offices intervene? Do they differ depending on the culture or country of origin of the potential rule-breaker or rule-bender? A better understanding of rule-breaking and rule-bending behavior, and how this behavior may vary within and between country offices, is important for our understanding of country-office performance and crucial for the development of training and human resource reform strategies that aim to enable more effective peacebuilding.

Why do country office headquarters, governing boards, and donors permit "bad behavior"?[80] In several of the case studies discussed in this book, headquarters was not aware of the existence of informal local accountability routines or the related circumvention of formal accountability routines, either because headquarters did not receive reports about their existence or because it did not read the reports that it received. In other cases, headquarters was aware of informal local accountability routines and the related rule-breaking or rule-bending behavior and argued against it, but the country office ignored these

---

[80] See Sarah Bush, *The Taming of Democracy Assistance* (Cambridge, UK: Cambridge University Press, 2015) for an excellent discussion of the incentive structure at headquarters.

requests. In still other cases, headquarters claimed to fully support informal local accountability routines, even if it could not directly incentivize them. What explains this variation? Is rule-bending behavior simply a result of the willingness and ability of country-office staff to bend the rules? Or does it require rule-bending by well-placed headquarters or donor staff as well? How does the strength of compliance-focused accountability influence the degree of individual agency potentially possessed by headquarters or donor staff, determining the necessary degree of rule-breaking behavior? How does the degree of centralization of decision-making influence rule-breaking behavior and informal local accountability? Does the cultural similarity between the headquarters or donor and the country-office staff matter? Does the country of origin, training, or work experience of key headquarters or donor staff matter? To what degree are formal accountability routines fixed or socially constructed, influencing the degree to which they need to be bent or broken?

Can positive peacebuilding performance happen in all conflict-affected contexts? In the case studies discussed in this book, peacebuilding performance was concentrated in two phases in Burundi's war-to-peace transition: specifically, 2001–2003 and 2003–2005, just after the inauguration of its transitional government and prior to its first democratic elections respectively. During this transitional period, many actors in Burundi prioritized peacebuilding above humanitarian and development assistance, influencing country offices' formal accountability routines. It was also a period when there were arguably more opportunities for peacebuilding because the Burundian government was more open to international peacebuilding efforts than it would be in later years. Yet, peacebuilding performance happened in all but one of the six phases in Burundi's war-to-peace transition. Peacebuilding performance can thus happen in the midst of violence and in the midst of increased authoritarianism.

The BLTP's experience during Burundi's transition suggests that it may be better to have positive peacebuilding performance in the midst of violence than nothing at all, at least so that interventions can take advantage of opportunities to influence change that may arise. But, as the earlier discussion of South Sudan and Sudan shows, the difficulty of prioritizing peacebuilding and establishing informal local accountability makes positive peacebuilding performance less likely in these contexts. Relatedly, if an organization is unable to establish informal local accountability or prioritize peacebuilding above other aims, then it should probably stop attempting to do peacebuilding in that particular context because it will be ineffective and may do harm.

Does positive peacebuilding performance of a single country office matter for longer-term outcomes? The relationship between the case studies and Burundi's war-to-peace transition suggests that positive peacebuilding performance might be pivotal for long-term conflict and cooperation outcomes, for example if it enables political inclusion that otherwise would not have existed. But is it really necessary to have such a large number of country offices operating in conflict-affected countries? If many country offices are achieving positive peacebuilding performance, then it may be more likely that they will contribute to pivotal change that influences longer-term outcomes. But, if these offices are not establishing informal local accountability routines and are instead fomenting discord, then the harm of many country offices may outweigh the potential good of a few high performers. As this discussion reveals, further examination of the influence of the heterogeneity of country-office behavior and performance on longer-term outcomes is a fruitful area for further research.

How does the behavior of the host government influence the behavior and performance of country offices? The influence of the host government on the behavior of country offices, which was particularly visible in the UN Mission case studies, points to the opportunity for more research into the ways that different host governments use the power of their sovereignty at the local level to influence the behavior of global governance institutions operating in their country.[81] Relatedly, the importance of informal local accountability points toward the opportunity for greater research into the different forms and functions of informal governance by global governors at the subnational level and how individual agents within these organizations may alter the behavior of IOs, INGOs, and states.[82] Investigating these and related questions could provide crucial insights into factors that increasingly determine the legitimacy and performance of global governors in the growing number of complex situations in which they intervene.

By raising these questions and hopefully spurring more, this book aims to inspire new research that systematically examines the behavior of country offices both within and outside conflict-affected

---

[81] Michael Barnett and Raymond Duvall, "Power in International Politics," *International Organization* 59, no. 1 (2005): 39–75.

[82] Deborah D. Avant, Martha Finnemore, and Susan K. Sell, eds., *Who Governs the Globe?* (Cambridge, UK: Cambridge University Press, 2010): 356; Randall W. Stone, "Informal Governance in International Organizations: Introduction to the Special Issue," *Review of International Organizations* 8, no. 2 (2013): 121–36; Stone, *Controlling Institutions: International Organizations and the Global Economy* (Cambridge, UK: Cambridge University Press, 2011).

environments. Future examination of the subnational behavior of international actors should lead to new findings about the potential importance of individual agency within country offices and at headquarters. It should help us better understand the relationship between formal and informal systems within and between global governance organizations. It should enable scholars to identify when and how the micro-level interactions between global and local actors are mutually constitutive and contribute to transnational and multi-level governance. In a world where the global and local are increasingly embedded, the study of global governance at the local level provides an important opportunity for greater scholarly understanding and more effective policy engagement.

Bibliography

Abbass, Julie. "Peace Education Project: Grassroots Community Research, Final Summary." Bujumbura, Burundi: CARE Burundi, June 10, 2001.

Acharya, Amitav. "How Ideas Spread: Whose Norms Matter? Norm Localization and Institutional Change in Asian Regionalism." *International Organization* 58, no. 02 (2004): 239–75.

Advisory Group of Experts. "The Challenge of Sustaining Peace Report of the Advisory Group of Experts for the 2015 Review of the United Nations Peacebuilding Architecture." New York: United Nations, June 29, 2015.

Agence France-Presse. "AFP: Western Envoys Raise Concerns over Burundi Killings." June 3. 2011.

"Burundi Negotiators to Meet for Consultations." October 1, 1999.

"S. African Troops Arrive in Burundi for VIP Protection Force." October 28, 2001.

Ahmed, Rafeeudin, Manfred Kulessa, and Khalid Malik. *Lessons Learned in Crises and Post-Conflcit Situations: The Role of UNDP in Reintegration and Reconstruction Programmes.* New York, NY: United Nations Development Programme Evaluation Office, 2002. Accessed December 21, 2017. www.researchgate.net/publication/44832533_Lessons_learned_in_crises_and_post-conflict_situations_the_role_of_UNDP_in_reintegration_and_reconstruction_programmes.

Alesina, Alberto and David Dollar. "Who Gives Foreign Aid to Whom and Why?" *Journal of Economic Growth* 5, no. 1 (March 1, 2000): 33–63.

All Africa Press Service. "Regional Leaders to Impose Sanctions on Burundi." August 8, 1996. Accessed December 28, 2017. http://reliefweb.int/report/burundi/regional-leaders-impose-sanctions-burundi.

Anderson, Mary B., *Do No Harm: How Aid Can Support Peace – or War.* Boulder, CO: Lynne Rienner, 2010.

Anderson, Mary B., Dayna Brown, and Isabella Jean. *Time to Listen: Hearing People on the Receiving End of International Aid.* Cambridge, MA: CDA Collaborative Learning Projects, 2012.

Andrews, Matt, Lant Pritchett, and Michael Woolcock. *Building State Capability: Evidence, Analysis, and Action.* Oxford, UK: Oxford University Press, 2017.

Argyris, Chris. *On Organizational Learning.* Boston, MA: Blackwell, 1992.

Argyris, Chris and Donald A. Schon. *Organizational Learning: A Theory of Action Perspective.* Boston, MA: Addison-Wesley, 1978.

"Participatory Action Research and Action Science Compared." *American Behavioral Scientist* 32, no. 5 (1989): 612–23.

Autesserre, Séverine. "Hobbes and the Congo: Frames, Local Violence, and International Intervention." *International Organization* 63, no. 02 (2009): 249–80.

"International Peacebuilding and Local Success: Assumptions and Effectiveness." *International Studies Review* 19, no. 1 (2017): 114–32.

"Paternalism and Peacebuilding: Capacity, Knowledge, and Resistance in International Intervention." In *Paternalism beyond Borders*, edited by Michael N. Barnett, 161–84. Cambridge, UK: Cambridge University Press, 2017.

Peaceland: Conflict Resolution and the Everyday Politics of International Intervention. Cambridge, UK: Cambridge University Press, 2014.

The Trouble with the Congo: Local Violence and the Failure of International Peacebuilding. Vol. 115. Cambridge, UK: Cambridge University Press, 2010.

Avant, Deborah D., Martha Finnemore, and Susan K. Sell, eds. *Who Governs the Globe?* Cambridge, UK: Cambridge University Press, 2010.

Ayindo, Babu. "Demystifying Theory of Social Change: Reflections on the Praxis of Select CARE Programs in Burundi." Care Burundi, July 26, 2008.

Ayoob, Mohammed. "State Making, State Breaking, and State Failure." In *Leashing the Dogs of War: Conflict Management in a Divided World*, edited by Chester A. Crocker, Fen Osler Hampson, and Pamela Aall, 95–114. Washington, DC: United States Institute of Peace, 2007.

Banbury, Anthony. "I Love the U.N., but It Is Failing." *New York Times* (New York), March 18, 2016. Accessed December 28, 2017. www.nytimes.com/2016/03/20/opinion/sunday/i-love-the-un-but-it-is-failing.html?_r=0.

Barma, Naazneen. *The Peacebuilding Puzzle: Political Order in Post-Conflict States.* Cambridge, UK: Cambridge University Press, 2016.

Barnett, Michael. "Accountability and Global Governance: The View from Paternalism." *Regulation and Governance* 10, no. 2 (June 2016): 134–48.

"Building a Republican Peace: Stabilizing States after War." *International Security* 30, no. 4 (2006): 87–112.

"Humanitarianism Transformed." *Perspectives on Politics* 3, no. 04 (2005): 723–40.

Barnett, Michael, ed. *Paternalism beyond Borders.* Cambridge, UK: Cambridge University Press, 2017.

Barnett, Michael and Raymond Duvall. "Power in International Politics." *International Organization* 59, no. 1 (2005): 39–75.

Barnett, Michael, Songying Fang, and Christoph Zürcher. "Compromised Peacebuilding." *International Studies Quarterly* 58, no. 3 (2014): 608–20.

Barnett, Michael and Martha Finnemore. "The Politics, Power, and Pathologies of International Organizations." *International Organization* 53, no. 4 (1999): 699–732.

Rules for the World: International Organizations in Global Politics. Ithaca, NY: Cornell University Press, 2004.

Barnett, Michael, Hunjoon Kim, Madalene O'Donnell, and Laura Sitea. "Peacebuilding: What Is in a Name?" *Global Governance* 13, no. 1 (2007): 35–58.

Barnett, Michael and Christoph Zürcher. "The Peacebuilder's Contract: How External State-Building Reinforces Weak Statehood." In *The Dilemmas of Statebuilding: Confronting the Contradictions of Postwar Peace Operations*, edited by Timothy Sisk and Roland Paris, 23–52. Abingdon, UK: Routledge, 2009.

Baulch, Bob. "Aid Distribution and the MDGs," *World Development* 34, no. 6 (June 2006): 933–50.

Beardsley, Kyle and Kristian Skrede Gleditsch. "Peacekeeping as Conflict Containment." *International Studies Review* 17, 1 (2015): 67–89.

Benn, Hillary. "Testimony by Hilary Benn on DFID's Support for Education in Burundi." *House of Commons Hansard Written Answers for 23 May 2007 (pt 0012)*, 2007. Accessed December 22, 2017. https://publications .parliament.uk/pa/cm200607/cmhansrd/cm070523/text/70523w0012.htm.

Benner, Thorsten, Stephan Mergenthaler, and Philipp Rotmann. *The New World of UN Peace Operations: Learning to Build Peace?* Oxford, UK: Oxford University Press, 2011.

Bennett, Andrew. "Causal Mechanisms and Typological Theories in the Study of Civil Conflict." In *Transnational Dynamics of Civil War*, edited by Jeff Checkel, 205–30. Cambridge, UK: Cambridge University Press, 2014.

"*Complexity, Typological Theory, and Research Design*." Power Point. Georgetown University. May 2015.

Berthoin-Antal, Ariane, Uwe Lenhardt, and Rolf Rosenbrock. "Barriers to Organizational Learning." In *Handbook of Organizational Learning and Knowledge*, edited by M. Dierkes, A. Berthoin-Antal, J. Child, and I. Nonaka, 865–85. Oxford, UK: Oxford University Press, 2000.

Beyna, Larry, Michael Lund, Stacy Stacks, Janet Thuthill, and Patricia Vondal. "Greater Horn of Africa Peace Building Project – the Effectiveness of Civil Society Initiatives in Controlling Violent Conflicts and Building Peace: A Study of Three Approaches in the Greater Horn of Africa." Evaluation. Washington, DC: Management Systems International, June 2001.

BINUB. "Stratégie integrée d'appui des nations unies à la consolidation de la paix au Burundi – 2007–2008." Bujumbura, Burundi: United Nations, 2006.

"UN Integration in Burundi in the Context of a Peacebuilding Office BINUB: Lessons Learned from June 2006 to Oct 2007." Bujumbura, Burundi: United Nations, February 2008. Accessed December 28, 2017. http://reliefweb.int/report/burundi/un-integration-burundi-context-peacebuilding-office-binub-lessons-learned-jun-2006

BLTP. "Fabien Nsengimana | Burundi Leadership Training Program." Bujumbura, Burundi: Burundi Leadership Training Program. Accessed November 23, 2011. https://bltprogram.wordpress.com/lequipe/fabien-nsengimana/.

"Note sur l'école de la democratie." Bujumbura, Burundi: Burundi Leadership Training Program, November 2011.

"Note sur le projet 'Renforcement du leadership feminin.'" Bujumbura, Burundi: Burundi Leadership Training Program (BLTP), November 2011.

Boshoff, Henri, Waldemar Vrey, and George Rautenbach. "ISS – Monograph 171: The Burundi Peace Process, from Civil War to Conditional Peace, Henri Boshoff, Waldemar Vrey and George Rautenbach." Pretoria: Institute for Security Studies. Accessed December 28, 2017. https://issafrica.s3 .amazonaws.com/site/uploads/Mono171.pdf.

Boutros-Ghali, Boutros. *Agenda for Peace: Preventive Diplomacy, Peacemaking and Peacekeeping. Report of the Secretary-General Pursuant to the Statement Adopted by the Summit Meeting of the Security Council on 31 January 1992.* New York, NY: United Nations, 1992.

Supplement to an Agenda for Peace: Position Paper of the Secretary General on the Occasion of the Fiftieth Anniversary of the United Nations. New York, NY: United Nations, 1995.

Branch, Adam and Zachariah Mampilly. *Africa Uprising: Popular Protest and Political Change.* London, UK: Zed, 2015.

Brown, M. Leann and Michael Kenney. "Organizational Learning: Theoretical and Methodological Considerations." In *Organizational Learning in the Global Context*, edited by M. Leann Brown, Michael Zarkin, and Michael Kenney, 1–20. Hampshire, UK: Ashgate, 2006.

Brown, William. "Sovereignty Matters: Africa, Donors, and the Aid Relationship." *African Affairs* 112, no. 447 (2013): 262–82.

Browne, Angela and Aaron Wildavsky. "Implementation as Exploration." In *Implementation: How Great Expectations in Washington Are Dashed in Oakland*, edited by Jeffrey L. Pressman and Aaron Wildavsky, 232–53, Berkeley, CA: University of California Press, 1984.

"Burundi: Donors Pledge $440 Mn." *Africa Recovery, United Nations* 14, no. 4 (January 2011). Accessed December 15, 2017. www.un.org/en/ africarenewal///subjindx/144aidf.htm.

Burundi Réalités. "Burundi: Half of the National Budget Embezzled within Two Years." *All Africa Press Service.* February 2, 2008. Accessed December 22, 2017. http://allafrica.com/stories/200802020014.html.

Bush, Sarah. *The Taming of Democracy Assistance,* Cambridge, UK: Cambridge University Press, 2015.

Call, Charles T. *Why Peace Fails: The Causes and Prevention of Civil War Recurrence.* Washington, DC: Georgetown University Press, 2012.

Call, Charles T. and Elizabeth M. Cousens. "Ending Wars and Building Peace: International Responses to War-Torn Societies." *International Studies Perspectives* 9 (2008): 1–21.

Call, Charles T. and Vanessa Wyeth. *Building States to Build Peace.* Boulder, CO: Lynne Rienner, 2008.

Campbell, Susanna P. "Independent External Evaluation: Peacebuilding Fund Projects in Burundi." Evaluation. Bujumbura, Burundi: BINUB, 2010. Accessed December 21, 2017. www.unpbf.org/wp-content/uploads/ Independent-Evaluation-Burundi.pdf.

"Organizational Barriers to Peace: Agency and Structure in International Peacebuilding" (PhD dissertation). Tufts University, 2012.

"Routine Learning? How Peacebuilding Organizations Prevent Liberal Peace." In *A Liberal Peace? The Problems and Practices of Peacebuilding*, edited by

Susanna P. Campbell, David Chandler, and Meera Sabaratnam, 89–105. London, UK: Zed, 2011.

"When Process Matters: The Potential Implications of Organizational Learning for Peacebuilding Success." *Journal of Peacebuilding and Development* 4, no. 2 (2008): 20–32.

Campbell, Susanna P., David Chandler, and Meera Sabaratnam, eds. *A Liberal Peace? The Problems and Practices of Peacebuilding.* London: Zed, 2011.

Campbell, Susanna P., Tracy Dexter, Michael G. Findley, Stephanie Hofmann, Josiah Marineau, and Daniel Walker. "Independent External Evaluation: UN Peacebuilding Fund Project Portfolio in Burundi, 2007–2013." New York: United Nations Peacebuilding Support Office, 2014.

Campbell, Susanna P. and Jenny Peterson. "Statebuilding." In *Handbook of Peacebuilding*, edited by Roger Mac Ginty, 336-46. London: Routledge, 2013.

Campbell, Susanna P. and Lisa Schirch. "UNDP's Role in Peacebuilding: Issues and Strategies." *Internal UNDP Report.* September 17, 2012.

Campbell, Susanna P. with Michael G. Findley, and Kyosuke Kikuta. "An Ontology of Peace: Landscapes of Conflict and Cooperation with Application to Colombia." *International Studies Review* 19, no. 1 (2017): 92–113.

CARE Burundi. "Analysing the Causes of Poverty – a Process and Change of Attitudes: Care Burundi's Story." Bujumbura, Burundi: CARE Burundi, 2008.

"A Journey of Empowerment: CARE Burundi's Rights-Based Learning Program Approach." Bujumbura, Burundi: CARE Burundi, 2010. http://pqdl.care.org/sii/compendium/Original%20documents/CARE%20Burundi%20Learning%20Program%20Approach_final.pdf.

"Burundi Country Profile." Accessed February 28, 2012. www.care.org/country/burundi.

"CARE International in Burundi Strategic Plan Document, 2002–2005." Bujumbura, Burundi: CARE Burundi, 2001.

"Learning from Peace and Conflict Monitoring (LCPM) Bi-Annual Narrative Report, November 2007–April 2008." Bujumbura, Burundi: CARE Burundi, April 2008.

CARE International. "Care International Structure." Accessed October 25, 2011. www.care-international.org/Structure.

CARE International–Burundi. "Strategic Journey 2007–2011." Bujumbura, Burundi: CARE International, November 2006.

Carnegie Commission. *Preventing Deadly Conflict: Final Report.* New York, NY: Carnegie Corporation of New York, 1997.

CDA Collaborative Learning Projects. *Reflecting on Peace Practice (RPP): Participant Training Manual.* Cambridge, MA: CDA Collaborative Learning Projects, 2008.

Chandler, David. "Back to the Future? The Limits of Neo-Wilsonian Ideals of Exporting Democracy." *Review of International Studies* 32, no. 3 (2006): 475–94.

Chapman, Nick and Charlotte Vaillant. "Synthesis of Country Programme
    Evaluations Conducted in Fragile States." Evaluation. London: Department
    for International Development, February 2010. Accessed December 28,
    2017. www.gov.uk/government/uploads/system/uploads/attachment_data/
    file/67709/syn-cnty-prog-evals-frag-sts.pdf.
Chigas, Diana, and Peter Woodrow. "Assessment of BCPR-Supported Conflict
    Prevention Initiatives." Cambridge, MA: CDA Collaborative Learning
    Projects, December 9, 2009.
Christiansen, Thomas and Christine Neuhold, eds. "International Handbook
    on Informal Governance." *Journal of Common Market Studies* 51, no. 6
    (2013): 1196–1206.
Church, Cheyanne and Mark Rogers. *Designing for Results: Integrating Monitoring
    and Evaluation in Conflict Transformation Programs.* Washington, DC:
    Search for Common Ground, 2006.
Cluster Working Group on Early Recovery, and UNDG-ECHA Working
    Group on Transition. "Guidance Note on Early Recovery." Geneva,
    Switzerland: United Nations Development Programme Bureau for Crisis
    Prevention and Recovery (BCPR), April 2008. Accessed December 28,
    2017. https://docs.unocha.org/sites/dms/Documents/Guidance%20note
    %20on%20Early%20Recovery.pdf.
Colgan, Jeff and Robert Keohane. "The Liberal Order Is Rigged." *Foreign Affairs*,
    April/May 2017. Accessed December 28, 2017. www.foreignaffairs.com/
    articles/world/2017-04-17/liberal-order-rigged.
Collier, David, Jody LaPorte, and Jason Seawright. "Putting Typologies to
    Work: Concept Formation, Measurement, and Analytic Rigor." *Political
    Research Quarterly* 65, no. 1 (2012): 217–32.
Collinson, Sarah and Mark Duffield with Carol Berger, Diana Felix da Costa,
    and Karl Sandstrom. "Paradoxes of Presence: Risk Management and
    Aid Culture in Challenging Environments." *Research Reports and Studies*.
    London, UK: Overseas Development Institute Report, 2013. Accessed
    December 23, 2017. www.bristol.ac.uk/media-library/sites/global-
    insecurities/migrated/documents/riskreport.pdf.
Committee to Protect Journalists. "CPJ Condemns Continuing Harassment of
    Radio Journalists." *Committee to Protect Journalists: Defending Journalists
    Worldwide*, October 2, 2006. Accessed December 20, 2017. https://cpj.org/
    2006/10/cpj-condemns-continuing-harassment-of-radio-journa.php.
Cooley, Alexander and James Ron. "The NGO Scramble: Organizational
    Insecurity and the Political Economy of Transnational Action." *International
    Security* 27, no. 1 (2002): 5–39.
Cousens, Elizabeth M. "Introduction." In *Peacebuilding as Politics: Cultivating Peace
    in Fragile Societies*, edited by Elizabeth M. Cousens, Chetan Kumar, Karin
    Wermester, and Karin Wermester, 1–20. London: Lynne Rienner, 2001.
de Waal, Alex. "Mission without End? Peacekeeping in the African Political
    Marketplace." *International Affairs* 85, no. 1 (2009): 99–113.
Denyer, Simon. "Analysis: Burundi Slides Back towards All-out War."
    Reuters AlertNet. May 15, 2001. Accessed December 20, 2017. http://relief
    web.int/report/burundi/analysis-burundi-slides-back-towards-all-out-war.

Department for International Development. "Building Peaceful States and
    Societies: A DFID Practice Paper." London: Department for International
    Development, 2010. Accessed December 28, 2017. www.gov.uk/
    government/publications/building-peaceful-states-and-societies-a-dfid-
    practice-paper.
"Building the State and Securing the Peace." Emerging Policy Paper.
    London: Department for International Development, June 2009. Accessed
    December 22, 2017. www.gsdrc.org/document-library/building-the-state-
    and-securing-the-peace/.
*The Closure of DFID's Aid Programme in Burundi: Written Evidence Submitted
    by the Department for International Development.* London: UK Parliament –
    International Development Committee, 2011. Accessed December 28,
    2017. https://publications.parliament.uk/pa/cm201012/cmselect/cmintdev/
    writev/burundi/bu09.htm.
"DFID Burundi, 2009–2011: Issues and Choices Paper – Burundi's Options
    for 2009–11." Bujumbura, Burundi: Department for International
    Development, 2009.
House of Commons – International Development – Fifth Special Report. London:
    United Kingdom Parliament, 2008. Accessed December 22, 2017.
    www.publications.parliament.uk/pa/cm200708/cmselect/cmintdev/592/
    59204.htm.
"Multilateral Aid Review: United Nations Development Programme
    (including the Bureau for Crisis Prevention and Recovery)." London: UK
    Aid, March 2011. Accessed December 21, 2017. www.gov.uk/government/
    uploads/system/uploads/attachment_data/file/214119/UNDP-response.pdf.
Dijkzeul, Dennis. "Programs and the Problems of Participation." In *Rethinking
    International Organizations. Pathology and Promises*, edited by D. Dijkzeul
    and Y. Beigbeder, 197–233. Oxford, UK: Berghahn, 2004.
DiMaggio, Paul and Walter Powell. "The Iron Cage Revisited: Institutional
    Isomorphism and Collective Rationality in Organizational Fields." In
    The New Institutionalism in Organizational Analysis, edited by Paul DiMaggio
    and Walter Powell, 64–5. Chicago, IL: Chicago University Press, 1991.
Doyle, Michael and Nicholas Sambanis. "International Peacebuilding:
    A Theoretical and Quantitative Analysis." *American Political Science Review*
    94, no. 4 (December 2000): 779–801.
Making War and Building Peace: United Nations Peace Operations. Princeton,
    NJ: Princeton University Press, 2006
East Africa Living Encyclopedia. "Burundi – Ethnic Groups." Accessed July 24,
    2015. Accessed December 21, 2017. www.africa.upenn.edu/NEH/
    bethnic.htm.
Easterly, William. *White Man's Burden: Why the West's Efforts to Aid the Rest
    Have Done So Much Ill and So Little Good.* Oxford, UK: Oxford University
    Press, 2006.
Ebrahim, Alnoor. "Accountability in Practice: Mechanisms for NGOs." *World
    Development* 31, no. 5 (2003): 813–29
"Accountability Myopia: Losing Sight of Organizational Learning." *Nonprofit
    and Voluntary Sector Quarterly* 34, no. 1 (2005): 56–87.

NGOs and Organizational Change: Discourse, Reporting, and Learning.
Cambridge, UK: Cambridge University Press, 2003.

"Economic Sanctions against Burundi Suspended." *Africa Recovery, United Nations* 12, no. 4 (April 1999). Accessed December 20, 2017. www.un.org/en/africarenewal/subjindx/124sanc.htm.

Economist Intelligence Unit. "Burundi Economic and Political Outlook." Economist Intelligence Unit. February 2012.

Eden, Lynn. "'Getting It Right or Wrong': Organizational Learning about the Physical World." In *Organizational Learning in the Global Context*, edited by M. Leann Brown, Michael Kenny, and Michael Zarkin, 197–216. Aldershot, UK: Ashgate, 2006.

Whole World on Fire: Organizations, Knowledge, and Nuclear Weapons Devastation. Ithaca, NY: Cornell University Press, 2004.

Elman, Colin. "Explanatory Typologies in Qualitative Studies of International Politics." *International Organization* 59, no. 02 (2005): 293–326.

Englebert, Pierre and Denis M. Tull. "Postconflict Reconstruction in Africa: Flawed Ideas about Failed States." *International Security*, 32, no. 4 (2008): 106–39.

Esser, Daniel. *Do No Harm: International Support for State Building.* Paris: Organization for Economic Cooperation and Development, 2010.

Executive Board of the United Nations Development Programme and of the United Nations Population Fund. "Extension of the First Country Cooperation Framework for Burundi." Note by the Administrator. New York: United Nations Development Programme, December 20, 2000. Accessed December 28, 2017. web.undp.org/execbrd/pdf/bdiextI.pdf.

"Role of UNDP in Crisis and Post-Conflict Situations." New York: United Nations Development Programme, 2000. Accessed December 28, 2017. www.gsdrc.org/document-library/role-of-undp-in-crisis-and-post-conflict-situations/.

"Second Country Cooperation Framework for Burundi (2002–2004)." New York: United Nations Development Programme, July 24, 2001. Accessed December 28, 2017. web.undp.org/execbrd/archives/sessions/eb/2nd-2001/DP-CRR-BDI-2.pdf.

Executive Representative of the Secretary General. "2010 Resident Coordinator Annual Report: Burundi." New York: United Nations Development Group, 2010. http://goo.gl/IFsgqp.

Feldman, Martha S., and Brian T. Pentland. "Reconceptualizing Organizational Routines as a Source of Flexibility and Change." *Administrative Science Quarterly* 48, no. 1 (2003): 94–118.

Ferguson, James. *The Anti-Politics Machine: "Development," Depoliticization, and Bureaucratic Power in Lesotho.* Minneapolis, MN: University of Minnesota Press, 1994.

Ferlie, Ewan, Laurence E. Lynn Jr., and Christopher Pollitt. *The Oxford Handbook of Public Management.* Oxford, UK: Oxford Handbooks Online, 2007.

Finnemore, Martha and Kathryn Sikkink. "International Norm Dynamics and Political Change." *International Organization* 52, no. 4 (1998): 887–917.

Fortna, Virginia Page. "Does Peacekeeping Keep Peace? International
    Intervention and the Duration of Peace after Civil War." *International Studies
    Quarterly* 48, no. 2 (2004): 269–92.
Does Peacekeeping Work? Shaping Belligerents' Choices after Civil War. Princeton,
    NJ: Princeton University Press, 2008.
"Peacekeeping and Democratization." In *From War to Democracy*, edited by
    Anna Jarstad and Timothy Sisk, 39–70. Cambridge, UK: Cambridge
    University Press, 2008.
Fox, Jonathan and L. David Brown, editors. *The Struggle for Accountability:
    The World Bank, NGOs, and Grassroots Movements.* Cambridge, MA:
    MIT Press, 1998.
Gerring, John. "Case Selection for Case-Study Analysis: Qualitative and
    Quantitative Techniques." In *The Oxford Handbook of Political Methodology*,
    edited by Janet M. Box-Steffensmeier, Henry E. Brady, and David Collier,
    645–84. Oxford, UK: Oxford University Press, 2008.
Case Study Research: Principles and Practices. Cambridge, UK: Cambridge
    University Press, 2007.
Ghani, Ashraf and Clare Lockhart. *Fixing Failed States: A Framework for
    Rebuilding a Fractured World.* Oxford, UK: Oxford University Press, 2008.
Gibson, Clark C., Krister Andersson, Elinor Ostrom, and Sujai Shivakumar.
    The Samaritan's Dilemma: The Political Economy of Development Aid. Oxford,
    UK: Oxford University Press, 2005.
Gilligan, Michael and Ernest J. Sergenti. "Do UN Interventions Cause Peace?
    Using Matching to Improve Causal Inference." *Quarterly Journal of
    Political Science* 3, (2008): 89–122.
Goodhand, Jonathan. *A Synthesis Report: Kyrgyzstan, Moldova, Nepal, and
    Sri Lanka.* London, UK: Conflict, Security, and Development Group, 2001.
Gourevitch, Philip. "Coming to Terms." *The New Yorker*, June 22, 2015,
    sec. Comment. Accessed December 28, 2017. www.newyorker.com/
    magazine/2015/06/22/coming-to-terms-africas-succession-problem.
Government of Burundi. "Letter Dated 1 February 1999 from the Permanent
    Representative of Burundi to the United Nations Addressed to the
    President of the Security Council – S/1999/106." New York, NY: United
    Nations Security Council, February 2, 1999.
Grant, Ruth W. and Robert O. Keohane. "Accountability and Abuses of
    Power in World Politics." *American Political Science Review* 99, no. 1 (2005):
    29–43.
Gutner, Tamar and Alexander Thompson. "The Politics of IO Performance:
    A Framework." *Review of International Organizations* 5, no. 3 (2010):
    227–48.
Haas, Peter. *Saving the Mediterranean: The Politics of International Cooperation.*
    New York, NY: Columbia University Press, 1990.
"Introduction: Epistemic Communities and International Policy
    Coordination." *International Organization* 46, no. 1 (1992): 1–35.
Haggard, Stephan and Lydia Tiede. "The Rule of Law in Post-Conflict
    Settings: The Empirical Record." *International Studies Quarterly* 58, no. 2
    (June 2014), 405–17.

Hawkins, Darren G., David A. Lake, Daniel L. Nielson, and Michael J. Tierney. *Delegation and Agency in International Organizations.* Cambridge, UK: Cambridge University Press, 2006.

High-Level Panel on Humanitarian Financing Report to the Secretary General. "Too Important to Fail: Addressing the Humanitarian Financing Gap." Istanbul, Turkey: World Humanitarian Summit, January 2016.

Houngbo, Gilbert Fossoun, and Ramadhan Karenga. "Consultations between the Government of Burundi and the United Nations on the Post-ONUB Period, Bujumbura, 21–24 May 2006." Bujumbura, Burundi: United Nations, May 24, 2006.

Hovland, Ingie. "Knowledge Management and Organisational Learning: An International Development Perspective." Working Paper. London, UK: Overseas Development Institute, August 2003.

Howard, Lise Morjé. *UN Peacekeeping in Civil Wars.* Cambridge, UK: Cambridge University Press, 2008.

Huber, George. "Organizational Learning: The Contributing Processes and the Literatures." *Organization Science* 2, no. 1 (1991): 88–115.

Human Rights Watch. "Closing Doors? The Narrowing of Democratic Space in Burundi." New York, NY: Human Rights Watch, November 23, 2010. Accessed December 20, 2017. www.hrw.org/report/2010/11/23/closing-doors/narrowing-democratic-space-burundi.

"Find the Killers of Anti-Corruption Activist." New York, NY: Human Rights Watch, April 15, 2009.

"Pursuit of Power: Political Violence and Repression in Burundi." New York, NY: Human Rights Watch, May 2009.

"'We'll Tie You Up and Shoot You.'" New York, NY: Human Rights Watch, May 14, 2010. Accessed December 20, 2017. www.hrw.org/report/2010/05/14/well-tie-you-and-shoot-you/lack-accountability-political-violence-burundi.

Integrated Regional Information Networks. "Burundi: Free Schooling Starts with Huge Logistical Problems." *Integrated Regional Information Networks.* September 19, 2005. Accessed December 22, 2017. www.irinnews.org/news/2005/09/19/free-schooling-starts-huge-logistical-problems-0.

"Burundi: A New Rebellion?" *Integrated Regional Information Networks.* November 30, 2011. Accessed December 28, 2017. http://peacenews.org/2011/11/30/burundi-a-new-rebellion-irin-africa/.

"Burundi: IRIN Focus – Containing the Crisis." *Integrated Regional Information Networks.* June 28, 2001. Accessed December 20, 2017. https://reliefweb.int/report/burundi/burundi-irin-focus-containing-crisis.

"Burundi: Nkurunziza Announces Free Maternal Healthcare, Pay Rise for Workers." *Integrated Regional Information Networks.* May 1, 2006. Accessed December 28, 2017. http://allafrica.com/stories/200605010081.html.

"Burundi–South Africa: SA Troops Face 'Delicate Mission.'" *Integrated Regional Information Networks.* October 30, 2001 edition. Accessed February 9, 2012. http://reliefweb.int/report/burundi/burundi-south-africa-sa-troops-face-delicate-mission.

"Burundi: UN Suspends Missions after Staff Killed." *Integrated Regional Information Networks.* October 13, 1999. Accessed December 28, 2017. www.irinnews.org/report/9700/burundi-un-suspends-missions-after-staff-killed.

International Alert. *The Closure of DFID's Aid Programme in Burundi.* London, UK: UK Parliament. Accessed October 2, 2011. http://goo.gl/d183kA.

International Alert, Saferworld, and FEWER. "Conflict Sensitive Approaches to Development, Humanitarian Assistance and Peacebuilding: A Resource Pack." London, UK: Africa Peace Forum/CECORE/CHA/fewer/ International Alert and Safer World, 2004. Accessed December 28, 2017. www.participatorymethods.org/resource/conflict-sensitive-approaches-development-humanitarian-assistance-and-peacebuilding

International Crisis Group. "A Framework for Responsible Aid to Burundi." *Africa Report,* no. 57. Brussels, Belgium: International Crisis Group, February 21, 2003. Accessed December 20, 2017. www.crisisgroup.org/africa/central-africa/burundi/framework-responsible-aid-burundi.

"Burundi after Six Months of Transition: Continuing the War or Winning Peace?" *Africa Report.* Brussels, Belgium: International Crisis Group, May 24, 2002. Accessed December 20, 2017. www.crisisgroup.org/africa/central-africa/burundi/burundi-after-six-months-transition-continuing-war-or-winning-peace.

"Burundi: Breaking the Deadlock, The Urgent Need for a New Negotiating Framework." *Africa Report.* Brussels and Nairobi: International Crisis Group, May 14, 2001. Accessed December 28, 2017. www.refworld.org/docid/3de220844.html.

"Burundi: Democracy and Peace at Risk." *Africa Report.* Brussels, Belgium: International Crisis Group, November 30, 2006. Accessed December 20, 2017. www.crisisgroup.org/africa/central-africa/burundi/burundi-democracy-and-peace-risk.

"Burundi: Ensuring Credible Elections." *Africa Report.* Brussels, Belgium: International Crisis Group, February 17, 2010. Accessed December 28, 2017. www.crisisgroup.org/africa/central-africa/burundi/burundi-ensuring-credible-elections.

"Burundi: From Electoral Boycott to Political Impasse." *Africa Report.* Brussels, Belgium: International Crisis Group, February 7, 2011. Accessed December 20, 2017. www.crisisgroup.org/africa/central-africa/burundi/burundi-electoral-boycott-political-impasse.

"Burundi: Internal and Regional Implications of the Suspension of Sanctions – International Crisis Group." *Africa Report.* Brussels, Belgium: International Crisis Group, May 4, 1999. Accessed December 28, 2017. http://old.crisisgroup.org/en/regions/africa/central-africa/burundi/003-burundi-internal-and-regional-implications-of-the-suspension-of-sanctions.html.

"Burundi: One Hundred Days to Put the Peace Process Back on Track." *Africa Report.* Arusha, Bujumbura, Nairobi, and Brussels: International Crisis Group, August 14, 2001. Accessed December 20, 2017. www.crisisgroup.org/africa/central-africa/burundi/burundi-one-hundred-days-put-peace-process-back-track.

"Burundi: Proposals for the Resumption of Bilateral and Multilateral Co-Operation." *Africa Report.* Brussels, Belgium: International Crisis

Group, April 13, 1999. Accessed December 20, 2017. www.crisisgroup.org/
africa/central-africa/burundi/burundi-proposals-resumption-bilateral-and-
multilateral-co-operation.

"Burundi: Restarting Political Dialogue." *Africa Briefing*. Brussels, Belgium:
International Crisis Group, August 19, 2008. Accessed December 20,
2017. www.crisisgroup.org/africa/central-africa/burundi/burundi-restarting-
political-dialogue.

"Burundi under Siege: Lift the Sanctions Re-Launch the Peace Process."
Africa Report. Brussels, Belgium: International Crisis Group, April 28,
1998. Accessed December 20, 2017. www.justice.gov/sites/default/files/
eoir/legacy/2014/09/29/icg_04271998.pdf.

"Elections in Burundi: The Peace Wager." *Africa Briefing*. Brussels, Belgium:
International Crisis Group, December 9, 2004. Accessed December 20,
2017. www.crisisgroup.org/africa/central-africa/burundi/elections-burundi-
peace-wager.

"End of the Transition in Burundi: The Home Stretch." *Africa Report*.
Brussels, Belgium: International Crisis Group, July 5, 2004. Accessed
December 20, 2017. www.crisisgroup.org/africa/central-africa/burundi/end-
transition-burundi-home-stretch.

International Development Committee. "The Closure of DFID's Bilateral Aid
Programme in Burundi - Tenth Report of Session 2010–2012." House of
Commons Report. London, UK: House of Commons, October 28, 2012.
Accessed December 22, 2017. www.publications.parliament.uk/pa/
cm201012/cmselect/cmintdev/1730/1730.pdf.

Jackson, Stephen. "The United Nations Operation in Burundi (ONUB):
Political and Strategic Lessons Learned." Independent External Study.
New York, NY: Conflict Prevention and Peace Forum, July 2006. Accessed
June 6, 2017. http://goo.gl/YdYbO5.

Jackson, Tony. "Equal Access to Education a Peace Imperative for Burundi."
International Alert. June 2000. Accessed December 22, 2017. www
.international-alert.org/sites/default/files/publications/burun_ed_en.pdf.

Jennings, Kathleen. "Blue Helmet Havens: Peacekeeping as Bypassing in
Liberia and the Democratic Republic of the Congo." *International
Peacekeeping* 23, no. 2 (2016): 302–25.

"Life in a 'Peace-kept' City: Encounters with the Peacekeeping Economy."
Journal of Intervention and Statebuilding 9, no. 3 (2015): 269–315.

Johnson, Erica and Aseem Prakash. "NGO Research Program: A Collective
Action Perspective." *Policy Sciences* 40, no. 3 (2007): 221–40.

Johnson, Tana. *Organizational Progeny*. Oxford, UK: Oxford University Press,
2014.

Johnson, Tana and Johannes Urpelainen. "International Bureaucrats and the
Formation of Intergovernmental Organizations: Institutional Design
Discretion Sweetens the Pot." *International Organization* 68, no. 01 (2014):
177–209.

Jones, Stephen, Katarina Kotoglou, and Taylor Brown. "The Applicability of the
Paris Declaration in Fragile and Conflict-Affected Situations." Evaluation
of the Implementation of the Paris Declaration. Paris, France: OECD,
August 2008. Accessed December 22, 2017. www.oecd.org/development/
evaluation/dcdndep/41149294.pdf.

Kahler, Miles, ed. *Networked Politics: Agency, Power, and Governance.* Cornell Studies in Political Economy. Ithaca, NY: Cornell University Press, 2009.

Kalyvas, Stathis N. *The Logic of Violence in Civil War.* New York, NY: Cambridge University Press, 2006.

"The Ontology of 'Political Violence': Action and Identity in Civil Wars." *Perspectives on Politics* 1, no. 03 (September 2003): 475–94.

Kaplan, Oliver. *Resisting War: How Communities Protect Themselves.* Cambridge, UK: Cambridge University Press, 2017.

Keck, Margaret E. and Kathryn Sikkink. *Activists beyond Borders: Advocacy Networks in International Politics.* Ithaca, NY: Cornell University Press, 1998.

Keeton, Claire. "Burundi Still Volatile Despite Transition Installation: Analysts." *Agence France-Presse.* October 31, 2001.

Kelley, Judith G. and Beth A. Simmons. "Politics by Number: Indicators as Social Pressure in International Relations." *American Journal of Political Science* 59, no. 1 (2015): 55–70.

Keohane, Robert O. "International Institutions: Two Approaches." *International Studies Quarterly* 32, no. 4 (December 1988): 379–96.

Knack, Stephen. "Building or Bypassing Recipient Country Systems: Are Donors Defying the Paris Declaration?" *Journal of Development Studies* 50, no. 6 (June 3, 2014): 839–54.

Koremenos, Barbara, Charles Lipson, and Duncan Snidal. "The Rational Design of International Institutions." *International Organization* 55, no. 4 (October 2001): 761–99.

The Rational Design of International Institutions. Cambridge, UK: Cambridge University Press, 2004.

Krasner, Stephen D. and Thomas Risse. "External Actors, State-Building, and Service Provision in Areas of Limited Statehood: Introduction." *Governance* 27, no. 4 (October 2014): 545–67.

Lake, David A. "Delegating Divisible Sovereignty: Sweeping a Conceptual Minefield." *Review of International Organizations* 2, no. 3 (2007): 219–37.

"Rightful Rules: Authority, Order, and the Foundations of Global Governance." *International Studies Quarterly* 54, no. 3 (2010): 587–613.

Lake, Milli. "Building the Rule of War: Postconflict Institutions and the Micro-Dynamics of Conflict in Eastern DR Congo." *International Organization* 71, no. 2 (2017): 281–315.

"Organizing Hypocrisy: Providing Legal Accountability for Human Rights Violations in Areas of Limited Statehood." *International Studies Quarterly* 58, no 3, (2014): 515–26.

Lawry-White, Simon. "Review of the UK Government Approach to Peacebuilding and Synthesis of Lessons Learned from UK Government Funded Peacebuilding Projects 1997–2001." London, UK: DFID, 2003. Accessed December 22, 2017. www.gov.uk/government/publications/review-of-the-uk-government-approach-to-peacebuilding-and-synthesis-of-lessons-learned-from-uk-government-funded-peacebuilding-projects-1997-2001-ev646s.

Lederach, John Paul. *Building Peace: Sustainable Reconciliation in Divided Societies.* Washington, DC: United States Institute of Peace, 1997.

Lemarchand, Rene. *Burundi: Ethnic Conflict and Genocide*. New York, NY: Woodrow Wilson Center Press and Cambridge University Press, 1994.

Levitt, Barbara and James G. March. "Organizational Learning." *Annual Review of Sociology* 14, no. 1 (1988): 319–40.

Levy, Jack S. "Learning and Foreign Policy: Sweeping a Conceptual Minefield." *International Organization* 48, no. 2 (1994): 279–312.

Lipson, Michael. "Performance under Ambiguity: International Organization Performance in UN Peacekeeping." *Review of International Organizations* 5, no. 3 (September 2010): 249–84.

"Peacekeeping Reform: Managing Change in an Organized Anarchy," *Journal of Intervention and Statebuilding* 6, no. 3 (2010): 279–98.

Lund, Michael S., Barnett R. Rubin, and Fabienne Hara. "Learning from Burundi's Failed Democratic Transition, 1993–1996: Did International Initiatives Match the Problem?" *Cases and Strategies for Preventive Action* 2 (1998): 47–91.

Mac Ginty, Roger. "Hybrid Peace: The Interaction between Top-Down and Bottom-Up Peace." *Security Dialogue* 41, no. 4 (2010): 391–412.

"Hybrid Peace: How Does Hybrid Peace Come About?" In *A Liberal Peace? The Problems and Practices of Peacebuilding*, ed. Susanna P. Campbell, David Chandler, and Meera Sabaratnam, 209–25. London, UK: Zed, 2011.

International Peacebuilding and Local Resistance. London, UK: Palgrave, Macmillan, 2011.

Mahmoud, Youssef. "Partnerships for Peacebuilding in Burundi: Some Lessons Learned." Unpublished Paper, October 15, 2009.

Makoroka, Stanislas and Oliver Le Brun. "La revue du projet d'appui au Programme National de Gouvernance Démocratique." Evaluation Report. Bujumbura, Burundi: United Nations Development Programme, February 2004. Accessed December 21, 2017. https://erc.undp.org/evaluation/documents/download/144.

Mankell, Henning. "The Art of Listening." *New York Times*, December 10, 2011, sec. Opinion. Accessed December 12, 2011. www.nytimes.com/2011/12/11/opinion/sunday/in-africa-the-art-of-listening.html?src=me&ref=general.

March, James G. "Learning and the Theory of the Firm." In *Explorations in Organizations*, edited by James G. March, 15–35. Stanford, CA: Stanford Business Books, 2008.

The Pursuit of Organizational Intelligence. Oxford, UK: Blackwell Business, 1999.

March, James G. and Herbert Simon. *Organizations*, Second Edition. Cambridge, UK: Blackwell Business, 1993.

Martens, Bertin, Uwe Mummert, Peter Murrell, and Paul Seabright. *The Institutional Economics of Foreign Aid*. Cambridge, UK: Cambridge University Press, 2002.

Mason, David and Sara McLaughlin Mitchell, eds. *What Do We Know about Civil Wars?* New York, NY: Rowman and Littlefield, 2016.

McCune, Marianne. "Relearning the Peace (Interview with Howard Wolpe)." Homelands Productions. Accessed November 23, 2011. http://homelands.org/theme/peace-conflict/.

Menkhaus, Ken and Ben K. Fred-Mensah. "Institutional Flexibility in Crises and Post-Conflict Situations: Best Practices from the Field." New York, NY: United Nations Development Programme Evaluation Office, November 2004. Accessed December 21, 2017. http://web.undp.org/evaluation/evaluations/documents/CPC_evaluation_2004.pdf.

Minorities at Risk. "Chronology for Hutus in Burundi." 2010. Accessed December 20, 2017. www.mar.umd.edu/chronology.asp?groupId=51601.

Morgenthau, Hans. "A Political Theory of Foreign Aid." *American Political Science Review* 56, no. 2 (1962): 301–9.

Mosse, David. *Adventures in Aidland: The Anthropology of Professionals in International Development.* New York, NY: Berghahn, 2011.

Moss, Todd, Gunilla Pettersson, and Nicolas van de Walle. "An Aid-Institutions Paradox? A Review Essay on Aid Dependency and State Building in Sub-Saharan Africa." Working Paper. Washington, DC: Center for Global Development, January 2006.

Mukhopadhyay, Dipali. *Warlords, Strongman Governors, and the State of Afghanistan.* Cambridge, UK: Cambridge University Press, 2014.

Murdie, Amanda and David R. Davis. "Shaming and Blaming: Using Events Data to Assess the Impact of Human Rights INGOs." *International Studies Quarterly* 56, no. 1 (2012): 1–16.

Murphy, Craig. *The United Nations Development Programme: A Better Way?* Cambridge, UK: Cambridge University Press, 2006.

National Audit Office. "Department for International Development: Operating in Insecure Environments – National Audit Office." London, UK: National Audit Office, October 16, 2008. Accessed December 22, 2017. www.nao.org.uk/report/department-for-international-development-operating-in-insecure-environments/.

Natsios, Andrew. "The Clash of Counter-Bureaucracy and Development." Washington, DC: Center for Global Development, 2010.

Newby, Vanessa. "Power, Politics and Perception: The Impact of Foreign Policy on Civilian–Peacekeeper Relations." *Third World Quarterly* (2017): 1–16.

Nielson, Daniel L., Michael J. Tierney, and Catherine E. Weaver. "Bridging the Rationalist–Constructivist Divide: Re-Engineering the Culture of the World Bank." *Journal of International Relations and Development* 9, no. 2 (2006): 107–39.

Nsengimana, Fabien. "Briefing on BLTP Activities." Washington, DC: Woodrow Wilson Center, January 16, 2008. Accessed December 20, 2017. http://goo.gl/Hm8SUu.

Olsen, Johan P. "Democratic Order, Autonomy, and Accountability." *Governance: An International Journal of Policy, Administration, and Institutions* 28, no. 4 (2015): 425–40. doi:10.1111/gove.12158.

Oppenheim, Ben and Johanna Soderstrom. "Citizens by Design? Explaining Ex-Combatant Satisfaction with Reintegration Programming." *Journal of Development Studies* (2017):1–20.

Organization for Economic Cooperation and Development. "Paris Declaration and Accra Agenda for Action." *Development Cooperation Directorate (DCD-DAC)*. Paris, France: Organization for Economic Cooperation and

Development. Accessed October 17, 2011. www.oecd.org/dac/effectiveness/
parisdeclarationandaccraagendaforaction.htm.

Principles for Good International Engagement in Fragile States and Situations.
Paris, France: Organization for Economic Cooperation and Development,
2007.

State Building in Situations of Fragility: Initial Findings. Paris, France:
Organization for Economic Cooperation and Development, August 30,
2009. Accessed September 8, 2011. www.oecd.org/dataoecd/62/9/
41212290.pdf

"Supporting Statebuilding in Situations of Conflict and Fragility: Policy
Guidance." *DAC Guidelines and Reference Series.* Paris, France: Organization
for Economic Cooperation and Development, February 28, 2011.
Accessed December 28, 2017. www.oecd-ilibrary.org/docserver/download/
4311031e.pdf?expires=1498101426&id=id&accname=guest
&checksum=AEA55B27563C7689125E0E58F21C841E.

"United Kingdom Development Assistance Committee (DAC) Peer Review."
Peer Review, 2006. Accessed December 28, 2017 www.oecd.org/
development/pcd/37010997.pdf.

"United Kingdom Development Assistance Committee (DAC) Peer Review."
Peer Review, 2010. Accessed December 28, 2017. www.oecd.org/
development/peer-reviews/45519815.pdf.

Organization for Economic Cooperation and Development – Development
Assistance Committee. "QWIDS – Query Wizard for International
Development Statistics." Accessed February 9, 2012. http://stats.oecd.org/
Index.aspx.

Pan African News Agency. "80% des Burundais préoccupés par la guerre
civile dans le pays." June 5, 2001. Accessed December 20, 2017.
https://reliefweb.int/report/burundi/80-des-burundais-préoccupés-par-la-
guerre-civile-dans-le-payss.

Paris, Roland. *At War's End: Building Peace after Civil Conflict.* Cambridge, UK:
Cambridge University Press, 2004.

"Saving Liberal Peacebuilding." *Review of International Studies* 36, no. 02
(April 2010): 337–65.

Paris, Roland and Timothy D. Sisk. *Managing Contradictions: The Inherent
Dilemmas of Postwar Statebuilding.* New York, NY: International Peace
Academy, 2007.

Parties to the Arusha Agreement. "Arusha Peace and Reconciliation Agreement
for Burundi." Arusha, Tanzania, August 28, 2000.

"United Nations Peacekeeping Operations: Principles and Guidelines."
Peacekeeping Best Practices Section, Division of Policy, Evaluation and
Training, Department of Peacekeeping Operations, UN Secretariat, 2008.

Petrie, Charles and Adrian Morrice. "Scrambling and Pulling Together the
UN's Civilian Capacities in Conflict-Prone States." In *Peacebuilding
Challenges for the UN Development System,* edited by Stephen Browne and
Thomas G. Weiss, 39–52. New York, NY: Future United Nations
Development System, 2015.

Pollack, Mark A. and Emilie M. Hafner-Burton. "Mainstreaming International
Governance: The Environment, Gender, and IO Performance in the

European Union." *Review of International Organizations* 5, no. 3 (July 31, 2010): 285–313. doi:10.1007/s11558-010-9091-4.

Pouligny, Beatrice. "Civil Society and Post-Conflict Peacebuilding: Ambiguities of International Programmes Aimed at Building 'New' Societies." *Security Dialogue* 36 (2005): 495–510.

Peace Operations Seen from Below: UN Missions and Local People. London, UK: Hurst, 2005.

Powell, Walter W. "Expanding the Scope of Institutional Analysis." In *The New Institutionalism in Organizational Analysis*, edited by Walter W. Powell and Paul J. DiMaggio, 183–203. Chicago, IL: University of Chicago Press, 1991.

"Presidential Special Issue on Exploring Peace." *International Studies Review* 19, no. 1 (2017). Accessed December 28, 2017. https://academic.oup.com/isr/issue/19/1.

Pressman, Jeffrey and Aaron Wildavsky, eds. *Implementation: How Great Expectations in Washington Are Dashed in Oakland.* Berkeley, CA: University of California Press, 1984.

Pritchett, Lant and Michael Woolcock. "Solutions When the Solution is the Problem: Arraying the Disarray in Development." *World Development* 32, no. 2, (2004): 191–212.

Radcliffe, Vaughan S. "Knowing Efficiency: The Enactment of Efficiency in Efficiency Auditing." *Accounting, Organizations and Society* 24, no. 4 (May 1999): 333–62.

Ramalingam, Ben, Miguel Laric, and John Primrose. "From Best Practice to Best Fit: Understanding and Navigating Wicked Problems in International Development." London, UK: Overseas Development Institute Report, September 2014.

Refugees International. "Give Burundi a Chance." Refugees International, November 30, 1999. Accessed December 20, 2017. https://reliefweb.int/report/burundi/give-burundi-chance

Reimann, Kim D. "A View from the Top: International Politics, Norms and the Worldwide Growth of NGOs." *International Studies Quarterly* 50, no. 1 (2006): 45–68.

Reinsberg, Bernhard. "Foreign Aid Responses to Political Liberalization." *World Development* 75 (2015): 45–61.

Reno, William. *Warlord Politics and African States.* Boulder, CO: Lynne Rienner, 1998.

Report of the High-Level Panel on Threats, Challenges and Change. "A More Secure World: Our Shared Responsibility," no. A/59/565, December 2, 2004.

Report of the Secretary-General. "An Agenda for Peace: Preventive Diplomacy, Peacemaking and Peacekeeping." New York, NY: United Nations, 1992.

Reuters. "Burundi Peace Talks End in Deadlock." *Reuters AlertNet*, July 16, 1999. Accessed December 20, 2017. http://reliefweb.int/report/burundi/burundi-peace-talks-end-deadlock.

Reyntjens, Filip. *Again at the Crossroads: Rwanda and Burundi, 2000–2001.* Current African Issues. Uppsala, Sweden: Nordic Africa Institute, 2001.

Richmond, Oliver. *A Post-Liberal Peace.* New York, NY: Routledge, 2012.

Richmond, Oliver and Jason Franks. "Liberal Hubris? Virtual Peace in Cambodia." *Security Dialogue* 38, no. 1 (2007): 27–48.

Liberal Peace Transitions: Between Statebuilding and Peacebuilding. Edinburgh, UK: Edinburgh University Press, 2009.

Robiolle, Tina and Steve McDonald. "The Burundi Leadership Training Program | Wilson Center." Accessed November 25, 2011. www .wilsoncenter.org/the-burundi-leadership-training-program.

Roper, Laura, Jethro Pettit, and Deborah Eade, eds. *Development and the Learning Organisation*. Boulder, CO: Lynne Rienner, 2003.

Rubin, Barnett R. *Blood on the Doorstep: The Politics of Preventive Action*. New York, NY: Century Foundation Press, 2002.

"What I Saw in Afghanistan." *The New Yorker*, July 1, 2015. Accessed December 28, 2017. www.newyorker.com/news/news-desk/what-have-we-been-doing-in-afghanistan?intcid=mod-latest.

Rwegayura, Anaclet. "Burundi: Famine Hits Hard as Fighting Continues in Burundi." *Pan African News Agency*, October 4, 2000. Accessed December 20, 2017. http://reliefweb.int/report/burundi/famine-hits-hard-fighting-continues-burundi.

Sabaratnam, Meera. "A Liberal Peace? An Intellectual History of International Conflict Management, 1990–2010." In *A Liberal Peace? The Problems and Practices of Peacebuilding*, edited by Susanna P. Campbell, David Chandler, and Meera Sabaratnam, 13–30. London, UK: Zed, 2011.

Samii, Cyrus. "Perils or Promise of Ethnic Integration? Evidence from a Hard Case in Burundi." *American Political Science Review* 107, no. 03 (August 2013): 558–73.

Scott, W. Richard. *Institutions and Organizations: Ideas and Interests*, Third Edition. London, UK: Sage, 2008.

Senge, Peter. *The Fifth Discipline*. New York: Doubleday, 1990.

Serwer, Daniel, and Patricia Thomson. "A Framework for Success: International Intervention in Societies Emerging from Conflict." In *Leashing the Dogs of War: Conflict Management in a Divided World*, edited by Chester A. Crocker, Fen Osler Hampson, and Pamela Aall, 369–88. Washington, DC: United States Institute of Peace Press, 2007.

Simon, Herbert. *Administrative Behavior*, Fourth Edition. New York, NY: Free Press, 1997.

Sinduhije, Alexis. "Burundi Faces Economic Woes Despite Sanctions End." *Reuters AlertNet*, 1999. Accessed December 20, 2017. http://reliefweb.int/report/burundi/burundi-faces-ecomomic-woes-despite-sanctions-end.

Smith, Dan. "Development Thinking Develops – DFID's White Paper and What Comes Next." *Dan Smith's Blog*, August 21, 2009. Accessed December 28, 2017. https://dansmithsblog.com/2009/08/21/development-thinking-develops-dfids-white-paper-and-what-comes-next/.

"Towards a Strategic Framework for Peacebuilding: Getting Their Act Together – Overview Report of the Joint Utstein Study of Peacebuilding." Brattvaag, Norway: Royal Norwegian Ministry of Foreign Affairs, April 2004. Accessed December 22, 2017. www.regjeringen.no/globalassets/upload/kilde/ud/rap/2000/0265/ddd/pdfv/210673-rapp104.pdf.

Stone, Randall W. *Controlling Institutions: International Organizations and the Global Economy*. Cambridge, UK: Cambridge University Press, 2011.

"Informal Governance in International Organizations: Introduction to the Special Issue." *Review of International Organizations* 8, no. 2 (2013): 121–36.

Suhrke, Astri. *The Limits of Statebuilding: The Role of International Assistance in Afghanistan.* San Diego, CA: Chr. Michelsen Institute, 2006.

"Reconstruction as Modernisation: The 'Post-Conflict' Project in Afghanistan." *Third World Quarterly* 28, no. 7 (2007): 1291–1308.

When More Is Less: The International Project in Afghanistan. New York, NY: Columbia University Press, 2011.

Talentino, Andrea Kathryn. "Perceptions of Peacebuilding: The Dynamic of Imposer and Imposed Upon." *International Studies Perspectives* 8, no. 2 (2007): 152–71.

Tankari, Oumar. "Projet Sasagaza Amahoro: répandre la paix – Rapport Finale." Evaluation. Bujumbura, Burundi: Care Burundi and USAID, March 2010.

Terry, Fiona. *Condemned to Repeat? The Paradox of Humanitarian Action.* Ithaca, NY: Cornell University Press, 2002.

Tilly, Charles. "War Making and State Making as Organized Crime." In *Bringing the State Back In,* edited by Peter B. Evans, Dietrich Rueschemeyer, and Theda Skocpol, 169–91. Cambridge, UK: Cambridge University Press, 1985.

Transparency International. "Policy_research/surveys_indices/cpi." *Transparency International Corruption Perceptions Index.* Accessed April 20, 2012. www.transparency.org/research/cpi/overview.

Trudeau Foundation. "Carolyn McAskie." Accessed December 14, 2011. www.trudeaufoundation.ca/en/community/carolyn-mcaskie.

Turner, Mark. "Special Reports/Responsible Business 2001." FT.com. Accessed October 23, 2001. http://goo.gl/bS0CG0.

United Kingdom Parliament. "Statements by Clare Short, Secretary of State for International Development." *House of Commons Hansard Written Answers for 4 Nov 2002 (pt 8).* London, UK: U.K. Parliament, 2002. Accessed December 22, 2017. https://publications.parliament.uk/pa/cm200203/cmhansrd/vo021218/text/21218w14.htm.

House of Commons Hansard Written Answers for 17 Dec 2002 (pt 8). London, UK: U.K. Parliament, 2002. www.publications.parliament.uk/pa/cm200203/cmhansrd/vo021217/text/21217w08.htm.

House of Commons Hansard Written Answers for 18 Dec 2002 (pt 14). London, UK: U.K. Parliament, 2002. Accessed December 22, 2017. https://publications.parliament.uk/pa/cm200102/cmhansrd/vo021104/text/21104w08.htm.

House of Commons Oral Evidence Taken before the International Development Committee – Working With Fragile and Conflict-Affected States: DRC, Rwanda and Burundi. London, UK: UK Parliament, 2011. Accessed December 22, 2017. www.publications.parliament.uk/pa/cm201012/cmselect/cmintdev/c1133-i/c113301.htm.

United Nations. "Carolyn McAskie Appointed Special Representative of Secretary-General for Burundi." Press Release. New York, NY: United Nations, May 26, 2004. www.un.org/press/en/2004/sga874.doc.htm.

"Overview." UN Department of Political Affairs website. Accessed November 9, 2015. www.un.org/undpa/en/in-the-field/overview.

"Report of the Technical Assistance Mission to BINUB." UN Restricted. New York, NY: United Nations, September 19, 2007.

"UN Entities." New York, NY: United Nations Department of Political Affairs, 2011.

United Nations Country Team. "Burundi: les défis du processus de transition." Bilan Commun de Pays [Common Country Assessment (CCA)]. Bujumbura, Burundi: United Nations, February 2004.

"Press Statement on the Incident Resulting in the Deaths of Two UN Staff Members in Rutana Province (Burundi) 12 Oct 1999." Burundi: United Nations, October 13, 1999. Accessed December 20, 2017. http://relief web.int/report/burundi/press-statement-incident-resulting-deaths-two-un-staff-members-rutana-province.

United Nations Data. "Burundi Country Profile," 2015. Accessed December 20, 2017. http://data.un.org/CountryProfile.aspx?crName=burundi#Social.

United Nations Department of Public Information. "Briefing by Humanitarian Coordinator for Burundi." Press Briefing. New York, NY: United Nations, December 3, 1999. Accessed December 20, 2017. http://reliefweb.int/report/burundi/briefing-humanitarian-coordinator-burundi.

"ONUB: United Nations Operation in Burundi." Peace and Security Section. New York: United Nations, 2006. www.un.org/en/peacekeeping/missions/past/onub/.

"Press Briefing by Special Representative on Burundi." Bujumbura, Burundi: United Nations, October 19, 1999. Accessed December 28, 2017. http://reliefweb.int/report/burundi/press-briefing-special-representative-burundi.

"Press Conference by Permanent Representative of Burundi." Press Release. Burundi: United Nations, January 14, 2000. Accessed December 28, 2017. http://reliefweb.int/report/burundi/press-conference-permanent-representative-burundi-0.

United Nations Development Group. "UN Resident Coordinator Generic Job Description," February 6, 2014. Accessed December 28, 2017. www.humanitarianresponse.info/system/files/documents/files/approved_rc_job_description_feb_2014.pdf.

"UNDAF or Common Programming Tool," 2015.

United Nations Development Programme. "Burundi Country Profile: Human Development Indicators." Accessed July 24, 2015. http://hdr.undp.org/en/countries/profiles/BDI

"Évaluation du programme d'appui à la réhabilitation, réintégration des sinistrés et de lutte contre la pauvreté." Bujumbura, Burundi: United Nations, September 2009. Accessed December 28, 2017. http://goo.gl/4MAsPW.

"Evaluation of Results-Based Management at UNDP." New York, NY: Evaluation Office, December 2007. Accessed December 28, 2017. web.undp.org/evaluation/documents/thematic/rbm/rbm_evaluation.pdf.

"Evaluation of UNDP Support to Conflict-Affected Countries." New York, NY: Evaluation Office, 2006. Accessed December 28, 2017. www.government.nl/documents/reports/2006/01/01/evaluation-of-undp-support-to-conflict-affected-countries.

"Programme de pays pour le Burundi (2010–2014)." Bujumbura, Burundi : United Nations, August 2009.

"Rapport de la mission d'évaluation externe du PCAC II." Evaluation Report. Bujumbura, Burundi: United Nations, January 30, 2005. Accessed December 21, 2017. https://erc.undp.org/evaluation/documents/download/147.

"Strategic Review of the Bureau for Crisis Prevention and Recovery." Final Report. New York, NY: United Nations, March 10, 2010.

"UNDP and Electoral Assistance: Ten Years of Experience." New York, NY: United Nations, 2000.

"UNDP to Support Burundi Elections." September 23, 2009. Accessed December 28, 2017. www.undp.org/content/undp/en/home/presscenter/articles/2009/09/23/undp-to-manage-usd-44-million-fund-for-burundi-elections.html.

United Nations Development Program–Burundi. "Appui à la réintégration durable des ex-combattants." Accessed September 20, 2011.

United Nations Development Programme and Republic of Burundi. "Plan d'action du programme de pays 2005–2007." Bujumbura, Burundi: United Nations, May 2005.

United Nations Development Programme Bureau for Crisis Prevention and Recovery (BCPR). "Bureau Strategy 2007–2011." New York, NY: United Nations, January 2007.

United Nations General Assembly Security Council. "The Report of the Panel on United Nations Peace Operations." Report. New York, NY: United Nations, November 13, 2000. Accessed December 23, 2017. www.un.org/en/events/pastevents/brahimi_report.shtml.

United Nations Information Service. "Secretary-General Appoints Berhanu Dinka as His Special Representative for Burundi." Biographical Note. New York, NY: United Nations, July 24, 2002. Accessed December 20, 2017. www.unis.unvienna.org/unis/pressrels/2002/sga811.html.

United Nations News Centre. "Ban Lauds Burundians for Gains in Consolidating Peace," June 9, 2010. Accessed December 20, 2017. www.un.org/apps/news/story.asp?NewsID=34964&Cr=burundi#.WUtHGWjys2w.

"Burundi Outlook Good 'in Many Regards' as It Turns to Economic Development – UN." *UN News Service,* December 9, 2010. Accessed December 21, 2017. www.un.org/apps/news/story.asp?NewsID=37005&Cr=burundi&Cr1=&Kw1=petrie&Kw2=&Kw3#.WUtHL2jys2w.

United Nations Office for the Coordination of Humanitarian Affairs. "What Is the Cluster Approach?" New York, NY: United Nations, 2015. Accessed December 28, 2017. www.humanitarianresponse.info/en/about-clusters/what-is-the-cluster-approach.

United Nations Peacebuilding Commission. "Strategic Framework for Peacebuilding in Burundi." New York, NY: United Nations, July 30, 2007.

United Nations Peacebuilding Fund. Accessed December 28, 2017. www.unpbf.org/application-guidelines/what-is-peacebuilding.

United Nations Peacekeeping Website. "About the Fifth Committee." UN General Assembly website. Accessed 9 November 2015. www.un.org/en/ga/fifth/about.shtml

"Department of Field Support." New York, NY: United Nations. Accessed
    November 9, 2015. www.un.org/en/peacekeeping/about/dfs/).
"Peacekeeping Budgets." New York, NY: United Nations. Accessed
    November 9, 2015. www.un.org/en/ga/fifth/Presentations/67th%20session/
    peacekeepingfinance.pdf.
"What Is Peacekeeping?" New York, NY: United Nations. Accessed November
    9, 2015. www.un.org/en/peacekeeping/operations/peacekeeping.shtml.
United Nations Secretary-General. "Decision of the Secretary-General: 25 June
    Meeting of the Policy Committee." New York, NY: United Nations, 2008.
"United Nations Political Missions: Report of the Secretary-General."
    New York: United Nations, 2014, Accessed December 21, 2017.
    www.unis.unvienna.org/pdf/0_Regular_Updates/Political_Missions_
    Report.pdf.
United Nations Security Council. "First Report of the Secretary-General on
    the United Nations Operation in Burundi (ONUB)." New York, NY:
    United Nations, August 25, 2004. Accessed December 20, 2017. https://
    documents-dds-ny.un.org/doc/UNDOC/GEN/N04/467/77/IMG/
    N0446777.pdf?OpenElement
"Interim Report of the Secretary-General to the Security Council on the
    Situation in Burundi." New York, NY: United Nations, November 14,
    2001. Accessed December 28, 2017. https://documents-dds-ny.un.org/doc/
    UNDOC/GEN/N01/625/83/PDF/N0162583.pdf?OpenElement.
"Letter Dated 2 November 1999 from the Secretary-General Addressed
    to the President of the Security Council." United Nations Security
    Council S/1999/1138, November 5, 1999. Accessed December 21, 2017.
    https://documents-dds-ny.un.org/doc/UNDOC/GEN/N99/332/22/PDF/
    N9933222.pdf?OpenElement.
"Report of the Secretary-General on Burundi." New York, NY: United
    Nations, March 16, 2004. Accessed December 20, 2017. https://documents-
    dds-ny.un.org/doc/UNDOC/GEN/N04/269/25/IMG/N0426925.pdf?
    OpenElement.
"Resolution 1545 (2004) Adopted by the Security Council at Its 4975th
    Meeting, on 21 May 2004." New York, NY: United Nations, May 21,
    2004. Accessed December 21, 2017. https://repositories.lib.utexas.edu/
    bitstream/handle/2152/5802/3067.pdf?sequence=1&isAllowed=y.
"Resolution 1719 (2006) Adopted by the Security Council at Its 5554th
    Meeting, on 25 October 2006." New York, NY: United Nations, October
    25, 2006. Accessed December 21, 2017. http://reliefweb.int/report/burundi/
    burundi-resolution-1719–2006-adopted-security-council-its-5554th-
    meeting-25-october.
"Resolution 1959 (2010) Adopted by the Security Council at Its 6451st
    Meeting on 16 December 2010." New York, NY: United Nations,
    December 16, 2010. Accessed December 21, 2017. www.un.org/press/en/
    2010/sc10120.doc.htm.
"Second Report of the Secretary-General on the United Nations Operation in
    Burundi." New York, NY: United Nations, November 15, 2004. Accessed

December 21, 2017. https://documents-dds-ny.un.org/doc/UNDOC/GEN/
N04/604/38/PDF/N0460438.pdf?OpenElement.

"Seventh Report of the Secretary-General on the United Nations Integrated
Office in Burundi." New York, NY: United Nations Security Council.
Accessed September 19, 2011. http://reliefweb.int/report/burundi/seventh-
report-secretary-general-united-nations-integrated-office-burundi-
s2010608.

"Sixth Report of the Secretary-General on the United Nations Integrated
Office in Burundi." New York, NY: United Nations Security Council,
November 30, 2009. Accessed December 21, 2017. www.un.org/en/ga/
search/view_doc.asp?symbol=S/2009/611.

"Sixth Report of the Secretary-General on the United Nations Operation in
Burundi." New York, NY: United Nations Security Council, 21 March
2006.

"Statement Issued by the Government Following the Fifteenth Summit
Meeting of the Regional Peace Initiative on Burundi (S/2001/752)." Letter
to the Security Council. Bujumbura, Burundi: United Nations, July 31,
2001. Accessed December 20, 2017. http://reliefweb.int/report/burundi/
statement-issued-government-following-fifteenth-summit-meeting-
regional-peace.

United Nations System in Burundi. "Lettre de présentation de l'équipe de pays."
Resident Coordinator Annual Report Introductory Letter. Bujumbura,
Burundi: United Nations, 2005.

United States Agency for International Development. "Evidence Base for
Collaborating, Learning, and Adapting: Summary of the Literature Review."
August 2016. Accessed December 28, 2017. https://usaidlearninglab.org/
sites/default/files/resource/files/eb4cla_literature_review_20160831.pdf

Unsworth, Sue. "Is Political Analysis Changing Donor Behavior?" London, UK:
Global Development Research Center, 2008. Accessed December 22, 2017.
www.gsdrc.org/document-library/is-political-analysis-changing-donor-
behaviour/.

An Upside Down View of Governance. Washington, DC, and London, UK:
Institute of Democracy Studies, 2010. Accessed December 28, 2017.
www2.ids.ac.uk/gdr/cfs/pdfs/AnUpside-downViewofGovernance.pdf

Uvin, Peter. Aiding Violence: The Development Enterprise in Rwanda.
West Hartford, CT: Kumarian Press, 1998.

"Corruption and Violence in Burundi." New Routes no. 3, 2009. Accessed
December 20, 2017. http://fletcher.tufts.edu/Alumni/Fletcher-News-Flash/
829D5F88159949928D7A84886390272D.aspx

"Difficult Choices in the New Post-Conflict Agenda: The International
Community in Rwanda after the Genocide." Third World Quarterly 22, no. 2
(2001): 177–89.

Life after Violence: A People's Story of Burundi. London, UK: Zed, 2009.

Uvin, Peter and Susanna P. Campbell. "The Burundi Leadership Training
Programme (BLTP): A Prospective Assessment." Washington, DC: World
Bank, 2004.

Valters, Craig, Clare Cummings, and Hamish Nixon. "Putting Learning at the Centre." London: UK: Overseas Development Institute Report, March 2016.

van Trier, Lukas. "Lessons Learned and Challenges Faced in Community-Based Peacebuilding in Burundi." The Hague: Care Nederland, October 2010.

Vaughan, Dianne. *The Challenger Launch Decision: Risky Technology, Culture, and Deviance at NASA.* Chicago, IL: University of Chicago Press, 1996.

von Billerbeck, Sarah B. K. *Whose Peace? Local Ownership and United Nations Peacekeeping.* Oxford, UK: Oxford University Press, 2016.

Walter, Barbara F. *Committing to Peace: The Successful Settlement of Civil Wars.* Princeton, NJ: Princeton University Press, 2002.

Whalan, Jeni. *How Peace Operations Work: Power, Legitimacy and Effectiveness.* Oxford, UK: Oxford University Press, 2013.

Wilson, Dr. Gregory. "What Is Adaptive Management?" Washington, DC: United States Agency for International Development website, November 2016. Accessed December 28, 2017. https://usaidlearninglab.org/lab-notes/what-adaptive-management

Wolpe, Howard. "Response to Draft Evaluation of the BLTP by Peter Uvin and Susanna P. Campbell." Washington, DC: Woodrow Wilson International Center for Scholars, July 2004.

Wong, Wendy H. "Pushing Against Boundaries: How Non-Governmental Organizations Link the Politics of Human Rights to Poverty." *International Studies Review* 13, no. 4 (2011): 660–2.

Woodrow Wilson International Center for Scholars. "Proposal for Renewing and Expanding the World Bank/WWICS Partnership in Post-Conflict Burundi." Proposal. Washington, DC: Woodrow Wilson International Center for Scholars, July 2004.

Woodward, Susan. "Do the Root Causes of Civil War Matter? On Using Knowledge to Improve Peacebuilding Interventions." *Journal of Intervention and Statebuilding* 1, no. 2 (2007): 143–70.

World Bank. "Data Catalog." Accessed February 9, 2012. http://goo.gl/NsPR.

World Development Report 2011: Conflict, Security, and Development. Washington, DC: World Bank, 2011.

Yin, Robert K. *Case Study Research: Design and Methods.* Thousand Oaks, CA: Sage, 2009.

Zartman, William I. "Ripeness: The Hurting Stalemate and Beyond." In *International Conflict Resolution after the Cold War*, edited by Paul C. Stern and David Druckman, 225–50. Washington, DC: National Academy Press, 2000.

Index

For EU product safety concerns, contact us at Calle de José Abascal, 56–1°,
28003 Madrid, Spain or eugpsr@cambridge.org.